£10

Sex, Wives, and Warriors

Sex, Wives, and Warriors

*Reading Old Testament Narrative
with Its Ancient Audience*

PHILIP F. ESLER

CASCADE *Books* · Eugene, Oregon

SEX, WIVES, AND WARRIORS
Reading Old Testament Narrative with Its Ancient Audience

Cascade Books
A Division of Wipf and Stock Publishers
199 W. 8th Ave., Suite 3
Eugene, OR 97401

www.wipfandstock.com

ISBN 13: 978-1-60899-829-6

Cataloging-in-Publication data:

Esler, Philip Francis.

Sex, wives, and warriors : reading Old Testament narrative with its ancient audience / Philip F. Esler.

p.; cm. Includes bibliographical references and index.

ISBN 13: 978-1-60899-829-6

1. Narration in the Bible. 2. Bible. O.T.—Social scientific criticism. 3. Bible. O.T. Genesis—Criticism, interpretation, etc. 4. Bible. O.T. Samuel, 1st—Criticism, interpretation, etc. 5. Bible. O.T. Samuel, 2nd—Criticism, interpretation, etc. 6. Bible. O.T. Apocrypha. Judith—Criticism, interpretation, etc. I. Title.

BS1171.2 E85 2011

Manufactured in the U.S.A.

To Bernard Carey

Contents

Preface

The genesis of this book lies in four essays I published between 1998 and 2006 that all explored the meanings that particular Old Testament narratives conveyed to their original audiences using cultural anthropology to provide resources to interrogate and interpret the textual data (chapters 4, 5, 8, and 9). Courtesy of a semester of sabbatical leave kindly granted me by the University of St Andrews from September 2009 to January 2010, I was able to articulate and develop the methodological presuppositions underlying these essays—both why and how we should read Old Testament narrative and also in relation to the original context of such texts (chapters 1 and 2). In addition, I was able to write on four more narratives (chapters 3, 6, 7, and 10). My hope is that I have set out a reasonably coherent methodology and a sufficient number of case studies to illustrate its usefulness. With the permission of the original publishers, I have at times lightly edited the four essays already published to update them or to accommodate them more closely to the overall thrust of the book. Although there are many other narratives in the Old Testament that I could have examined, the book is already long enough with the eight I have discussed.

Over the years I have benefited from extremely helpful feedback on earlier versions of various parts of this volume from my friends in the Context Group, especially Zeba Crook, Dennis C. Duling, John H. Elliott, Anselm Hagedorn, and Gary Stansell. Professor J. Cheryl Exum encouraged me in the production of the first essay, on Saul. During the publication of this book I also profited from useful suggestions made by K. C. Hanson. I am grateful to all these colleagues for their assistance, while acknowledging that I alone bear responsibility for the book's contents. The contents of the book were completed while I was on the staff of the University of St Andrews, in its divinity school, St Mary's

College. Throughout my time at St Andrews, from my arrival there on 1st October 1992 until my departure on 30th September 2010, I profited from the friendship and assistance of my friends at St Mary's (especially Professor Ron Piper, who was head of school for much of my time at St Andrews; and Miss Susan Millar in the college office) and also from the university's overall commitment to excellence. Many were the times when St Andrews enabled me to attend conferences abroad at which I presented papers underlying chapters in this book or on other subjects. Although I have now moved on to another St Mary's, I will not forget this support over so many years.

The book is dedicated to Dr. Bernard Carey, solicitor of the New South Wales Supreme Court. Bernard and I got to know one another when we were working at a department store in Sydney in December 1970 before we started Arts and Law degrees at Sydney University early in 1971. We have been close friends ever since. When I found myself looking for the thesis for a New Testament doctoral dissertation in Oxford in the summer of 1982, a book he had mentioned to me approvingly several years before—Peter Berger and Thomas Luckmann's *The Social Construction of Reality*—came into my head. I was working on Luke-Acts at the time, and when I began to read Berger and Luckmann I found in it a new, social-scientific approach suitable for this text and the thesis I was looking for. Without Bernard's help in this way, my life would probably have gone off in quite a different direction.

Acknowledgments

I am grateful to the following publishers for permission to reprint the essays listed:

"The Role of Hannah in 1 Samuel 1.1—2.21: Understanding a Biblical Narrative in Its Ancient Context." In *Kontexte der Schrift. Band II: Kultur, Politik, Religion, Sprache. Festschrift für Wolfgang Stegemann*, edited by Christian Strecker, 15-36. Stuttgart: Kohlhammer 2005.

"The Madness of Saul: A Cultural Reading of 1 Samuel 8–31." In *Biblical Studies/Cultural Studies. The Third Sheffield Colloquium*, edited by Cheryl J. Exum and Stephen D. Moore, 220–62. Sheffield, UK: Sheffield Academic Press, 1998. Continuum.

"'By the Hand of a Woman:' Culture, Story and Theology in the Book of Judith." In *Social Scientific Models for Interpreting the Bible: Essays by the Context Group in Honor of Bruce J. Malina*, edited by in John J. Pilch, 64–101. Leiden: Brill, 2001.

"2 Samuel—David and the Ammonite War: A Narrative and Social-Scientific Study of 2 Samuel 10–12." In *Ancient Israel: The Old Testament in Its Social Context*, edited by Philip F. Esler, 191–207. Minneapolis: Fortress Press, 2006.

Reading Old Testament Narrative

THE PHENOMENON OF NARRATIVE IN THE OLD TESTAMENT

Many of the world's best-known stories are found in the Old Testament: the stories of Adam and Eve, the worldwide flood and the salvation of Noah and his family, Abraham's sacrifice of Isaac, David and Goliath, David and Bathsheba, Absalom and Ahithophel, Jonah, Daniel in the lions' den, Judith and Holofernes, and many more. Indeed, to think of the Old Testament is, unavoidably, to think of narrative. Of the thirty-nine books in the Hebrew Bible, thirteen are entirely narrative in form, constituting about one-third of its total length.[1] Several more, such as Exodus, Numbers, and Deuteronomy, have extensive narrative passages, while narrative features in many other books, such as some of the Psalms, many of the Prophets, and Job. This additional material means about half the total text is narrative.[2] Of the eight extra works that are included in the form of the Old Testament recognized by Roman Catholics (as translated by Jerome into Latin in the fifth century CE), four of them

---

1. Genesis, Joshua, Judges, Ruth, 1 and 2 Samuel, 1 and 2 Kings, 1 and 2 Chronicles, Ezra, Nehemiah and Esther. In the Revised Standard Version these occupy 298 pages of a total of 843, or 35 percent. In Kittel's *Biblica Hebraica* these texts occupy 527 pages out of 1434, or 37 percent.

2. When Yairah Amit notes that "those who love measurements tell us that stories occupy fully one-third of the Bible" (*Reading Biblical Narratives*, 1), I assume she is referring only to these texts that consist entirely of narrative.

are narratives, approximately 45 percent of their total length.[3] When
the individual authors of Old Testament works and those who compiled
them into collections that became canonical wanted to speak of God's
ways with the universe and with his chosen people, Israel, they did so
largely through narrative.

The stories of the Old Testament also have an immense cultural
significance, since they have inspired the production of paintings and
sculptures; poems, fiction, and drama; musical compositions; and, since
the very early twentieth century, numerous films. While we can thus
distinguish between the religious and cultural arenas in which Old
Testament narratives have been immensely influential, we must also
recognize how religious and cultural impetuses to their appropriation
are often closely interconnected. For example, regular exposure to Old
Testament narratives that are read in churches and synagogues helps to
generate and maintain an audience for films on biblical themes.

This book is written both in the conviction that these biblical narratives have an abiding value and deserve the closest attention—across
a very broad range of readers—and with the aim of encouraging and
assisting close engagement with them. It is encouraging to see that
Don C. Benjamin's recent textbook, *The Old Testament Story*, provides
an introduction for students that focuses on the way the Bible works
through story, so the book moves away from introductions in the past
(like Bernard W. Anderson, *Understanding the Old Testament*), which
Benjamin submits had too much history and too little criticism of the
biblical texts.[4]

In this volume the expression "Old Testament" rather than the
"Hebrew Bible" is used of the corpus in view to emphasize that the
somewhat larger collection of texts recognized as canonical (or at least
deuterocanonical) in the Roman Catholic and Orthodox communities

---

3. In addition to the works in the Hebrew Bible recognized as canonical for Jews
and followed by most Protestants, the Council of Trent recognized as canonical the
Additions to Daniel, the Additions to Esther, Baruch and the Epistle of Jeremiah, 1
and 2 Maccabees, Judith, Tobit, Ecclesiasticus, and Wisdom. The Greek Church, at the
Synod of Jerusalem in 1672, recognized as canonical, in addition to those of the Jamnia
canon, four extra works: Wisdom, Ecclesiasticus, Tobit, and Judith. For all of these details, see Eissfeldt, *The Old Testament*, 568–73. By way of contrast, about 70 percent of
the New Testament is in narrative form (the narrative texts are the four Gospels, the
Acts of the Apostles and the Apocalypse.).

4. Benjamin, *Old Testament Story*, 18–19. In this work Benjamin utilizes the findings of narrative criticism, social-scientific criticism, and feminist criticism.

(which both include the book of Judith, for example) fall within our purview. While there is no perfect way of referring to this corpus, I particularly seek the indulgence of Jewish readers for including what they call the Tanakh under the rubric "Old Testament."

The first section of this chapter addresses the question of why we should read Old Testament narratives, by first modeling four groups of potential or actual readers and by then offering a range of reasons attuned to the interests and needs of the very different readers these groups encompass. The second section offers a particular answer to the question of how we should read these narratives—in particular by seeking to understand the meanings they would have conveyed to their original audiences in ancient Israel. This entails adopting a position in contrast to (and sometimes in critique of) other approaches currently in vogue in the scholarly marketplace that are not concerned with reading for original meaning and that at times positively disparage that exercise. In chapter 2 I set out the broad lineaments of that context for application in the examination of specific narratives that occupy chapters 3 to 10.

WHY READ OLD TESTAMENT NARRATIVE?

Modeling Readers of the Old Testament

The assertions just made for the significance of Old Testament narratives and for the claim they make on us for attention are large ones and require some justification. The essential starting point is the recognition of the huge variety of actual and potential readers. There is no single answer to the questions, why are people interested, or why should they be interested, in reading Old Testament narratives? There are likely to be as many different answers to the questions as there are respondents. Probably even these questions should be expanded to include those who listen to Old Testament passages being read aloud (at church or synagogue services, for example). Nevertheless, it is possible to identify the broad categories of audience and then to consider the varying types of significance that the narratives in question do or should have for them. We can begin to articulate the meaningfulness of Old Testament narratives for various audiences by forming a simple model arranged around two axes. The vertical axis differentiates readers or hearers who encounter Old Testament narratives by reason of religious belief from those who approach them for nonreligious reasons (of whatever kind). The horizontal axis differentiates nonprofessional readers from those who read for professional reasons. These two axes then generate a model of four quadrants, which I have lettered A to D to correspond to the order in which they are each considered.

A MODEL OF READERS OF THE OLD TESTAMENT

Readers for Religious Reasons

C.	**A.**
*Believing Jewish and Christian Biblical critics	*Practicing Christian and Jewish lay people
*Believing undergrads and postgrads in biblical studies	
*Priests, ministers, rabbis	
*Believing artists, composers, etc.	

Professional Readers / **Non-Professional Readers**

D.	**B.**
*Agnostic/Atheist biblical critics	*One-time Jews and Christians
*Comparative Lit critics and students	*Curious people and searchers
*Literary critics and art historians	
*Artists	
*Filmmakers	
*Composers	
*Journalists	

Readers for Non-religious Reasons

I will now consider the four broad groups identified in turn.

Far and away the largest group in numerical terms is A. The practicing Christian and Jewish lay people who are directly exposed to Old Testament narratives, either by hearing passages read at church or synagogue (possibly as they follow lectionary passages from service sheet, Bible or missal), or by reading them privately, must be numbered in their hundreds of millions. A primary aim of this book is to legitimate, that is, to explain and justify, particular ways of reading Old Testament narrative to this, the largest group. For those who regularly encounter the Old Testament passages read at services during the liturgical year, there is an inevitable connection between the biblical narratives and the life and identity of their faith communities that will require particular attention below.

The second-largest group numerically is B. Here we are dealing with millions of people falling into two subgroups. First are those who, having practiced Christianity or Judaism in the past, do so no longer yet are still attracted to these narratives, largely from a sense of nostalgia for their past affiliation and its continuing bearing on their life and identity. Second are those in the community who have never had an institutional link with Christianity or Judaism but are genuinely curious about the nature of Old Testament narratives for their story value or for their impact on art and culture, or who are searching for assistance in their own life journeys. This book also aims to assist readers like these to discover in biblical narratives a greater resource than they had imagined for satisfying the interests with which they come to those texts.

The third-largest group numerically is group C. Here we are dealing with the large number of persons, probably to be numbered in the hundreds of thousands, who are practicing Christians or Jews, but who also have a professional role in relation to the Old Testament writings: either as biblical interpreters in universities (such as the present writer) or as undergraduate or postgraduate students in biblical studies; or in their own religious communities as priests, ministers and rabbis; or those who are inspired by Old Testament stories to create works of art or musical compositions. My aim for these readers is the same as for those in Group A but additionally includes the provision of a fresh approach to the interpretation of Old Testament narrative within the vibrant current scholarly debate on the texts in question (to which we will return shortly).

While the fourth group, D, professional people reading Old Testament narrative for nonreligious reasons, is the smallest in number, it features many high-profile researchers in fields as various as biblical studies, art history, and comparative literature, while also including artists, film makers, composers, journalists, and others who find in these texts stimuli and resources for the various types of artistic and cultural production in which they engage. For those readers in this group who are academic researchers, my aim is to contribute to the scholarly debate over these texts, while for the artistic and cultural producers among them I seek to explain how Old Testament narrative, understood in the manner set out in this book, has a richer capacity to stimulate their creative instincts than they may have anticipated.

Now that I have outlined these four groups, the next step is to consider particular reasons for reading Old Testament narrative and to indicate for which of the four groups identified each reason has relevance.

Reasons for Reading Old Testament Narrative

Religion as a Chain of Memory

Peter Berger and Thomas Luckmann once noted, "The individual's biography is apprehended as an episode located within the objective history of the society."[5] This means we human beings must inevitably acknowledge that our own autobiographical experiences fall within the larger histories of the groups to which we belong—be they family, religion, nation, or ethnic group, to name only a few of the possibilities. These groups existed before we were born, continue during our lifetimes, and will persist after our death. Current members of groups bring past members or events (both real and created) into recollection, even into life as it were, in the present by the process of remembering. They remember both persons and events they personally experienced in the past, or those they have heard about from others, even if the people in question lived, or the events occurred, long before they were born. It was the great achievement of French sociologist Maurice Halbwachs to explain the extent to which we connect with groups that preexisted us by the processes of collective memory.[6] Collective memory embraces a number of related phenomena, such as the contents of what is remembered, the situations

5. Berger and Luckmann, *Social Construction of Reality*, 77–78.
6. Halbwachs, *Collective Memory*.

in which memory is mobilized and the process by which this happens.[7] It is difficult to imagine a community in which collective memory is not central to its identity and experience.[8] In the last decade collective-memory theory has begun to find a place in New Testament interpretation, both exegetically and theologically.[9] As far as the Old Testament is concerned, its narratives are the source of a major component of the collective memories of Christians and Jews. Jan Assmann, an Egyptologist from the University of Heidelberg, has developed Halbwachs's ideas on collective memory by development of the notion of "cultural memory" (*Kulturelle Gedächtnis*) that, inter alia, brings out very strongly the importance of material culture in the process.[10]

Yet, with help from another French sociologist, Danièle Hervieu-Léger, we are able to say much more about their significance than this, and in a general enough way to embrace both Christians and Jews in their relationship to biblical narrative. In her work *Religion as a Chain of Memory,* Hervieu-Léger aims to establish an analytical method that will enable religion, in spite of the condition of modernity in which we find ourselves, to be considered a proper subject matter for sociology.[11]

Many practicing Christians and Jews will probably regard Hervieu-Léger's definition of religion as helpful, in that it fixes upon some aspects of what it means to be religious, having an orientation to the divine while also belonging to a community whose members share a similar orientation, but as also a rather narrow one. This will especially be the case if they have ever encountered what Rudolf Otto described in *The Idea of the Holy* in 1917 (English translation 1923) as the "numinous" (from the Latin *numen* for undifferentiated divinity). This means the experience of something very strange that makes our hair stand on end, the nonrational apprehension of something lying outside the self, a mystery (*mysterium*) that is both terrifying (*tremendum*) and fascinating (*fascinans*) at the

---

7. Billig, "Collective Memory," 60.

8. Middleton and Edwards, "Introduction," 10.

9. For some early examples, see Esler, *Conflict and Identity in Romans*, 171–94; Esler, *New Testament Theology*, 213–28; and Kirk and Thatcher, *Memory, Tradition, and Text.* For an excellent recent review of this area, see Duling, "Memory, Collective Memory."

10. Assmann, *Kulturelle Gedächtnis.*

11. Hervieu-Léger, *Religion as a Chain of Memory*, 4. This work was published in 2000, but translating a 1993 French original. Modernity has proved more of a problem for religion in Europe than the United States.

same time.[12] Otto's notion of the numinous established an approach to religion as a nonreducible, original category in its own right. He brings out
the importance of direct experience of God by individuals or groups, with
respect to which memory that allows them to connect with their tradition
and its account of God's relationship with humanity through time may
not carry the same weight. William James once noted, "Knowledge about
a thing is not the thing itself," or, even more vividly, "A bill of fare with
one real raisin on it instead of the word 'raisin,' with one real egg instead
of the word 'egg,' might be an inadequate meal, but it would at least be a
commencement of reality."[13]

Nevertheless, Hervieu-Léger's proposal for identifying the nature
of religion with memory is extremely useful here because she focuses
upon an aspect of religion richly relevant to the role of narrative in
Bible-based or Bible-informed faith, whatever else such faith might encompass, and does so in a way that applies to both Christians and Jews.

She adopts a view of religion as a particular form of belief that specifically implies reference to the authority of a tradition.[14] Her approach
is to "describe any form of believing as religious which sees its commitment to a chain of belief it adopts as all-absorbing."[15] She thus offers the
following definition: "a religion is an ideological, practical and symbolic
system through which consciousness, both individual and collective,
of belonging to a particular chain of belief is constituted, maintained,
developed and controlled."[16]

In this perspective, *tradition* refers to the "body of representations,
images, intelligence, behavior, attitudes and so on that a group or society
accepts in the name of the *necessary* continuity between the past and the
present."[17] While serving present interests, she notes, tradition "confers
transcendent authority on the past."[18] Citing another researcher (Joseph

---

12. See Otto, *Idea of the Holy*, for his views on the *tremendum* dimension of the
numinous (12–24), the *mysterium* dimension (25–30) and the *fascinans* dimension
(31–40).

13. James, *Varieties of Religious Experience*, 488 and 500 (= Lecture 20). I am indebted to Dr. Georgia Frank of Colgate College for this reference.

14. Hervieu-Léger, *Religion as a Chain of Memory*, 4.

15. Ibid., 81.

16. Ibid., 82.

17. Ibid., 87.

18. Ibid., 86.

Moingt), she adds that a tradition implies "assenting to a past, determination to prolong it in the present and the future, the act of receiving a sacred, intangible trust, humble and respectful resolve to repeat something already said."[19] For present purposes, it is clear that the narratives in the Old Testament constitute a large part of the *tradition* in this sense for believing Christians and Jews. Once tradition is placed at the center of the nature of religion, "the future of religion is immediately associated with the problems of collective memory." Individuals or groups, to some extent at least, will see themselves as part of a chain or lineage so long as there is "mention of the past and memories that are consciously shared with and passed on to others."[20] This will inevitably come into tension with modern society that, by and large, is more "a society of change" than "a society of memory."[21] Paul Connerton has recently written on the extent to which modernity has a particular problem with forgetting.[22] Nevertheless, in a religious community, the continuity of the lineage of believers, which is for Hervieu-Léger the source of religious belief

> is affirmed and manifested in the essentially religious act of recalling a past which gives meaning to the present and contains the future. The practice of *anamnesis*, of the recalling to memory of the past, is most often observed as a rite. And what characterizes a religious rite in relation to all other forms of social ritualization is that the regular repetition of a ritually set pattern of word and gesture exists in order to mark the passage of time (as well as the transience of each individual life incorporated in the chain) with the recall of the foundational events that enabled the chain to form and/or affirm its power to persist through whatever vicissitudes have come, and will still come, to threaten it.[23]

While Christian and Jewish liturgies and services, with their oral proclamation of Old Testament stories in regular yearly cycles that have been repeated for centuries, represent anamnetic rituals of the type she has in mind, we should add that anamnesis also occurs outside ritual contexts, when individual Christians and Jews take up their Scriptures and read these mighty tales for themselves.

19. Ibid., 86.
20. Ibid., 123.
21. Ibid, 125.
22. Connerton, *How Modernity Forgets*.
23. Hervieu-Léger, *Religion as a Chain of Memory*, 125.

Finally, in a context where I will be seeking to release new meanings from Old Testament narratives—new to us at least in the individualistic cultures of North America, northern Europe, and Australasia, but well appreciated by their original audiences in ancient Israel—Hervieu-Léger fully acknowledges that a religious tradition is not static or calcified but continually reveals fresh and unexpected aspects of itself in new contexts: "any tradition in its relationship to a past, given actuality in the present, always incorporates an imaginative strain. The memory it invokes is always, in part at least, a reinvention. This reinvention is most often effected through successive readjustments of memory."[24]

For this reason, the fresh readings proposed in this book represent not merely reinterpretations of the tradition but readjustments of the collective memory that the narratives in question embody and nourish.

This perspective constitutes a significant reason for those in both Groups A (practicing Christian and Jewish laypeople) and C (practicing Christians and Jews in professional roles related to Israelite Scriptures) to read Old Testament narrative. In addition, representatives of the first subgroup of Group B (one-time Christians and Jews reading Old Testament narrative with nostalgia for its contribution to their sense of who they are) will also find that the process impacts upon the collective memories that they still hold by virtue of their previous affiliation. Only now the effect will be greatly diminished because they no longer consider that—to cite the approach of Hervieu-Léger—they belong to this particular chain of belief or have an all-absorbing commitment to it. Previously they were insiders and now they are outsiders, although well-informed ones. Nevertheless, to the extent that they are still interested in biblical narrative as helping, at least in part, to tell them who they are, the approach adopted in Hervieu-Léger's book will give them new food for thought.

It might be helpful if, as a representative of Group C myself, I provide a brief autobiographical reminiscence of a personal experience of religion as a chain of memory embracing Old Testament narrative. The incident in question concerns my first conscious memory of encountering an Old Testament story. It is 1957 and I am five years of age, sitting with some forty other kindergarten children on tiny wooden chairs in a Roman Catholic primary school in an outer, semirural suburb of Sydney, Australia. The school is run by Daughters of Charity nuns, still

24. Ibid., 145.

dressed—in those far-off, pre–Vatican II days—in a black habit with a huge and elaborate starched white bonnet. We cluster in a semicircle around one of the nuns who is telling us the story from Exodus 32 of Moses coming down from Mount Sinai with the two tablets of the law, only to find the Israelites dancing around a golden calf. She is using a visual aid, a large colored print of this scene (one of many such prints in soft paper on a frame that can be turned over as appropriate). I still have a vivid recollection of the angry look on Moses's face. This was happening in a context of intense Roman Catholic religious practice in my family and in the school: prayers several times a day (including before and after meals and before lessons); evening recitation of the Rosary; and Mass on Sundays, feast days, missions, and the first Fridays of each month; all punctuated occasionally by more notable events, such as the entry into religious life or ordination to the priesthood of a close relative or family friend. Exposure to the stories of the Old Testament was part and parcel of this identity. For me, and I know I am not alone, to immerse oneself again in an Old Testament narrative is to reconnect with this chain of belief, to be reimmersed in a particular orientation to the ultimate realities that we inherited from those who went before us, our parents especially, which leaves an indelible mark on who we are, and that will live on in those who come after us. Perhaps, more specifically, my own career in biblical criticism, including the interest I have in the Bible and the visual arts,[25] owes something to this early exposure to biblical narrative mediated through visual representation.

Disclosing More Ample Possibilities for Being Human

In an essay published in 2000 John Barton has asked, and sought to answer, the question, "How do stories 'work' in communicating to us the revelation of God: that is, God's revelation of himself?"[26] Plainly this concern, as it relates to the stories of the Old Testament, will be of primary interest to people falling within Groups A and C: believing Christians and Jews, whether approaching the texts with a professional or nonprofessional interest, who regard these narratives as part of a

25. See Boyd and Esler, *Visuality and Biblical Text*; Esler, "Paul and the Agon"; Esler and Piper, "Raising of Lazarus in Early Christian Art"; and Esler, "Biblical Paintings of Ivor Williams (1908–82)."

26. Barton, "Disclosing Human Possibilities," 54; this essay draws on Barton, "Reading for Life."

canon containing God's revelation of himself. Nevertheless, the answer Barton provides to his question is broad enough to carry weight even for readers who do not have religious faith.

In this context, the critical question is how can God reveal himself, that is, communicate his reality and plans to us in a story (as opposed to, say, a law code or a prayer). Barton has suggested that the Old Testament narratives do this, paradoxically perhaps, "by opening up to us the possibilities and the problems of being human in God's world."[27] In taking this line he has been prompted by two works of Martha Nussbaum (*The Fragility of Goodness* and *Love's Knowledge*). Nussbaum argues there is no fixed boundary between the people we meet in fiction and the people we meet every day. One aspect of this is that well-drawn characters in fiction are almost real and so can offer insight into real people like us. More characteristic of Nussbaum is her suggestion that "real people" are just as fictional as the characters in a novel, meaning that all our encounters with other people depend on our ability to "fictionalize" them. And others see us as characters too. "Thus the possibility of turning to literature for insight into life rests, not on the closeness of good fiction to reality, but on the closeness of any reality we can grasp to fiction."[28] Nussbaum thus argues that we can "Read for life." In other words, "Stories can disclose for us the possibilities of being human." Barton goes on, "We learn from stories how to live because we discover from them how voluntary decisions interact with unpredictable occurrences to generate moral character."[29]

Although Nussbaum's examples come from Greek tragedy and modern fiction (especially Charles Dickens and Henry James), Barton reasonably proposes that many biblical narrative texts are quite similar to the events in Greek tragedies and could easily be treated in a similar way. Stories, such as those of Joseph in Genesis 37–50 and the Succession Narrative (2 Sam 8–20 and 1 Kings 1–2) achieve a "disclosure of human possibilities (and human limitations) that is arguably not available in any other way." For example, we see a David who "is inhuman, superhuman or subhuman, but all-too-human and therefore susceptible to temptations and disasters, just was we are ourselves." As a result, "these stories are not reducible to a set of ethical principles, as if they were

27. Barton, "Disclosing Human Possibilities," 54.

28. Ibid, 55.

29. Ibid, 55.

sermon exempla." Although principles can be seen as exemplified by the stories, "the story cannot be replaced by a statement of principles, which are disclosed through the interplay of characters and situations and not in any other way." The stories draw us in and "ensure that we will never again be quite the same people that we were before we read these classic stories." In short, "There is an irreducibility about the narrative character of these works."[30]

It is clear from this account that, while practicing Jews and Christians will interpret the disclosure of human possibilities in Old Testament stories as a mode of divine revelation, even nontheists will be able to learn from them factors that either promote or stifle human flourishing.

Promoting Intercultural Understanding

At first sight it might appear that the type of historical approach adopted in this volume stands in the road of achieving my aim of encouraging the various types of readers who are modeled above to pursue their interest in reading Old Testament narratives. The potential problem is that interpretations of the Bible that stress its social and temporal distance from us, such as will be offered in chapters 3 to 10 below, are sometimes said to create an unbridgeable gap between the biblical texts and the present and prevent them speaking to us here and now. Not only is this a misconception, but the very fact of the social distance of these texts from modern readers means both that they can speak to us in new and unsuspected ways and that by attending to such meanings our capacity for intercultural understanding and sensitivity is enhanced.[31]

People who do embed themselves in a foreign culture, which means making a deliberate and socially sensitive effort to understand its social script, frequently return to their homelands. When they do, they will generally seek to explain what they have learned about the foreign culture to themselves and other members of their own culture. To do this, they will need to be able to translate from the foreign culture into the local one in language and concepts that will be understood. This is the cross-cultural stage in the meeting of cultures that necessarily involves

---

30. Ibid, 56.

31. For a detailed expression of my views on this matter, see Esler, *New Testament Theology*, 38–66.

a process of translation. Where the translation moves from the culture of an indigenous, preindustrial people to a modern, postindustrial one informed by social-scientific analysis of social realities, the movement is from what has become usefully described as the "emic" (indigenous) to the "etic" (outsider, generalized, and social-scientific) levels.[32] The presentation of the context of ancient Israel in the light of modern anthropological research into the Mediterranean region offered in chapter 2 will enable readers of this volume to make just this sort of transition.

Furthermore, once people who have habituated themselves to a foreign culture come home and engage in the process of translation, they tend to find that they now stand with their feet in both cultures and are able to assess and interpret each with respect to the other. This mediating experience can be a very rich one, although it will vary from individual to individual. Those who have it may be called "intercultural."[33] To become intercultural means both to have sought to penetrate the strangeness of the foreign culture in the first place, to have set emic meanings within more etic conceptual frameworks, and then to have brought the understanding so garnered into active relationship and tension with one's own cultural context. There is a growing literature on this notion of interculturalism, although its application to the realm of biblical criticism began fairly recently.[34] It offers a powerful mode of communion between those ancient Israelites who produced these texts, people whom the members of Groups A and C will regard as their ancestors in faith,[35] and whom members of all Groups will rightly regard as well worth attending to for other reasons.

The Power of Story as Story

"Stories are a staple of human life. And stories abound in the Hebrew Bible."[36] So say David Gunn and Danna Fewell at the start of their book *Narrative in the Hebrew Bible*. They go on to affirm that these "biblical

32. See Headland et al., *Emics and Etics*.

33. See the discussion in Gudykunst and Kim, *Communicating with Strangers*.

34. Esler, *Galatians*, 2–28 and 234–39.

35. For my attempt to explore the significance of intercultural communication and communion in relation to New Testament texts, see Esler, *New Testament Theology*, 47–52.

36. Gunn and Fewell, *Narrative*, 1.

stories, like stories everywhere, can powerfully shape people's lives."[37] That line of argument is somewhat similar to John Barton's. In fact, however, stories are a staple of human life whether they shape human lives or not. This is because of our love of mimesis, of our being able—by hearing or reading a story—to enter a created, imaginative realm that draws on our everyday world but transmutes it into a reality having its own independent existence in reliance on aesthetic not physical laws. As I have argued elsewhere in substantial agreement on this point with Hans-Georg Gadamer, the experience of reading an imaginative work is connected with the idea of play.[38] Yet this is not to suggest that play is an escape from reality. As Gadamer so astutely phrased it, when we read a novel, play or poem (or, we might add, an Old Testament narrative), "all those purposive relations which determine active and caring existence have not simply disappeared, but in a curious way acquire a different quality."[39] Being immersed in a novel, or an Old Testament story, bears "strong similarities to the experience of being temporarily withdrawn from the mundane world of purpose and responsibility that characterizes play or the time during which one gazes upon an accomplished painting or sculpture."[40] To repeat, our desire to engage in such experience is driven by our human love of mimesis and representation, whether we are personally shaped by it or not.

It is perfectly possible to read Old Testament narratives simply in this sense, that is, from an aesthetic viewpoint that is uninterested in or denies the existence of God and hence his actual participation in the events described, as well as in claims that such stories tell us who we really are or change us existentially or morally. While there is inevitably more in these narratives than this for those of Christian or Jewish faith, for many people in Groups B and D, this type of interest might be a significant factor in their motivation to read these texts and in the satisfaction that they derive from them. On the other hand, those who are reading the text for religious reasons cannot simply isolate themselves from their human delight in mimetic experience, and they will also participate in this type of engagement with Old Testament narrative. Finally, many Old Testament stories (as we will see throughout this

---

37. Ibid., 1.
38. Esler, *New Testament Theology*, 94–96.
39. Gadamer, *Truth and Method*, 91.
40. Esler, *New Testament Theology*, 95.

volume) bear structural similarities to other well-known stories outside the Bible. It seems to be the case that the aesthetic pleasure that readers derive from prose narratives (as contrasted, say, with lyric poems) originates, at least in part, from such narratives usually exemplifying particular story elements or story structures that also outcrop in other narratives, a subject that has attracted considerable attention both from scholars and more popular writers. We will defer further consideration of this issue, however, until the next section of this chapter, which moves on from the big question of, "Why should we read Old Testament narrative?" to the equally significant question of "How should we read such narrative?"

HOW SHOULD WE READ OLD TESTAMENT NARRATIVE?

The question of the literary character of Old Testament narratives, here meaning their quality and impact as stories, constitutes one of the great curiosities in the way biblical interpretation has developed. In short, there has been an unfortunate shift from one extreme to the other, from a long-standing focus on history unconcerned with final literary form to a recent interest in final literary form that is largely insouciant to history. How did this come about, and is there an alternative to this strange polarization of research?

History but Not Literary Form?

For most of its course, the historical interpretation of the Old Testament in the modern period (starting in the eighteenth century and largely led by German scholars) has taken a very particular, in fact decidedly narrow, approach to the literary qualities of the biblical texts. Its initial interest lay in "source criticism" (*Literarkritik*), meaning the exercise of differentiating earlier and later strata in the various books and wherever possible dating them. Historical criticism directed to discovering the sources of biblical texts was thought to allow its practitioners to construct a history of Israel's religious development.[41] The crowning achievement of this research was the four-document hypothesis for the Pentateuch developed by Julius Wellhausen (1844–1918). In contrast to such source-critical investigations, Hermann Gunkel (1862–1932) took

---

41. See Golka, "German Old Testament Scholarship," 259.

a different approach, by applying a new methodology of "form criticism" (*Formgeschichte*), notably in his commentary on Genesis (1901; 3rd ed. 1910).[42] Form criticism involved examining texts for smaller units, literary genres (*Gattungen*) in fact, such as sagas and aetiologies, which were each situated within an original setting in the life of Israel (*Sitz im Leben*).[43] Form criticism was helpful in tracing tradition back behind the sources to historical realities. Yet even Gunkel's literature interest was reductionist, since he was not so much concerned with the literary form of the final text as with the fragments of which he thought it was composed. It should be noted, however, that while some critics who were influenced by Gunkel, for example Martin Noth (1902–1968), pursued a similarly reductionist path,[44] Gerhard von Rad (1901–1971) was rather different in his concern for the literary genre of the entire Hexateuch and its particular *Sitz im Leben*.[45] By and large, however, source critics and form critics ignored the final form of Old Testament narratives and were indifferent to fundamental narrative characteristics since they really wanted to understand the historical actuality to which the text allowed access, not the text in itself.[46] This was in spite of the fact, noted at the beginning of this chapter, that narrative composed nearly half the entire corpus.

Literary Form but Not History?

In due course, and not surprisingly, such neglect of the obvious elicited a reaction. In her 2001 volume on how to read biblical narratives, Yairah Amit identifies Franz Rosenzweig (1887–1929) and Martin Buber (1878–1965) as the initiators of the study of the aesthetic dimensions of biblical texts in the 1920s and 1930s.[47] During the years 1925 to1929, at a time when a major assault on the Old Testament was developing in Germany, Rosenzweig and Buber were working on a new type of translation of the Hebrew Bible into German and set out their approach to this task in a number of working papers, which Buber published in 1936 (Rosenzweig

42. Gunkel, *Genesis*.

43. Golka, "German Old Testament Scholarship," 261.

44. Noth, *History of Pentateuchal Traditions*.

45. Von Rad, "Problem of the Hexateuch."

46. See Clines and Exum, "New Literary Criticism," 11–12.

47. Amit, *Reading Biblical Narratives*, 11.

having died in 1929).[48] One of these papers was Rosenzweig's 1928 essay
"The Secret of Biblical Narrative Form."[49] Central features of their approach were a regard for the Bible in its final form as an organic whole,
a belief in the Bible as an essentially spoken document (so that the way
it sounded really mattered), and the highlighting of the "leading-word"
(*Leitwort*) technique, where the repetition of paronyms of a Hebrew root
are a guide to the thematics of numerous biblical passages.[50]

Yet, as Amit has noted, it was not until 1962 that there appeared
a work that sought to launch a systematic analysis of the formal aspects of biblical literature by applying the approach of the new science of literature—such as the Anglo-Saxon "New Criticism" and the
Werkinterpretation of central Europe. This was Meir Weiss's methodological work, *The Bible from Within: The Method of Total Interpretation*,
originally published in Hebrew.[51] It is worth noting that Weiss himself
acknowledged that independently of him Alonso-Schökel had been
moving to a stylistic analysis of Hebrew prophecy also under the inspiration of New Criticism and *Werkinterpretation*.[52] Weiss was following in a tradition that went back to the early twentieth century and
that demanded the study of poetry should concentrate on the poem
itself, should see the poem as an end in itself, not just as means to understanding something else, such as history.[53] Or, moving beyond the
poem, a literary creation "is considered a unique entity which should
be therefore contemplated for its own sake."[54] Weiss acknowledged but
minimized the role of historical knowledge: "we must remember that
historical erudition is not itself an interpretation but the preparation for
one. Interpretation begins only where historical research leaves off."[55] In
a manner typical of the New Critics' passion for "close reading," Weiss

48. Fox, "Book in Its Contexts," xiii–xiv. For the essays themselves, see Buber and
Rosenzweig, *Scripture and Translation*.

49. Rosenzweig, "Secret of Biblical Narrative Form."

50. See Fox, "Book in Its Contexts," xviii–xxii. On the *Leitwort* technique, see Buber,
"Leitwort and Discourse Type."

51. Amit, *Reading Biblical Narratives*, 11–12. An English translation of Weiss's book,
Bible from Within, appeared in 1984.

52. See Weiss, *Bible from Within*, 40–41, with reference to Alonso Schökel's *Estudios
de poética hebrea* (1963).

53. Weiss, *Bible from Within*, 4.

54. Ibid., 6.

55. Ibid., 11–12 (italics added).

advocated paying "close attention to the text, to every word, to the word order and syntax, to synonyms and metaphors, to unusual syntactical phenomena, to the structure of every sentence and to the structure of the work as whole."[56]

Thus Amit is correct in stating that Weiss's method was a "literary synchronic approach, as opposed to the dominant historical diachronic one, which means it ignores the history of the text and its stratification, and concentrates on the story's meaning in relation to its formal design."[57] This distinction between the diachronic approach of the historical critics and the synchronic approach of the literary critics, which has actually become a major fault-line in the field (even if there are some who seek to bridge it), appears frequently in recent discussions of Old Testament criticism.

Many significant works of literary criticism of the Old Testament have been published in the fifty years since Weiss. Perhaps most influential has been Robert Alter's 1981 publication, *The Art of Biblical Narrative*, for which he had published a programmatic essay in 1975. Alter aimed "to throw some new light" on the Hebrew Bible by bringing a literary perspective to bear on it.[58] He wanted his argument to be intelligible to the general reader and expressed "the belief that it is possible to discuss complex literary matters in a language understandable to all educated people." Not surprisingly, therefore, he found the usefulness of the new narratology limited, and was "particularly suspicious of the value of elaborate taxonomies and skeptical as to whether our understanding of narrative is really advanced by the deployment of bristling neologisms like analepsis, intradiegetic, actantial." He differed from narratologists in wanting to move "from the analysis of formal structures to a deeper understanding of the values, the moral vision embodied in a particular kind of narrative." For this reason he thought he had something to say to readers trying to make sense of the Bible as "a momentous document of religious history."[59]

While I am in sympathy with this aim and appreciative of Alter's exegesis of texts from the Hebrew Bible, more is needed to comprehend the values and moral vision embodied in a biblical narrative than the

56. Ibid., 26.

57. Amit, *Reading Biblical Narratives*, 12.

58. Alter, *Art*, ix.

59. Ibid, x.

astute investigations of a contemporary interpreter.[60] For the insistent questions inevitably intrude: Whose values? Whose moral vision? Or more broadly, whose assumptions as to the meaning of social interactions in a particular setting? Are they those of humane and highly literate interpreters from our modern era typically habituated to North American and northern European ways of seeing the world, or those of the people by whom and for whom Old Testament narratives were written? How do we actually tell the difference?

Yairah Amit, for her part, also draws a distinction between the older "historical" interests in issues such as who wrote a biblical text and when, meaning the history of its composition, on the one hand, and the much more recent focus on its form and aesthetic features on the other, a focus especially stimulated by Robert Alter.[61] Accordingly, she advocates the synchronic approach, "which examines the story as we find it and pays no attention to its history."[62] She even accepts that once a biblical text is being investigated using literary-critical techniques the "age of the text makes no difference."[63] The only means of bridging the gap between historical and literary approaches that she envisages is that "the historian who seeks to reconstruct the realities behind the narrative finds that in order to elucidate the historical core, it is necessary to observe the formal design."[64]

Historical Context and Literary Form

In this volume, however, I will challenge this dichotomy between the historical and the literary/aesthetic by proposing a different, and integrated, model of interpretation and applying it to the eight narratives considered in chapters 3 to 10. My approach is historical in that it seeks

60. For a structural semiotic explanation of the Judah and Tamar narrative in Genesis 38 (considered in chapter 3, below) that is not characterized by the rebarbative technical language Alter decries and that produces significant insights into the text, see Sharon, "Some Results."

61. Amit, *Reading Biblical Narratives*, 10–11. Meir Sternberg's 1985 work *The Poetics of Biblical Narrative* has also had a significant influence on biblical literary critics.

62. Ibid., 12.

63. Ibid., 13; citing Menahem Perry and Meir Steinberg from an essay in Hebrew that appeared in 1968.

64. Ibid. For a recent literary study of the David and Saul narratives that is not much interested in their ancient context, see Borgman, *David*.

to ascertain what these texts meant when they were produced or appeared in their current form at some point in the history of Israel, but this approach is also literary in paying close attention to the narratives as narratives, as story.

It is worth noting that as long ago as 1753 Robert Lowth, in his epochal work, *On the Sacred Poetry of the Hebrews*, published in Latin, advocated a rather similar fusion of, on the one hand, literary form and, on the other hand, as complete a grip as possible on the way ancient Israelites would have understood these texts:

> He who would perceive the peculiar and interior elegancies of the Hebrew poetry, must imagine himself situated as the persons for whom it was written, or even as the writers themselves; he is to feel them as a Hebrew . . . nor is it enough to be acquainted with the language of this people, their manners, discipline, rites and ceremonies; we must even investigate their inmost sentiments, the manner and connexion of their thoughts; in one word we must see all things with their eyes, estimate all things by their opinion: we must endeavour as much as possible to read Hebrew as the Hebrews would have read it.[65]

While laudable in its aims, even if Stephen Prickett wonders if this statement was "more an off-the-cuff reflex than a considered agenda,"[66] to understand people from another time and culture has proved a formidably difficult task. With the rise of the social sciences, especially anthropology, in the last two centuries, however, we are now better equipped for the task than Lowth could ever have imagined, even if the complete understanding of the type he envisaged is likely always to elude us.

The Historical Context of Ancient Israel

While it is true, as noted above, that much traditional biblical scholarship of a historical kind has interested itself in the process that led to the texts in the form we now have, typically through source and form criticism, it is an unfortunate error to believe that these approaches exhaust the historical dimensions of a biblical text that are capable of scrutiny. Writing in 1992 Francis Watson was able to claim, "It has been agreed that the primary task of biblical scholarship is to reconstruct the

65. Prickett, *Origins of Narrative*, 113–14, citing Lowth, *Lectures*, 113–14.
66. Prickett, *Origins of Narrative*, 113.

diachronic historical processes underlying the text as it now stands."[67]
If there was such widespread agreement on that point two decades ago,
the position is very different today. Indeed, observations directed to how
the text came into existence from various sources can be a distraction
from interpretation devoted to what it meant when it had reached its
present form. Such is the case, for example, with the common view that
the so-called Psalm of Hannah in 1 Sam 2:1–10 possibly dates from the
tenth century BCE and has been inserted into the narrative (which is of
later date).[68] From the perspective of this volume, the relevant question
is rather what function that passage serves in the narrative as we have it
before us (a question addressed in chapter 4). Historical interpretation
of the sort advocated here is sociolinguistic, not archaeological, by in-
stinct: it explores the meaning of a particular narrative text in the social
setting in which it appeared rather than excavating the strata of tradition
and sources that underlie it.

Nor am I focused on the historical realities "behind the narrative"
(Amit's expression cited above), but with understanding the narrative
in relation to the social setting prevailing when it first appeared in its
current form, which is a properly historical interest. In fact, a common expression like the world "behind" a narrative represents a highly
misleading metaphor that separates text and context and thus obscures
the tight interpenetration of a narrative and the world in which it first
appeared. Thus, it is not relevant to my purpose here to assert or deny
that events reported in the biblical texts actually occurred or that the
characters described there actually existed; this is a valuable historical
investigation of a different kind that has attracted very lively debate in
recent years.[69]

I wish to concentrate on a different issue. The present investigation
is committed to exploring how an ancient Israelite audience would have
understood the eight narratives analyzed in this volume around the time
they were first put into the form we now have in the Hebrew Bible (the
"Masoretic Text"), except for Judith, which is only extant in Greek (and
later translations into other languages). I am focusing on the narratives

67. Watson, *Text, Church and World*, 15.

68. See McCarter, *I Samuel*, 74.

69. On this area see Davies, *In Search*; Dietrich, *Samuel*, 12–64; Halpern, *David's Secret Demons*; Isser, *Sword of Goliath*, 5–21; and Kratz, *Composition*; Römer and de Pury, "Deuteronomistic Historiography," 141; and Lemche, *Old Testament*.

in their Hebrew Bible version since this is the form most familiar to readers of this volume, especially (but not only) to those who read their Bible
in translation. In addition, trying to deal with other ancient versions in
their original languages would unnecessarily complicate the argument I
will be seeking to make, especially because of the textual variation in the
Hebrew and Greek versions of 1 and 2 Samuel. In addition, statements
in this volume as to what motivated characters in the various narratives
to do what he, she, or they did must not be taken as directed to the historical realities referred to by the text, but to the manner in which such
narrative details might have made sense to an ancient Israelite audience.

The texts in this volume come from Genesis, 1 and 2 Samuel and
the book of Judith. Genesis in its final form probably dates to the sixth
century BCE or later, even though it contains traditions that could be
much earlier.[70] The question of the date of composition of 1 and 2 Samuel
is still heavily under the influence of the view expressed by Martin Noth
in 1943 in *The Deuteronomistic History*,[71] that a single writer who lived
in Palestine during the period of the exile, compiled a history of Israel
from the viewpoint of the theology of Deuteronomy that included
Deuteronomy, together with Joshua, Judges, 1 and 2 Samuel, and 1 and
2 Kings. Yet other possible dates of composition, pre- and postexilic, are
possible.[72] Callaway has argued for a date in the early postexilic years.[73]
Although there is a lively general discussion concerning the existence,
character, and consequences of Noth's Deuteronmistic History,[74] it is not
relevant to this volume, for the reason that my focus is historical in the
sense that I am concerned to explore what these narratives meant to
their original audiences, not the history of development of the text or
the historical reality of characters and events mentioned in those narratives. Finally, the book of Judith was probably written in the Hasmonean
period.[75]

There is no need, however, to determine in this volume the precise
date or period of composition of these biblical texts since the features

---

70. See Whybray, "Genesis," 39–40 and von Rad, *Genesis*, 13–28.

71. Noth, *The Deuteronomistic History*.

72. See Klein, 1 *Samuel*, 2nd ed., xxviii–xx, for a succinct summary of the main
possibilities.

73. Callaway, *Sing, O Barren One*, 55.

74. See the essays in de Pury et al., *Israel Constructs Its History*.

75. See Cowley, "The Book of Judith," 245 and Moore, *Judith*, 67–70.

of the social context that will concern us are general enough to have been familiar to an ancient Israelite at any time from 900 to 100 BCE. Nothing said about the ancient Israelite context in this volume is tied to any particular historical event or period; we are looking at very general cultural and social features that persisted over centuries. That is to say, even though it is clear that there were developments in social structure and literary output across the pre- and postexilic periods, the broad features of context relevant to this study, especially the type of relationships between elite and non-elite; the patterns of patrilineality, patrilocality, and polygyny; group-orientation; honor and shame; patron and client relations; and the limited good—all of which are considered in chapter 2 with the benefit of comparison with recent social-scientific research into similar phenomena from modern (mostly preindustrial) cultures—persisted throughout this period in general form, whatever local variation they may have received.

Nor do we need to know if these four texts were "published" to an audience when they were put into their present form, or if they remained in the possession of the scribes or other persons who had composed or compiled them. This uncertainty is not germane to our argument, since each of them made sense to at least one ancient Israelite, namely, to the persons responsible for the final form of the texts in question, their respective authors or editors in their own historical settings within the broad chronological period in view here.

Although the approach advocated in this volume for interpreting Old Testament narrative is uncommon, it has some recent precedents apart from my own earlier essays in this area.[76] In the New Testament field, analysis directed to what the text in question meant to a particular ancient audience was central to redaction criticism from the late 1940s onwards, although attention to narrative was not prominent in that exercise.[77] The enterprise of making sense of the narrative flow of short segments of texts—in discrete passages such as parables—with respect to a context understood using the social sciences has become reasonably

76. See various publications by Victor Matthews and Don C. Benjamin (such as Matthews, *Social World of Ancient Israel*; and Benjamin, "Amnon and Tamar"), Ken Stone's *Sex, Honor, and Power in the Deuteronomistic History*; and the essay by Richard DeMaris and Carolyn Leeb, "(Dis)Honor and Ritual Enactment in the Jephthah Story."

77. See Günther Bornkamm's classic essay, first published in 1948, "The Stilling of the Storm at Sea in Matt. 8.23–27."

well established only in the last two decades, for example in publications by William Hertzog and Richard Rohrbaugh.[78]

The Literary Dimension

But what about the literary dimension of my textual investigations, given my aim of examining how these biblical narratives work *as narrative* within their ancient cultural context? I am initially fortified by the fact that so perceptive a literary interpreter of biblical narrative as Cheryl Exum has sought to explore the tragic dimension of several Old Testament texts in a manner that respects their "ancient character" and "cultural assumptions" and does not wrench "them wholly or violently out of their ancient context" to make them fit modern notions of the tragic.[79] But what about the literary dimension itself? The fact that we are dealing with texts in the form of narrative and not some other form? The fundamental answer is that exploring how the first audience of a biblical narrative, listeners rather than readers, would have understood and related to it means paying close attention to the details of the story. Close reading of texts is probably the main contribution that literary critical approaches have made to biblical interpretation in the last fifty years, and some form of this practice is necessary if we are to attend sufficiently to the qualities of the narratives as narratives. I find myself largely in agreement with a view Phyllis Bird expressed in 1989: "I am convinced that literary art and social presuppositions are so interrelated in any literary work that adequate interpretation requires the employment of both literary criticism and social analysis. Neither alone suffices."[80]

In the present volume, however, the characteristics subjected to close scrutiny will not be so much the formal or stylistic aspects of the texts favored in some reaches of literary criticism (although they will not be ignored) as those features of plot development and character portrayal that both resonate most strongly within the distinctive context of ancient Israel and have parallels in narratives from other cultures.

Yet, is this enough for the literary dimensions of these texts? Is some form of narratological theory necessary as well? Robert Alter, at

---

78. See Herzog, *Parables as Subversive Speech*; and Rohrbaugh, "A Dysfunctional Family and Its Neighbors."

79. Exum, *Tragedy and Biblical Narrative*, 13.

80. Bird, "The Harlot as Heroine," 99.

least, thought not. As we have noted above, he wanted to produce readings untroubled by the technical language of narratology that would be
accessible to all educated readers; he sought to understand not the deep,
formal structures but the values and moral vision of biblical narratives,
parts of a momentous document in religious history.[81] Ken Stone, the
author of some extremely perceptive interpretations of various narratives in the Deuteronomistic History, is of the view that "the use of a
specific method of literary analysis . . . is an essential safeguard against
implausible anthropological readings: it forces interpreters to consider
particular textual features, to incorporate those features into the interpretation, and to communicate to their audience some idea about the
ways in which this process takes place."[82]

For his "specific method" he opts for "a narratological model of
textual analysis developed by Dutch literary theorist Mieke Bal,"[83] especially because Bal is interested in the relations between literary analysis
and cultural context. Any interpreter, however, who is engaged in a close
reading of a text is able to address particular textual features, incorporate them into his or her analysis, and explain how this was done without recourse to a specific method of literary analysis. A little later Stone
acknowledges that he considers it preferable to employ a single model
of narrative discourse (Bal's) that he can explain and use consistently
"rather than appealing to a potpourri of narrative theorists whose theories are often different from or incompatible with one another."[84] While
his choice of Bal is reasonable, the situation he describes does leave
hanging the question, "So why use any narratological theory?" When
Stone does move on to interpreting narratives, moreover, his use of Bal
is fairly light and much of the analysis consists of the deployment of anthropological perspectives coupled with close reading to produce strong
interpretations. In his illuminating fifteen-page treatment of Judges 19,
for example, he introduces many anthropological perspectives but does
not utilize Bal's narratology at all.[85] These considerations suggest that a
specific literary critical method or theory is not necessary for the inves-

---

81. Alter, *The Art*, x.

82. Stone, *Sex, Honor, and Power*, 50. See Bal, *Death and Dissymmetry*.

83. Stone, *Sex, Honor, and Power*, 50.

84. Stone, *Sex, Honor, and Power*, 54.

85. Ibid, 69–84. Stone does refer to particular biblical interpretations by Bal on two
occasions in these pages.

tigation of the narratives that follows in this volume; a social-science informed understanding of the context coupled with a close examination of the Hebrew text (or the Greek, in the case of Judith) will be the central requirements.

Nevertheless, there is one area of literary study that will be of assistance for the reason that it will allow us to situate certain Old Testament narratives within a wider context, namely the study of typical elements in stories and broad story-structures that occur in folktales and written literature across the world. A consideration of this subject (the significance of which in relation to the aesthetic pleasure we derive from stories was raised at the end of the section above, on the question, "Why read Old Testament narrative?") will bring the current chapter to an end.

Story Elements and Story Structures[86]

Identifying Story Elements and Story Structures

During the second half of the nineteenth century, many ethnologists and students of folklore began to discover that the same motifs and characters appeared in myths and stories from numerous cultures around the world. The influence of such research in biblical criticism can be seen in Hermann Gunkel's important 1917 work *The Folktale in the Old Testament*. Perhaps the most influential researcher in this area was Sir James Frazer (1854–1941), who, in *The Golden Bough* (1890), argued that beneath a huge variety of ancient myths and religion lay fertility cults involving a king who was periodically put to death in sacrifice only to rise again; hence the notion of the dying and rising god that was to become hugely influential in anthropology (with Polish-British anthropologist Bronislaw Malinowski claiming that Frazer inspired him to develop the notion of functionalism) and literature.

While modern anthropologists are deeply skeptical of Frazer's project, because, for example, of the violent ripping of stories from their original contexts that it entailed, it paved the way for other attempts to develop taxonomies for myth, folklore, and story generally.

The American scholar Stith Thompson (1885–1976) devoted much of his career (spent largely at Indiana University in Bloomington) to

---

86. I gratefully acknowledge the assistance from discussion with Prof. Dennis C. Duling in relation to the material in this section, but I alone bear responsibility for its contents.

classifying motifs in folktales. The main product of this work was his six-volume *Motif-Index of Folk-Literature: A Classification of Narrative Elements in Folktales, Ballads, Myths*, originally published between 1932 and 1937.

Perhaps most significant, however, was the work of the Russian scholar Vladimir Propp (1895–1970). Inspired by Russian Formalism, a technique of literary analysis that involved breaking sentences into smaller elements ("morphemes") that were capable of analysis, Propp proceeded, in *Morphology of the Folktale* (1928) to break down folktales into their smallest narrative units ("narratemes") by analyzing some 150 Russian folktales and then to develop a typology of what he had found. Propp, in fact, identified thirty-one such units and the first five and last two such units will give some flavor of the project.[87] After the initial situation is depicted, there is "Absentation," where a member of a family leaves the security of the home environment and the hero is introduced. Then the hero is given an "Interdiction," such as "Don't do this," which he or she promptly ignores, producing a "Violation of Interdiction." The villain appears and makes a "Reconnaissance." In the next function, "Delivery," the villain gains information about the victim.[88] After the sequence of units is complete, the victim receives "Punishment," and the hero marries and ascends the throne (= "Marriage").[89] From the one hundred folktales he analyzed, Propp identified seven broad types of character:

1. The villain
2. the donor (who prepares the hero or gives him some magical object)
3. the (often) magical helper of the hero
4. the princess and her father
5. the dispatcher (who makes the lack or problem known to the hero and sends him off)
6. the hero
7. the false hero (who takes credit for the hero's actions or tries to

---

87. See Propp, *Morphology*, 25–65, for the 31 narrative units (after the initial situation) that he identified.

88. Ibid, 26–29.

89. Ibid, 63–65.

marry the princess).[90]

It is fundamental to Propp's approach that the structure or formal organization of a folktale is developed "following the chronological order of the linear sequence of elements in the text as reported by an informant." If a tale consists of narrative units from A to Z, "the structure of tale is delineated in terms of this same sequence."[91]

In the 1960s the Lithuanian linguist A. J. Greimas relied heavily on Propp in developing what he called his "actantial" model for the analysis of stories. He argued that stories could be broken down into six facets or "actants." These are:

1.   the subject

2.   and object (which can be a person)

3.   the sender (who instigates the action)

4.   the receiver (who benefits from the action)

5.   a helper (either person or useful object)

6.   an opponent (either personal or impersonal).[92]

The French Structuralist Claude Lévi-Strauss also argued that myths could be broken down into their constituent parts ("mythemes").[93] Yet he was critical of Propp[94] and proposed a very different approach. He sought to identify the patterns alleged to underlie myths and folktales, patterns that were "usually based upon an a priori binary principle of opposition."[95] He argued that binary oppositions (such as life and death, male and female) formed the deep structure of myths, and that myths resolved these oppositions.[96] His essay "The Story of Asdiwal" is a powerful and concise illustration of his method.[97] Lévi-Strauss was not

90. Ibid, 79–83.

91. Dundes, "Introduction," xi.

92. See Greimas, *Sémantique structurale*, especially 172–91. See Crossan, *Dark Interval*, for an application to biblical narrative.

93. For a succinct and sympathetic account of the structuralism of Lévi-Strauss, see Sturrock, *Structuralism*, 40–54.

94. See Lévi-Strauss, *La structure*. For the relationship between Propp's work and structuralism, see Olshansky, "Birth of Structuralism."

95. Dundes, "Introduction," xi.

96. See Lévi-Strauss, "Structural Study of Myth."

97. For an English translation, see Lévi-Strauss, "Myth of Asdiwal." In 1974 Robert

interested in the narrative progression of particular myths. In fact, his position was essentially that "linear sequential structure," of the type proposed by Propp, is merely the apparent or manifest content, whereas he was concerned with the deep, schematic structure, which constituted "the more important latent content."[98] A significant criticism of Lévi-Strauss concerns the arbitrariness of the structures that he claimed to have discovered.[99] In addition, the underlying structures that Lévi-Strauss purported to discern in myths will not be detected by anyone not considering them from his structuralist vantage point and will be alien to a nonspecialist audience listening to or reading them. Propp's structures, on the other hand, and indeed any approach that seeks to uncover the elements of narratives in sequential order, are at least capable of comparison with actual myths, folktales, and stories, can also be used as a model for the creation of new narratives and are more in tune with the way nonspecialists listen to or read narratives. His third character, the helper, for example, finds resonances in Sancho Panza in *Don Quixote*, Dr Watson in the Sherlock Holmes novels, and Obi Wan Kenobi in *Star Wars*. Indeed, if one looks at popular fiction and the story-lines of many movies, one or more of Propp's seven characters usually appear, and his identification of them helps us to appreciate the structure of the work in ways that allow it to be related to a wider literary universe.

A question of critical importance for both Propp's and Lévi-Strauss's differing approaches to the structure of myths and folktales is that of the relationship of the structures they produce to context. According to Alan Dundes, and with some justification, Propp's approach "has unfortunately dealt with the structure of text alone, just as literary folklorists generally have considered the text in isolation from its social and cultural context." To this extent he sees the "pure formalistic structural analysis" as probably "every bit as sterile as motif-hunting and word-counting."[100] Lévi-Strauss, on the other hand, according to Dundes, has "bravely" attempted to relate the deep structures he finds in myth "to the world at large, that is, to other aspects of culture such as cosmology and

---

Funk edited an important collection of essays on structuralist approaches to the parables (*A Structuralist Approach*).

98. Dundes, "Introduction," xii.

99. Clarke, *Foundations of Structuralism*, 202–5.

100. Dundes, "Introduction," xii.

world view."[101] There is a strong probability, however, that at least some of the structures Lévi-Strauss claimed to have found in myths he studied were actually his as a modern, Western intellectual rather than those of the indigenous peoples whose mythical productions he studied—for example his insistence on the constitutive opposition between nature and culture.[102] Accordingly, while Dundes is absolutely right to insist on the need for consideration of how myths, folktales, and other stories are contextualized in the cultures in which they appeared, he is wrong to consider that Lévi-Strauss addressed this issue whereas Propp did not. We will return to the importance of contextualization below.

In addition to these serious, scholarly works, semipopular works by two other writers are worth consideration: Joseph Campbell (1904–1987) and Christopher Booker (b. 1937). Campbell was an American lecturer and author who worked extensively in comparative religion and comparative mythology, arguing that recurrent, archetypal patterns appeared in myths and stories across the world. He believed the same universal truths were to be found in both Eastern and Western religions and gave particular priority to the role of the hero. In *The Hero with a Thousand Faces*, published in 1949, he introduced the idea of the "monomyth." Campbell's ideas have been widely influential, including on film makers such as George Lucas in his creation of the *Star Wars* series of films. More like Propp and unlike Lévi-Strauss, Campbell described the sequence of events through which myths advance and which other writers have found directly useful in crafting their own narratives. The second popularizer, Christopher Booker, is a prominent and controversial British journalist, who in 2005 published *The Seven Basic Plots: Why We Tell Stories*, the product of thirty years' work aimed at demonstrating that underlying the world's stories are seven basic story-lines, which he called:

a. "Overcoming the Monster"

b. "Rags to Riches"

c. "The Quest"

d. "Voyage and Return"

---

101. Ibid., xii–xiii. For applications of structuralist analysis to Ugaritic literature and the Old Testament respectively, see Rummel, "Narrative Structures" and Kunin, *Logic of Incest*.

102. Clarke, *Foundations of Structuralism*, 205–6.

e. "Comedy"

f. "Tragedy"

g. "Rebirth"

The first part of *The Seven Basic Plots* (pages 21 to 235) consists of an analysis of about 450 stories (mainly from Europe and the Middle East) in the light of one or more of these plots (some stories illustrate more than one). While a number of reviewers criticized the book, it found favor with many academics, playwrights, and novelists, including Beryl Bainbridge, John Bayley, and Fay Weldon.[103] Although Booker goes on to try to account for why these seven plots exist (with considerable reliance on Jung's theory of archetypes), and why we read stories (to see the ultimate defeat of good over evil that is the underlying structure in all of them), only the typology in this first section that will be utilized in this volume. His application of a Jungian framework in the second part of the book is unexamined and is not particularly persuasive.[104] Nor is his castigation of much literature written in the last two hundred years.[105] Finally, his work, of necessity and in a manner not dissimilar to that of Propp and Lévi-Strauss, largely involves decontextualizing the stories he discusses from the cultural matrices in which they were created, and in which they conveyed meaning to their original audiences.

The Significance of Story-Elements and Story-Structures

What are we to make of these various attempts to identify story elements and story structures? And since, of their nature, the same elements and structures can be shown to outcrop in stories and myths from many different cultures (even if the claim by the exponents of some of them to be worldwide in their scope needs to be taken with care), how are they to be reconciled with the dominant interest in the present volume to understand the eight narratives under discussion in the very specific culture of ancient Israel? These questions really involve digging into the tension generated by integrating (as in this volume) close attention to narratives

103. As seen in the commendations of the work published with it.

104. See Denis Dutton's critique of the Jungian dimension to the book, "Are There Seven Basic Plots?"

105. See Carolyne Larrington's review, "Downhill since Milton."

within their original contexts and the comparability of the plots of those narratives to other stories told or written in very different contexts.

Bruce Malina has observed, "all human beings are entirely the same, entirely different, and somewhat the same and somewhat different at the same time."[106] He means by this that all people are 100 percent the same in relation to "nature," that is our physiological character, our biological "hard-wiring," as a particularly advanced species of bipedal primates capable of interbreeding with one another across the globe. Second, all people are 100 percent different at the level of the individual, with a distinct personhood and subjectivity. Third, all people are partly the same and partly different in the area of culture, which for this purpose (the word *culture* is a very slippery one!) he defines as "an organized system of symbols by which persons, things, and events are endowed with rather specific and socially shared meanings, feelings, and values."[107] Human knowing embraces, simultaneously, these natural, individual/subjective, and cultural dimensions of our existence.

One of the exciting advances in the study of religion in the last two decades has been produced by the arrival of cognitive science, which "focuses on cross-culturally recurrent patterns in religious thought, experience and practice, explaining those regularities in terms of the architecture of the human mind."[108] This new research covers a subset of that aspect of human beings identified by Malina as 100 percent the same: our physiological makeup. These insights have now begun to permeate New Testament studies, as a 2007 collection of essays shows, edited by Luomanen et al.[109] I have argued in my essay in that work, on the basis of explorations into the nature of human cognition stretching back into the 1930s, that the physiological capacity that all human beings have for remembering is frequently expressed in the generation of narrative.[110] In the 1930s, British psychologist F. C. Bartlett, for example, showed how his experimental subjects, when required to transmit information from person to person using memory alone, transmitted folktales with greater fidelity than other material.[111]

---

106. Malina, *New Testament World*, 3rd ed., 8.

107. Ibid., 8.

108. Luomanen et al., "Introduction," 1.

109. Luomanen et al., *Explaining Christian Origins and Early Judaism*.

110. Esler, "'Remember My Fetters.'"

111. Bartlett, *Remembering*, 118–76, especially 171–76.

It is also probable that similarities in folktales and stories across times and very different cultures (as identified in their various ways by Frazer, Propp, Greimas, Lévy-Strauss, Campbell, Thompson, Booker, and others) connect with our fundamental cognitive processes. The existence of a set of cognitive structures and processes common to all human beings would explain why a tale has either appeared independently in different places or, alternatively, has been told in one place and traveled widely to others where it was retold to and by people of very different cultures because it struck some deep chord.[112] There is potentially a rich seam of research here for specialists in folklore and story to collaborate with cognitive scientists to determine if human beings are indeed "hard-wired" to generate and appreciate stories developed using certain elements/motifs and structures.

For the purposes of this volume, however, it is enough to rely upon the sheer existence of similar story types across cultures and the comparative framework they provide within which to consider the eight narratives in chapters 3–10. Most useful will be Christopher Booker's typology of seven plots, for two reasons: first, all the narratives discussed in chapters 3 to 10 are comparable with one or more of his plots, which helps us to appreciate the significance of aspects of their narrative progression; second, Booker's typology allows us to situate these biblical narratives in relation to a wide range of literary works so that by the processes of comparison and contrast, we can appreciate their distinctiveness and yet also see how well they stand up against the other works in terms of literary power. The problem of the decontextualization that tends to beset any form of structural comparison of a range of stories will be addressed by paying the closest attention to the way these storylines are contextualized in the culture of ancient Israel. To that particular cultural context we now turn.

---

112. For an encyclopedic description of folktales, see Thompson, *Motif-Index of Folk-Literature*.

2

The Original Context of Old Testament Narrative

UNDERSTANDING THE CONTEXT OF ANCIENT ISRAEL

In the previous chapter I have outlined my aim of reading Old Testament narratives within their cultural contexts in ancient Israel, that is, reading them with the understanding of their original Israelite audiences. Is this possible? If we are speaking of putting ourselves fully into the lives of these ancient Israelites, plainly not. It is hard enough for an ethnographer engaged today in the participant observation of the people of another culture to do this, let alone for us fully to assimilate our understanding to that of a long-dead people who have left only fragmentary documentary and physical evidence of their presence on this earth. Yet the problem is not just the limited nature of the surviving textual and material remains. Since the social world of ancient Israel was radically different from the one with which I and (presumably) most of the readers of this volume are personally familiar (assuming they were raised and socialized in the societies of North America and northern Europe, Australia, and New Zealand), to undertake the *historical* task of investigating what biblical narratives written in that setting meant when they first appeared represents quite a challenge. The risk is that we will interpret the extant evidence in accordance with unexamined assumptions and prejudgments that are based on our own social experience and that are inappropriate for Israelite culture. To attempt to read such a biblical narrative for its original meaning without vectoring in the distinctive ancient social scenarios it embodies risks obscuring its depths with anachronistic and ethnocentric misreadings.

In spite of these difficulties, the interpretation of the texts discussed later is based on the view that we can realistically aim for a general approximation of the culture in which ancient Israelites were immersed, and that is everywhere presupposed in the literature they have left behind, that is quite sufficient for the purpose of reading the narratives with their original audiences. While we cannot achieve the highest level of comprehension of their culture, we can learn enough to give us the general sense of the meanings these narratives would have conveyed to their original audiences in ancient Israel.

Moreover, the meanings we obtain from the narratives in this way are often radically different (as we will see repeatedly during the course of this volume) from those derived from interpretations that do not take seriously the need to attend to the cultural distance between our world and theirs, that make the mistake, in Cheryl Exum's words (noted in chapter 1), of wrenching "them wholly or violently out of their ancient context" to make them fit modern notions.[1]

How do we avoid this danger of reading our values into these ancient texts? As the ideal way for us to come to grips with the social setting of ancient Israel—a time-traveling team of ethnographers projected back to Jerusalem and its hinterland in the eighth century or so BCE—is, alas, denied us,[2] what means are available? Traditional biblical scholarship proceeds by the rigorous examination of all surviving sources of evidence, archaeological and documentary, to generate a picture of what Israel was like at this period. This sounds sensible but can involve a deep methodological flaw. Although close familiarity with the ancient data is necessary, all data has to be interpreted. A major problem with the traditional approach is that those who practice it usually bring to the task unrecognized and unacknowledged assumptions and beliefs about how societies work that stem from their upbringing and socialization in very different, modern cultures. These assumptions and beliefs often become embedded in traditions of interpretation that can create real impediments to understanding.

1. Exum, *Tragedy*, 13.

2. For an imaginative and highly revealing study of what such an expedition to first century CE Judea might be like see Malina, *Windows on the World of Jesus.*

The interpretation of the eight narratives set out in chapters 3 to 10 of this volume rests on the premise that the best way, probably the only way, we can step out of our habitual social frameworks is to draw upon anthropological resources and undertake comparative reference to social systems reasonably close to that in which these biblical texts are embedded, or at least much closer than those of North America and northern Europe. Such an approach, combined with the use of archaeology, has also been advocated by Carol Meyers in relation to families in early Israel (and families will be very prominent in the interpretations set out below):

> The value of ethnoarchaeology for reconstructing the early Israelite family merges with the general use of *social science methodology*. Again, precisely because so little information is available, knowledge of visible agrarian cultures provides important clues about early Israel. This is especially true in considering families. To be sure, cross-cultural variations are manifold and divergences even within a society are the norm. Yet, despite such differences, the very ubiquity of the family as an institution—as a small, kinship-structured domestic unit—allows theorists to suggest certain commonalities for families living in similar environmental niches and with corresponding subsistence regimes.[3]

All this fits in closely with the extent to which the interpretations offered in this volume are historical (in the sense of seeking to explain the meaning they would have conveyed to their original audience) even though I am not concerned with the historicity of the events described or with the history of the traditions that culminated in the various narratives considered. As Thomas Overholt has observed, "The object of using anthropology to assist in the interpretation of Old Testament texts is not, however, to argue that such narratives are historically accurate, let alone normative. What one looks for in the texts and seeks to understand is more basic patterns of behavior . . . The objective is not to establish 'reality' in some positivistic sense—this or that actually happened—but to suggest a broader social reality that was part of the context in which the texts were produced and that continues to be reflected in the texts, despite their subsequent literary history."[4]

3. Meyers, "The Family," 7 (italics original).
4. Overholt, *Cultural Anthropology*, 18–19.

ANTHROPOLOGY AND THE ANCIENT CONTEXT

Since the late 1970s an increasing number of biblical interpreters have turned to the social sciences to provide modes of interpreting the primary data in ways that are methodologically self-conscious and that depend upon the disciplined examination of similar social phenomena to allow us to escape the otherwise automatic importation of our own (often wildly inappropriate) prejudgments and presuppositions. In fact, however, the use of social-scientific ideas to understand the Old Testament has precursors going back to the nineteenth century, especially in the work of Scottish academic William Robertson Smith (1846–1894).[5] This is now a flourishing field.[6]

Since a burgeoning body of literature explains the use of the social sciences in biblical interpretation,[7] only brief remarks on the methodology need to be made here. The use of the social sciences in relation to biblical texts inevitably entails the process of comparison. Given that we cannot have direct access to the people of Israel in the first millennium BCE, we bring the data we do have about them into comparison either with particular works of ethnography or with theoretical resources that have been generated by anthropologists (or other social scientists) from empirical data, in the form of typologies, models or theories, or perspectives derived from theories.

In so doing we are not seeking to fill holes in ancient data from these theoretical resources; that is entirely inapposite, not least for the reason that it is precisely where lacunas exist in the ancient evidence that the phenomena in question may have differed from modern circumstances.[8] No, the reason to use anthropological resources is twofold. First, it has a heuristic function, enabling us to appreciate data that may be unexpectedly significant in the light of the social-scientific perspective being deployed. Second, it allows us to organize the data in ways that make

5. See Esler and Hagedorn, "Social-Scientific Analysis of the Old Testament," 16.

6. For a recent review, see Esler and Hagedorn, "Social-Scientific Analysis of the Old Testament."

7. See Elliott, *Social-Scientific Criticism*; Esler, "Introduction: Models, Context and Kerygma"; and Esler, "Social-Scientific Models"; Horrell, *Social-Scientific Approaches*; Malina, *The New Testament World*; and Overholt, *Cultural Anthropology*.

8. On this point I part company with Thomas Overholt when he writes, in speaking of the gaps in our knowledge of the society that produced the Hebrew Bible (*Cultural Anthropology*, 22), "insights derived from anthropology can often allow us to make inferences that at least provisionally fill in some of these gaps."

more sense than if we just employed our own homespun understanding of social phenomena (in other words, "to draw lines between the dots" more convincingly). I have recently defended such an approach by reference to the social-scientific methodology of Max Weber.[9]

In this volume the main area of the social sciences to be utilized is that of cultural anthropology (including ethnography). Although anthropology hardly exhausts the social sciences available for use in biblical criticism (and in my own work on the New Testament in recent years I have relied extensively on social psychology and the largely sociological field of collective memory), it does offer resources highly apt for interpreting Old Testament narrative. This is particularly the case with the ethnographies written in the second half of the twentieth century of various Mediterranean peoples and with the theorization that anthropologists produced based on this ethnographical research. Before considering this work, it is worth mentioning that it had some antecedents, with one notable Finnish pioneer—Hilma Granqvist—in the 1920s and 1930s (whose work we will utilize extensively later) and some French researchers in the 1930s and 1940s.[10] Raphael Patai was a shrewd observer of Middle Eastern cultures, and published a work in 1959, *Sex and Family in the Bible and the Middle East,* that contains still useful information.[11] Given that the use of anthropological perspectives from the Mediterranean in biblical interpretation has come under some criticism in recent years, a brief review and defense of the project is called for.

MEDITERRANEAN ANTHROPOLOGY AND THE BIBLE

The emergence of the Mediterranean as a distinct field of anthropological study dates from 1959, when Julian Pitt-Rivers organized the first conference devoted to the subject at Burg Wartenstein in Austria, bringing together anthropologists from the UK and continental Europe (both northern and southern), the USA, and Egypt.[12] Another conference

9. See Esler, "Social-Scientific Models."

10. See Albera and Blok, "The Mediterranean," 17, who mention Marc Bloch, Charles Parain, J. Weulersse, and Fernand Braudel.

11. Patai (1910–1996) was the first person to receive a doctorate from the Hebrew University in Jerusalem (in 1936). Also worth noting here is Johannes Pedersen, an Old Testament critic who was convinced of the importance of setting the texts in their social contexts; see *Israel: Its Life and Culture.*

12. On the background to this conference, see Pitt-Rivers, "La conférence."

involving a similar group was held in Athens in 1961, organized by John
Peristiany.[13] These meetings led to the publication of two important collections of essays. First came *Mediterranean Countrymen: Essays in the
Social Anthropology of the Mediterranean* in 1963, edited by Julian Pitt-
Rivers, which was concerned with "social structure," in particular "the
rural Mediterranean family and land tenure" that had been the main
interest of the 1959 conference.[14] Second was *Honour and Shame: The
Values of Mediterranean Society* in 1965, focusing on the values honor
and shame in the Mediterranean and edited by John Peristiany.[15] Most
of the essays were based on ethnographic research conducted by the
authors in the 1950s and early 1960s that had appeared or that would
subsequently appear in published monographs.[16]

The work undertaken in the 1960s involved the highlighting of a
number of themes: social structure and organization (including family
structure, kinship and inheritance, and patron-client relations), social
values (especially including honor and shame—and their close connection with male competitiveness, sexuality and the separation of the
sexes—but also hospitality, sanctity and impartiality), city and country,
internal and external migration, and social change.

The exploration of honor and shame was important but did not
dominate these proceedings. On the other hand, honor and shame—
understood in extremely diverse ways yet still recognizably honor and
shame—were central to the social values of many rural communities this group of anthropologists were investigating right around the
Mediterranean (including in Andalusia, Corsica, Cyprus, Thessaly
and Boeotia, central Turkey, Lebanon, Egypt, Morocco, and the Atlas
mountains) in ways that have long disappeared in the societies of North

13. See Peristiany, "Introduction," 9 and Albera and Blok, "The Mediterranean," 11
and Silverman, "Defining," 45–50.

14. See Pitt-Rivers, "Foreword and Acknowledgement," in *Mediterranean Countrymen*
(for "social structure"); and Friedl, "Some Aspects of Dowry," 114.

15. Also, from a meeting in Athens in 1963, came *Contributions to Mediterranean
Sociology: Mediterranean Rural Communities and Social Change* in 1968, edited by J.
G. Peristiany. Papers presented at a meeting in Canterbury in 1967 were published in a
special issue of *Anthropological Quarterly* 42:3 (1969).

16. This ethnography included Pitt-Rivers, *People of the Sierra* (1954), on the agrarian people living in a town in Andalusia; Campbell, *Honour, Family and Patronage*
(1964), on the Sarakatsani (transhumant shepherds of central Greece); and Paul Stirling,
A Turkish Village (1965).

America and northern Europe. On this matter their published ethnography speaks for itself. It is thus disappointing to discover H. V. Harris endorsing a throwaway remark of Sir Kenneth Dover (in a book review) in relation to honor and shame that "I find very little in a Mediterranean village which was not already familiar to me in a London suburb."[17] Dover (who died in St Andrews on 7th March 2010, aged 89 and greatly loved) was in his time the greatest Hellenist alive, but on this matter he was simply (and seriously) wrong. Yet even *bonus dormitat Homerus.*[18] Was Dover (or Harris?) familiar with young women in a London suburb (except perhaps among immigrant families from the Middle East) being killed by their fathers or brothers for besmirching the family honor by having sexual intercourse out of wedlock with a man of whom they did not approve (or for the mere suspicion of such activity)? This phenomenon is quite common in some Middle Eastern countries, and it reflects an attitude to honor utterly unlike that held by most people in the UK, northern Europe, the USA, Canada, Australia or New Zealand.[19] To refuse to acknowledge that cultural difference can be real, and that more extreme cultural forms can be fatal to those caught up in them will not assist the advance of scholarship in this area.

For a number of reasons this early research retains its importance, even though anthropology has changed greatly since the 1960s. First, it has a high value as ethnography, since it is characterized by close observation and penetrating analysis and discrimination. Second, it was largely conducted in rural areas that were already beginning to experience major social change that has now led to the modification or even disappearance of some of the phenomena studied by Julian Pitt-Rivers, John Campbell, Pierre Bourdieu, and the rest.

This area of anthropology continued to develop in the 1970s and 1980s. Notable ethnographic studies included Juliet DuBoulay's *Portrait of Greek Mountain Village* (1974), Jane and Peter Schneider's *Culture and Political Economy in Western Sicily* (1976), David Gilmore's *The People of the Plain* (1980), and Lila Abu-Lughod's *Veiled Sentiments: Honor and Poetry in a Bedouin Society* (1986).

---

17. Harris, *Rethinking the Mediterranean.*

18. "The great Homer nods," Horace, *Ars Poetica* 1.359.

19. On the subject of honor killings as a context for Joseph's remarkable attitude toward Mary in Matt 1;19, see Marohl, *Joseph's Dilemma.*

A major aspect of the 1960s Mediterranean ethnography was its emphasis on unrelenting competition between males for honor, including over women and sexual access to them.[20] Pitt-Rivers argued that Mediterranean honor involved the domination of other men: one achieved honor by defeating someone else, whereby his honor became yours.[21] Since honor "was always implicitly the claim to excel over others," it was the basis of precedence in what Pitt-Rivers called the "pecking-order" theory of honor.[22] Other ethnographers encountered similar attitudes. Thus Campbell observed that among the Sarakatsani there was no cooperative activity among men who were not related: everything else was competition: "outside the family and the kindred a man meets and expects only hostility and suspicion . . . Confidence, trust, and an altruistic concern about another individual's welfare can only exist between kinsmen."[23] As for non-kin, "the opposed families of this fragmented community are related through competition for prestige."[24] Pierre Bourdieu set out the "rules of the game" of challenge and response that governed how the men of the Kabyle tribe in Algeria competed with one another over matters of honor in a wide variety of situations from insults to gift giving.[25]

In 1981 Bruce Malina published *New Testament World: Insights from Cultural Anthropology*, a short work, modestly aimed at students "beginning to study the New Testament," [26]—a work that has nevertheless since had an enormous influence on biblical research. Malina's aim was to help those reading the New Testament documents understand their original meaning more accurately by emphasizing how different was the cultural context in which they were written from that familiar to most North American and northern European readers of the Bible. To achieve this he used the findings of Mediterranean ethnographers Pierre Bourdieu, J. G. Peristiany, and Julian Pitt-Rivers (but also of several other social scientists, such as Mary Douglas, Clifford Geertz, M.

20. Gilmore, "Introduction," 5.

21. See Pitt-Rivers, *The Fate of Shechem*, 3, 92.

22. Pitt-Rivers, "Honour and Social Status," 23.

23. Campbell, *Honour, Family and Patronage*, 38.

24. Ibid., 39.

25. Bourdieu, "The Sentiment of Honour," with "rules of the game" mentioned at 197.

26. Malina, *The New Testament World*, iii.

A. K. Halliday, and Edmund Leach) to develop a reading strategy and theoretical pictures of subjects like honor and shame, personality, kinship and marriage, and purity for comparison with New Testament data. A striking feature of the book was the extent to which Malina adopted the theme of competition between men over honor that had been an important topic in the early Mediterranean ethnography. At one point he noted, "nearly every interaction with non-family members has undertones of a challenge to honor."[27]

As Mediterranean anthropology matured, it inevitably became subject both to methodological critique and a heightened degree of self-reflection on the part of those engaged in it. In 1977 John Davis critically reviewed the field, taxing it with failure to be sufficiently comparative (that is, with continuing to produce ethnographies of particular communities that did not relate to other ethnographic research), with ignoring historical development among the peoples studied, with focusing on marginal (mainly rural) communities, and with neglecting links between city and country, region and nation.[28]

In 1980 Michael Herzfeld criticized the use of "honour" and "shame" as representing "inefficient glosses" and "massive generalizations" on a wide variety of indigenous terminological systems—glosses that had become counterproductive, especially because they facilitated comparison between phenomena in different cultures that might not be comparable. Yet while concepts like "honor" and "shame" represent terminology at a certain level of abstraction that facilitates comparison between similar phenomena and should never be allowed to distort our understanding of such phenomena in their particular settings, Herzfeld went too far with this critique. At the outset, for example, he conceded that the earliest work (Peristiany's 1965 collection of essays, *Honour and Shame*) "avoided facile correlations through its scrupulous attention to the details of particularistic ethnographic description."[29] If Pierre Bourdieu was able to conjoin the general expression "honour" with the most finely observed account of the Arabic terminology of its various elements among the Kabyle,[30] as did other contributors to the 1965 collection, why cannot Herzfeld? In short, Herzfeld's approach on this point

---

27. Malina, *The New Testament World*, 1st ed., 30.

28. Davis, *People of the Mediterranean*, 5–10.

29. Herzfeld, "Honour and Shame," 339.

30. Bourdieu, "The Sentiment of Honour."

is unpersuasively "particularistic," as a number of other anthropologists have pointed out.[31] He is also inconsistent in ditching *honor* as a general comparative term, only to adopt *hospitality* instead, in relation to which just the same kind of objection could be made.[32]

The tendency in the early Mediterranean anthropology to view "honor" and "shame" essentially as balanced opposites attracted valuable criticism from Unni Wikan in 1984. Although she did not dispute the role of the two concepts as useful abstractions,[33] Wikan argued on the basis of her research in Cairo and Oman that often "shame" rather than "honor" was the more important value, and that people were more tolerant of "shameful" behavior than previous ethnographic research might suggest. Wikan also argued against the idea that had been expressed by the early ethnographers that only men, not women, could have or strive for honor.[34] She also showed how in Oman women who were friends with another woman who had sex with other men while her husband was away were largely willing to overlook her behavior because in other respects she was kind, hospitable, and helpful.[35] Wikan's work with communities in Cairo and Oman is an object lesson in the need to ensure that abstract language useful for comparative purposes is never allowed to supplant the realities of a situation discovered by close observation.

The increasing maturity of Mediterranean anthropology surfaced in a collection of essays edited by David Gilmore that appeared in 1987: *Honor and Shame and the Unity of the Mediterranean*. Most of the contributors continued employing "honor" and "shame" as useful concepts for comparable (although highly diverse) phenomena appearing in societies around the Mediterranean.[36] Nevertheless, they objected (with

31. See Gilmore, "Introduction," 6–7; Davis, "Family and State," 23 ("His refreshing skepticism leads to an extremely particularist position . . . to which few people pay more than lip service, although they do admire the discriminating precision of his ethnography"); and Giovannini, "Female Chastity Codes," 61.

32. See Herzfeld, "'As in Your Own House.'"

33. Wikan, "Shame and Honour." At page 637 she notes that she is not throwing doubt "on the overall importance of a concept of honour in many societies of the Mediterranean and the Middle East."

34. Ibid., 638–9. Pitt-Rivers, for example, had expressed the view in relation to women and honor that their "feminine status precludes their striving for it by might" ("Honor," 505).

35. Wikan, "Shame and Honour," 640.

36. Those of this view were David Gilmore, John Davis, Carol Delaney, Michael Marcus, Maureen Giovannini, Mariko Asano-Tamanoi, and Stanley Brandes; Michael

good cause) to the reification of these concepts, especially if that entailed homogenized versions of honor and shame substituting for finely focused and discriminating ethnography in particular contexts. Several of them commented upon the impact of social change, with Giovannini noting that a useful research question was the differential survival of the Mediterranean cultural codes "in contexts of urbanization, industrialization, migration, and political change."[37]

A number of the contributors in the 1987 collection took issue with the picture of unremitting male competition that had characterized some of the work in the 1950s and 1960s and argued that other moral principles (such as generosity and honesty) were at times more prominent than honor as a masculine ideal.[38] Pitt-Rivers had himself attempted to circumvent this objection by distinguishing between the competitive "precedence honor" and the noncompetitive "virtue honor" that covered values like honesty and loyalty.[39] Peristiany expressed a somewhat similar view.[40] In 1992 they confirmed the distinction yet now referred to it as a "paradox."[41] There are, however, real problems with this distinction.[42] Chief among them, as Gilmore has noted, is that this "arbitrary division is probably logically valid, but it begs the question of what Mediterranean honor is by dividing it up into contrasting categories and by calling different things honorable."[43] It would have been preferable for Pitt-Rivers and Peristiany to have reserved "honor" for the aggressive ideal and behavior of masculine competition, and to have simply conceded that it coexisted with other ways of valuing males that

Herzfeld was the solitary exception.

37. Giovannini, "Female Chastity Codes," 71.

38. So Gilmore, "Introduction," 3; and Marcus, "Horsemen," 50.

39. See Pitt-Rivers, "Honour and Social Status," 61; and Pitt-Rivers, "Honor," 510.

40. Peristiany, "Honour and Shame," 189–90.

41. Pitt-Rivers and Peristiany, "Introduction," 5.

42. Louise Lawrence has utilized "virtue honor" quite extensively (*Ethnography, passim*) but without giving much attention to the problems inherent in the concept. Lawrence's *Ethnography* is an important book that critically engages with existing scholarship applying Mediterranean anthropology to biblical interpretation and then uses fresh anthropological and literary-critical perspectives to interpret Matthew's gospel. Zeba Crook has published two substantial reviews of *Ethnography*, in 2006 and 2007: "Method and Models" and "Structure vs. Agency," the second of which has attracted a response from Lawrence, "Structure, Agency and Ideology."

43. Gilmore, "Honor, Honesty, Shame," 90.

were different in character and, furthermore, not necessarily distinctive to the Mediterranean area. On the other hand, the foregrounding in the early ethnography of gender separation, female chastity, and the shame incurred through loss of premarital virginity was endorsed by several of the contributors.[44]

Julian Pitt-Rivers and J. G. Peristiany themselves returned to the character of Mediterranean anthropology in the introduction to a volume of essays they edited that appeared in 1992: *Honor and Grace in Anthropology*. While mainly concerned with the connection between honor and the sacred, which had been neglected in the 1960s (except by J. K. Campbell), they commented on a number of other issues. On honor, for example, they noted how warring conceptions of honor (representing the "varied and conflicting interests of rival groups") appeared in communities, with their respective champions. As a result, it was "an error to regard honor as a single constant concept rather than a conceptual field within which people find the means to express their self-esteem or their esteem for others."[45] They insisted that when they had associated "the Mediterranean concept of honor" with "a tendency to associate masculine honor with female sexual purity," they had been speaking "rather vaguely," since in some areas near the Mediterranean (as in northern Spain) or in parts of Algeria this connection was not made at all. There was also considerable variety within what was loosely described as "the Mediterranean concept of honor."[46]

The role of women in Mediterranean societies has come to be seen as much more active and influential than the 1950s and 1960s ethnography allowed, especially because so many female anthropologists have worked in the area and gained access to women in a way that would have been very difficult for their male colleagues, especially in Muslim communities. Finnish anthropologist Hilma Granqvist (whose ethnography will be used heavily in chapter 4, below) had shown the possibilities here as long ago as the 1920s and 1930s, as had Elizabeth Fernea, who, as her husband finished his own anthropology book, distilled into the celebrated book, *The Guests of the Sheik*, published in 1969, her experience of Iraq during the two years they lived in a village there. Ernestine

44. See Gilmore, "Introduction," 3–4; Delaney, "Seeds of Honor," 35–36; Giovannini, "Female Chastity Codes."

45. Pitt-Rivers and Peristiany, "Introduction," 4.

46. Ibid.," 6.

Friedl was the only woman among the anthropologists who published in the collections of 1963 and 1965 edited by Pitt-Rivers and Peristiany respectively, her subject being aspects of dowry and inheritance in Boeotia. Even at that early stage Friedl was able to show an intersection between virtue and financial considerations ("an ugly, older girl, with a bad reputation would have to bring a large dowry to compensate for her personal deficiencies"), and that among the Boeotian farmers, "male honor depends not only on male protection of the chastity of women, but also more explicitly and obviously on the provision by men of adequate dowries for their women."[47] More recent ethnography, conducted by anthropologists like Unni Wikan (1984), Susan Carol Rogers (1975 and 1985), Lila Abu-Lughod (1986), Alice Schlegel (1990), Sally Cole (1991), and Jill Dubisch (1995), has continued to show that the cultures in view are more complex than was previously thought, by bringing out the important role of women in the domestic economy, the economic dimensions of their procreativity, the power they can exercise in particular local settings, and their capacity to form social networks to achieve their ends. Having reviewed much of this material, Carolyn Osiek concluded recently that honor and shame must be understood within a complex matrix of other societal factors.[48] On the other hand, it does women in particular contexts a disservice not to recognize that sometimes the type of culture Pitt-Rivers and Peristiany described in the 1950s and 1960s can persist as far as they are concerned with almost their full vigor and effect. Such was the case with the Iraqi women closely interviewed by British sociologist Sana Al-Khayyat, herself born in Iraq, in the early 1980s.[49] Similarly, although it has been asserted that "Lila Abu-Lughod's celebrated *Veiled Sentiments* illustrates how Egyptian Bedouin women assert their acceptance or defiance of the system of social hierarchy through poetic discourses on emotion that are linked to the ideology of modesty,"[50] the subject matter of many of the songs in question is how a woman was in love with a man only to be compelled to marry her cousin![51]

---

47. Friedl, "Some Aspects of Dowry," 124 and 133.
48. Osiek, "Women, Honor, and Context."
49. Al-Khayyat, *Honour and Shame*, especially 21–55.
50. Lawrence, *An Ethnography*, 48.
51. See Abu-Lughod, *Veiled Sentiments*, 208–13.

In an article published in 1989 João de Pina-Cabral took issue with a number of the contributors to the 1987 volume, especially with Gilmore himself.[52] Pina-Cabral was particularly critical of the attempt to describe the Mediterranean as a "culture area" and linked that attempt to the demands of academic politics (this point, however, clearly being irrelevant to the merits of the argument).[53] He also (and with good cause) rejected Gilmore's attempt to link particular cultural features of the Mediterranean to individual psychological development. Yet whatever one thinks of the Mediterranean as a "culture area," a notion originally developed by Conrad Arensberg and recently defended by Sydel Silverman,[54] it is possible to benefit from the individual essays in Gilmore's 1987 book without subscribing to this idea. Pitt-Rivers and Peristiany have observed that the notion of "culture area" played no part in their ethnography in the 1960s, since "our aim in treating the Mediterranean as a whole was epistemological only and we never attempted to define it geographically."[55]

Since the 1980s fine works of Mediterranean anthropology have continued to be produced, some of them ethnographic and others more theoretical in character. They include an important collection of essays edited by Peter Loizos and Evthymios Papataxiarchis, *Contested Identities: Gender and Kinship in Modern Greece* (1991); Anne Meneley's *Tournaments of Value* (1996); and David E. Sutton's *Remembrance of Repasts: An Anthropology of Food and Memory* (2001). Sutton states that the latter "is not meant as an ethnography of food and social life on Kalymnos." Rather, he is using "grounded ethnography to consider issues of current theoretical concern," in the belief "that such a grounded and simultaneous consideration of the topics of food and memory will shed light on current diverse theoretical approaches, ranging from structure and history, to 'embodiment,' to consumption."[56] A major collection of

52. Pina-Cabral, "The Mediterranean."

53. For further criticism of the Mediterranean as a "culture area," see Herzfeld, "The Horns."

54. See Arensberg, "The Old World Peoples"; and Silverman, "Defining the Anthropological Mediterranean," 48–50.

55. Pitt-Rivers and Peristiany, "Introduction," 6.

56. Sutton, *Remembrance of Repasts*, ix. David Horrell misreads the intention of this work (against the clearly expressed aim of its author) when he states "Sutton's book is primarily an ethnographic study of 'the relationship between food and memory on the island of Kalymnos, Greece" ("Whither Social-Scientific Approaches," 14).

essays and review of the field, *L'anthropologie de la Méditerranée*, edited by Dionigi Albera and others appeared in 2001.[57] This work (and the conference that preceded it) marked a fresh start for Mediterranean anthropology, avoiding the pitfalls of the past and pushing on in new directions. Since 2001, indeed, review essays and contributions on particular topics have continued to appear, with Dionigi Albera, in his judicious way, suggesting in 2006 that Mediterranean anthropology was located "between crisis and renewal."[58]

Where does all this leave the use of Mediterranean ethnography in the task of biblical exegesis? *First*, Carolyn Osiek has recently made this important observation: "many newer anthropological studies now focus on the changes brought about by globalization and economic transformation in traditional societies . . . Thus there is the dilemma that in most cases the older ethnographic studies are more directly helpful for the study of ancient cultures that were not at all influenced by similar phenomena, yet the newer ones bring the reader up to date in anthropological thinking and research."[59]

Accordingly, the Mediterranean ethnography from the 1950s and 1960s—undertaken largely in relation to rural and peasant communities at an agrarian stage of development, but which have now been greatly influenced, if not utterly transformed, by the forces of modernization—is likely to retain its usefulness. This is especially true of Old Testament narratives, which have a largely rural setting, unlike most New Testament documents, which were written for urban communities. *Second*, the use of this ethnography in no way implies, let alone necessitates, any historical link between the biblical data we will be examining and the ethnography of recent times. Certainly a reasonable fit is needed between the anthropology and the biblical material for the comparison to have any point, but that is all. *Third*, Mediterranean anthropology can either be deployed at a reasonably high level of generality, as when we use theoretical perspectives or models derived from the ethnography (and we will see this particularly in relation to the pattern of challenge-and-riposte), or at more empirical level, by comparing ethnographic research

57. See Albera et al., *Anthropology of the Mediterranean*.

58. See Sant Cassia, "Review Article: Navigating" Albera, "Anthropology of the Mediterranean"; Bromberger, "Towards an Anthropology"; Bromberger, "Bridge, Wall, Mirror"; and Hauschild et al., "Syncretism in the Mediterranean."

59. Osiek, "Women, Honor, and Context" 324.

into a particular community or communities with Old Testament data. The latter type of comparison is essentially immune from the criticisms that have been made against tendencies in Mediterranean anthropology to reify concepts like honor and shame since such abstractions are not required in this comparative mode. *Fourth*, and this applies especially when we are employing the former of the two modes just mentioned, abstract conceptions must never ride roughshod over the detailed evidence in the text under consideration. We should be alert to the possibility, for example, that shame rather than honor will reflect the dominant mode in which the worth of individuals is assessed by the local community that we are presupposing as the audience for the narrative. While theoretical perspectives are useful in uncovering important phenomena and patterns in the text, and in helping us organize the data we find there in plausible ways, they must not substitute for or supplant the data or its close examination. The plausibility of a reading will continue to depend on close examination and analysis. *Fifth*, although we must be alert to ensure that strongly competitive interpretations of interactions in a given narrative are closely based on the textual data and not merely assumed to exist there, the fact that more recent ethnographers have discerned noncompetitive values (like honesty and generosity) operative in some Mediterranean communities must not divert us from recognizing and responding to instances of "honor precedence" when they appear in the text before us. Thus, Gary Stansell has taken up the issue of honor and shame in relation to certain narratives concerning David (1 Sam 18:23; 20:30–34; 25; 2 Sam 6; 10:1–6; 19:1–9; 13; and 16:20–23) in an essay that offers new and culturally realistic interpretations of these texts.[60] *Sixth* and last, while issues relating to gender separation, sexuality, and female chastity remain prominent themes in Mediterranean ethnography, we should be open to the possibility of women engaging in competition over honor. A number of the narratives considered in this volume will show women taking the initiative when their honor is threatened.

THE SOCIAL CONTEXT OF ANCIENT ISRAEL

The time has now come to set out a broad profile of the social context of ancient Israel that I will return to repeatedly in discussing the narratives considered below. I will move from the microcosmic to the macrocos-

---

60. Stansell, "Honor and Shame."

mic, first exploring the physical realities of life for families in the villages of Israel; then the strong group bonds, social structures, and values that held them together in a world where all goods were thought to exist in finite and stable quantities; then patterns of kinship, inheritance and marriage; before moving to the macro level: to the broad set of relationships whereby the elite controlled and appropriated the surplus of the non-elite in a manner typical of "agrarian" and "advanced agrarian" societies (terms explained below). The chapter will conclude with a consideration of Israel as a high-context culture and what this means for the mode of representation we encounter in biblical narratives.

Material Conditions: Families and Villages

The ancient Israelite audience probably imagined that Judah was living in the sort of villages known to us now through archaeological surveys and excavations of Iron I settlements conducted after the Six-Day War (1967) in what was western Canaan. Victor Matthews and Don Benjamin have noted that "archaeologists have identified more than 300 village sites in the hills which date from the Iron I period (1250–1000 BCE)." In the next two centuries the population expanded to about eighty thousand, and "more than 100 new villages were founded in the hills of Samaria, Galilee to the north and Beersheba to the south."[61] The archaeological findings have been invaluable because, as Benjamin and Matthews note, the "Bible seldom explains farming, but simply assumes the audience knows it so well that no additional details are needed."[62] Apart from well-watered parts of Galilee, in most places farming conditions were very difficult, with crop failures frequent. In spite of this, Israelite farmers built up a close understanding of the land and its often harsh ecological niches, as Ellen Davis has brilliantly explained.[63] The Israelites grew wheat and barley; figs, grapes, and olives; and raised sheep, goats, donkeys, and some other animals. A remarkable glimpse of the ancient Israelite agricultural cycle for crops is provided by a text scratched on an archaic Hebrew potsherd from about 1000 BCE from Gezer, in which someone was practicing writing Hebrew. The so-called Gezer almanac provides for the picking of olives in August and September, sowing bar-

61. Matthews and Benjamin, *Social World of Ancient Israel*, 4.
62. Ibid., 37.
63. Davis, *Scripture, Culture, and Agriculture*.

ley in October, sowing wheat in December and January, pulling flax in February, harvesting barley in March and April, harvesting wheat and feasting in April, pruning the vines in May and June, and picking the summer fruit in July.[64] Technology was developing, for example, by farmers introducing new dry-farming techniques like terraces on hillsides and cisterns to increase agricultural production and to improve the viability of life in the hill country.[65]

According to Carol Meyers, the archaeological investigations since 1967 "have provided a wealth of new information about the dwellings, artifacts, subsistence strategies, and other aspects of daily life of the agrarian communities in which virtually all the early Israelites lived."[66] These Israelites lived in small villages, with the area most of them occupied ranging only from about half an acre to two and half acres, with some fifty inhabitants in the smaller ones (more like hamlets) and 150 in the larger. Probably the majority were agglomerative in character, made up of an irregular collection of clusters of homes roughly arranged in an oval, while others showed some planning, with an elliptical ring of houses spread around a central space.[67] These villages seem to have been coterminous with the *mišpaḥah*, which is hard to translate but refers to a kinship group, a group of related families usually sharing a common male ancestor.[68] Most of the houses in such villages were small rectilinear structures, with access through a door leading to the main room, with a row of pillars often appearing on one or both sides of the door. At the end of this room, one or more doorways led to one, two, or three more rooms. Stairways, frequently attached to outside walls, indicate the original presence of upper stories. Probably the ground floor was for animal and storage needs associated with subsistence agriculture,

64. A drawing of the potsherd and an interpretation of the text are provided by Matthews and Moyer, *The Old Testament*, 83, in a useful summary of life on the land at this time (81–86). See also "The Gezer Almanac" online: www.kchanson.com/ANCDOCS/westsem/gezer.html.

65. Matthews and Benjamin, *Social World of Ancient Israel*, 43, in a chapter on the "The Farmer" (37–51)

66. Meyers, "The Family," 7. For conditions during the First Temple period, see Blenkinsopp, "The Family."

67. See Meyers, "The Family," 12, relying on Shiloh, "Population"; and Finkelstein, *Archaeology*, 238–50. Also illuminating is Finkelstein's report of the excavation of a single village, *'Izbet Sartah*.

68. Meyers, "The Family," 13.

while the living quarters were upstairs. Cooking seems to have taken place in sheltered, outdoor space.[69] These dwellings constitute evidence for a family unit larger than that of the nuclear family (which matches with biblical data on patrilineality, to be discussed in more detail below), suggesting that the core of the compound family in one of these houses would have been a senior married pair with their children and grand-children.[70] But what was life like for the people who lived in such houses in these villages?

Group Orientation

Unfortunately, we can learn little of the character of the relationships between the family members who inhabited such houses merely from the archaeological remains. Nevertheless, comparative experience from elsewhere suggests, and literary evidence from biblical texts confirms, that ancient Israelites were group-oriented and not individualistic. This should really not cause us too much surprise, given that individualistic cultures are fairly uncommon in the world and really only appeared in comparatively modern times, initially in northern Europe. Yet this is so important a feature of the context of the texts and so alien to the experience of most of those reading this book that it is necessary to spend a little time on this issue.

Collectivistic cultures require that individuals belong to groups that provide protection and identity in return for loyalty. Assertions of identity are usually linked to groups like families, tribes, and villages. Collectivistic cultures emphasize the aims and needs of the ingroup over those of the individual and seek to maximize collaboration between members rather than achievements by individuals. Indeed, individual initiative and innovation are generally not encouraged in collectivistic cultures. One aspect of the pronounced ingroup/outgroup differentiation typical of collectivistic cultures is the tendency to apply different standards to the behavior of members of the ingroup, on the one hand, and of outgroups on the other, with ingroup members favored and outgroup members negatively stereotyped and discriminated against. By way of contrast to all this, in individualistic cultures (like those of North

---

69. Ibid.,14–15, citing Shiloh, "The Four-Room House"; Holladay, "House" and "Stable"; Herzog, *Beersheba II*; and Braemer, *L'architecture domestique*.

70. Meyers. "The Family," 16–17.

America, northern Europe, Australia, and New Zealand) individuals aim for self-realization and self-fulfillment; for example, leaving home when of a certain age is seen as a necessary and desirable step in the process of maturation. People look after themselves and their immediate family. Individual initiative is positively encouraged. Statements of identity are likely to focus on the qualities of the individual, not his or her important ingroups. Value systems are regarded as universalistic and do not discriminate between ingroup and outgroup.[71] Harry Triandis has noted a good indicator of the difference between the individualistic USA and the collectivistic Japan: in the USA delinquent children are punished by being "grounded" (made to stay in the home), but in Japan they are punished by being put out of the house.[72]

It is worth noting, however, that while cultures tend to be predominantly collectivistic or individualistic, both types of behavior can occur in any given culture. Harry Triandis has explored some of the complexities here. He uses the words "idiocentric" and "allocentric" to refer to the orientations adopted by individuals in, respectively, individualistic and collectivistic cultures. He points out that sometimes we find idiocentric individuals in collectivist cultures and allocentric individuals in individualistic cultures. Individuals like this may be countercultural, but they do occur. Collectivist cultures have a preponderance of allocentric responses, and individualistic a preponderance of idiocentric responses.[73]

We actually have some evidence for the appearance of individualistic phenomena in collectivistic contexts in the modern and ancient Mediterranean. A. M. Abou-Zeid, one of the leading figures in social-scientific research in the Middle East (and a participant at the meetings convened by Julian Pitt-Rivers and J. G. Peristiany in the 1960s), has described what happened when the Kharga Oasis, lying in a low depression 150 kilometers to the west of the Nile and largely inaccessible to the Nile valley, was connected to Cairo by railway around the beginning of the twentieth century. In essence, this meant that young men could now leave the tightly collectivistic villages of the oasis, where

71. See Triandis, "Collectivism vs. Individualism" and "Cross Cultural Studies" for the views expressed in this paragraph. For group-oriented personality in the New Testament, see Malina, *New Testament World*, 3rd ed., 60–67.

72. Triandis, "Theoretical and Methodological Approaches," 49.

73. Ibid., 41–51.

they were subject to their fathers and to village sheikhs, to seek work in Cairo or other Nilotic towns. Sometimes they went with the approval of their family with the aim of making money and eventually returning, but sometimes they went for the "individualistic" reason that they were in conflict with "the family or the whole community." Thus there were two contrasting situations—one reinforcing group orientation, the other a rebellion against it: "The planned type of migration (sc. of young men to the Nile valley) manifests the solidarity of the family and its integrity as one corporate unit, while the individualistic type is a manifestation of the struggle within the family and an expression of its disintegration."[74]

Influenced by Harry Triandis's identification of individualistic pockets in otherwise collectivistic Latin America, and writing in relation to the first century CE, Bruce Malina has pointed to what he calls "quasi-individualist" behavior exhibited by two types of people: the extremely wealthy and the extremely downtrodden. The first group indulges in "all kinds of conspicuous consumption, carnivals, trade, luxury goods, and so on," which is motivated by pleasure, personal needs, or aspirations.[75] Malina could have cited the freedman Trimalchio, immortalized by Petronius, as an excellent case in point. Such people have left group belonging and loyalty far behind them. At the other end of the spectrum, we find people who cannot maintain their social status and are forced to fend for themselves: "beggars, prostitutes, disinherited sons, family-less widows, orphans or children that families cannot support who are abandoned to the streets to fend for themselves." These are the most marginalized people in their societies who are cut from their usual ingroups that would otherwise guarantee their survival.[76]

Old Testament narratives offer numerous signs that they originate in and assume a collectivistic culture, and it will be useful to set out some of the evidence here. The way characters are introduced, the first information that we receive, which the narrator obviously considers that his readers or listeners need to know, takes us straight into a group-oriented world. We are so used to such introductions in the Bible that we have probably become quite blasé about how much they tell us of ancient Israel. Consider the very first verse of 1 Samuel: "There was a certain man of Ramathaim-zophim of the hill country of Ephraim, whose name

74. Abou-Zeid, "Migrant Labour," 49.

75. Malina, "Collectivism," 23.

76. Ibid.

was Elkanah the son of Jeroham, son of Elihu, son Tohu, son of Zuph, an Ephraimite" (1 Sam 1:1, RSV).

Here we have five descriptors of a man, only one of which is personal (his own name), whereas all the rest are group-oriented: his village, his region (hill country), his tribe and his family—with the latter described in terms of his patrilineage. His male forebears are mentioned back to his great-great-grandfather, "the sign of a noble and well-known family,"[77] a good example of both the patrilineality and the honor attached to it that we consider in more detail below. Nothing is said about his age, physical attributes, character, or interests, such as one would expect if he were being described in an individualistic context.

Or consider the following description: "There was a man of Benjamin whose name was Kish, the son of Abiel, son of Zeror, son of Becorath, son of Aphiah, a Benjaminite, a man of wealth" (1 Sam 9:1, RSV). Once again the family of Kish, in terms of his patrilineage, is taken back four generations. We learn his tribe (Benjamin), although not at this point his village (Gibeah), and also the fact that he was wealthy. Nothing is said about his age, personality, appearance, or interests.

The next verse may seem to contain a surprise, however, in the description of the son of Kish: "[A]nd he had son whose name was Saul, a handsome young man. There was not a man among the people of Israel more handsome than he; from his shoulders upward he was taller than any of the people" (2 Sam 9:2, RSV). At first sight this might seem to be the description of someone in terms of his individual appearance that we would expect to find in an individualistic culture. But appearances can be deceiving (as God will remind the prophet Samuel later in the narrative; see 1 Sam 16:7). These details are only provided because they serve to differentiate Saul from all other male Israelites in such a way that will serve to explain why God should have directed Samuel to anoint him as king (1 Sam 10:1). Even here, moreover, we learn nothing about Saul's character. A further sign of a collectivistic mindset appears in David's reflecting what the rest of Israel could be expected to think of him given his origin in an insignificant family: "Who am I, and who are my kinsfolk, my father's family (*mišpaḥah*) in Israel, that I should be son-in-law to the king?" (1 Sam 18:18, RSV); and later, "Does it seem a little thing to become the king's son-in-law, seeing that I am a poor man and of no repute?" (1 Sam 18:23, RSV).

77. Hertzberg, *I & II Samuel*, 22.

Another revealing indication that this was a group-oriented culture, where the family was the most important group of all, is that individual members shared with their relatives any success or good fortune they enjoyed, or any disaster they suffered. Thus, in Isa 22:23 the appointment of Eliakim to high office means that he has become "a throne of glory for his father's house." In Joshua 7, on the other hand, the sin of Achan in keeping something that was under the ban results in disaster not only for him but for his whole family (Josh 7:15, 24).

The recognition of the distinction between societies that are mainly collectivistic and those that are mainly individualistic does not, however, entail denying that *individuality* occurs in group-oriented societies (which is a charge sometimes heard against those like the present writer, who have the temerity to suggest that ancient Israelites were not individualistic like us). *There is big difference between individuality and individualism.* The action of David in accepting Goliath's challenge in 1 Samuel 17 (discussed in chapter 6) illustrates this difference. The narrator certainly portrays David as a robust individual, in fact the *only* Israelite willing to take on the huge Philistine. Yet while this is about as pure an expression of individuality as one could imagine, it is not at all a sign of an individualistic streak in David. For what motivates David to fight the Philistine is not the chance for him to achieve self-realization but the desire to stand up for his people and his people's God. David is actually the most loyal Israelite present, the one who feels most strongly the slight Goliath has offered to Israel and to Yahweh. That is why he asks, in 1 Sam 17:26 (RSV), "What shall be done for the man who kills this Philistine, and takes away the disgrace from Israel? For who is this uncircumcised Philistine, that he should challenge the armies of the living God?"

Another aspect of a strongly group-oriented culture is that ingroup members may have no compunction about deceiving representatives of outgroups. This possibility forms an important aspect of Bruce Malina's model. He proposes that in relation to a group-oriented and honor-focused culture like that of the ancient Mediterranean, "moral commitment in telling the truth unambiguously in such honor cultures derives from the social commitment or loyalty to persons to whom such commitment is due." In the first-century-CE context "there was no such thing as universal, social commitment . . . Lying and deception are or can be honorable and legitimate. To lie in order to deceive an outsider, one who has no right to the truth, is honorable."[78] This view reflects the strongly competitive streak in the Mediterranean ethnography of the 1950s and 1960s, and other evidence for the existence of such an attitude has emerged subsequently, including from DuBoulay and Gilsenan, both in 1976.[79] Further support can be found in the literature that has appeared on cross-cultural approaches to secrecy (1980), on secrecy in religions (1987), on the prevalence of deceit (1991), and on deception in biblical and postbiblical Judaic tradition itself.[80] John Pilch brought much of this work together in two articles in 1992 and 1994.[81] Nevertheless, we can affirm from our earlier discussion that it is necessary to ensure that in any given context we do not neglect the possibility that other values, of a noncompetitive or even group-transcending type, are active within the social dynamics in view. A model such as Malina's is not a description of empirical reality but a simplification, at a particular level of abstraction, used for heuristic and data-organizing purposes. Thus, for Malina to include the manner in which deception often functions in a strongly group-oriented culture like that of the ancient Mediterranean does not mean that different attitudes were not possible, for example in philosophical circles that were less tied to loyalty to *polis* or *ethnos*. In this connection it is worthwhile noting that Freund has argued that Philo considerably watered down the numerous lies in Genesis, although Josephus did not go nearly so far in this direction.[82]

Honor and Shame

We have seen that the values of honor and shame figured prominently in the early Mediterranean ethnography and still have a role as useful abstractions as long as they are employed carefully, in particular by not being allowed to supplant actual data revealed by close observation. We know that honor has different connotations in various parts of the contemporary Mediterranean, and we would expect that these have changed through history. Nevertheless, it still has certain broad characteristics

78. Malina, *New Testament World*, 3rd ed., 41.

79. DuBoulay, "Lies, Mockery and Family Integrity"; and Gilsenan, "Lying, Honor, and Contradiction."

80. See Tefft, *Secrecy*; Bolle, *Secrecy in Religions*; Bailey, *The Prevalence of Deceit*; and Freund, "Lying and Deception."

81. See Pilch, "Lying and Deceit"; and Pilch, "Secrecy."

82. Freund, "Lying and Deception."

that operate generally at a certain level of abstraction, in spite of local variations. To reiterate the view of Pitt-Rivers and Peristiany articulated in 1992 and cited earlier, it is a conceptual field within which diverse notions of esteem and self-esteem can be expressed. Moreover, the picture of honor that I am about to provide should be seen as a model, as a tool of use in the heuristic interrogation and then in organization and interpretation of data: a process that might well lead to modifications of the model; the model should not be viewed as an ontological or nomic description. I have set out my approach to models in this sense elsewhere and will not go into detail here.[83]

Honor is the value someone has in his or her own eyes and in the eyes of his community. It denotes a person's own assessment of his or her worth and the recognition of that claim by a relevant social group.[84] Honor often has shame as its opposite, but (as noted above) we must avoid the notion that they are always binary opposites and be alive to situations when shame may be more prominent in local discourse than honor. Honor and shame, Peristiany reasonably suggests, are the constant preoccupations of individuals in "small-scale, exclusive societies where face to face personal, as opposed to anonymous, relations are of paramount importance and where the social personality of the actor is as significant as his office."[85] A person who is making a claim for honor must get himself (and in this culture claimants are usually male but sometimes female) accepted at his own valuation, must receive the honor he seeks, or else the claim is an empty one that will attract ridicule, with the result that the claimant will be shamed rather than honored.[86] Our word *boasting*, which always has negative implications, is not appropriate when applied to the Mediterranean. There is nothing wrong with claiming to be honorable, since the problem only arises in relation to a claim that lacks foundation.

Social groups as well as individuals are capable of possessing honor. The members of an honorable social group share its honor and, on the other hand, a group will be shamed by the dishonorable conduct of its members.[87] Although relevant groups include one's nation, tribe, city or

---

83. Esler, *Community and Gospel*, 6–12; and Esler, "Introduction: Models," 4–8.

84. Pitt-Rivers, "Honour and Social Status," 21.

85. Peristiany, "Introduction," 11.

86. Ibid.

87. Pitt-Rivers, "Honour and Social Status," 35.

town, army unit and artisans' association, the most significant repository for collective honor in Mediterranean culture is the family. Many
Mediterranean societies distinguish sharply between those who are one's
kin, or fictive kin (for example, those in a patron-client relationship)
and those who are not. "Help your own kinsmen," runs a proverb of
the Kabyle, a contemporary North African people, "whether they are
right or wrong,"[88] for between kin and fictive kin trust, confidence, and
unselfish assistance are the rule. Among the Sarakatsani tribe in Greece,
similarly, an entirely different attitude is maintained toward those who
are not kin; relationships are determined not merely by self-interest but
with the objective of gaining honor by defeating or even deceiving non-
kin in any possible situation.[89]

Finally, the honor of women is closely tied up with their sexuality
and role in procreation. Carol Delaney and Maureen Giovannini regard
this connection as something distinctively Mediterranean, while Mariko
Asano-Tamanoi has confirmed that whereas similar notions of honor
linked to the family are found in Japan, the sexual dimension is much
less prominent.[90] Giovannini has observed that in spite of considerable
variety in the moral-evaluative systems of the Mediterranean, some
striking parallels exist: "One of these is the cultural emphasis on female
chastity as an indicator of social worth for individuals and their respective kin groups. Consistent with this pattern is male control over female
sexuality since men are usually responsible for protecting the chastity of
their female relatives."[91]

In addition, in such contexts a suitable marriage is very important
for the social status, even identity, of women. Speaking of the situation in
the Turkish village she studied, but with parallels in many Mediterranean
communities, Delaney observed, "Most girls want to marry since it is
the only means of achieving something like a social identity. Through
marriage her existence is socially acknowledged; unmarried women are
socially invisible."[92]

---

88. Bourdieu, "The Sentiment of Honour," 229.

89. Campbell, *Honour, Family and Patronage*, 316.

90. See Delaney, "Seeds of Honor," 36; Giovannini, "Female Chastity Codes," 61;
and Asano-Tamanoi, "Shame, Family, State."

91. Giovannini, "Female Chastity Codes," 61.

92. Delaney, "Seeds of Honor," 36.

But one should add to this that it is really only when a married woman produces children, sons preferably, that her position is fully secure. Nor should one forget the other ways mentioned above that women can achieve power and influence in their own settings, even if such a capacity probably requires marriage and motherhood to be exercised.

Challenge and Response

Among some Mediterranean peoples the various arenas of social interaction, including warfare, sporting contests, dinner invitations, gift giving, buying and selling, marriage arrangements, and commercial agreements, even public discussions, provide an opportunity for those involved to enhance their honor at someone else's expense. Because of its marked competitiveness, cultures like these can be designated "agonistic,"[93] from the Greek *agon*, meaning, "contest."

Pierre Bourdieu, writing of the Kabyle tribe of Algeria, has modeled the process whereby honor is acquired (the *agon*) in terms of "challenge and response."[94] Bruce Malina has adroitly applied this model for use in interpreting the New Testament, and it continues to provide interpretative traction for both Old and New Testaments.[95] The worth of the model can only be determined by close attention to the details of the text in question. In response to a claim by Jerome Neyrey that they reveal the pattern of challenge-and-riposte, Louise Lawrence has closely analyzed passages in Matthew's gospel that focus on controversy between Jesus and his opponents, and has reached the view that (with the exception of Matt 12:9–14) they do not fit the challenge-riposte pattern but rather are illustrative of honor virtue.[96] Such an argument, however, even if accepted for these Matthean passages, does not settle the issue in relation to other examples. Each case must be looked at on its merits (which, in any event, is the logic of Lawrence's position). Since the New Testament, even given its first-century-CE context where there existed philosophic and religious traditions that countered male competitiveness and display, does indeed provide clear examples of data suitable for compari-

---

93. Peristiany, "Introduction," 14.
94. Bourdieu, "'The Sentiment of Honour."
95. Malina, *New Testament World*, 3rd ed., 33–36.
96. Lawrence, *The Ethnography*, 145–66.

son against the pattern of challenge and riposte,[97] we may be sanguine
that the Old Testament will also provide suitable comparable material.
Indeed we will see that challenge and response will help us identify and
explain important features in several of the narratives discussed below,
including those concerning Hannah (chapter 4), David and Goliath
(chapter 6); Judith and Holofernes (chapter 8); the war between Israel
and Ammon (chapter 9); and Tamar, Amnon and Absalom (chapter
10). Insisting on the usefulness of this model for these narratives does
not deny the possibility that other values apart from highly competitive
honor may be present in such narratives.

The dynamic of challenge and response has four stages. First comes
the challenge. A usual condition of any challenge is that one's adversary
is equal in honor to oneself.[98] The challenge itself, issued by word or
deed or both, constitutes a claim to enter the social space of another. A
person of honor is ever on the alert to issue such a challenge, in order to
promote the honor of himself and his group, such as family, tribe, city, or
ethnic group. Someone who never made such claim on another would
be unlikely to be a person of honor.[99] The claim may either be positive,
with a view to gaining a share in valuable social space or at least a mutually beneficial foothold, in which case it will usually take the form of a
word of praise or a gift; or negative, aimed at dislodging another from
his or her social space, in which case it will consist of an insult, threat,
or physical assault.

The second stage of the challenge and response focuses on how the
challenge is treated. With a reasonable equality of honor, as between the
maker and receipient of the challenge, the recipient must consider the
harm that the challenge will occasion to his or her honor if it goes unan-
swered. In cases where there is, in fact, nothing like equality of status, or
when an inferior has broken an obligation owed to a superior (instances
that, strictly speaking, do not constitute challenge and response), the
superior may well visit some punishment on the other party.

The third stage of the challenge and response is the receiver's response, and covers three possibilities: first, an intentional refusal to act,

97. Examples include Gal 2:1–14 (on which see Esler, "Making and Breaking an
Agreement Mediterranean Style"; and *Galatians*, 126–40); and John 8:31–59 (see Esler,
"Introverted Sectarianism," 84–90).

98. Bourdieu, "The Sentiment of Honour," 197.

99. Ibid., 199.

communicated by disdain or scorn; second, acceptance of the challenge, expressed in a counterchallenge, either positive or negative, by word or action; and, third, a passive refusal to act, which may cause dishonor.

The fourth stage of the challenge and response is the public verdict. Either the successful challenger will be publicly credited with the honor he has stripped from the recipient of the challenge, or the challenger will forfeit his honor to the recipient. Such a conclusion is the aim of the whole process, for the pursuit of honor is "the basis of the moral code of an individual who sees himself always through the eyes of others, who has need of others for his existence, because the image he has of himself is indistinguishable from that presented to him by other people."[100]

While an honorable man in such a culture must respond to all slights and dishonors to himself or to his relevant social group, a period of time will sometimes elapse before a response becomes possible. In the meantime, the person slighted will nurse a desire for vengeance toward his adversary, since "to leave an affront unavenged is to leave one's honour in a state of desecration."[101] The longer the time that passes, the less effective is the response, unless good reasons exist that prevent the offended party from making his response. This outlook means that it may well be honorable for a man to have enemies who are hoping to exact some form of vengeance against him, since this shows that he has successfully shamed them at some time in the past. Hence a proverb current among the Kabyle runs as follows: "The man without enemies is a donkey."[102]

It will be helpful to offer a demonstration of the prima facie relevance of this model to the Old Testament with reference to one example outside of the narratives to be considered in this volume. Second Chronicles 32 recounts the events surrounding Sennacherib's invasion of Judah. From Lachish the Assyrian king first sends envoys to Hezekiah in Jerusalem to tell him that Hezekiah is deluded if he thinks Yahweh will save them and then dispatches a letter in which he says, "Just as the gods of the nations in other countries have failed to save their peoples from me, so will the god of Hezekiah fail to save his people" (2 Chr 32:17; JB). The text explicitly says that Sennacherib wrote this letter "to challenge" or "insult" (MT *leharef*; LXX *oneidizein*) the Lord God (2 Chr

---

100. Ibid., 211

101. Pitt-Rivers, "Honour and Social Status," 26.

102. Bourdieu, "The Sentiment of Honour," 199.

32:17); this word we will see has great prominence in the contest between David and Goliath (chapter 6, below). In the terms of the model,
from Sennacherib's perspective this letter may be seen as a negative
challenge by Sennacherib, aimed at dislodging Yahweh from his social
space, especially the relationship he has with the Judeans. The challenge
suggests God's honor is on the line. Sennacherib impudently assumes
an equality of status with the Israelite god, as if Yahweh must respond
or risk suffering disgrace before his people and the Assyrians! God's response is devastating, since his angel kills many of the Assyrian host, as
commemorated in the well-known poem by Byron, "The Destruction of
Sennacherib," which ends with this verse:

> And the widows of Ashur are loud in their wail,
> And the idols are broke in the temple of Baal;
> And the might of the Gentile, unsmote by the sword,
> Hath melted like snow in the glance of the Lord!

From Yahweh's point of view, Sennacherib is hardly his equal in
honor, so this slaughter should be seen as the punishment against inso-
lence. But from the king's perspective, he has fallen into the trap of having his boasting shown to be foolish and empty. The model suggests that
this will result in his dishonor, and this is just what we find in the text.
We are actually informed that Sennacherib returned home with "shame
on his face" (MT *bebošet panim*; LXX *meta aischynēs prosōpou*, 32:21),
and he was killed by some of his own children in the temple of his god.
The exhibition of Sennacherib's shame physically upon his face reminds
us of a modern Arabic expression "to blacken someone's face," meaning
"to shame" the person, "to make a fool of him."

Limited Good

In an important essay first published in 1965, George Foster developed
the idea of "limited good" as an essential feature of peasant life; he primarily focused on peasants from Mexico and other Central American
countries (but also referred to some other parts of the world).[103]
Although limited good was not strictly one of the major themes in the
Mediterranean ethnography of the 1950s and 1960s considered above,
it certainly has a place in the region. Stanley Brandes noted in 1987 that
honor (which he suggested could be translated as "esteem, respect, pres-

---

103. Foster, "Image of Limited Good."

tige, or some combination of these attributes, depending on local usage") was treated throughout the Mediterranean area "as a sort of limited
good in George Foster's sense." He then went on to say, "Wherever we
look, Mediterranean honor appears to be related to control over scarce
resources, including, of course, land and property, political power, and,
perhaps most notably, female sexuality, with its procreative potential."[104]
The notion of limited good was picked up and applied by Malina in *The
New Testament World* in 1981.[105]

Foster proposed that peasants were characterized by a cognitive
orientation, that is, "an unverbalized, implicit expression of their understanding of the 'rules of the game' of living imposed upon them by
their social, natural and supernatural universes, best described as 'the
image of limited good.'"[106] This meant that they viewed their social, economic, and natural universes, their total environment in fact, as one in
which all the desired things in life, such as land, wealth, health, friendship, love, honor, status, power, and influence, existed in finite and short
supply.[107] Moreover, there is no way in which the available quantities of
such goods can be increased. This carries the corollary an individual or
family can only improve its position at the expense of others.[108] Thus,
anthropologists working in peasant villages soon find that they must
be very careful not to show excessive favor or friendship towards some
families, lest they alienate others who will feel deprived and reluctant to
help the research.[109]

Peasants, in Foster's view, are always on the alert for individuals
within families or families themselves who try to improve their position
at the expense of other family members or other families, phenomena
that nevertheless do occur despite of the social disapproval they attract.
Widespread expressions of sibling rivalry in peasant society indicate
that even a mother's ability to love her children is viewed as limited in
quantity. Very often older siblings are envious of younger ones, espe-

---

104. Brandes, "Reflections on Honor and Shame," 121–22.

105. Bruce Malina has shown the importance of the idea of limited good for understanding the New Testament (*New Testament World*, 3rd ed., 81–107).

106. Foster, "Peasant Society," 304.

107. Ibid., 300.

108. Ibid., 305.

109. Ibid., 307.

cially for the reason that they are attracting too much attention from their parents.[110]

Preferred behavior in this context is that by which a peasant maximizes his security, his relative position in the traditional social order.[111] Individuals or families who appear to violate the customary norms of behavior stimulate cultural responses aimed at redressing the balance. Such responses usually begin with envy, anger, and dislike and may develop into outright aggression toward more fortunate people.[112] In this context the ideal peasant is a man who feeds and clothes his family, who fulfills his obligations to the community, who minds his own business, who does not seek to be outstanding, but who protects his rights when necessary. He avoids presumption, lest this be seen as an attempt to take something that belongs to another.[113]

One exception to these attitudes, where positive changes of fortune, for example by a sudden accretion of wealth, might not incur community censure, arises where rises in fortune are caused by an unexpected outside intervention. Sometimes, for example, peasants luckily discover (or purport to discover) treasure buried on their property![114]

This exposition of limited good, aimed at helping to understand and organize data in the texts (and never to substitute for such data) can now be illustrated from four Old Testament passages as a prelude to its appearance on a number of occasions in the eight narratives considered in subsequent chapters. *First*, the story of Cain and Abel in Gen 4:1–16 offers an instructive biblical illustration of a number of these aspects of limited good. The firstborn son, Cain, encounters a situation where for unexpressed reasons Yahweh shows favorable regard for the offering of his younger brother, Abel, but has no regard whatever for Cain's. Like all goods in this context, Yahweh's favor is finite, and Abel experiences it to the detriment of Cain. In a typical expression of sibling rivalry toward a younger brother, Cain becomes angry with Abel and actually murders him in consequence and is cursed by God (Gen 4:8–16). *Second*, Isaac only has one blessing to give, as Esau learns to his cost: "'Have you but one blessing, my father? Bless me, even me also, O my father.' And Esau

110. Ibid., 308.

111. Ibid., 310.

112. Ibid, 312.

113. Ibid, 313.

114. Ibid, 316. For a similar New Testament example, see Matt 13:44.

lifted up his voice and wept" (Gen 27:38, RSV). *Third*, that there is only so much honor to be won from defeating Midian, and that Yahweh prefers that he gets it and not Israel is offered in Judges 7, for example, as the explicit justification for his requiring Gideon to reduce his army from 32 thousand to three hundred—comprising the remnant who drink in the (dishonorable) manner of dogs: "There are too many people with you for me to put Midian into their power; Israel might claim the credit for themselves at my expense: they might say, 'My own hand has rescued me'" (Judg 7:2, JB).

Yahweh's motivation for this action in this incident makes little sense in modern Northern European or North American culture, where the notion of an expanding gross national product, in vogue since the days of Adam Smith, has rendered obsolete previous acceptance of the finite nature of goods; but it made good sense in the ancient biblical world. *Fourth*, and perhaps most revealingly, we have what Saul says to Samuel at one point in the lead-up to the prophet's anointing Saul "prince" (*nagid*) over Israel (1 Sam 10:1). Having in mind the wealth that will flow to Saul and his family once Saul is king, Samuel tells him not to worry about the asses he has been looking for, since they have been found, and then adds, "And for whom is all that is desirable in Israel? Is it not for you and for all your father's house?" As we would expect for someone socialized in a limited-good society, this sentiment immediately set alarm bells ringing in Saul's head and he replied, "Am I not a Benjaminite, from the least of the tribes of Israel? And is not my family the humblest of all the families of the tribe of Benjamin. Why then have you spoken to me in this way?" (1 Sam 9:21, RSV).

In Yahweh's choosing a son from the lowest family among Israel's lowest tribe—and later selecting David, the youngest son among the sons of Jesse, to replace his first choice—readers learn, and not for the last time in the Old Testament, that Israel has a God who subverts the local honor code to work his purposes in his own way. Indeed, one cannot appreciate the gratuitous nature of God's action without paying regard to the cultural context in which it occurs.

It is worth noting here one final issue related to limited good. There was a rich vocabulary in the ancient Mediterranean world, which I will return to below in relation to the version of the David and Goliath story in the Hebrew Bible (chapter 6), for people who failed to keep within proper social roles and modes of behavior, and who transgressed the so-

cial space of another by insult or physical aggression. In Hebrew this type
of misbehavior in the context of limited good was designated by nouns
such as *zadon* (and its cognate verb *zod* and adjective *zed*) and *gaon* (and
its cognates) and in Greek by the noun *hubris* (and its cognates).[115]

Patron and Client Relationships

One way in which a member of a limited-good society can improve
his or her position, or at least make the best of things as they stand, is
by entering into a relationship with someone who has more resources
and more prestige. Patronage is an asymmetrical relationship between
persons known to one another in which the patron provides his or her
clients with various types of resources in return for their loyalty and
loyal service to him or her. Sometimes a third party, a "broker" serves as
an intermediary between a patron and a client. To the client the broker
will appear to be a patron (although one facilitating access to another
patron on a higher social level), while to the patron the broker will be a
client, but one who allows access to clients at lower social levels through
the direct agency of the broker. The benefits provided by a patron can
be material but can also involve the exercise of protection, power, and
influence on behalf of the client. In return, the clients do such services as
may be required of them, including helping to maintain the status of the
patron. [116] Patronage is one aspect of a broader set of relationships that
constitute reciprocity.[117] It is important to realize that patron-broker-
client relationships can exist even in spite of the lack of a specific terminology to describe them as is largely the case with the Hebrew Bible
but not in Latin, since the Romans had a developed language relating to
patrons and clients.[118]

---

115. For the Hebrew vocabulary, see Bertram, "*hubris*"; and for *hubris*, see Dover, *Greek Popular Morality*, 147 ("the violent or contumelious treatment of a fellow-citizen").

116. On patron-client relations, see Moxnes, "Patron-Client Relations"; and Stewart, "Social Stratification and Patronage."

117. On reciprocity and its relation to patronage, see Crook, *Reconceptualising Conversion*, 53–89.

118. On Roman patronage, see Saller, *Personal Patronage under the Early Empire*.

Patrilineality, Patrilocality, and Polygyny

"Patrilineality" (or "patrilinearity"), also known as "agnatic kinship," means a system where kinship is through the father's line, so that male offspring inherit (land especially) and take their names from their father's lineage. "Patrilocality" refers to that aspect of a social system in which married couples reside with the husband's parents.[119] In relation to patrilocality, it is important to acknowledge that at any given time in a certain community, it is likely that only a minority of households will constitute a patrilocal household (consisting of a man, his wife or wives, all his sons and their wives and children, and his unmarried daughters), because the man will have died before his sons have children, or will have died when those children were very young. David Stirling discovered that of two villages in Turkey where he had conducted research, and where this three-generation type was the ideal, one had only 15 percent of households of this type, and the other had 22 percent.[120] "Polygyny" denotes the form of marriage in which a man has two or more wives at the same time. All three household types were important features of life in ancient Israel. There is most evidence for patrilineality and patrilocality, but as Ralph Klein notes, "though monogamy predominates in the OT, there is occasional evidence that men had two or more wives."[121]

For anyone reading the Old Testament brought up in social systems not characterized by such features, however, they will require explanation. We must make a deliberate effort to fertilize our interpretative imagination in relation to them if we are to have any chance of understanding the meaning a narrative containing such features conveyed to its original audience. The best way to do this is to familiarize oneself with patrilineal, patrilocal and polygynous cultures from the contemporary or near-contemporary world known to us from ethnographic research. Of particular assistance in this volume (especially in chapters 3 and 4) will be the research conducted by Finnish anthropologist Hilma Granqvist among certain Arab villagers in Palestine in the 1920s and 1930s, since all three features (patrilineality, patrilocality, and polygyny) were present in the social system that she observed. Using Granqvist's research does not entail any (clearly unsustainable) claim that life in an-

119. For much of the biblical data on the patrilineal inheritance of property in the Old Testament, see Greenspahn, *When Brothers Dwell Together.*

120. Stirling, "The Domestic Cycle," 204.

121. Klein, *1 Samuel,* 6.

cient Israel was the same as life in Palestine in the 1920s and 1930s, but
the combination of all three features in early twentieth-century Palestine
makes this culture very useful for comparative purposes to pose relevant
questions to, and to understand, the data we find in Old Testament narratives (such as Genesis 38 and 1 Samuel 1–2, considered in chapters 3
and 4). I will also occasionally cite other research into patrilineal and
patrilocal cultures in other parts of the Mediterranean world.

The Broad Socioeconomic and Political Structure of Ancient Israel: Elite and Non-Elite

Here we are addressing the fundamental question: how were political
power and economic resources allocated at the broadest level across society? The study of the socioeconomic and political structures of ancient
Israel has advanced rapidly in the last forty years, with the initial stimulus
of a magnificently provocative article by George Mendenhall in 1962.[122]
Gerhard and Jean Lenski made an important theoretical contribution to
this developing research in their macrosociological model of the various
phases through which society develops as modes of production improve
through innovation.[123] The work of Mendenhall found significant responses in the writings of Norman Gottwald, Marvin Chaney, Robert
Coote, and Keith Whitelam, to name just a few, while Chaney, Coote,
and Whitelam were also heavily influenced by the Lenskis.[124]

In its earliest period ancient Israel represented what Lenski and
Lenksi call the "agrarian" stage of development, which is characterized
by the use of ploughs that produce a surplus over the needs of each family and the consequent rise of armed elites, living in cities and served by
retainers, who take control of that surplus. The "advanced agrarian" stage
is reached when the introduction of iron-tipped ploughs produces even
greater surpluses. In *The Politics of Aristocratic Empires* John Kautsky
has gathered and analyzed data from many agrarian empires and has

122. Mendenhall, "The Hebrew Conquest."

123. Lenski and Lenski, *Human Societies*. The 11th ed. is authored by Patrick Nolan
and Gerhard Lenski (2009).

124. See Gottwald, *Tribes of Yahweh*; Chaney, "Ancient Palestinian Peasant
Movements"; Chaney, "Bitter Bounty"; and Chaney, "Study of the Israelite Monarchy,"
(in all three of which essays he employs the understanding of an agrarian society developed by Lenski and Lenski); and Coote and Whitelam, *Emergence of Early Israel*,
especially 22.

shown how their politics was shaped by conquest and exploitation of the peasantry, with fundamental changes in this system only emerging with commercialization.[125]

The Israel depicted in 1 and 2 Samuel (which contain six of the eight narratives considered in this volume) exists at the agrarian stage of development, evident (merely to cite one example) from the produce mentioned in 1 Sam 1:24 (bullocks, flour, and wine). Even before and apart from the establishment of the monarchy there was potential for other elite members of society, such as priests, to act unjustly and oppressively toward the non-elite, and I will consider the behavior of the sons of the priest Eli (1 Sam 2:12–17) in this light in chapter 4. Samuel gives a highly revealing speech in 1 Samuel 12 when, as an old man, he asks the Israelites, "Whose ox have I taken? Or whom have I defrauded? Whom have I oppressed? Or from whose hand have I taken a bribe to blind my eyes with it? Testify against me and I will restore it to you" (1 Sam 12:3, RSV).

Although the Israelites immediately confirm that he has done none of these things, their specification in this way shows the sort of behavior that would be expected from someone in authority. The whole issue of elite/non-elite relations and the burdens placed by the former on the latter bursts to the surface of the text with even more remarkable clarity in 1 Sam 8:10–18, in Samuel's warnings to the Israelites concerning what it will be like if they acquire a king, and this passage deserves close consideration. Rarely can the picture of what social reality might be like proffered by an etic (outside, social-scientific) perspective have found such closely comparable data at an emic (indigenous and insider) level.

The prophet Samuel had given the Israelites ample and vivid warning of what a king would be like if they persisted in their desire to have one:

> These will be the ways of the king who will reign over you: he will take your sons and appoint them to his chariots and to be his horsemen, and to run before his chariots; and he will appoint for himself commanders of thousands and commanders of fifties, and some to plough his ground and to reap his harvest, and to make his implements of war and the equipment of his chariots. He will take your daughters to be perfumers and cooks and bakers. He will take the best of your fields and vineyards and olive

125. Kautsky, *Politics.*

orchards and give them to his servants. He will take the tenth of
your grain and of your vineyards and give it to his officers and to
his servants. He will take your menservants and your maidservants, and the best of your cattle and your asses, and put them to
his work. He will take the tenth of your flocks, and you shall be
his slaves. (1 Sam 8:11–17, RSV)

One thing that Samuel failed to mention, probably because it went
without saying (cf. Judg 8:22–23), is that Saul would be followed in the
office of king by his son. Yet the Israelites refused to listen: they wanted
to be like other nations, with a king to govern them and to lead them
out and fight their battles (1 Sam 8:19–20). When Saul, son of Kish from
Gibeah (a man of wealth), of the tribe of Benjamin, the tallest and most
handsome Israelite (1 Sam 9:1–2) was anointed king of Israel (1 Sam
10:1), he became a leader with all the powers and entitlements described
by Samuel. It made no difference that Benjamin was the least of the tribes
of Israel or Saul's family the humblest of all the families of the tribe of
Benjamin (1 Sam 9:21).

J. Mendelssohn has noted similarities between Samuel's description and the incidents of kingship known from the records of the near-
contemporary peoples of Alalakh and Ugarit.[126] The surviving records
of these two cities (covering the eighteenth to the thirteenth centuries
BCE) delineate a system in which there was an army composed of professional warriors drawn from the local aristocracy, with superior military
equipment (especially the horse-drawn chariot) and conscripted foot
soldiers from the common people. This is very similar to what Samuel
says, on the reasonable assumption that the king's senior military leaders
went to war in chariots. From Ugarit comes much information about
the royal domains owned by the king and granted to his family, to high
state officials, and to other persons, in return for services or tax, which is
very similar to what is said in 1 Sam 8:14: "He will take the best of your
fields and vineyards and olive orchards and give them to his servants."
At Ugarit there was also a one-tenth royal tax on the products of the
field and on cattle (as 1 Sam 8:15 reports). Finally, at Ugarit the common
people were subject to corvée labor, essentially as described in 1 Sam
8:12b–13 and 16.

Nevertheless, Mendelssohn goes too far in seeing in the similarities
between 1 Samuel's account and records of contemporary kingship as evi-

---

126. Mendelssohn, "Samuel's Denunciation."

dence of a very early date for the passage,[127] since the picture that emerges from what 1 Samuel says is, at a reasonably general level, very similar to that of most kingdoms in the ancient Near East (and elsewhere, for that matter) at an agrarian or advanced agrarian level of development.[128]

The key elements in this form of kingship are as follows: First, the king controls a properly equipped army. While the surrounding context of the passage points to the role of the king and army in fighting external enemies of the people (1 Sam 8:20), the army (by necessary implication that is fully realized later in 1 Samuel) also gives the king the means to control (or attempt to control, as Saul tries with David) dissident elements among his own people. Second, the king is entitled to extract resources of various kinds from his people, including personnel for his army, his court, and his administration; land, crops, and livestock. Third, the king acts as a patron (as described above) to those upon whom he principally relies (his clients) to keep the entire system working, especially military leaders and senior officials at his court.

This is how kingship in Israel (and in surrounding Near Eastern countries) worked. The king, together with the most senior people under him, constituted the elite in that society. The rest of the population, including the soldiers, and artisans who served the king and the elite; the peasantry; and slaves made up the non-elite component in the system. Samuel had warned the Israelites that a king would take best of their fields, vineyards, and olive orchards, and a tenth of their grain and vineyards and give them to his officers and servants. Saul behaves in just this way. As patron, he provides senior positions in his army and administration to chosen Israelites by making them military leaders, administrative officials, and other personnel he needs to keep the system operating—men like Doeg the Edomite, the chief of his herdsmen (1 Sam 21:7) and the women serving as "perfumers and cooks and bakers" mentioned in 1 Sam 8:13—and also land and agricultural produce. In a group-oriented society like this, we would expect Saul to favor the two groups closest to him, his family and his tribe, in providing the benefits of patron to client.

As mentioned above, even before Samuel had anointed Saul as prince over Israel (1 Sam 10:1), he had indicated to him the wealth that would flow to Saul *and his family* when—in telling Saul to give no

127. Ibid., 22.

128. See Kautsky, *The Politics.*

thought to the asses that he had been seeking, for they were found—he
went on to ask, "And for whom is all that is desirable in Israel? Is it not for
you and *for all your father's house*?" (1 Sam 9:20). Unequivocal evidence
that Saul had received "all that is desirable" in Israel and distributed it
to those closest to him emerges in 1 Sam 22:6–10. Saul is seated on the
height of Gibeah under a tamarisk tree with his spear in hand with all
his "servants" standing about him, the most senior figures among them
no doubt composing (with Saul) the newly emerged elite of Israel, and
makes the following complaint to them: "Hear now, you Benjaminites;
will the son of Jesse give every one of you fields and vineyards, will he
make you all commanders of thousands and commanders of hundreds,
that all of you have conspired against me?" (1 Sam 22:7–8, RSV). This
passage reveals that Saul is providing largesse in the form of land and
military positions to all the Benjaminites who are his "servants" ("every
one of you"), the fellow members of his tribe. One is reminded of the
statement by Auda Abu Tayi, leader of the Howeitat tribe, in the film
Lawrence of Arabia (1962): "I am a river to my people."

HIGH-CONTEXT CULTURES

We must now consider one very general aspect of the nature of biblical
since it fundamentally affects the way the stories are told. This is that biblical texts emerged from what anthropologists (beginning with Edward
T. Hall in 1976) refer to as a "high-context culture," which is one where
the large amount of relevant information possessed by a particular ingroup that shares similar experiences and expectations means that a few
words can convey a complex message and much can be left unsaid.[129]

    Hall and Hall distinguished high- and low-context cultures as fol-
lows: "A high context (HC) communication or message is one in which
most of the communication is already in the person, while very little is
in the coded, explicit, transmitted part of the message. A low-context
(LC) communication is just the opposite; i.e., the mass of the information is vested in the explicit code. Twins who have grown up together

129. For the origin of the notion of 'high' and 'low' contexts, see Hall, *Beyond Culture*;
and Hall, *The Dance of Life*; and Hall and Hall, *Understanding Cultural Differences*,
with further development by Copeland and Griggs, *Going International*, 106–7; and
Samovar et al., *Communication between Cultures*,158–60. Bruce Malina introduced
Hall's distinction between high- and low-context cultures into New Testament research
in 1991 (see Malina, "Reading Theory Perspectives, 19–21).

can and do communicate more economically (HC) than two lawyers in a courtroom during a trial (LC), a mathematician programming a computer, two politicians drafting legislation, two administrators writing regulation."[130]

Gudykunst and Kim note that "members of individualistic cultures predominately use low-context communication and tend to communicate in a direct fashion, and members of collectivistic cultures predominately use high-context messages when ingroup harmony is important and tend to communicate in an indirect fashion."[131]

A major reason for meanings often not needing "to be stated verbally in high-context cultures is that the people are very homogeneous. They have similar experiences, information networks, and the like. High-context cultures, because of tradition and history, change very little over time."[132] This is the underlying social explanation for the phenomenon Eric Auerbach identified from a literary perspective in the celebrated first chapter of *Mimesis: The Representation of Reality in Western Literature*,[133] namely, the cryptic conciseness of biblical narrative. Robert Alter has suggested, however, what Auerbach observed in one part of Genesis does not apply in all parts of the Hebrew Bible: His key notion of biblical narrative as a purposefully spare text "fraught with background" is at once resoundingly right and too sweepingly general. Distinctions have to be made for narratives by different authors, of different periods, and written to fulfill different generic or thematic requirements.

Alter notes that while what Auerbach says works brilliantly for the story of the binding of Isaac (where we have an "arresting starkness of foreground, an enormous freight of background"), in Esther, on the other hand, there is a "high degree of specification in the foreground of artifacts, costume, court customs, and the like."[134] While this may be true, it probably reflects the fact that the subject being described was one of which most Israelites did not have firsthand experience, so that the author needed to provide more descriptive help. Most Israelites were more familiar with life in small rural villages than with royal courts. It is also possible that while quite late texts like Esther might well reflect

130. Hall and Hall, *Understanding Cultural Differences*, 6.
131. Gudykunst and Kim, *Communicating with Strangers*, 69.
132. Samovar et al., *Communication between Cultures*, 158–59.
133. Auerbach, *Mimesis*.
134. Alter, *The Art*, 17.

a more developed and complex social, especially urban setting and one that was somewhat less high-context, the style of writing in the texts from Genesis and 1 and 2 Samuel we will be considering (and most narrative in the Hebrew Bible) is much closer to Genesis 22 than to Esther. It is indeed "fraught with background." We are now in a position to begin reading Old Testament narratives with their ancient audience.

PART 1

Wives

Chapters 3 and 4 cover two narratives that focus upon the position, or rather the plight, of two wives in ancient Israel—Tamar in Genesis 38 and Hannah in 1 Samuel 1–2. The common dimension to their stories, and one that sharply outlines distinctive features of this culture, was the personal and social need of Tamar and Hannah to have children and how they eventually overcame obstacles in their path and succeeded in doing so.

In modern Western cultures, if a couple wanting to have children are unable to do so, it will usually be a cause of sadness to them and their families and friends. It will not, however, bring them shame. In ancient Israel the experience of a woman's childlessness and shame were closely connected. While the causes of Tamar and Hannah's not producing children initially were different, the shame so produced was very similar.

Tamar was denied the possibility of having children by the early death of her first husband (Er), the sexual practices and then death of her second (Er's brother Onan), and the fact that her father-in-law (Judah) then denied her the opportunity to marry his remaining son, Shelah, by sending her back to her father's house. Rather than living in her father-in-law's house and bearing children, sons especially, to one of his sons, Tamar found herself in the anomalous and shameful position of being back home with her birth family and with no real prospect of becoming a mother. Hannah, on the other hand, did have a husband, Elkanah, who loved her, but she was barren. To make matters worse, Elkanah had another wife, Peninnah, who had given birth to several children, and who each year during the family's visit to the sanctuary at Shiloh publicly insulted Hannah for her barrenness. To most modern readers of this text, the frequently poor relations between co-wives in a polygynous marriage will come as a complete surprise, but Mediterranean ethnography provides illuminating comparative material.

Tamar and Hannah find the solution to their problem in quite different ways—Tamar by a cunning ruse that leads to Judah himself fathering twins with her, and Hannah by very deliberately casting herself upon the mercy of God in the temple at Shiloh. Both of them had sons, the prime requirement for a woman's honor and happiness in this culture, and thus ended the shame in which they had been immersed. And what sons! Tamar's would father a line that led to David, while Hannah's son, Samuel, was to become a great judge and prophet through whom God would establish a kingdom in Israel.

3

Judah and Tamar (Genesis 38)

JUDAH AND TAMAR: CULTURAL SPECIFICITY AND CROSS-CULTURAL APPEAL

The account of Judah and Tamar in Genesis 38 represents a brief yet powerfully realized and highly memorable biblical narrative. The description of a daughter-in-law tricking her father-in-law into having sexual intercourse with her so that she may give birth to the progeny his actions would have otherwise denied her is likely to be provocative, if not shocking, in most human contexts in which the story is told. Yet my aim is to explore the impact the narrative is likely to have had in one very particular context: the ancient one in which and to which it was written. The story was composed at some time in the first millennium BCE in a particular Israelite cultural setting (within the broader Mediterranean world) and must have made sense to its author and to its intended audience in that setting.

In this chapter, as with the others in this volume, I will seek to demonstrate the benefits that flow from seeking to read biblical narrative in its ancient Israelite context, with its distinctive moral and cultural contours, and to show that to do this we must take definite steps to move outside our own taken-for-granted understandings of how society works and how and why people act as they do. When we make this effort, the texts seem unexpectedly new and, paradoxically, have a far greater capacity to impact upon our contemporary world than when they are read tightly wrapped in a cultural cocoon that comes from our habit (usually unreflective) of viewing them on our terms rather than on their own. To illustrate this point I will at times refer to contemporary literary analyses of Genesis 38, including that of Esther Menn,[1] which while often making illuminating observations on the narrative structure of this passage, nevertheless by failing to attend to its ancient context, contain views that are ethnocentric and anachronistic.

This last point requires some unpicking. How could a narrative produced in a context remote from us in time and culture still hold an imaginative sway over us? Is it simply the power of cultural difference, the shock of the new, that touches us in striking ways? Or is there something that we have in common with the ancient Israelites who produced and listened to stories like those of Judah and Tamar that allow us to be affected emotionally and intellectually in spite of the cultural differences? Or, perhaps most likely, are both of these questions to be answered in the affirmative? In this chapter I aim to show both that to understand the particular dynamics of its telling in ancient Israel it is necessary to grasp the cultural context in which it was produced, and that the story of Judah and Tamar a contains narrative structure that has been found appealing across a range of human societies. There is no contradiction between acknowledging that to comprehend the particular ways in which the story of Judah and Tamar would have made sense to ancient Israelites it is necessary to pay the closest attention to distinctive features of the social context in which it appeared and also to recognize a cross-cultural appeal in the type of narrative it represents. As to the question of its underlying narrative structure, the story in Genesis 38 certainly has parallels in other times and other places, which suggest a cross-cultural appeal inherent in its structure. I will now open up this topic, before returning to it in the conclusion of this chapter.

One of the benefits of a typology is that it requires the interrogation of relevant data to determine how comparable it is with one or more types in the typology, and this process itself produces interesting questions to ask. At first sight, the story of Judah and Tamar is comparable to two of Booker's plots, and the decision as to which has the closer degree of comparability cannot be determined in advance of a detailed examination of the text. The two types are "Rags to Riches" and "Comedy." "Rags to Riches" starts with the hero or heroine in a disadvantaged position but then called out into the wider world to enjoy

---

1. Menn, *Judah and Tamar.*

some initial success before encountering a crisis where everything goes wrong. But the hero or heroine then discovers in himself or herself hidden resources that allow him or her to take on the major opponent and win, so that they reach final fulfillment.[2] "Comedy," on the other hand, concerns a little world where people are subjected to difficulties and confusion, which gets worse and worse until everyone is in a terrible tangle before, with the unveiling of things previously hidden, perceptions are changed, the knots untied, and at the end everyone is brought into a happy state, frequently by marriage. That is to say, the resolution of a comedy involves a group of people, not just an individual. Thus Northrop Frye notes that the "tendency of comedy is to include as many people as possible in its final society."[3] Comedy often involves the disguising and then disclosing of identity and basically good people who go astray before being led back into the light again.[4] In brief, Tamar needs to be the heroine or protagonist of the narrative for the "Rags to Riches" plot to be more applicable, whereas if Judah is the hero, "Comedy" may represent the more comparable plot.[5] On either interpretation, however, we must be open to the possibility that the narrative represents a fusion of the two plots, even if one seems more appropriate. We will return to this question at the conclusion of the analysis of the text. In undertaking this process we should not forget that Booker's seven plots are types, which we are using for comparative purposes. In using types we are not engaged in a pigeonholing exercise but are rather employing them to ask particular questions of the text and to situate it in a larger context of cultural productions.

READING GENESIS 38

Genesis 38 and the Joseph Narrative

Genesis 38 represents an interruption to the story of Joseph. Genesis 37 ends with the Midianites having sold David to Potiphar, one of Pharaoh's officers, after Judah had suggested to his brothers selling Joseph to them,

2. For Booker's understanding of "rags to riches," see *Seven Basic Plots*, 51–68.

3. Frye, *Anatomy of Criticism*, 165.

4. For Booker's understanding of "comedy," see *Seven Basic Plots*, 107–52.

5. I am grateful to Dr. Zeba Crook for focusing my attention on this issue when he responded to a paper containing an earlier version of this chapter at a meeting of the Context Group in Portland, Oregon, in March 2010.

rather than letting him die in the dry well into which they had thrown him. Genesis 39 will resume the story of Joseph under Potiphar's control. The events of Genesis 38 occur when Judah is separated from his brothers and, by necessary implication, from his father (38:1). A debate goes on today as to how integrated Genesis 38 is into the rest of Genesis. E. A. Speiser regards Genesis 38 as a "completely independent unit" having no connection with the drama of Joseph, apart from building a sense of suspense.[6] Richard Clifford, on the other hand, makes a strong case for connections between the events in Genesis 38 and the later story of the family of Jacob (especially in Egypt), but his argument that Judah and not Tamar is the central actor in this particular narrative is not convincing, for reasons that will emerge in the course of this essay.[7] Aaron Wildavsky also connects Genesis 38 to the Joseph stories but gives far more prominence to Tamar, for example by setting her in contrast to Potiphar's wife.[8]

Issues of Social Context

For many critics the Israelite law relating to Levirate marriage is the only, or at least the dominant, aspect of context necessary to interpret Genesis 38. While that is a prominent issue to which we will return below, there are other significant contextual dimensions to Genesis 38. In the course of the discussion below I will refer to and expand upon a number of features of Mediterranean culture that were explained in chapter 2, such as the centrality of honor in what were very group-oriented or collectivistic societies and the role of patrilineality and patrilocality.

Interpreting the Narrative in the Light of Its Israelite Social Context

Verses 1–6 are notably terse, with von Rad of the view that vv. 1–11 give "the reader the most necessary facts in a rather dry enumeration and without particular vividness," and that "the narrator dispenses with all causes and motivations in this section."[9] Yet in a text that originates in a

---

6. Speiser, *Genesis*, 299.

7. Clifford, "Genesis 38." For further observations on the relation of Genesis 38 to the Joseph story, see Smelik. "Genesis 38 Revisited."

8. Wildavsky, "Survival."

9. Von Rad, *Genesis*, 352.

high-context culture, this feature of the text should occasion no surprise. Gen 38:1 states that Judah "went down" (*yarad*) away from his brothers and "turned aside towards" (*wayyeṭ*; the consecutive Qal imperfect of *naṭah*) an Adullamite named Hirah. Thus Judah has left his brothers in the hill country of Hebron (Gen 37:14), one of the highest points in southern Canaan (at 3,040 feet above sea level), to travel down to Adullam, a Canaanite city in the northern sector of the Judean lowland (*shephelah*), usually identified with Tell esh-Sheikh Madhkur, southwest of Bethlehem and northwest of Hebron.[10] Uncertainty surrounds the precise nature of the relationship initiated between Judah and Hirah by the word *naṭah* (also used at 38:16), but whatever its nature, twice later in the text Hirah is described as his friend (38:12, 20), and it is clear from the narrative that they are on very close terms. The fact that Judah forms such a friendship with a man who is a Canaanite and of no relation to him means that the culture envisaged in this text differs from that of some contemporary Mediterranean societies investigated by ethnographers and discussed in chapter 2—cultures in which relationships with non-kin were often unfriendly if not downright hostile. It might be thought that this simply reflects Judah's having left his own family behind and having little choice but to forge links with the local people, but this impression is contradicted by the closeness of his links with Hirah and by the fact that he seems to have no trouble in marrying a local woman himself and in arranging a similar wife for his son Er. Here, therefore, we have a good example of the continuing need not to let views formed on the basis of contemporary ethnography relating to some Mediterranean cultures blind our eyes to differences that may be found in the world presupposed in the biblical narratives.

We are not told whether Judah (or Hirah for that matter) is living in a tent[11] or had a house (like Tamar's father, as we learn in v. 11). The original audience, however, would probably have assumed that Judah lived in a house, since the only type of edifice mentioned in the text is a house and Judah has quite an establishment, including flocks four miles from Adullam at Timnah (v. 12), where he could surely have pitched his tent if that had been what he was living in. Most probably we should

10. See Sarna, *Genesis*, 265; Wenham, *Genesis 16–50*, 366; and Hamilton, *Book of Genesis*, 432.

11. As Hamilton supposes (*Book of Genesis*, 431), although many commentators do not even ask this question.

understand that Judah is living in Adullam in a house, just like the Canaanites who are his neighbors.

A house of the sort described in chapter 2, in a village arranged as an oval, is probably how an ancient Israelite would have imagined Judah's abode. Judah is somewhat unusual, however, in two respects. First, he is a single person about to start a family. It is probable that local families were patrilocal by inclination, since Judah himself is intent on setting up a family where his sons' wives would live in his house, even if (as we saw in chapter 2) this ideal may have been achieved in only one-fifth of households. Second, Judah was not already related to people in the village. Whereas there was a preference in Israelite society (as in patrilineal cultures generally) for marriage to a daughter of a father's brother, especially as this kept property within the male line,[12] this option was not available to Judah. Rather, Judah came across a Canaanite woman, the daughter of Shua, probably to be understood as living in the same village as himself, whom he saw and took as his wife, and with whom he had sexual relations (v. 2). Wenham notes that although "'take' is a perfectly proper term for marriage, the combination of "see" and "take" has in Genesis overtones of illicit taking (cf. 3:6; 6:2; 12:15; 34:2; cf. Judg 14:1–2), "suggesting Judah's marriage may have been based on mere lust." Wenham considers that the fact that Judah's wife's name is not mentioned, only her father's, points in the same direction.[13] While this is a shrewd observation from a modern perspective, a rather different interpretation emerges if we probe into marriage arrangements in a patrilineal and patrilocal society such as this, arrangements also relevant to the marriage of Tamar a little later in the text.

Among the Palestinian Arabs with whom Finnish anthropologist Hilma Granqvist lived in the 1920s and 30s, it was the father who procured a bride for this son. But if a man's father was dead, his mother stepped into this role, and if she too was deceased, his brothers had a duty to assist.[14] While Judah did indeed procure a wife for his son Er later, none of this was possible for Judah himself when he was seeking

12. Meyers ("The Family," 36) notes the importance of cross-cousin marriage, but errs in suggesting that the ideal partner was the daughter of the brother of one's mother; this did occur (as with Jacob marrying Leah and Rachel, the daughters of Laban, his mother, Rebekah's, brother [Gen 29:10]), but far better the daughter of your father's brother, since this kept property in the male line.

13. Wenham, *Genesis 16–50*, 366.

14. Granqvist, *Marriage Conditions*, 46.

to marry, since he was physically separate from his father and brothers (Gen 38:1), and, additionally, his mother Leah (Gen 35:23) may have been dead.[15] Among Granqvist's *fellahin* (peasants), the man seeking to procure a wife (usually for his son, but sometimes for himself) normally had to negotiate with the father of the bride-to-be, who had power over her.[16] This is what Judah must be understood to have done when the text states, in the typically compressed fashion of a high-context culture, "and he took her" (*wayyiqqaḥeha*). This means he married Shua's daughter by agreement with Shua. The bride might have been quite young, little would be known of her, and her views on the matter were essentially irrelevant. Even if she did not like the bridegroom, her father's will in the matter normally prevailed; the significant actor in the marriage as far as she was concerned was her father, or her brother if her father was dead.[17] That is why Shua's daughter is not named in this narrative, not because she is a victim of Judah's lust.

But much more needs to be said of Judah's wife, especially as the same considerations apply with equal force to Tamar. Although the text—once again probably because of its origin in a high-context culture—says nothing directly about the domestic circumstances, these would have been very familiar to the original audience of this narrative. The first point is that the daughter of Shua must have moved to Judah's house when he married her. This is necessitated by the explicit statement later that Judah sent Tamar back to her father's house, which establishes what must have been the local pattern: the same must be implied for Judah's wife as well. We are dealing, after all, with a patrilocal culture.

Those of us familiar with the nuclear family—where a young man and woman who have married or decided to begin living together usually set up a household of their own—need to put this cultural experience behind them and take steps to become familiar with the very different social dynamics at work in a patrilocal society. It is usually quite traumatic for a young girl to leave her father's home and move to that of her father-in-law or husband, especially because she must leave behind par-

---

15. The time of Leah's death is not given in the Old Testament. She died before Jacob (Gen 49:31) and is not mentioned as having gone with him to Egypt.

16. Granqvist, *Marriage Conditions*, 52–53.

17. Ibid., 54–55. And note this statement (56–57): "A woman has no external power. What could she do against her family? She is completely in their hands. If she does not wish to be expelled from society she cannot, nor will she, break with them who are and will remain all her life her natural protectors, her father and her brother."

ents and siblings who know her and love her, and settle among people who may not. The betrothal and wedding songs of Palestinian Arabs often contained laments that the young girl must leave her father's home.[18] Granqvist explains that

> the wife is not dependent only on her husband but is absorbed into the new home ('eilitha) as a supplement to the man, of course with her special tasks but in any case only a small part of a much larger complex. And yet—and probably just therefore—it is the woman for whom marriage means the greatest change. Uprooted from her own circle (ahelha), she is transplanted to a quite different environment—her husband's father's house—where she must adapt herself to her new position in relation to the members of the new home ('eilitha), who are her husband's relatives (ahlo).[19]

The Palestinian wedding songs bring this out clearly: the bride goes from the house of joy to misery, from her own people to strangers.[20] Carol Meyers has recognized this factor in relation to ancient Israelite society: "Even if daughters-in-law maintained respect for their husbands' mothers—a value strongly present in the book of Ruth—their position as outsiders, at least in the early years of their marriage, may have made life difficult at times."[21] Both Judah's unnamed wife and then Tamar must have experienced this lonely separation from their own families. The disruption would have been intensified by the fact that the household to which the women moved did not even share the religion of their fathers. Often the relation between mother-in-law and daughter-in-law was particularly fraught, as the older woman saw in the younger a rival for her son's love,[22] a not uncommon sentiment magnified in this setting by the domestic propinquity of the two women. At least Judah's wife did not have to deal with a father-in-law and mother-in-law.

If the new wife produced a child, especially a son, everything changed. Hilma Granqvist had not been very long in Palestine before she realized "how important it was for a married woman to bear a son and by this means confirm her position in her husband's house."[23] To bear a

18. Ibid., 60.
19. Ibid., 2:142–43.
20. Ibid., 2:143.
21. Meyers, "The Family," 36.
22. Granqvist, *Marriage Conditions* 2:146–47.
23. Granqvist, *Child Problems*, 60.

child (a son especially) was regarded as the greatest honor that a woman could receive.[24] Data from another contemporary Mediterranean culture that is patrilineal and patrilocal—that of the Sarakatsani shepherds of the Greek mountains—provides further valuable comparative material on this point. Before the birth of the child, although full membership of her new family was extended to the woman, "in an affective sense she remained a stranger even in the eyes of her own husband." When the child was born, however, it is said that "the new bride 'takes root in the new family.'" The joy that surrounds the birth means that the attitude of the family towards the woman "shifts from tolerance to acceptance and affection for her as the mother of their tiny kinsman."[25] In relation to the position in the Bible, Joseph Blenkinsopp has accurately noted that the "women on whom our sources report exhibit an invincible desire for marriage and children, not because they were ideologically naïve and unenlightened but because they had few, if any, other options."[26]

Judah's wife was in an unusual position, since she had married a man who worshiped a different God and who, without any relatives locally, was establishing his own family. Nevertheless, she amply fulfilled the social expectations of her in a patrilineal culture by producing three sons, Er, Onan, and Shelah (Gen 38:3–5), and her husband could not have faulted her in this regard. We know Judah was fond of his wife, since he needed consolation when she died (Gen 38:12); but not as fond as Jacob was for Joseph, since when he thought his son had died he was inconsolable (Gen 37:34–35). As already noted, however, to understand what happens in the narrative, we have to read the brief account of these births quite closely, paying careful attention to every detail in this text from a high-context culture where compression and understatement were the rule.

Our starting point is that Judah names his firstborn Er (38:3), while his wife names Onan and Shelah (38.4–5). There is a textual issue here, since in a number of witnesses Judah's wife names Er.[27] We will stick with the Hebrew Bible version, the Masoretic Text (here as elsewhere). It is usual for commentators, even when following the Masoretic Text,

---

24. Granqvist, *Marriage Conditions* 2:166.

25. Campbell, *Honour, Family, and Patronage*, 69.

26. Blenkinsopp, "The Family", 77.

27. These witnesses are the Samaritan Pentateuch, Targum Jonathan and twelve Hebrew manuscripts.

not even to mention the fact that Judah named Er but that his wife named Onan and Shelah.[28] Esther Menn notices that Judah's wife does not name Er, but instead of reflecting on the significance of Judah doing so, destroys the point by translating the Hebrew word as an impersonal expression: "his name was called Er."[29] Even some critics working with the Hebrew text are of the mistaken view that Judah's wife names Er.[30] These responses show the gap between modern Western and ancient Mediterranean sensibilities that hinder us from seeing what is actually happening in the text. Among the Palestinian Arabs observed by Hilma Granqvist, the naming of a child was a matter of considerable interest in the family.[31] Although there was no firm rule, the father usually chose the name for a boy and the mother for a girl. At times, other relatives (such as grandparents) chose the name. In general, however, either the name reflected a situation current at the birth of the child (for example, the death of a recent relative after whom the baby could be named), or the child was called after a certain person. In the Old Testament there are forty-six occasions when children are named, with twenty-eight named by the father and eighteen by the mother.[32] There is no norm even in relation to firstborn sons: Abraham names Ishmael (Gen 16:15) and Isaac (Gen 21:3), both names given at God's command (Gen 16:11; 17:19), while Leah and Rachel, not Jacob, name all the sons of themselves and their maidservants. Nevertheless, the fact that Judah did name his firstborn, while leaving it to his wife to name his second and third sons, does indicate a direct and interested role by him in that first birth.

Another aspect of the text supports the view that Judah was mainly focused on his firstborn. For we are told in the Masoretic Text that Judah was in Chezib when she bore Shelah.[33] What is the significance of this detail? Chezib is probably to be equated with Achzib (Josh 15:44; Mic 1:14), three miles west of Adullam.[34] Judah was only at Chezib temporarily, not

---

28. For example, the point is not noted by Rad, *Genesis*, Wenham, *Genesis*, Hamilton, *Book of Genesis* and Sarna, *Genesis*.

29. Menn, *Judah and Tamar*, 17 n10.

30. So Alter, *The Art*, 6; and Bos, "Out of the Shadows," 44.

31. See Granqvist, *Child Problems*, 11–14.

32. Löhr, *Die Stellung des Weibes*, 24; Blenkinsopp ("The Family," 68) goes astray in suggesting, "it also seems to have been the mother's prerogative to name the child."

33. The LXX says it was Judah's wife who was in Chezib.

34. So Wenham, *Genesis 16–50*, 366; and Sarna, *Genesis*, 265.

permanently,[35] since in v. 20 Hirah is still Judah's friend and near enough to do him a favor. One possible reason for the reference to Chezib here is that one of Shelah's five sons (as recorded In 1 Chr 4:21–22) settled there.[36] A better interpretation, however, is that Judah was not very interested in the birth of his third son and could not be bothered to be with this wife at this time, since he had absented himself from her and their home at the time of her delivery. Some commentators, indeed, have noted that the Hebrew words used here for the city and clan, *k-z-v* and *sh-l-h* both mean "to deceive, disappoint," and may refer to the disappointment felt by his wife at Judah for his absence.[37] Certainly this view is consonant with the broader picture of Judah's focus on his elder son. In a narrative written in an extremely economical fashion its author added this feature about Chezib more likely to say something directly relevant to one of the two major characters in the plot rather than to make a point about one of the five sons of Shelah (himself a minor character)—a point that has no bearing on the narrative. Accordingly, it is not the case that "all is well in this family," as Johanna Bos suggests.[38]

In making an argument for the dominant concern of Judah with his firstborn, however, we must not be distracted by any notion that Er would have inherited all Judah's estate upon his death, to the exclusion of Onan and Shelah, by operation of the law of primogeniture. Robert Alter has spoken of "the iron law of primogeniture," and Joseph Blenkinsopp also considers that in "normal situations, continuity was assured through primogeniture."[39] In fact, primogeniture institution did not exist in ancient Israel, as Frederick Greenspahn has conclusively shown.[40] A father divided his estate among his sons (as in Luke 15:11–32), although sometimes the elder son received a double portion (cf. Deut 21:15–18; 2 Kings 2:9). If there are a number of sons, the fact that the firstborn gets twice the share of each of the others is hardly consistent with the central idea of primogeniture, which is that the eldest inherits the estate.

At a very general level, it is clear that Judah now had the heirs he needed to keep his property within his growing family, and he also had

35. As Hamilton, *The Book of Genesis*, 434, suggests.

36. Sarna, *Genesis*, 265.

37. Ibid., 266.

38. Bos, "Out of the Shadows," 44.

39. Alter, *The Art*, 6; Blenkinsopp, "The Family," 72.

40. Greenspahn, *When Brothers Dwell Together*, 36–59.

family members to provide labor, rather than having to rely solely on paid servants. A man in his position within his culture would have been very happy with the way his family was growing, and happy with his wife for producing three sons. As the boys began to grow up, Judah inevitably gave thought to the next step in the development of his family, to secure wives for his sons. The typically terse, high-context statement in Gen 38:6 ("And Judah took a wife for Er his firstborn, and her name was Tamar") needs some unpacking.

First, since we are dealing with an ancient patrilocal family and not a modern nuclear one, there is no point to be made from the fact (although Menn seeks to make one)[41] that the text does not depict Er as leaving home and seeking a woman. That Judah had done so was exceptional; Er simply fits into the normal pattern in a patrilineal and patrilocal culture where his father arranges his marriage and his wife comes to reside with them in the father's home.

Second, we should notice that it is for Er first that Judah procures a wife. This may seem inevitable, yet Onan was probably also capable of fathering children at this time (since Judah marries him off to Tamar when Er dies). Accordingly, Judah's action reflects his predominant concern for his firstborn, the primacy of Er in Judah's eyes. This concern is reflected in the fact that v. 6 expressly notes that Judah took a wife for Er, his firstborn (*bekor*) and her name was Tamar. An ancient Israelite audience would have understood that Judah entered into a negotiation with Tamar's father to secure her as Er's wife—a negotiation probably involving payment of a brideprice (cf. Gen 31:15). This is the first of two occasions in the text where Er is specifically referred to as the firstborn (*bekor*); the next instance comes in v. 7. Although, as Frederick Greenspahn has shown,[42] *bekor* was at times a socially, not a biologically, determined status, it is here clearly attributed to Er in his capacity as Judah's firstborn son. It is difficult to avoid the conclusion that Judah's primary concern was with his firstborn, and that he was less interested in the next two. This is in keeping with a common idea in the Old Testament that the firstborn of a man is the most valuable child, "the firstfruits" of a man's strength (Gen 49:3; Deut 21:17; and Ps 78:51). Often in the Old Testament, however, younger siblings become preeminent in spite of this cultural expectation, and the relationship

41. Menn, *Judah and Tamar*, 20.

42. Greenspahn, *When Brothers Dwell Together*.

between brothers is generally characterized by rivalry and conflict, as Greenspahn has carefully explained.[43]

Third, how old was Er at the time at the time of his marriage? There is no expression of a passage of time between the birth of Shelah and this event, and subsequent events would indicate that the main requirement was that Er had reached puberty, so that he was capable of having effective intercourse with Tamar. Presumably Tamar had reached puberty as well. Both Er and Tamar could have been in their early teens.

The text tells us nothing about Tamar's experience in this new household, but from the text it does seem that she was a Canaanite,[44] so that she had ethnic and religious differences between herself and her new family to deal with. In addition, for reasons set out in more detail above, we are able to raise questions from comparable experience elsewhere. How did she get along with her husband's family? Mediterranean ethnography is replete with evidence for the way in which a new wife in such a patrilineal culture could have a very difficult time indeed. The new wife, often a young girl, could be quite lonely and miss the love and comfort previously provided to her by her parents and siblings. She was likely to be in a very subordinate position in the household.[45] In addition, she could have a very strained relationship with her mother-in-law. One reason for this, as Granqvist observed among the Palestinian Arabs, is that the mother-in-law might have lost her own daughter and her daughter's children to another house but would have to be a grandmother to her daughter-in-law's children. A Palestinian mother-in-law referred to her daughter-in-law as "her enemy."[46]

Some ethnographic material suggests that the position of the bride improves dramatically once she has a child, especially if her firstborn is a boy.[47] An ancient Israelite audience would no doubt expect someone in Tamar's position to look forward eagerly to the day when she would give birth to her first child, a son preferably, and thus acquire a position of honor and respect in her father-in-law's household, where her status

---

43. Ibid.

44. Some later Israelite texts attempt to avoid the strong implication in the Masoretic Text that Tamar, just like her mother-in-law, was a Canaanite (see *Jubilees* 41:1–2; *Testament of Judah*, 10:1).

45. Campbell, *Honour, Family, and Patronage*, 63–65.

46. See Granqvist, *Child Problems*, 143–44.

47. See Campbell, *Honour, Family, and Patronage*, 56, 69–70.

was insecure until this event. (The position of Hannah in 1 Sam1:1–18 indicates one type of problem for a wife who had not produced a child— a problem that we will consider in chapter 4.)

Unfortunately, while Tamar was in this difficult initial period, living among her new family, disaster struck for Judah, his wife and surviving sons, and for her: "But Er, Judah's first-born, was wicked in the sight of the Lord; and the Lord slew him" (Gen 38:7). We do not know what evil Er had done to warrant the Lord's slaying him, but we should steer clear of the highly improbable view, which goes back to Rashi, that Er's evil was the same as Onan's; that is, spilling his seed upon the ground, meaning to engage in *coitus interruptus* when he had intercourse with Tamar.[48] As we will see below, Onan's reason for so acting was related to his father's wish that he raise sons for Er; no such issue affected Er himself. There is no reason in Israelite culture why Er would have wanted anything other than that his wife produce sons; Rashi's suggestion that he did not want her to become pregnant lest she lose her looks is not to be taken seriously![49]

Whatever the nature of Er's wickedness, as we have already noted, there is considerable evidence in the text for the centrality of Er in Judah's affections and concern. And now he was dead. This would have been a heavy blow for Judah, even though the text does not specifically mention Judah's grief for his son's death.[50] Moreover, although not specifically mentioned in the text, it is impossible to ignore the impact that Er's death must have had on his mother. While it is likely that Judah's preoccupation with his firstborn had pushed her closer to her second and third sons (especially, perhaps, the youngest), she must also have nursed a special love for her firstborn, whose arrival had cemented her husband's regard for her and secured her place of honor in his house. We must imagine both father and mother entering a period of grief over the death of their firstborn.

In addition, it is important to ask how Judah and his wife would have felt toward Tamar in consequence of the death of Er. Palestinian Arabs in the first few decades of the twentieth century quite easily blamed a woman for her husband's death.[51] An ancient audience would probably

48. See Rashi on Gen 38:7 in Rosenbaum and Silbermann, *Rashi's Commentary*, 185.

49. Ibid.

50. As noted by Hamilton, *The Book of Genesis*, 434–35.

51. Granqvist, *Marriage Conditions*, 2:307.

have assumed that people in the position of Judah and his wife would have had a discussion as to whether Tamar was to blame. In challenging the whole notion of "patriarchy" as applied to ancient Israelite society, Carol Meyers has pointed out that Israelite women were powerful actors in "daily affairs and family decisions."[52] Judah's wife would have discussed Er's death with him. Since Judah goes on to have Onan take Tamar as his wife, however, the conversation must have been settled in Tamar's favor. Indeed, the whole Levirate law, which required a man to marry his brother's widow when she had not had children, could not have worked if the death of the first brother was blamed on the wife. Nevertheless, we should not draw the conclusion that the evil that the narrator attributes to Er as the reason for his death at God's hands also played a part in Judah's thinking. For Onan too is described as being killed by God for his evil actions, yet this does not stop Judah from preventing Shelah's marriage to Tamar (Judah presumably could have steered Sheela away from such wickedness, had he been aware of it). The unspecified evil of Er and the specified evil of Onan are known to narrator and audience but not, apparently, to Judah (or to his wife).

Fortunately for Judah and his wife, not everything is lost because of Er's death, since an Israelite social and legal practice was available to him that provided some amelioration of the consequences, by means of which Judah would be able to have children from Er (and grandchildren for him) fathered by Onan: "Then Judah said to Onan, 'Go into your brother's wife, and perform the duty of a brother-in-law to her and raise up offspring for your brother'" (38:8).

Although the Pentateuch forbids marriage between a man and his brother's wife (Lev 18:16), an exception was made when the brother died without leaving a son, and where he was living with a brother or brothers, as set out in Deut 25:5–6. Deuteronomy states the reason for this law as being to insure that "the name of the dead man may not be blotted out of Israel" (25:6). Herbert Brichto and Theodore Lewis have provided a context for statements such as this by showing how important it was for ancient Israelites to perpetuate the memory of deceased ancestors, who were actually known as "gods" (*'elohim*), and to invoke them during funerary rites.[53]

---

52. Meyers, *Discovering Eve*, 24–26; Meyers, "The Family," 34. Blenkinsopp, "The Family," 76, also finds 'patriarchy' an unsatisfactory term.

53. Brichto, "Kin, Cult, Land"; and Lewis, "The Ancestral Estate." Their views are

Such a rationale makes most sense for the father of the deceased, whose love for his son would be expressed by his arranging for the birth of progeny who would bear his son's name. The dead man would, in a sense, live on in those children, and that thought would be very gratifying to a grieving parent. But for the deceased's brother the situation was very different. The son or sons produced by a union with his dead brother's wife would inherit their father's share of their grandfather's estate, so that the living brother would inevitably receive less. That is why Deut 25:9 includes a statement indicating that the brother who does produce children with the dead man's wife is building up the dead man's house (*bet*). To the father of the deceased, at least where his sons live together (Deut 25:5), it really makes no difference to him which of his children or grandchildren fathered by his sons inherit his estate, since it is still being kept within the male line in accordance with the principles of patrilineality. The operation of the Levirate law, therefore, opens up lines of tension between the interests of the father and those of the surviving brothers of the deceased.[54] That Levirate marriage was not necessarily attractive to a dead man's brother is clear from Deuteronomy 25, since there provision is made for a man publicly to renounce this responsibility (vv. 7–10). Such renunciation is presented as a disgraceful action on the man's part, but this was no doubt a case where property mattered more than reputation.

Not surprisingly, therefore, Onan, decided to avoid the responsibility of the Levirate law: "But Onan knew that the offspring would not be his; so when he went into his brother's wife he spilled the semen on the ground, lest he should give offspring to his brother" (Gen 38:9). Onan was having intercourse with Tamar but also practicing *coitus interruptus* so that she would not fall pregnant. His probable reason is the risk of diminishing the property he stood to inherit from his father, as just discussed. This view is in accord with that of Sarna, who comments that because of

---

endorsed by Blenkinsopp, "Family," 63: "What was fundamentally important was paternity and inheritance, the extension of the man's 'house' into the future, the preservation of his name and that of his ancestral house."

54. Palestinian Arabs also practice marriage to a widow by the dead man's brother, which has some similarities to the Israelite law but differs in being applicable even when there are children of the first marriage. Here the subsequent marriage has the advantage of allowing the widow to stay in her husband's house with her children, whom she would have to leave there if she returned to the house of her father (Granqvist, *Marriage Conditions*, 2:303–6).

Er's death, Onan stood to inherit one-half of his father's estate, but this share diminished if he had children by Tamar for Er.[55] This explains why Onan did not wish to "give offspring to his brother." Another factor possibly in play here is Onan's resentment at his father's predominant interest in Er as the firstborn.

Unfortunately for Onan, God was displeased with his actions and killed him as well. It was now inevitable that Judah and his wife, with two of their three sons dead, would consider that Tamar had played some causative role in the deaths of their sons. While one could write off to coincidence the death of Er following his marriage to Tamar, the fact that Onan too died after he had started to have sex with her would be much harder to regard as coincidental. It is highly probable that an ancient audience would assume that Onan had not told his father or mother that he was engaging in *coitus interruptus* with Tamar (since this practice frustrated Judah's purpose in giving him Tamar as his wife), so that Judah and his wife would not be in a position to blame him for his own death.

The comparative experience of the Palestinian Arabs among whom Hilma Granqvist lived is illuminating. They considered that it was extremely grave if a woman lost several husbands who were brothers, with the same family having to bear repeated losses, and that the woman concerned had introduced a dangerous element into the family.[56] Granqvist actually learned of one case where a woman's first husband died, so she married a brother of her husband, and he died too. At this a third brother stepped forward who was willing to marry her (allegedly under the influence of a love potion!), but she died before he could.[57]

An ancient Israelite audience would probably have imagined Judah and his wife giving careful thought on what to do in this situation.

---

55. Sarna, *Genesis*, 267. Sarna is presumably assuming that with the death of Er, Onan would inherit equally with Shelah. It is probably more accurate just to say that Onan's share will be reduced, rather than to fix the his increased portion as one-half rather than one-third, since this depends on an equal shares division between surviving sons, for which the Old Testament does not provide evidence, nor the New Testament, where even the size of the portion taken by the prodigal son is not specified (Luke 15:11–32). Hamilton (*Book of Genesis*, 435) wrongly suggests that Onan stands to inherit "the family" estate, but this view presupposes the law of primogeniture that did not exist in Israel.

56. Granqvist, *Marriage Conditions*, 2:310.

57. Ibid., 307–9.

Although they had one son left, Shelah (admittedly still too young for marriage), the prospect of him marrying Tamar and then suffering the same fate as his brothers would almost certainly have prompted Judah and his wife to prevent their son's marrying her. There is one feature of the text, hitherto unnoticed (on my current inquiries), that seems to point to Judah and his wife's having had just such a discussion. The text records events after the death of Onan as follows: "Then Judah said to Tamar his daughter-in-law, 'Remain a widow in your father's house, till Shelah my son grows up'—for he feared that he would die, like his brothers. So Tamar went and dwelled in her father's house" (Gen 38:11).

This is the RSV, which obscures the important fact that the Hebrew text literally reads: "for he said (ki 'amar) otherwise he will die (pen yam-ut), him as well, just like his brothers." Although 'amar here is frequently interpreted as "he thought" or "he feared" (thus timebat in the Vulgate, for example), there is no need to interpret this other than with the most common meaning of the word as "he said" (as also the LXX: eipen). For the plain meaning of the statement makes excellent sense as the central feature of what Judah said to his wife when they were discussing what to do with Tamar to prevent Shelah from dying like Er and Onan had.

Rather than being honest with Tamar by explaining to her his fears, Judah decided instead to deceive her. He asked her to remain a widow until Shelah grew up, even though he had no intention of letting Shelah marry her. This direction from her father-in-law, who had authority over her, means, inevitably, that she could not marry anyone else or have children by anyone else. He thus subjected Tamar to a marginalized life where she would be living at her father's house while still subject to Judah and hence unable to find honor as a wife and mother, an essential aspect of womanhood in Israelite culture. Tamar's widow's clothes (see v. 14), which she must continue to wear, symbolize the permanently diminished existence and status to which Judah is intent on consigning her.[58]

It is highly likely that the original Israelite audience would have understood that Judah's wife was very active in relation to Tamar and

---

58. For discussions of the status of widows in Israel see Coats, "Widow's Rights"; Hiebert, "'Whence Shall Help Come to Me?'"; and Leeb, "The Widow" (although her description of a widow, almanah, who is past the age of childbearing and is not part of a male-centered household does not really work for the Tamar, who is described as being in such a household in Gen 38:11).

her role in the family, and the plausibility of this interpretation is cor-
roborated in two ancient witnesses—both of which diverge from the implication in the Masoretic Text by presenting Tamar as Aramean and not
Canaanite but also by showing Judah's wife as having a very active role.

First, *Jubilees*, a work from the second century BCE, retells the story
of Judah and Tamar in a manner that introduces some very negative views
towards non-Israelites. *Jubilees* 30:7 provides: "And if there is any man in
Israel who wishes to give his daughter or his sister to any man who is
from the seed of the gentiles, let him surely die, and let him be stoned
because he has caused shame to Israel."[59] Later in the text, in the account
of Judah and Tamar, we are told that Tamar was "from the daughters of
Aram," that is from the same people as Abraham, and that Er did not
want to marry her because his mother was a Canaanite, and he wanted
a Canaanite wife, but Judah compelled him to marry her. According to
Jubilees, Judah would have let Shelah marry Tamar when he had grown
up, but when this happened, "Bedsuel, Judah's wife, did not permit Selah,
her son, to marry."[60] This version assumes that Judah's wife was active in
the decision that Shelah not marry Tamar, probably because (in this text)
she was not a Canaanite like Judah's wife, although also possibly because
Bedsuel did not want to expose her third and only surviving son in marriage to a woman implicated in the death of the first two, a reading of the
narrative that accords with the interpretation presented above.

Second, there is a similar feature in the *Testament of Judah*, one
of the testaments in the work known as the *Testaments of the Twelve
Patriarchs*, probably to be dated to the second century BCE.[61] In this text,
Er brings Tamar, an Aramean, from Mesopotamia, but a problem arises
because she was not a Canaanite, namely, that his wicked Canaanite
mother did not want him to have children by Tamar. So Er and then
Onan die because of their wickedness, and although Judah wanted to
give Shelah (Shelom in this work) to Tamar, his wife would not allow
it, for the reason that Tamar was not a Canaanite as she was. Although
Judah's wife is not said to act out of fear that Shelah would die like his
brothers, this text confirms the interpretation set out above to the extent
that it suggests an ancient audience would have been open to the idea of

---

59. *Jubilees* 41:1–2; English translation in Wintermute, "Jubilees," 112.

60. *Jubilees* 41:6–7; English translation in ibid., 130.

61. See Kee, "Testaments," 777–78.

her being far more active in Judah's house than one would gather from
the bare words of the account in Genesis 38.

Returning to the text of Genesis 38, it is clear that for Tamar the
deaths of Er and Onan and Judah's sending her back to her father's
house represent a major crisis in her life, when everything suddenly goes
wrong. Because of the earlier improvement in Tamar's fortunes through
marriage to Er, and because Tamar is now so powerless, this is close to
being her worst moment and lowest point in the story. Yet things do, in
fact, get worse, when Tamar realizes that although Shelah has grown up,
Judah has not honored his commitment to have Shelah marry her. But
this brings us to the next phase in the story: Tamar seizes the initiative
and grasps her destiny and that of her children in her own hands.

Some time passes and Judah's wife, the daughter of Shua, dies.
When Judah's period of mourning is over, he heads off to Timnah to his
sheepshearers with his old friend, Hirah the Adullamite (Gen 38:12).
Sheep shearing was a time of feasting and drinking.[62] Esther Menn
comments that "the objective record of Judah's wife's death and his engagement in routine seasonal activities in Gen 38:12 suggests (sic) the
passage of time in a narrative world that has forgotten Tamar."[63] Perhaps
Tamar has been forgotten by Judah, but not by everyone in this narrative. For someone tells Tamar that Judah is going to Timnah; we do not
know who, but in Middle Eastern villages word flies fast through gossip
in a setting where everyone knows everyone else.[64] Now Tamar springs
into action (Gen 38:13–14) to ensnare Judah on his way to Timnah. The
fact that she hears of Judah's intentions in good time to take such action
suggests we are to understand that her father's house was very close to
his, possibly in the same village. Verse 14 first describes what she did
(taking off her widow's garb, putting on a veil, and sitting like a prostitute at the entrance to Ennaim, on the road to Timnah), and then why
she did it: "for she saw that Shelah was grown up and she had not been
given to him in marriage."

---

62. Cf. 1 Sam 25:4–8 and 2 Sam 13:23–29.

63. Menn, *Judah and Tamar*, 31.

64. Hamilton (*Book of Genesis*, 440) suggests that she owes the information about
her father-in-law's movements to an anonymous informer, but the natural spreading of
the news through a small community by gossip provides a more plausible explanation;
for the function of gossip in Middle Eastern villages today, see Rohrbaugh, "Gossip in
the New Testament."

The speed and decisiveness of Tamar's actions are worth noting. Probably we should imagine her waiting to see what would transpire when Judah's period of mourning for his wife had ended: would he call for her then? The news that he was going off to the vinous joy of the sheepshearing at Timnah and plainly had no intention of arranging the promised union between herself and Shelah answered her question. She had either already planned to have a child by Judah in this eventuality and now seized her chance to implement that plan, or her realization of his opposition to her marrying Shelah came simultaneously with her suddenly deciding what she could do about it: she would have a child by Judah himself.

The contrast between the initiative that she shows at this point in the story and the prior depiction of her is stark.[65] Previously she has been entirely passive; negotiated by Judah from her father and out of his house to marry Er, then offered to Onan in Er's stead. She has been treated by Judah essentially as an object, as a woman whose primary function was to produce male heirs for Er and hence for Judah himself (and no doubt also to do the cooking, cleaning, and spinning). Judah does not even use Tamar's name in referring to her; she is just the wife of his son(s). This instrumental treatment of women is what we should expect in a patrilinear and patrilocal culture such as this one. This expectation, in fact, forms the necessary context within which we can appreciate just how remarkably Tamar turns the tables on Judah and secures her own position. For now we see a different Tamar (or just a different side to her): a woman whose action is capable of analysis within the trickster tradition,[66] someone who reveals the independent strength within her.

With Tamar sitting at the entrance to Ennaim on the road to Timnah (v. 14), her trap is set. She will show even greater wile, however, in the way she springs it. There now occurs what Gordon Wenham aptly describes as "a wonderfully businesslike exchange."[67] Judah sees her and assumes she is a prostitute (*zonah*) because her face is covered (v. 15). He goes over to her at the side of the road and requests sex with her.[68] The text explains this request on the basis that he did not know

---

65. For a detailed description of the change in Tamar, see Wenham, *Genesis 16–50*, 367.

66. See Nicholas, *The Trickster Revisited*, 62.

67. Wenham, *Genesis 16–50*, 367.

68. On the role of the *zonah*, see Niditch, "Wronged Woman Righted," 147.

who she was, but such ignorance was produced only by the veil! Even though they have a conversation, Judah apparently knows his daughter-in-law so little that she can rely on the fact (correctly, as it turns out) that he will not recognize her voice! She replies by asking what he will pay her (v. 16). He offers a kid from his flock, but she wants a pledge for its delivery (v. 17). He agrees to her quite audacious request of his seal, his cord and his staff. The seal was a small cylindrical object with a hollowed-out center to hang around the neck, and engraved with ornamentation distinctive to its owner that was rolled over clay to legitimate documents. Sarna notes the significance of the seal: "It was a highly personal object that performed the function of a signature in modern society, a kind of extension of the personality. Judah leaves part of himself with Tamar when he gives her his seal."[69] In addition, Judah's staff may also have had an identifying sign.[70] Or, more probably, it was elaborately carved like the walking sticks that were owned by every Babylonian, according to Herodotus.[71] Judah was plainly going to look quite a sight as he proceeded on to Timnah without seal or staff and without even a cord around his waist. But so desperate was he that he handed over these objects and had sex with the "prostitute," as a result of which she conceived (v. 18). Tamar then went off and put her widow's clothes back on (v. 19), probably since they at least gave her a less anomalous place in the local community than she would have without them, and she was also assured of a few more months of her usual life until her pregnancy began to show.

Judah now sends his Adullamite friend to deliver the kid to "the hand of the woman" and thus to redeem his seal, staff, and cord from her (v. 20). Presumably, Judah is busy with his sheepshearing, has no interest in the woman and is probably also somewhat embarrassed by his having had sex with a *zonah*. He must also think the transfer will be easily effected, so that he can rely on Hirah to run this errand for him.[72] So Hirah goes off to the place (by necessary implication, carrying the kid!) but cannot find the woman. When he asks local men the whereabouts of

69. Sarna, *Genesis*, 268.

70. Ibid., 269.

71. Herodotus, *Histories*, 1.195; noted by Menn, *Judah and Tamar*, 24.

72. Some commentators, for example Hamilton (*Book of Genesis*, 446), make the point that Judah has not even bothered to learn the woman's name; but a woman who was concealing her identity with a veil would hardly want to give a customer her name.

the "cult prostitute," using a word (*qedešah*) that denotes a rather more up-market prostitute than the common whore (*zonah*), Judah thought he was resorting to, they reply that there had been no cult prostitute there (v. 21). Tamar's transaction with Judah had taken only minutes, after all, and she was apparently gone before anyone else in the vicinity could witness her presence. When Hirah has carried this news back to his friend (v. 22), Judah comments: "Let her keep the things as her own, lest we be laughed at; you see, I sent this kid, and you could not find her" (v. 23, RSV)

There is a touch of comedy here, since we must understand this conversation going on while one of them (probably Judah) is holding the kid ("this kid"). In the Hebrew text the words translated by the RSV here as "lest we be laughed at" are: "lest we be for contempt," "for ridicule" (*pen niyeh labuz*). Judah is concerned that their reputations—and note how easily he draws Hirah into the potential dishonor—will be damaged.

But what precisely is the nature of the ridicule or contempt (*buz*) that Judah fears? What is the source of Judah's concern that he would be made a laughingstock? Bird suggests that it was not a "sacred act of love-making with the hierodule of a Canaanite cult," since the people of the place are understood to be Canaanite and would find no cause for contempt in that. She suggests it is surely the fact that Judah was outwitted and, more specifically, "taken" by a common prostitute.[73] This seems a step in the right direction, but it is hardly a full explanation.

We need to recall that we are dealing with the consequence of a social interaction in an honor-bound culture that had a very rich vocabulary for pointing out that someone had been dishonored or shamed. E. Kutsch notes that this semantic field includes *herpa* ("reproach," "scorn"), *buz* ('contempt'), *bošet* ("shame"), *giddupim* ("reviling"), *dera'on* ("contempt"), *ḥesed* ("defamation"), *la'ag* ("derision"), *qeles* ("derision"), and above all *kelimma* and *kelimmut* (dishonor in the sense of "insult," "reproach").[74]

The word *buz* itself occurs eleven times in the Hebrew Bible. It principally refers to a social situation in which negative attitudes and verbal expressions are directed at those who have suffered dishonor, either through their behavior or through a fate that has befallen them, so

73. Bird. "Harlot," 104.
74. Kutsch, "*ḥrp' II*", 211.

that they have been diminished in public opinion. Particularly revealing is Job 31:34:

> because I stood in great fear of the multitude,
> and the contempt (*buz*) of families terrified me,
> so that I kept silence, and did not go out of doors. (RSV)

Here we see that one response to *buz* is to hide from those in whose eyes one stands dishonored. Job fears that if he goes outside, or even if he is heard within, he will be subjected to a barrage of verbal contempt. Because *buz* is an experience of shame suffered by someone in a particular social context, it can affect both the good and the bad. Thus, while sometimes righteous people experience *buz* (Pss 31:9; 119:22; 123:3, 4), so too can a man of perverse heart (Prov 12:8), while *buz* comes with wickedness (Prov 18:3) and God pours *buz* on princes (Job 12:21; Ps 107:40).

It is in this context, therefore, that we must explain Judah's apprehension at being laughed at. He fears that he will suffer a severe loss of reputation that will find expression in feelings of scorn towards him and verbal insults. It has not happened yet; but Judah fears that if the transaction becomes public, this is what will happen.

Yet what is it about that transaction that has caused this concern? The key lies in the statement, "you see, I sent this kid, and you could not find her" (v. 23). The arrangement between Judah and the woman was that she would give him sex in return for a kid. We can only surmise that the kid was a reasonable price for the service. In asking for, and getting, Judah's seal, staff, and cord, as security against delivery of the kid, the woman must have received items having a value far in excess of the kid. If Judah had bargained more cleverly, he would have offered only one of these items at least. Clearly his desire got the better of his judgment. When later he sends Hirah with the kid, he reaches the unpalatable conclusion that the woman would rather keep the items of greater value that he has left her. In other words, he has been tricked in the transaction. This would be bad enough if the other person was a man on his social level, it is doubly bad that he has been conned by a woman and triply bad that she is a prostitute. His statement, "you see, I sent this kid," does not operate in Israelite culture to provide a foundation for Judah's sense of grievance that the woman has disappeared with his property. Rather, it indicates the cause from which Judah can expect the ridicule. For it provides a scale for assessing just how completely Judah has been gulled by the woman. Here was Judah sending his friend Hirah with a kid and expecting the unknown woman from whom he had purchased sex to hand over Judah's much more valuable property in exchange for it, and (what a surprise) she was not to be found! Accordingly, the reason why it is better for Judah to take no more efforts to recover his property and simply to let the woman keep it is that this way no one will learn how he has been completely bested by the woman in their business negotiation.

Esther Menn misreads the narrative when she writes that this "humorous depiction of Judah's attempt to settle accounts with the woman he mistook as a prostitute appears to be a digression, since it does not forward the plot."[75] This incident is central to the plot, since if Judah had managed to retrieve his possessions, Tamar would have ended up burnt to death outside her father's house. It is also important in the presentation of Tamar as the real protagonist in Genesis 38 from vv. 13–30. It is Menn, after all, who usefully describes Tamar as a "marginal" or "unconventional" protagonist because of the way she takes the initiative in relation to producing an heir for Judah that none of his sons had managed to do,[76] and her action in relation to Judah's belongings provides significant evidence for the accuracy of this description.

The narrative now jumps three months and Judah is told, "Tamar your daughter-in-law has played the harlot; and moreover she is with child by harlotry" (v. 24a). The woman whom Judah has chosen to ignore and to leave as a widow in her father's house now once again becomes his daughter-in-law when it is alleged that she has prostituted herself and become pregnant as a result. He is angry because although she is now living in his father's house, her relationship to him, via his two dead sons and her virtual betrothal to Shelah, means his reputation has been damaged by her behavior. He is shamed because he has not been able to stop another man from having sex with her. Hence he says, "Bring her out and let her be burned" (v. 24b). Elsewhere in the Pentateuch (Deut 22:21) stoning, not burning, is envisaged for a woman who is found to have lost her virginity to someone before she marries her husband (although this is not quite the situation here); burning is restricted to a priest's daughter in these circumstances (Lev 21:9) and for

75. Menn, *Judah and Tamar*, 26.
76. Ibid., 28–29.

incest with one's mother-in-law (Lev 21:14). Judah is being exception-ally severe with Tamar.

His attitude is readily explicable in terms of wider patterns of Mediterranean culture, as explained in chapter 2. Maureen Giovannini has noted that across the Mediterranean region there is commonly a connection between female chastity and social worth. While this may not be a "universal," and similar concerns may crop up elsewhere, it is very pervasive in the Mediterranean region "where it is associated with institutionalized practices that both affect and reflect gender-based rela-tions of authority, dominance, and coercion." In particular, "Consistent with this pattern is male control over female sexuality since men are usually responsible for protecting the chastity of their female relatives."[77] Since Tamar is wearing widow's garb and betrothed (or very close to being betrothed) to his son Shelah, Judah is the man who has authority over Tamar and the one who has failed to protect her chastity against interlopers. His honor has been besmirched, and the only way to restore it is to have her killed, preferably in as gruesome a fashion as possible.

So we arrive at the point when they are bringing Tamar out to ex-ecute Judah's sentence of death by fire upon her. We must imagine a group of people gathered around her father's house, including no doubt the members of her own family (probably red faced with the shame she has brought on them) and other villagers. Some perhaps are sympathetic to Tamar as they await her fearsome death (perhaps women with whom she was on friendly terms, if present in ancient Israel were the positive attitudes—mentioned in chapter 2—that Unni Wikan observed among women in Oman toward another woman who engaged in illicit sex when her husband was away), while others are outraged by her breach of local convention.

At this moment, with all of them assuming her situation is desper-ate, Tamar suddenly derails the whole process, by sending word to Judah to say that she is pregnant to the man to whom belong this seal, cord, and staff (v. 25). One sees the crowd, at first wondering what difference it can possibly make for Tamar to proffer tokens that would reveal the identity of the man who had made her pregnant and then perhaps thinking that this revelation is an act of defiance or revenge on her part. Then comes the incipient astonishment as some of them realize that these items look like those belonging to Judah and tell the others.

77. Giovannini, "Female Chastity Codes," 61.

We must imagine Judah standing there, dumbfounded in front of her, the expression of anger and righteous indignation fading rapidly from his face. He makes no attempt to conceal the truth: "Then Judah acknowledged them" (v. 26). We must imagine the shock as Judah says, in the presence of the crowd, words to this effect: "Yes, they are mine." By so saying he confirmed the truth of Tamar's allegation; he was the father of her unborn child. Having been so completely bested, Judah realizes that the time had come for a frank admission of his culpability: "She is righteous, not I (*ṣadeqah mimmeni*), inasmuch as I did not give her to my son Shelah."[78] By these words Judah, if not exonerating Tamar of all blame for what has happened, recognizes that she has acted in accordance with local moral conventions and he has not. There is no judicial context in view here. As Hamilton notes, Judah's initial insistence that Tamar be burned "is simply an outburst of indignation, a spontaneous reaction, and hardly a reflection of actual juridical enforcement for sins relating to sexual behavior,"[79] even if the punishment of death by burning that he was seeking was known in Israel. To similar effect is Clifford's observation: "The scene is not a trial, however . . . Judah has acted as a *pater familias*, not as judge, in deciding that Tamar should be burned."[80]

The final statement in v. 26 raises a number of questions: "And he did not know her [that is, have sex with her] again." As Diane Sharon notes, "her status of motherhood is already perfectly realized."[81] But does this mean that she remained in her father's house and did not move back to Judah's? Almost certainly not. In Israelite culture it is highly unlikely, if not inconceivable, that Judah would have allowed his two sons by Tamar to live anywhere else than with him. Tamar must have been with them initially to suckle them and presumably would have stayed in Judah's household thereafter. Did she marry Shelah in the end? He did have children (1 Chr 4:21), but their mother is unspecified.

Tamar, as heroine, has now emerged fully into the light of day, with her exceptional qualities fully revealed, while the previously dominant

78. Here I follow Richard Clifford's translation of *ṣadeqah mimmeni* rather than the alternative, "she is more righteous than I" (Clifford, "Genesis 38," 530).

79. Hamilton, *Book of Genesis*, 449.

80. Clifford, "Genesis 38," 530; contra, Wenham, *Genesis 16–50*, 369. This is one of numerous places in the Old Testament where instances of *ṣaddiq/dikaios* do not have the "forensic" or "judicial" meaning so frequently and wrongly attributed to them (see Esler, *Galatians*, 159–69).

81. Sharon, "Some Results," 307.

figure, Judah in this case, has been discomfited and disappears from the culmination of the story, her delivery of twins; for her happy state is to become a mother and not just of one son but two: Perez and Zerah (vv. 27–30). This happy state, however, must be assumed since it is not described in the text. Indeed, as Esther Menn has pointed out, Tamar is given a notably passive role in the birth of her two sons. There are many details about the curious manner of their birth and the action of the midwife but nothing about Tamar herself except the fact of giving birth. She does not even name them.

The narrative does not tell us that one of her sons would turn out to have an illustrious destiny, although the original audience probably knew. Numbers 26:20 confirms that the three sons of Judah were Shelah, Perez, and Zerah, producing respectively the families of the Shelanites, the Perezites and the Zerahites. Perez produced two sons, Hezron and Hamul (Num 26:21), and Hezron is mentioned in the genealogical list that concludes the book of Ruth, which begins with Perez, then Hezron and then lists six more names, before concluding with Jesse and his son David (Ruth 4:18–22). So it was that Tamar would contribute to a genealogical line that would begin with Abraham and end with David, or, from a Christian point of view, with Jesus (see Matt 1:2–17). The long view, then, sees Tamar's happy state consisting not only in the production of two sons who themselves produced families (which happy day she was perhaps alive to see and take pride in) but also in something in addition to this motherly fulfillment—an immortal name among her adopted people and among another group that was to emerge from them but that would preserve her memory with similar fidelity (Matt 1:3).

CONCLUSION

Having investigated the narrative of Judah and Tamar in the light of its original context in Israel we now return to, and conclude this chapter with, a consideration of how the story relates to Christopher Booker's sevenfold plot typology, in particular with the "Rags to Riches" and "Comedy" plots. We must bear in mind, however, that since using a typology is a comparative exercise and not an attempt at pigeonholing, there is no reason why a particular narrative like this may not be comparable with more than one type; so we may find data in the text that corresponds to both of these plot types. And this, indeed, proves to be the case here.

Some aspects of comedy surface in Genesis 38. To be more precise, aspects of human character and interactions come in due course to characterize comic plots, even though Genesis 38 may well have been written before the beginnings of comedy in the Old Comedy of Aristophanes in Athens, performed between about 427 and 388 BCE. Of particular importance is the element that Booker shows has characterized comedy since its inception: that one of the characters is trapped in some dark state, which throws its shadows over other characters, before that character undergoes a change of heart or is exposed and punished.[82] Examples include Procleon in Aristophanes's *Wasps*, and the men of Athens in his *Lysistrata*; Katherina in Shakespeare's *The Taming of the Shrew*, and the four young men in his *Love's Labours Lost*; and Count Almaviva in Beaumarchais's *The Marriage of Figaro*. Judah's recognition that Tamar and not he is the one who has been acting justly accords with this sort of personal transformation. Another typically comic feature is the disclosure of disguised identity, the unveiling of what has been unclear; and that feature is represented in Tamar's tricking Judah and her ultimate revelation, using the physical tokens typical of this move, of who she really is. Yet in spite of these similarities, which certainly help us to situate Judah in a wider universe of comic narratives, two prominent features of comedy do not occur in Genesis 38. There is not, first of all, the complex skein of confusion involving several characters, which is eventually resolved, that features in most of the comedies summarized by Booker. There is no group of people brought to a happy resolution of their knots that previously held them. Rather, one man is misled and eventually brought to face the truth. Secondly, whereas comedy often ends in marriage, in the present case, the text expressly states that Judah and Tamar did not continue with a sexual relationship (v. 26), even if (as argued above) an ancient audience would have assumed Tamar ended up living with her twin sons in Judah's house. Judah and Tamar are not brought happily together at the end in the manner typical of comedy. Rather, the plot provides a strong sense of something unfinished, in the reference to the birth of Perez and his brother.

Instead, Genesis is more closely comparable with the "Rags to Riches" plot type known (from very diverse cultural settings) in other

---

82. See Booker, *Seven Basic Plots*, 107–29.

embodiments. As examples of this type of story Booker cites the story of Joseph in Genesis, the story of Aladdin, fairytales like "Cinderella" and "The Ugly Duckling," the character Eliza Doolittle in *Pygmalion*, novels like *David Copperfield* and *Jane Eyre*, and films such as Charlie Chaplin's *The Gold Rush* (1921) and *The Benny Goodman Story* (1956). Readers from the USA will be aware of another comparison in the novels of Horatio Alger (1832–1899), which have as their subject how impoverished boys manage to escape poverty through hard work, a moral life, and good fortune. The Horatio Alger novels made a significant contribution to the construction of the American dream.

Let us now progress through the five elements of Booker's "Rags to Riches" plot in comparison with Tamar.[83] First, we begin with a hero or heroine at a young age, or before he or she has ventured out into the world, or in some disadvantaged situation. The protagonist is at the bottom of the heap, seemingly inferior to those around him or her, more dominant figures who scorn or mistreat, and who can neither feel for the character nor perceive his or her true qualities. Second, something happens to call or send the hero or heroine into a wider world, where they have some initial success. They have a glimpse of the glorious state they may one day obtain. The nature of Genesis 38 means that elements 1 and 2 need to be addressed together. Since Tamar is not mentioned until v. 6, and then only as a passive actor in relation to an initiative by Judah (he takes her as a wife for his son Er), vv. 1–5 serve to supply information necessary to understand the nature of her initial condition and of her entry into the wider world. The second element as far as Tamar is concerned occurs with her marriage. Just being married represents initial success, and she has the bright prospect of becoming a mother to sons and a fully valued member of Judah's household. She need only begin producing sons for Er as her mother-in-law had for Judah and all will be well. But if that had been the result, we would not have had a story!

Third, however, there comes a "central crisis," when everything suddenly goes wrong. In Tamar's case this happens in Gen 38:7–12, with the deaths of her husbands (first Er and then Onan); with her dispatch by Judah to her father's house as a widow, allegedly to await the coming of age of Shelah; and then with her discovery that Judah is unlikely to allow her to marry Shelah.

83. See ibid., 51–68 for the "rags to riches" plot and 65–66 for this summary of its features.

For the protagonists in the "Rags to Riches" tale, because of the earlier improvement in their fortunes, and because they are so power-less, this is their worst moment and their lowest point in the story. So it is with Tamar. Yet as they emerge from the crisis (and this is the fourth trait of a "Rags to Riches" story), they begin to appear in a new light. They discover in themselves a new, independent strength. But this means that they must once again pit themselves against a figure who stands in the road of what they must achieve. This struggle with a powerful opponent forms the climax of the story. Only when they have successfully passed through this phase, and the shadow over their life is removed, are they liberated to move to the last phase. In Tamar's case her struggle with Judah (Gen 38:12–26) takes two phases: first, fooling him into impreg-nating her when he is unaware of her identity and, second, relying on the tokens she cleverly extracted from him on this occasion to protect her-self against his having her killed later when her pregnancy has become apparent. The result of all this is that Tamar has successfully passed through this fourth phase of the "Rags to Riches" story, and the shadow over her life has been removed, so that she is liberated to progress to the fifth and final phase, where she will be revealed as truly exceptional.

Fifth and finally, "Rags to Riches" heroes and heroines achieve ful-fillment. This often entails marriage, but it can also comprise attainment of some other happy state. The hero or heroine has emerged fully into the light of day, with his or her exceptional qualities fully revealed, while the previously dominant figures, on the other hand, either have been discomfited or have faded away. In Genesis 38 Tamar obtains the chil-dren she had desired (Gen 38:27–30) and, by implication, enters a happy state of fulfillment as their mother living in Judah's house, while Judah has had to acknowledge the lack of justice in his treatment of her.

In summary, we find in Tamar's story and in others like it a pat-tern of life that seems to have a particular fascination, to exert a strong grip on the human imagination: "We see," says Booker, "an ordinary, insignificant person, dismissed by everyone as of little account, who suddenly steps to the centre of the stage, revealed to be someone quite exceptional."[84] This is a common pattern in the Old Testament, and we will return to give it closer attention when we consider the case of David and how he came to greatness, in chapters 6 and 7.

84. Ibid., 51.

We must note, finally, how closely integrated are the structural connections that Genesis 38 has with other stories from different cultures and its particular context in ancient Israel. For it is impossible fully to appreciate the magnitude of Tamar's "Rags to Riches" transformation without knowing just how strongly the cards were stacked against a woman like her in a patrilinear and patrilocal setting such as ancient Israel, and how she triumphed in protecting her life and her honor in the face of a powerful opponent. While we may encounter the underlying structure of this type of story as an old friend known from many encounters in the world of literary imagination, the particular shape it takes here depends on a very distinctive mix of cultural features that give this narrative its particular imaginative power and resonance. In addition, to comprehend the particular shape this narrative has taken in its own culture, a deliberate effort has been required to replace the taken-for-granted assumptions about social relations that modern readers of Genesis 38 from the individualistic settings of northern Europe and North America would otherwise bring to this text with cultural understandings appropriate to its original context.

4

Hannah, Peninnah, and Elkanah
(1 Samuel 1–2[1])

Recent years have seen several literary readings of Hannah in 1 Samuel 1–2. Many of these readings, some of which I will interact with below,[2] seek to enlist this text in the important task of subverting contemporary interpretations that perpetuate dominant discourse and positions inimical to the interests of women. The interpretative approach taken in this chapter is literary in its concern with the *narrative qualities* of 1 Sam 1:1—2:21 in the Hebrew Bible version of story (the Septuagintal version differs in crucial respects),[3] both on its own terms and also as inaugurating the larger narrative which is 1 and 2 Samuel. Mary Callaway and Carol Meyers have both persuasively argued for the importance of Hannah in the early sections of 1 Samuel,[4] but even they have underestimated Hannah's significance. In particular, we will see that the fact that Hannah does not pass from the scene until 1 Sam 2:21, after the account of corrupt malpractice of the sons of the priest Eli in relation to sacrifices in vv. 12–17, is freighted with meaning for her role in the larger narrative of 1 Samuel in a manner that has not been appreciated hitherto. Additionally, in accordance with the broad approach of this volume,

---

1. This chapter originally appeared in a Festschrift in honor of Professor Wolfgang Stegemann.

2. See Amit, "'Am I Not More Devoted'"; Klein, "Hannah"; and Meyers, "Hannah and Her Sacrifice."

3. See Walters, "Hannah and Anna."

4. See Callaway, *Sing, O Barren One.*

the literary dimensions of 1 Samuel 1–2 also subsist in the relationship of the story to similar plot patterns in other narratives. Once again the plot type that Christopher Booker calls "Rags to Riches" will provide a comparison with Hannah's experience, although not with as many points of similarity as the story of Tamar in Genesis 38. The bulk of the interpretation offered in this chapter, however, will consist in reading the narrative in a manner that is closely related to the Israelite setting of its first audience by use of social-scientific ideas and perspectives.

UNDERSTANDING 1 SAMUEL 1:1—2:21

For this purpose, from a range of possible ethnography, including Haiti and Africa,[5] I will draw upon the results of research conducted by Finnish anthropologist Hilma Granqvist, who conducted ethnographic research among certain Arab villagers in Palestine from 1925 to 1931 and later published a number of volumes detailing her research.[6] Granqvist's gender allowed her unusual access to Palestinian women. This ethnography is attractive because of the richness of the data, and because it concerns an agricultural and sedentary group (as opposed to a nomadic and pastoral one) and was written long before Western influences reached their current level.[7] This was a population that also featured patrilineality, patrilocality, and polygyny and operated at the advanced agrarian stage of socioeconomic development. Clearly there are significant differences between this culture and that of Israel in the ancient period, but there are also similarities in social systems that meant these Palestinians were much closer culturally to ancient Israelites than are we who have been socialized into the cultures of northern Europe (and its colonial offshoots) and North America. I will deploy Granqvist's ethnography in the interpretation of 1 Sam

5. See Leeb, "Polygyny in the Biblical World." Also see Mbuwayesango, "Childlessness," 27–28.

6. See Granqvist, *Marriage Conditions*, vol. 1; *Marriage Conditions*, vol. 2; Granqvist, *Birth and Childhood*; and Granqvist, *Child Problems*. I am indebted to Bruce Malina for bringing Granqvist's under-appreciated work to my attention.

7. These three reasons make less applicable here the admittedly fine research represented in Abu-Lughod, "Polygyny." On the pressures on Arabs of Bedouin origin to move towards an increasingly Westernized lifestyle in Lebanon, see Hamadeh, "The Values and Self-Identity of Bedouin and Urban Women."

1:1—2:21 in the manner explained in chapter 2. I will begin by outlining relevant features of the Palestinian social system.

With this material providing comparative perspectives, I will then consider the text of 1 Sam 1:1—2:21 in some detail. During this phase of the argument I will frequently contrast the views I reach with those expressed in recent literary approaches (which often have the laudable aim of retrieving this passage from hegemonic, gendered readings)—not so much to criticize these views but rather to demonstrate how different is one's interpretation when the ancient cultural context of the narrative is given due prominence. Finally, I will offer some concluding observations that will include the resonances of Hannah's story with a wider range of narrative illustrating "Rags to Riches" plots.

A MODERN COMPARISON: PATRILINEALITY, PATRILOCALITY, AND POLYGYNY AMONG PALESTINIAN ARABS IN THE 1920S AND 1930S

The distinctive pressures created by patrilineality were continually evident among the Palestinian Arabs with whom Granqvist lived. To see how this system worked, we should imagine a single male with property, who is determined to preserve that property among his male issue. The first step is to provide that his sons inherit. But what about the next generation? The best he can do to put his purpose into effect is to have the children of his sons marry one another; that is, to have his grandchildren marry their paternal cousins. On this matter Henry Rosenfeld, one of the Mediterranean ethnographers of the 1960s, has observed, "Both Granqvist and I interpret the existence of (patrilateral) parallel cousin marriages as a means of protecting property . . . I see no reason not to believe that this was the original function of parallel cousin marriage at the time when rural agriculturalists transformed into a peasantry."[8]

Granqvist noticed that the pressures created by this patrilineal system were particularly felt in the area of inheritance. A man with property (land being the main asset) was required to pass it on to his nearest male relatives. In first place were his sons, but if he had no sons, it would pass to his daughter, but she would then usually be married by a cousin. If a man died without any children, his brothers had first claim, and through them their sons.[9] Here the principle behind these priorities

8. Rosenfeld, "The Contradictions," 250.
9. Granqvist, *Marriage Conditions*, 1:76.

of inheritance was clearly to preserve the property of a male among his male issue. Only if the deceased had no brothers, or if there were no sons of such brothers, could male relatives of his wife press a claim. A similar concern in ancient Israel to keep the inheritance in the family (and the tribe) was put into effect by the provisions of Num 27:1–11 and 36:1–9.

In relation to marriage partners, Granqvist observed that "today, as in former times, it seems that marriage with the father's brother's son (*ibn il-'amm*) is preferred to any other marriage in order to prevent a stranger taking possession of the property and inheritance of the family."[10] The rationale for cousin-marriage of this type is, as just noted, that by this arrangement a man ensures that his male issue retains his property.

Marriages were arranged by the families of the man and the woman (the bride being often, in fact, a young girl). The usual pattern was that a father procured a bride for his son.[11] Some betrothals occurred long before the girl had even reached puberty. Usually a girl agreed with her father's choice, although occasionally she resisted.[12] Upon marriage the bride left her father's home to go to live with her husband, who was usually residing in his father's house. This was the patrilocal dimension of this social system. Since the brides were often very young, and the transition could be quite traumatic, her father and brothers would console her with words to this effect: "We have not given you to any sort of people. We have given you to people upon whom we can depend."[13] This would especially be the case if she was marrying a cousin. One aspect of this patrilineal system was that it was usually the father who chose the name for a boy, and the mother who named a newborn girl. But this was not always the case; sometimes the procedure was reversed, or another close relative chose the name, or even an outsider.[14] In such cases, the person taking the initiative to name a child usually had a good reason for doing so, as when a grandmother named her grandson after the name of her recently deceased husband.[15]

Yet even when the property passed to the son of a brother there were serious disadvantages for the surviving relatives of the deceased. In

10. Ibid, 77–78, and 66–98 for the general position of cousins.

11. Ibid, 46.

12. Ibid, 54.

13. Ibid, 53.

14. Granqvist, *Child Problems*, 11.

15. Ibid, 13.

the usual course, if the deceased had left a daughter, a cousin with the right to the property married her but without paying a bride price (for there was no male to whom it could be given). In this way the incoming cousin acquired the property of the deceased and of the deceased it was said, "the heredity is lost."[16] Even apart from the question of property, the position of the surviving women could be quite catastrophic. Imagine a woman in her forties with a husband and children, including sons. If the husband died, she would grieve, but a son (with whom she would probably be on good terms) would inherit, and she would continue living in the family home in a position of love and respect. But if she had no son, she faced the arrival of cousin (marrying either her or one of her daughters), who may have had little time for her and who mainly wanted the estate. She faced marginalization at least, and possibly exclusion from the family home.[17] Such exclusion usually would compel her to return to the house of her father. If the daughter was thought to be at fault for not bearing a son, her return home would be regarded as shameful for her and her family.[18] If the woman's father and brothers were dead, she would have no one to turn for help, and her position was truly deplorable.[19]

Granqvist discovered a close connection between this patrilineal system and some cases of polygyny. Her research was stimulated by meeting a woman who had insisted that her husband (over his initial objections) take a second wife because upon his death his relatives would take possession of the property and force her to leave. This was not the only reason for polygyny. Sometimes the husband simply wanted a younger wife, and sometimes a man married again because his home needed more female labor and it was not the custom to keep women servants.[20] Nevertheless, the problem of what would happen to the property

---

16. Granqvist, *Marriage Conditions*, 1:74–76.

17. Granqvist, *Marriage Conditions*, 2:212.

18. Ibid, 248.

19. Ibid, 251–52.

20. Granqvist, *Marriage Conditions*, 1:3. Also note ibid., 2:211, where she reiterates two reasons that prompt one wife to disregard her dislike of having a co-wife: first, where the need for help in the house is so great and it is not the custom to use women servants; and, second, when she is childless or has only daughters.

if there were no sons to inherit constituted the most pressing reason for a man to take another wife.[21]

When lack of sons meant that a man was obliged to marry again, or when he did so for some other reason, the first wife had to adapt to a co-wife (*durra*) in her husband's house and possibly also to the second wife's children by her husband.[22] Granqvist offers a rich stock of information about the experience of wives in a condition of polygyny.[23] The attitude of the first wife was largely dependent on the reason for the second marriage. She would be most unhappy if she had sons and her husband simply wished to have a more attractive wife; indeed such an event might drive her to despair and vexation.[24] But if she had no sons, his taking a second wife would be an unfortunate necessity.

Relations between co-wives were generally poor. They tended to regard each other as troublesome and bitter. Even when a woman considered her co-wife was agreeable personally, she was still her rival for the attention of the husband. Many proverbs and songs among the villagers reflected this bitter rivalry between the co-wives.[25] Sometimes the rivalry was so fierce that co-wives practiced magic against one another.[26]

It was a custom among the Palestinian Arabs—a custom enforced locally by Islamic law—that a husband had to give his two wives a house or at least a room each. This increased the expense involved in taking on a second wife but no doubt did much to reduce the occasions of contention between them. A number of the songs brought out the poor position of an older, first wife in relation to a younger, second wife. Sometimes a new wife might displace the old to such an extent that she forced her husband to divorce the first wife.[27]

Yet it was not always the case that the new wife ended up with control. Granqvist noted that the new wife was not always the more

---

21. Note that in a survey of polygyny across many cultures Jack Goody observes ("Polygyny," 177), "in Europe and Asia, polygyny is largely but not exclusively an heir-producing device; often it is a way of replacing a barren wife."

22. Granqvist, *Marriage Conditions* 2:167.

23. Ibid, 2:174–217.

24. See the case discussed by Granqvist, ibid, 2:174–85.

25. Ibid, 186–87. Here is an example: "The co-wife (*durra*) is bitter even if she is only the handle of a water jar."

26. Ibid., 198–99.

27. Ibid, 190–91.

charming or the more adept at dealing with their joint husband. One first wife she knew greeted a second wife when she arrived at the house with a song that proclaimed, "Even if he takes a hundred wives, I am still the cover of the jar and all women are under my feet."[28]

As a general rule, the husband regarded one of the wives as the favorite, the "preferred one" (*il-mahdiyye*), the" beloved" (*il-mahbube*); and the other as the "not beloved" (*mus mahbube*), even the "hated" (*mabruda*). In addition, one of the co-wives usually had authority over the others; she was the "mistress" of the house, and any co-wife had to obey her. This was regarded as necessary for the proper running of the house.[29] Who filled this role seems to have depended on the respective strength of character of each of the co-wives.[30] A childless woman who was nevertheless the wife with authority even had the opportunity to win the affections of the children of her co-wife or co-wives.[31] The natural thing, however, was that the children would take their own mother's part against her co-wife (*durra*) so that in the latter, "her enemy," they would see their own enemy.[32]

If we ask what it was like to be a wife in this system who was incapable of producing children, who was "barren," to use the English word that conveys something of the seriousness of her situation (just as the clinical expression "infertile" most certainly does not), it is clear that the character of the patrilineal system explained above provides most of the answers. At best one's husband might have to marry a second wife, with all the potential for dissension and rivalry that would produce; while at worst the woman (without the sons needed to secure the inheritance and provide her with love and support) faced exclusion from her home.

Granqvist gathered some material directly on this issue. The value and status of a woman depended to a large extent upon her fruitfulness and the preservation of her children. Barrenness was considered a curse and a reproach.[33] It was regarded as good grounds for divorce or as necessitating the husband take a second wife. Barren women were

28. Ibid, 193.

29. Ibid, 194.

30. Ibid, 213–17.

31. Ibid., 214; see ibid., 213, for an instance in which a childless first wife held complete sway over a second wife who had two sons and two daughters.

32. Ibid., 216.

33. Granqvist, *Child Problems*, 224–25.

extremely sensitive to their condition and were distressed whenever they heard someone was expecting a child. As noted above, in some cases the woman herself had insisted that her husband take a second wife lest he die without heirs and his portion of land go to others:

> But in such cases the first wife must take the risk and danger that the new wife will be more than a substitute. How easily it may happen that he comes to love the other one and think more of her. Or, the second wife, having children, may look down upon her, like did the Egyptian handmaid, Hagar, upon her mistress Sarah. And when Sarah, contrary to all expectations bore a son, and drove Hagar away, it is possible that this was due to her fear lest the first-born son should set aside her own son, even it he was only the son of a handmaid.[34]

Granqvist notes that there was always a certain glory around the wife whose son would succeed his father: "If a childless wife is to raise herself and her position in relation to such a dangerous rival it requires unusual personal wisdom and strength of character."[35] And hers was always a fragile situation. Thus Granqvist noted one case of a husband with two wives, one with children and one without, but the barren wife was the "loved" one. As the barren wife had many attractive qualities, the husband generally said that he did not mind that she had no children. Yet there were also times when he became angry with her and said, "It is lawful to hew down a tree which does not bear fruit."[36]

Having set out this ethnographic material to provide a body of comparative material, we turn now to the narrative of 1 Sam 1:1—2:21.

INTERPRETING 1 SAMUEL 1:1—2:21

Setting the Scene: 1 Samuel 1:1–3

The first three verses of 1 Samuel 1, with the condensed quality typical of Old Testament narrative originating in a high-context culture, lay the foundations of a story brimming with drama and potential conflict at both the domestic and the social levels that will develop inexorably as the tale unfolds.

---

34. Ibid., 76–77.
35. Ibid., 77.
36. Ibid., 77–78.

The core of the situation described is that of two families, of different social levels and status and located in two locations, which are brought into proximity with one another once a year. First, there is Elkanah, an Ephrathite from Ramathaim-Zophim on Mount Ephrah, the son of Jeroham, the son of Elihu, the son of Tohu, the son of Zuph (1 Sam 1:1). Elkanah has two wives: Hannah, who has no children; and his second wife, Peninnah, who does (1 Sam 1:2). Second, there is Eli, and his two sons, Hophi and Phineas, who are the priests of Yahweh at Shiloh (1 Sam 1:3). Carol Meyers wrongly states that the "cast of characters in 1 Samuel 1 includes five individuals: the Ephraimite Elkanah; his two wives, Hannah and Peninnah; the priest Eli; and the infant Samuel."[37] By overlooking Eli's sons she misses their malpractice in 1 Samuel 2 and Hannah's role in condemning them, to which I will return below. Long ago Joseph Bourke astutely noticed that the theme of evil represented by Eli and his sons provided the contrasting refrain, the literary counterpoint, to the theme of good represented by Hannah and Samuel.[38]

To grasp how an Israelite of the Persian period (and indeed of the whole period from 950 to 250 BCE) would have understood this opening passage we must adopt the approach set out above, by trying to clear our minds of modern assumptions about human behaviour and by adopting a set of scenarios appropriate to the context. To do this I will rely upon the material on the context, set out in chapter 2, especially on the views on societies at an advanced agrarian stage of development formulated by Gerhard and Jean Lenski and on the Palestinian ethnography just described.

The reference in v. 3 to Eli, and his two sons, Hophni and Phinehas, who were the priests of Yahweh at Shiloh, is vital for the development of the narrative. This is not just because we are introduced to these figures as the custodians of a shrine to which Elkanah used to go every year to sacrifice, an event that will soon feature in the narrative. In addition, the position of Hophni and Phinehas would have given them great power and social eminence (far beyond that of Elkanah, although he was a man of very respectable lineage and clearly of some means; otherwise he could not have afforded to support two wives), both in terms of status and wealth, from the control they exercised over the cult and the share they could take from the sacrifices. They constituted part of the

---

37. Meyers, "Hannah and Her Sacrifice," 96.
38. Bourke, "Samuel and the Ark," 82.

local elite. On the other hand, it is reasonable to designate the family of
Elkanah as non-elite, since although Elkanah possessed a lineage and
resources, he and his family (like all other Israelites in the area) were
subject while visiting Shiloh to the power of Eli and his two sons, who we
soon learn engaged in the oppressive practices typical of other ancient
Near Eastern elites, discussed in chapter 2, with particular reference to
Samuel's warning of what Israel could expect from a king (1 Sam 8:11–
18). Any ancient Israelite audience, as soon as they heard this reference
to the priestly family in control at Shiloh, would probably have begun to
wonder whether Eli's sons were in the habit of abusing their position in
the interests of their personal enrichment, in line with the behavior of
other elites in their environment. This suspicion is amply confirmed in
the text. David Jobling has aptly pointed to the fact that we learn from 1
Sam 2:13–14 that the sons of Eli misappropriated part of the sacrificial
meat of *all* the Israelites who went there, including Elkanah, Hannah,
and Peninnah. This information inevitably affects the way we read the
mention of the two families in 1 Sam 1:1–3. Since the family had been
coming up every year, it follows that on each visit "Hannah experienced
the rottenness of the priestly regime."[39] Early in the twentieth century
Danish archaeolgists confirmed there was a cultic site at Shiloh (a site
lying between Bethel and Shechem).[40]

In relation to the Palestinian position described above, we note,
first of all, that the broad social system is patrilineal, since we find
Elkanah being designated in relation to a lineage traced back through
four generations of male ancestors. In other parts of the Old Testament
we find evidence for the fact that the male heirs, sons especially, inherited from their fathers.[41] As noted in chapter 2, however, the Old
Testament assumes no notion of primogeniture, of the elder son taking all.[42] Preference for cousin marriage, that we would consider possible from the Palestinian comparison to occur in such a setting, is not
mentioned in 1 Sam 1:1—2:21. Nevertheless, elsewhere the Bible gives
a number indications of the importance of marrying kinsfolk, and these

---

39. Jobling, "Hannah's Desire," 134.

40. See Kjaer, *The Excavation of Shiloh*.

41. Greenspahn, *When Brothers Dwell Together*.

42. Especially see Greenspahn, *When Brothers Dwell Together,* 54, with respect to
Deut 21:15–18.

would often be cousins (see Gen 24:1–4; Num 36:6 ["they shall marry within the family of the tribe of their father," RSV]).

An ancient Israelite would probably have regarded Elkanah as a man of some honor in this society, because of the length of his ancestry—"the sign of a noble and well-known family."[43] Another sign of Elkanah's being honorable is that he has the resources to support two wives, as already noted. From this detail, moreover, we learn that this is a social system where polygyny is practiced, and that it is patrilocal. There is evidence elsewhere for these customs having been features of the ancient Israelite social system (Gen 29:21–30; Deut 21:15), the presence of these features would have been recognized by any Israelite familiar with these texts.

As to the relationships between Elkanah, Hannah, and Peninnah, an ancient Israelite would probably have interpreted Hannah as Elkanah's first wife. This inference would have conformed with the Israelite habit of mentioning a person who is senior in time first.[44] Several commentators take this view.[45] That Hannah had failed to produce children put her husband and herself in a difficult position. The overriding need to preserve the family property was thus imperiled. Elkanah would also have faced the shame involved in his paternal line of five generations, including himself, coming to an end. In the meantime, he would not have sons to help him with the work. Hannah would certainly have also suffered on her own account. There are other instances in the Hebrew Bible of the shame and distress suffered by women who are barren. Thus, in Gen 16:4 Sarah's status in relation to Hagar is diminished when Hagar conceives, and in Gen 30:23 Rachel's first words as a mother are "God has taken away my shame."[46] Hannah's value and honor as a married woman were closely tied up in producing children. Instead, she was experiencing the curse of barrenness.[47]

43. Hertzberg, *I & II Samuel*, 22.

44. So elder sons are mentioned before younger ones—1 Sam 16:6–13.

45. See, as one example, Gordon (*1 & 2 Samuel*, 72), who says her being the first wife is "a fair inference."

46. On the shame of barrenness, see Chertok, "Mothers, Sons and Infertility." For a study of barrenness in relation to ecstatic states in the narratives of Sarah and Hannah, see Neufeld, "Barrenness."

47. To have children was a sign of God's blessing—see Exod 23:25–26 and Deut 7:14–15.

Under these circumstances, Elkanah had little choice but to take a second wife so he could father the sons that were necessary for the well-being of them all. The comparable material from Palestine invites us to imagine a woman in Hannah's situation seeing the wisdom in this and perhaps even pushing her husband to take such a step. This was, after all, similar to what Sarah said to Abraham when she had failed to produce children (Gen 16:1–4) and Rachel to Jacob (Gen 30:1–3), although in the second of these patriarchal examples any children of the maid were to be regarded as those of the wife.[48]

Yet this procedure, while it would satisfy Elkanah's need to secure his property and provide male labor, would have entailed the extra expense of a second wife and also the prospect of rivalry between his two co-wives. From Hannah's point of view, it was a solution that improved the likelihood that she would not be displaced if Elkanah died. Nevertheless, it did nothing for the disgrace she experienced because of her barrenness, and it meant that she would be in the center of a possibly difficult relationship with Elkanah's second wife. Not just in Palestine in the 1920s, as we have seen, but also in ancient Israel, as with Sarah and her servant Hagar in Genesis 16, relations between co-wives were generally poor. This was an almost inevitable result of two women competing for the attention and favour of one man. This is not to suggest that co-wives can't sometimes have a positive relationship and cooperate in their own joint interest,[49] but such a happy picture is not what Granqvist found, or what we see in this narrative.

So Elkanah took Peninnah as a second wife, and she bore him children. The hopes that he and Hannah had no doubt entertained beforehand concerning this union were realized in the birth of the children, but the likely problems that they had probably feared also came to pass. This brings us to the next section of the narrative, 1 Sam 1:4–8.

Relations between Elkanah, Hannah, and Peninnah (1 Samuel 1:4–8)

The setting of v. 4ff. is the occasion of one of the annual visits that Elkanah and his family made to Shiloh to offer sacrifice to Yahweh mentioned at the start of v. 3. The occasion was apparently a yearly feast also men-

48. On this issue see Van Seters, "The Problem of Childlessness."

49. For evidence for cooperation among co-wives in Africa, see Madhavan, "Best of Friends and Worst of Enemies." But note this article also recognizes the reality of competition between co-wives.

tioned in Judg 21:19–21. The details are richly illuminating: "On the day when Elkanah sacrificed, he would give portions (*manoth*) to Peninnah his wife and to all her sons and daughters. He would give Hannah one portion, (the portion) of the face,[50] for he loved Hannah, even though the Lord had shut her womb" (1 Sam 1:4–5).

The fact that Elkanah loved (*'aheb*) Hannah (although she was barren) sounds very similar to the phenomenon that Granqvist found to be common among Palestinian Arabs, whereby one wife was "loved" (*il-mahbube*) and the other was the "not beloved" (*mus mahbube*). While we are not told that Peninnah fell into this latter category, that seems a safe inference from the text. Indeed the Old Testament explicitly mentions this phenomenon. There is a close parallel in Gen 29:30–35, where we learn that Jacob loved Rachel but hated Leah, even though Rachel was barren. In Deut 21:15–17, a legal passage beginning with the words, "If a man has two wives, the one loved (*'ahubah*) and the other disliked (*senuah*), and they have both borne him children, both the loved and the disliked . . ." This passage differs from 1 Samuel 1 in that here both women have had children; nevertheless, that a law was needed to regulate the case of a man who loved one of two co-wives and disliked the other means this must have been a familiar feature of Israelite social life.

The fact that Elkanah loved Hannah lends support to the proposal advanced above that an ancient Israelite audience would have regarded Hannah as the first wife, and that Elkanah married Peninnah for the purpose of securing male heirs, possibly at her insistence and over his objections. It is also probable, given Hannah's seniority in the house and the fact that she and not Peninnah was the object Elkanah's love, that she was, similar to the custom of the Palestinian Arabs, the co-wife with authority in the household routines.

At this point we must consider the relationship between Hannah and Peninnah, especially in the presentation of Peninnah as Hannah's "rival," that we find in the next remarkable section of the narrative: "And her rival (*saratah*) used to provoke her sorely and to irritate her, because the Lord had closed her womb. So it went on year by year; as often as

---

50. The text is difficult: *papaya*, "nose," "wrath," or occasionally "face," may mean a large portion: see Hertzberg, *I & II Samuel*, 24. Bodner (*1 Samuel*, 15) is probably correct in suggesting the Elkanah only gave Hannah a single portion because she was barren and had no other mouths to feed.

she went up to the house of the Lord, she used to provoke her" (1 Sam 1:6–7, RSV).

I reiterate that I am concerned in this chapter only with the Masoretic Text, since the Septuagint lacks this element.[51] Lillian Klein has suggested that "jealousy" is one of the chief transgressions projected upon women in the Hebrew Bible.[52] She interprets Hannah as refusing to enter into jealous competition with Peninnah and as being marginalized in consequence.[53] Yet Hilma Granqvist observed that rivalry between co-wives in 1920s Palestine was routine. Does Hannah really stand apart from this form of interaction? With reference to the Palestinian comparison, we can envisage how an ancient Israelite audience would have made sense of the narrative, by imagining what it might have been like when, as a new bride, Peninnah arrived in Elkanah's house. Relations between co-wives among the Palestinian Arabs were generally poor, and we have just seen good reason to think that things were no different among the Israelites. While barren Hannah would have agreed with the necessity of Elkanah's second marriage, she could not have been happy at the prospect of sharing her husband with another woman, and she must also have been apprehensive that he might come to prefer Peninnah. Nor would she have relished giving up her position of authority in the house. Such apprehensions would probably ensure that she sought to keep Peninnah in her place, although this is not to suggest that she treated her harshly, for which there is no evidence. One can imagine courtesy and firmness on Hannah's part, but not warmth. In the months immediately after Peninnah entered Elkanah's house, she was in a very difficult position. Probably quite a young girl, she had suffered the trauma of separation from her father's house. These feelings may have been somewhat attenuated if Elkanah was related to her. But she must have soon realized that Elkanah loved Hannah, and she was probably under Hannah's authority. Until she produced a child, she had little honor in the house, and if she failed to bear one, she probably faced divorce. It is difficult to conceive that she got along well with Hannah.

The day Peninnah knew she was pregnant would have been a very happy one for her but would have fixed Hannah with ambivalent feel-

---

51. See the discussion on the difference between the Masoretic Text and the Septuagint on this point in Callaway, *Sing, O Barren One*, 48–49.

52. Klein, "Hannah," 78.

53. Ibid, 82.

ings. Her happiness and Hannah's ambivalence reached a climax when Peninnah produced her first son. Now Peninnah had a place of honor in the house, especially in relation to her rival, Hannah. Even if Elkanah did not love her, it was she who had secured his inheritance and would provide him with much-needed male labor, and for these reasons she must have had his respect and gratitude. She would also be able to bask in the affections and enjoy the protection of her son and then other children in the years ahead. For Hannah, however, while Elkanah's property would safely flow to his male progeny, her barrenness was now exposed in all its desolation in contrast to Peninnah's fruitfulness. At least she had not lost Elkanah's love. In this situation it was possible and probably imperative for Hannah to insist on her authority in the household even as Peninnah's position became more and more secure. On the other hand, in spite of bearing him children Peninnah had still not won Elkana's love, had still not been able to supplant Hannah in his affections; and this must have rankled.

Socially realistic scenarios of this sort help us understand the dramatic events in Shiloh. The venue is the trigger for what happens. The family has now left the comparative[54] privacy of their house (and no doubt farm) and come to the cultic shrine at Shiloh, a site open to Israelites where sacrifices are conducted in public. The sacrifice in view seems to be the "peace offering" (*zebah šelamim*) of Leviticus 3; this is the kind of sacrifice where the meat was eaten by the offerer and was often motivated by a sense of thanksgiving to the Lord.[55] Here the person making the sacrifice killed the animal, the priests threw its blood around the altar, while the fat was burnt on the altar as an offering to Yahweh (Leviticus 3). The sacrificer also brought cakes along with the sacrifice, one of which was supposed to go to the priest who sprinkled the blood, while the meat had to be eaten on the day of the sacrifice (Lev 7:11–21). From 1 Sam 2:13–14 the audience of this narrative would understand that the meat was cooked by boiling in a cauldron located in a public place in the precincts of the shrine.

To situate 1 Sam 1:4–7 within its ancient context, therefore, we must visualize Elkanah going through the sacrifice and then boiling the animal's flesh in a cauldron in some open space in the shrine. He then

---

54. "Comparative" because one must not underestimate the extent to which those living in preindustrial settings find it difficult to keep their affairs to themselves.

55. See Pagolu, *Religion of the Patriarchs,* 47.

handed out portions of the cooked meat to Peninnah and to all her sons and daughters, and a single, possibly generous, portion to Hannah. On such occasions Peninnah reacted in the way depicted in 1 Sam 1:6–7, publicly drawing attention to Hannah's barrenness in order to shame her. The result was that Hannah wept and did not eat (v. 7). To a modern reader unfamiliar with the personal politics of a patrilineal society (where honor is a primary value, and where people seek to avoid shame and the causes of shame), Peninnah's outburst and Hannah's response may come as a complete surprise. Yet the incident is explicable in light of Israelite culture as explained in chapter 2 and the interpretation of the narrative advanced so far. This biblical incident also corroborates the details of that interpretation.

First, we note that the text brings to the surface what we have argued, against the view of Lillian Klein, it implied all along by describing Peninnah as "her rival" (ṣaratah). Although this is the only instance of this noun in the Hebrew Bible, the cognate verb ṣarar, which generally means "to show hostility to," "to harass,"[56] is used to express the same idea in Lev 18:18, where a man is proscribed from taking as a "rival-wife" the sister of his existing wife in her lifetime.[57] When the use of the word "rival" is related to the reference to the loved and hated co-wives of Gen 29:30–35 and Deut 21:15–17, the resulting picture is very like that which prevailed among Granqvist's Palestinian Arabs.

But why does Peninnah choose the occasion of the distribution of the portions to provoke and vex Hannah? The answer to this question lies in the character of their relationship when back home and the nature of the social dynamic known as "challenge-and-response." As explained in chapter 2, this social dynamic was first described by anthropologist Pierre Bourdieu from his work among the Kabyle, a North African tribe, and subsequently systematized by Bruce Malina for application to biblical texts.[58] Challenge-and-response describes the principal way in which honor can be acquired in Mediterranean culture where it is a central, indeed often dominant, value. Normally such competition involved males of roughly equal status seeking to assert themselves and demonstrate

---

56. See, for example, Exod 23:22; Num 10:9; 25:17; and 33:55.

57. Words closely related to "rival" in 1 Sam 1:6 occur with the meaning "rival wife" in Syriac and Arabic—see Gordon, *1 & 2 Samuel*, 74.

58. See Bourdieu, "The Sentiment of Honour"; and Malina, *New Testament World*, 3rd ed., 27–56.

their honor in the eyes of the local public in a variety of social arenas. Yet the same cultural patterns also applied to women, given a suitable setting, as Malina has noticed.[59] First Samuel 1 is a very rare instance in which we do have a situation in which women are involved in a dispute over honor; although the evidence does not usually reach into such a context, this is a precious case in which it does.

The process begins with one party issuing a challenge, a claim to enter the social space of the other, which can be negative or positive. A negative challenge (and most challenges are negative) usually consists of an insult. A positive challenge consists of a gift or a word of praise. In either case the person challenged has to respond in an appropriate way or will be shamed before the audience present. Sometimes the response will take the form of a counterchallenge, thus putting the onus back on the challenger. When Elkanah distributed the portions, Peninnah "grieved Hannah sorely," which we could reasonably translate as "challenged" her in the sense just explained, in order to make her ashamed and despondent because the Lord had closed her womb. Peninnah was saying something like: "Look at how the Lord has blessed me with sons and daughters, while he has shut up your womb!" She did so in the shrine at Shiloh precisely because this was a public place. Unlike at the family house, here others would be present to see Peninnah compare her fruitfulness, which Elkanah must publicly acknowledge in the multiple portions that he provides to herself and her children, with the barrenness of Hannah, who received only one portion, generous or not. For Peninnah this was a glorious opportunity to take revenge for the fact that at home Hannah, in spite of her having no children, was the wife whom Elkanah loved and probably the wife with authority. When Hertzberg writes in relation to the portion Elkanah gives Hannah, "Hannah must have been treated by her husband in some special way to explain the taunts which Peninnah used to fling on such an occasion,"[60] he falls into the error of supposing that Peninnah's reaction was motivated merely by the size or character of Hannah's portion rather than by the whole course and nature of their relationship—the typically troubled one of co-wives in a patrilineal culture. Similarly, when Lillian Klein suggests that it is Elkanah who generates mimetic desire leading to jealousy between the

59. Malina, *New Testament World*, 3rd ed., 35: "Similarly, women among themselves compete in challenge-riposte interactions."

60. Hertzberg, *I & II Samuel*, 24.

two women by his practices with the portions,[61] she overlooks the probability that the relationship between Hannah and Peninnah was hardly likely to have been a good one when they were back at home. Peninnah's response is of a piece with that of Hagar, who, when she learned that she had conceived, meaning that the balance of power between mistress and maid had now shifted decisively, "looked with contempt upon her mistress" (Gen 16:4).

To Peninnah's challenge Hannah had no response. The shame it occasioned her affected Hannah deeply. Not only did she weep; she even stopped eating. Carol Meyers mistakenly suggests that Hannah's weeping was occasioned by the share of the sacrifice allotted to her by Elkanah.[62] The actual reason lay in her relationship with Peninnah. Hannah did not weep on these occasions because she was childless (which surely oppressed her just as much at home as in Shiloh), but because of the extra factor—that Peninnah used the occasions in the shrine to humiliate her publicly. Lillian Klein, on the other hand, has proposed that "nothing in the text suggests that Hannah wants a child because Peninnah has children or because Peninnah taunts her. Hannah's desire arises from within and is maintained as a personal, as yet unfulfilled wish."[63] Against this view, which might carry force in a modern Western context but is rather anachronistic when applied to ancient Israel, we have the consideration that Hannah's misery is triggered precisely by Peninnah's taunts, and that when she gives vent to her joy later in the text she indicates very clearly that she is intent on playing the same game as Peninnah, by deriding her enemies (1 Sam 2:1). Even more provocatively, Hannah observes that "the barren has borne seven, but she who has many children is forlorn"(1 Sam 2:5, RSV), which clearly reveals her glee at the reversal of roles that has occurred between herself and Peninnah.

At v. 8 begins an account of the last such occasion of misery and embarrassment for Hannah. Her husband is moved by her state to ask her why she weeps, why she does not eat, and why her heart is sad. Finally he asks, "Am I not better to you than ten sons?" He may have been motivated by kindness, but he was not particularly percipient. Presumably he is aware of how Peninnah taunted Hannah each year in Shiloh. Perhaps for his peace of mind he has decided not to intervene

61. Klein, "Hannah," 84–85.
62. Meyers, "Hannah and Her Sacrifice," 94.
63. Klein, "Hannah," 83.

in the difficult relationship between his two co-wives. He expresses his concern for Hannah solely in relation to the fact that she has no sons, not in relation to the shame that this allows Peninnah to heap upon her head. He also seems to consider only the factors of the love and support Hannah would have from sons, which he himself can provide. He ignores Hannah's shame, which Peninnah can trumpet, arising from the Lord's cursing her with barrenness, while Peninnah herself delights in sons and daughters. Elkanah also fails to consider what will happen if he dies and Peninnah and her children turn on Hannah and throw her out.

In some recent feminist criticism Elkanah is judged very severely. Yairah Amit, for example, suggests that Hannah's silence, her failure to eat, and her departure were actually motivated by her pain at what her husband had said, not by Peninnah.[64] This interpretation is implausible both because Hannah has begun weeping and stopped eating before Elkanah asks her why she is distressed, and also because of the terms of Hannah's song in 1 Sam 2:1–10, especially when she derides her enemies, who plainly include Peninnah (1 Sam 2:1). Joan Cook aptly questions Amit's interpretation of Elkanah by suggesting that "it makes Hannah very male-dependent by suggesting that she suffered from Elkanah's insensitivity but not from Peninnah's obnoxiousness."[65] But Lillian Klein is even harder on Elkanah than is Yairah Amit. She regards Elkanah's questions as delivered under the "blamer mode," where the questioner is interested in throwing his weight around rather than finding out anything. She sees his questions as a form of disguised verbal abuse made by a man against the woman he loves, because she is barren.[66] Yet it is most unlikely that an ancient Israelite audience would have judged Elkanah with such severity, since not only has he not divorced his barren wife, as he was entitled to do, but because he still loves her in spite of her failing to produce a son. The Israelite audience would probably have regarded him as doing his best to balance the interests of two rival co-wives, no light task for any husband. Nevertheless, that Elkanah's response does nothing to assuage Hannah's pain becomes apparent in the next verse.

64. Amit, "'Am I Not More Devoted,'" 74.

65. Cook, *Hannah's Desire*, 36.

66. Klein, "Hannah," 87–88.

Hannah and Eli in the Temple (1 Samuel 1:9–18)

Hannah waits until they have eaten and drunk. An ancient audience would have assumed that she had to play her part with Peninnah in ensuring that their husband and the children, none of them hers, had finished their meal. Then she rises up and, although the text does not say so explicitly, enters the temple, where, unobserved by her, Eli the priest sits upon a seat near a pillar (1 Sam 1:9). This sets the scene for the first encounter between representatives of the two families—one elite and one non-elite—that is actually described in this part of 1 Samuel. As we have noted, the narrative implies that Elkanah and his wives had met the family of the priest during their previous visits, and Hannah and Elkanah would go on meeting Eli in the years ahead (1 Sam 1:25–28; 2:19–20). Yet these meetings did not exhaust the possibilities of the conjunction between the two families established in 1 Sam 1:3, as we will soon see.

There follows a moving account of a distressed and weeping woman prayerfully pouring out her heart to her God, in whom she has a most fervent belief, to give her a son, whom she will give back to him (1 Sam 1:10–11). Hannah has been praying silently and Eli, mistaking her lip movements for those of a drunken woman, irascibly rebukes her (1 Sam 1:12–14). Immediately regaining her composure, Hannah rejects the charge with strength and dignity, but her address to him as "my lord" (ʾadoni; 1 Sam 1:15) and her designation of herself as his "maidservant" (šifḥah; 1 Sam 1:18) indicate the great social distance between him and her, between elite and non-elite in that culture. Joseph Bourke described Hannah as one of the anawim, "the lowly and righteous whom Yahweh loves."[67] Wisely accepting the truth of her explanation and assuming she has been making a petitionary prayer, Eli bids her go in peace with the wish that the God of Israel grant her prayer. Hannah leaves the temple, and, apparently comforted by her experience there, eats and loses her sad countenance (1 Sam 1:17–18). The picture we have of Eli is of a man apparently grown cynical of human nature, in that he mistakes a woman's silent prayer for drunkenness, but who is not so cynical as not to be able to recognize the truth when he hears it, or to invoke God's assistance for her, apparently with success.

---

67. Bourke, "Samuel and the Ark," 84, 87.

Hannah and Samuel (1 Samuel 1:19–28)

The ensuing events and how an ancient audience would have interpreted them may be briefly recounted. The family returns to their house in Ramah, where Elkanah has intercourse with Hannah. Just as she had prayed, the Lord remembers her, and she conceives and bears a son whom she calls Samuel (1 Sam 1:19–20).

Meyers suggests that the fact that it is Hannah who names the child attributes to her "exceptional status." Hannah is one of a series of biblical women who name their offspring. Yet although her naming Samuel certainly contributes to the picture of her as a woman who takes the initiative, perhaps we should not make too much of this. Among Palestinian Arabs, where fathers usually named sons, circumstances connected with the birth could produce a different result. Hannah had good reason to name the child here. In Luke 1:59–64, moreover, it is the previously barren Elizabeth who names her son John, a course in which her husband acquiesces.

An ancient Israelite audience would have recognized that Hannah's falling pregnant and then her delivery of Samuel would have raised her status in relation to Peninnah dramatically. Hannah, the loved wife, now has a son as well. Not surprisingly, neither Peninnah nor her children are mentioned thereafter. Thereafter Elkanah "and all his house" went up to offer their yearly sacrifice,[68] but Hannah stays behind at home with Samuel (1 Sam 1:21).

Hannah tells Elkanah she will stay behind, and that when Samuel is weaned she will bring him to Shiloh to serve the Lord there (1 Sam 1:22–23). That Elkanah accepts that the first son of his preferred wife will leave the family and live in the temple indicates the authority she has in the house and also no doubt the depth of his love for her. Whereas previously he had asked her inept questions aimed at budging her from her unhappiness, to which she failed to reply (v. 8), now she simply asserts what she will do and he consents. On all matters to do with Samuel the active parties are Hannah and the Lord; Elkanah is there to swell the scene. On the other hand, "all his house" who do go up to Shiloh (v. 21) no doubt includes the now unmentioned Peninnah. Previously this had been the occasion on which she shamed Hannah because of her barrenness. But no more! An Israelite audience would have understood

68. The Masoretic Text also refers to "his vow," but it is unclear to what this refers.

Elkanah continuing to provide portions to Peninnah and her children, but all the while with his mind firmly set on his favorite wife back home, suckling their son Samuel, so that Hannah's eminence as between the two wives was now complete.

Then, when Hannah has weaned Samuel, she takes him up to Shiloh to serve in the temple, with three bullocks, flour, and wine for a sacrifice (1 Sam 1:24).[69] Elkanah is not expressly mentioned but is presumably included in the statement "they slew a bullock and brought the child to Eli" (v. 25).[70] When the bull is slain, Hannah reminds Eli (presumably present to sprinkle blood around the altar as mentioned in Leviticus 3) of the earlier occasion when she met him in the temple and that now she is lending her son to the Lord in accordance with her prayer (1 Sam 1:25–28). Once again, in these three verses Hannah has the initiative. The audience is to understand that Elkanah is present, but looking on and acquiescing in silence in all that Hannah says and does. Hannah has not only reversed her previous disgrace of barrenness that probably caused Elkanah to take Peninnah as his second wife in the first place, but she has handed over to the Lord in a shrine some distance from their home the very son of herself and her husband whose birth had restored her honor. This represents a radical rewriting of the rules of a patrilineal and patrilocal society—a radical rewriting not diminished by the fact that (as we learn in due course) the Lord gave Hannah three more sons and two daughters (1 Sam 2:21), at which point she passes forever from the narrative of 1 Samuel. Yet before that we have material of critical importance in 1 Sam 2:1–21. I will begin with Hannah's Psalm (1 Sam 2:1–10).

Hannah's Psalm and Its Target (1 Samuel 2:1–17)

As noted in chapter 1, I am not concerned with how Hannah's Psalm in 1 Sam 2:1–10 came to be included in this text, but with what role it plays in the wider narrative. Even in spite of such an awkward feature as Hannah referring to the Lord giving strength to his king (v. 10) years

69. For a fine "ethnoarchaeological" analysis of the sacrifice mentioned in 1 Sam 1:24, see Meyers, "An Ethnoarchaeological Analysis of Hannah's Sacrifice."

70. Carol Meyers has argued for the importance of Hannah at Shiloh, and not her husband, who is described as bringing to the temple the sacrificial offerings mentioned in 1 Sam 1:24. Meyers sees this as an example of family religion where women played a role (ibid.).

before Israel had one, Callaway rightly advises concentration on the final form of the text as we now have it for its connection with the Israelite community when it appeared.[71]

The main observation to be made is that the content of Hannah's hymn clearly transcends the celebration of her happy new position now that Samuel has been born. The elements of her previous situation, her barrenness that was the basis for the status-degradation event that her rival co-wife, Peninnah, put her through each year in Shiloh, relate to some but not all the material. To account for the rest, we must look to the other dimensions of the narrative, especially at the tense relationship between the elite and non-elite in Israelite culture. This is a factor that is widely overlooked by commentators on 1 Sam 2:1–10.

First Samuel 2:1 evokes Hannah's newfound joy that the Lord has greatly increased her status, thus allowing her to deride her enemies (*'oybay*), who must include Peninnah and any others who had sided with her in deriding Hannah (Peninnah's children perhaps). As already noted, Lillian Klein's efforts to insulate Hannah from the rivalry between co-wives endemic to patrilineal and polygynous societies is unsuccessful. Verse 2 is a resultant prayer of praise. Verse 3, an injunction not to talk proudly and arrogantly, must refer to Peninnah's taunts, whatever else it might include. So far the prayer is readily explicable in terms of the domestic politics of the house of Elkanah.

With vv. 4–5, however, a remarkable change occurs, for Hannah begins speaking in a way that initially goes beyond her domestic circumstances, even though they reappear at the end of v. 5:

> The bows of the mighty are broken,
> but the feeble gird on strength,
> Those who were full have hired themselves out for bread,
> but those who were hungry have ceased to hunger.
> The barren has borne seven,
> but she who has many children is forlorn. (RSV)

While there is a clear reference to Peninnah in v. 5 (the "forlorn" mother of many children), the remainder of these verses propels the ancient audience beyond the house of Elkanah in Ephraim into the wider world of politics and military power. Two immensely revealing vignettes occur in which the position of the elite is subverted. First, in

---

71. Callaway, *Sing, O Barren One*, 51–52.

the phrase "the bows of the mighty" we have a reference to the military forces acting for the elite that kept the non-elite in a state of subjection and coerced them into handing over a proportion of their produce. But now their bows broken, while the non-elite become strong. This is a picture of radical social reversal. Second, the author deftly sketches the position of wealthy landowners ("those who are full") on the one hand, and, on the other, those who must hire themselves out to them on a daily basis to earn enough to feed themselves and their families. In this second scene of reversal, the elite landowners must change places with the hungry laborers they had previously employed, while the previously hungry laborers are now full. Yet the narrative conveys a more specific point to this aspect of Hannah's Psalm, since the reference to "Those who were full have hired themselves out for bread" of 1 Sam 2:5 is closely connected with what we later learn is in store for the house of Eli—its hungry surviving members will beg for a loaf of bread (1 Sam 2:36).

This theme continues in the rest of her psalm. The Lord raises the poor (*dal*) from the dust, and needy (*'ebyon*) from the ash heap to set them among princes and to inherit the throne of glory (v. 8). He will protect the feet of those who are faithful (*ḥasid*), but the wicked will be cut off in darkness (v. 9). We also learn that the adversaries of the Lord shall be broken in pieces (v. 10). It is necessary to note that in the broader narrative of 1 Samuel 1–2 this statement has a particular application—to the sons of Eli, who are later described as sinning against the Lord by the way they behave in his temple (1 Sam 2:25, 30).

Thus Hannah carries her message beyond the domestic realm to society at large, where there are pronounced differentials of wealth and status, which the oppressed long to see overturned. But why does she do this, when it has no relevance to her relationship with Peninnah?

The scholarly answers to this question to date have not been satisfactory. Entirely unpersuasive are interpretations that completely miss the connection between what Hannah says and the injustice of the sons of Eli. Hertzberg is a case in point. For him "the psalm puts the birth, and hence the life, of Samuel in the context of the all-powerful saving acts of God."[72] The critical encounter between the righteous non-elite and the unjust elite of Israel that the narrative began to set up as early as 1 Sam 1:1–3 passes unnoticed. Similarly, Joan Cook regards the reference to the barren woman (in 1 Sam 2:5) as "the only direct link between Hannah's

72. Hertzberg, *I & II Samuel*, 31.

Song and her particular situation."[73] Cook does not mention the sons of Eli in commenting upon 1 Sam 2:1–10. More persuasive are those critics who have at least noticed the link between the practices Hannah castigates in her psalm and the behavior of the sons of Eli. Thus R. A. Carlson correctly notes the link between "those who were full have hired themselves out for bread" of 1 Sam 2:5 and the fate of Eli's family described in 1 Sam 2:36,[74] yet without appreciating the significance of this link. For Carlson has a source-critical concern and argues that Hannah's Psalm is a deuteronomic insertion into the narrative that deepens the "ideological interpretation" of the events described in 1 and 2 Samuel. Similarly, Robert Gordon also notes that the hard times predicted in 1 Sam 2:5 are matched by the prophesied downfall of Eli's house in v. 36, and that 1 Sam 2:11—4:1 poignantly illustrates the theme of Hannah's Psalm in 1 Sam 2:7b ("he brings low, he also exalts"), but does not take these insights any further.[75]

The question remains of the precise function of the Psalm within the narrative of 1 Samuel 1–2 in light of such linkages. Callaway rightly insists on this point and offers the explanation that the psalm does not relate to Samuel and to his role as judge and prophet, "and it relates only partially to the fall of Eli and the rise of Zadok." According to her, it functions rather to "dramatize Hannah as the symbol of the *anawim*, the poor of Yahweh."[76]

Yet even this view largely misses the point of the narrative. The narrative is not just interested in the plight of the non-elite, Yahweh's *'ebyonim* and *dalim* in 1 Sam 2:8, but also depicts the larger social system that put them into this position at the hands of the powerful and wealthy members of society, whom it condemns. In addition, the narrative predicts that the two groups are about to find their roles reversed. This is the best answer to the function of Hannah's Psalm. That it is targeting the sons of Eli, as representatives of Israel's oppressive elite, is confirmed by the way the narrative develops immediately after this passage. Eli's sons were mentioned in 1 Sam 1:1 and now (after a brief reference in v. 11 to Elkanah's return and to Samuel's serving the Lord before Eli), they

73. Cook, *Hannah's Desire*, 45.

74. Carlson, *David*, 45–46.

75. Gordon, *1 & 2 Samuel*, 79–81; Bodner (*1 Samuel*, 28) notes Gordon's remarks but does not endorse them.

76. Callaway, *Sing, O Barren One*, 54.

reenter the narrative, in the shocking account of their avaricious and potentially violent acquisition of sacrificial portions from Israelites in the temple (1 Sam 2:12–17). The conjunction of the two families in the narrative since it began now becomes more insistent. Hannah is actually setting the standard against which the sons of Eli will be judged. While she acts to insert her son into the heart of God's plans, she establishes the basis for the eventual demise of Eli's sons from that place and role. As members of the elite, they will fall, while Hannah, from the non-elite, has been elevated to a place of honor, just as will be her son Samuel. None of this is to deny the powerful theological ideas at work in this narrative, but we cannot appreciate the character of God's action on behalf of those whom he loves if we do not understand the precise nature of the forms of bondage and oppression, both domestic and political, from which he liberates them.

Concluding the Story of Hannah (1 Samuel 2:18–21)

The story of Samuel in relation to his parents ends in vv. 18–21. Samuel ministers before the Lord; he is a child, yet clothed in an ephod. In the meantime, the yearly visits by Elkanah and his family to Shiloh to sacrifice continue; but now his mother brings him a little coat each year (v. 19). Thus has been modified the original picture of two families, living in two places who come together once a year. Now the family of Elkanah has a permanent presence in Shiloh. The reversal of the respective fortunes of elite and non-elite has begun. Hannah has regained her honor by the birth of Samuel and five other children (v. 21), and Samuel is growing up to assume a focal place in the life of Israel, while Eli and his sons are living on borrowed time. The fate in store for Eli's sons begins to emerge immediately after this, with Eli's warning to his sons to mend their ways, for they were sinning against the Lord (vv. 22–25). After a brief reference to Samuel (v. 26), a man of God comes to Eli, prophesying the death of his sons by the sword because of their sins, a fate that befalls them in 1 Sam 4:11.

CONCLUSION

By introducing social scenarios relating, first, to an agrarian society marked by a gulf between those at the top of the socioeconomic register (and their soldiers and other retainers) and the rest of the population and, second, to the cultural features of patrilinearity, patrilocality, and polygyny, I have sought to interpret the narrative that is 1 Sam 1:1—2:21 in a manner that would have made sense to an ancient Israelite. This form of interpretation contextualizes the narrative in a way that brings out the careful craft with which characters and events in the plot are integrated into a tight literary unity. It also reveals the provocative distance of the social world it presupposes from North American and northern European forms of economic organization, domestic life, and gender relationships. In addition, however, this approach helps us understand the developing narrative of 1 Samuel. For although the story continues after 1 Sam 2:21 without further mention of Hannah, the additional details of the sinfulness of the sons of Eli, of which we learn from 1 Sam 2:22 onward, and their ultimate fate all serve to fulfil her earlier prediction: "The adversaries of the Lord will be broken to pieces; against them he will thunder in heaven" (1 Sam 2:10, RSV).

Having closely investigated the text of 1 Sam 1:1–2:21 in relation to its original context, we may now return to a question raised at the start of this chapter and consider the similarities Hannah's story bears to other narratives that Christopher Booker has identified as belonging to the "Rags to Riches" plot type. I have already mentioned the five elements of this plot in connection with Tamar in Genesis 38 (see chapter 3, above). We see a compressed version of this plot in the case of Hannah, with three elements rather than five.

Element 1 (the initial disadvantageous state) and then element 2 (some early success) are missing. If the story had described how Hannah had come into Elkanah's house as his wife, probably as a young girl of largely unknown character and qualities who was at the bottom of the heap, but had then won the love of her husband and was looking forward to giving him sons, we would see elements 1 and 2 (and the original audience probably imagined something very much like this had occurred in Hannah's case).

Instead, we find Hannah in the center of the crisis that constitutes element 3. It is not the case that *everything* is going wrong, since she retains the love of her husband in spite of being barren, but she must bear both her barrenness and the fact that she is subjected to deeply wounding, public scorn by her co-wife, Peninnah, each year on the occasion of the family's visit to God's shrine at Shiloh. She is deeply unhappy.

This brings us to element 4, defined by Booker as a struggle against a powerful opponent who stands in the road of what they must achieve, the successful conclusion of which will allow them to move to the final phase of the plot, element 5: a state of fulfilment. This aspect of the "Rags to Riches" plot and the comparison with Tamar and Judah is deeply instructive, mainly because of the ways Hannah diverges from what we might expect. Although Judah did fit the bill as a powerful opponent of the requisite sort and Tamar defeated him through her own intelligence, guile, and resolution in a narrative in which God is never mentioned, Hannah is very different. There is nothing more that Hannah *herself* can do to gain what she so sorely desires, a baby son. Only God can cause her to conceive. Similarly, there is no opponent who can prevent this happening, as long as she has marital relations with Elkanah. Although Peninnah is described as her rival (see above), there is nothing that Peninnah can do to stop Hannah conceiving. Then she encounters another "opponent," which is the appropriate context within which to view her encounter with Eli in the temple at Shiloh. His initial hostility to her, motivated by his mistaken belief that the is drunk (1 Sam 1:14), represents an attenuated version of the serious opposition that such a character, in other examples of the "Rags to Riches" plot, will mobilize against her to prevent her achieving her goal. But what happens here is that he rebukes Hannah, then discovers he has misunderstood her and actually ends with a blessing for her and a prayer that God will grant her petition (1 Sam 1:17). So Hannah does indeed encounter and overcome an a powerful opponent, but the happiness she seeks does not really depend on the outcome, unless it be the case that the original audience would have believed that God granted Hannah her wish in part at least because Eli had also prayed to God on her behalf. This is an intriguing possibility (and only a possibility, since we are told that the Lord remembered Hannah in 1 Sam 1:19, but Eli is not mentioned) and demonstrates the benefit of comparing the text with the "Rags to Riches" plot.

The fifth and final element, where the heroine achieves fulfilment, also takes an arrestingly different form in this narrative. Because Hannah knew she was dependent on God and not on her on her own strength or qualities for the blessing of a child she hoped to receive, she had vowed to God to dedicate her son to his service all the days of his life (1 Sam 1:11). This means she must actually give up the son whom she had so earnestly desired, as indeed she does, by bringing him to Eli in Shiloh as soon as the child (whose name, Samuel, first appears in the text in 1 Sam 1:20) is weaned (1 Sam 1:24–28). Yet she is additionally blessed, in the birth of three more sons and two daughters (1 Sam 2:21). Her first opponent, Peninnah, is completely discomfited, and her second, Eli, will soon see disaster overtake his family because of the corruption practiced by his two sons.

What other stories are like Hannah's? Generally "Rags to Riches" tales involve heroes and heroines who sink much lower than Hannah before their glorious elevation. Nevertheless, it is worth thinking of Hannah in connection with Cinderella (where all five elements are clearly present, however), mocked by her cruel stepmother and vain stepsisters, but who is enabled by her fairy godmother to attend the ball and meet the prince (= elements 1 and 2), whom, after more disappointment, she eventually marries.[77] The story of the ugly duckling, initially ridiculed by his brothers and sisters for his awkwardness and ugliness, but who eventually grows into the loveliest swan of all, provides another example.[78] So too does the account of Joseph in Genesis 37–50.[79]

Finally, we should briefly mention a particular theological ramification of this interpretation of 1 Sam 1:1—2:21. The picture is very different from that in Genesis 38, where although God does feature, by putting Er and Onan to death, he is not mentioned in connection with Tamar, who seems to achieve what she does by virtue of her own initiative and strength. Hannah, on the other hand, is expressly described as pouring out her soul (*nephesh*) before God in his temple (1 Sam 1:15), in distress, tears, and prayer. There is a strong sense here of Hannah hitting the absolute nadir of her human experience: unable to produce the child that would alone bring her fulfillment in her culture, and publicly ridiculed for her failure, and in this bleak night of forsakenness reaching out in hope to God to end her pain. Hannah's desolate prayer is answered, for "the Lord remembered her" (1 Sam 1:19), and she gives birth to Samuel. In Hannah's raw cry of anguish and in God's response we recognize a close bond between them that we will see again later in 1 Samuel in the account of the relationship between God and David. It is clear, however, that to consider this theological dimension of the narrative, to explore what it has to say about God's dealings with his people, relating

77. Booker, *Seven Basic Plots*, 52, 58.

78. Ibid, 51.

79. Ibis, 53.

the text to its ancient context has been indispensable. For it shows us what God did for Hannah in a way not otherwise available, where we can appreciate both the depth of her dishonor and hence the magnitude of the mercy that God bestows upon her, where we can discover what it truly means in Hannah's case to be raised from the dust and to be lifted from the ash heap (1 Sam 2:8).

PART 2

Warriors

The position of Israel—as a small nation clinging to hilly territory of variable agricultural quality between the major powers of Mesopotamia to the east and Egypt to the south, with significant peoples like the Philistines ensconced on the coastal plain to the west—meant that warfare was always going to be a major element in its continued existence. To survive in war meant that Israel needed warriors: outstanding ones to lead its armies and competent ones to fill the ranks. The Israelites actually exhorted Samuel to give them a king so that they would have someone to govern them and to lead them in battle like other nations (1 Sam 8:19–20). Chapters 5, 6, 7, and 8 in this volume deal with narratives concerning the warrior abilities of three Israelites: two men (Saul and David) and one woman (Judith). Saul and David were probably historical figures, Judith probably not.

Warfare is inevitably affected by the values of those who engage in it. It is not surprising, therefore, that the competition over honor common in social interactions in ancient Israelite culture emerges time and again in these narratives: in the clash between David and Goliath, in Saul's envy at David's success against the Israelites and in the shame brought upon Israel by Holofernes and his army before Judith's decisive intervention, to mention only a few examples. Challenges are offered and encounter powerful ripostes.

In such a heavily group-oriented society, every conflict between individuals also entails a conflict between the groups they represent. This is most clearly seen in the combat between David and Goliath (between Israel and the Philistines), and the encounter between Judith and Holofernes (between Israel and the Assyrians). But even in the long struggle for supremacy between Saul and David, the former is serving the interests of the tribe of Benjamin and the latter those of the tribe of Judah.

Finally, that some ancient Israelite author should have decided to retell the male game of war in a female key, in a story that pitted Judith, an Israelite widow, against the leader of a huge invading army, and have her triumph over him by a mixture of guile and homicidal violence is one of the big surprises in the Old Testament. Here is a female warrior who so clearly matches David's achievements that Western artists would later depict the two of them in juxtaposed scenes.

5

The Madness of Saul, a Warrior-King
(1 Samuel 8–31)

INTRODUCTION

Madness, which I will loosely define as a serious impairment of a person's mental and emotional connection with everyday reality accompanied by various forms of exaggerated affect, is not a very prominent phenomenon in the Old Testament. Yet it was known in ancient Israel. This emerges unambiguously in the famous incident (which I will return to in chapter 7) when David flees from Saul to Achish, king of Gath, where he is recognized as the slayer of tens of thousands and becomes greatly afraid: "So he changed his behavior before them; he pretended to be mad when in their presence. He scratched marks on the doors of the gate, and let his spittle run down his beard. Achish said to his servants, 'Look, you see the man is mad; why then have you brought him to me? Do I lack madmen, that you have brought this fellow to play the madman in my presence? Shall this fellow come into my house?'" (1 Sam 21:14–16, NRSV).

The last three references to being mad in the passage employ forms of the word *šagʿa*, which seems to match the phenomenon of madness as defined above. This word occurs ten times in the Hebrew Bible, seven times as a verbal form and three as a substantive.[1] It has cognates in

---

1. As a pual participle at Deut 28:34; 1 Sam 21:16; 2 Kgs 9:11; Jer 29:26; and Hos 9:7; in the hithpael at 1 Sam 21:15 and 16, and in the substantival form at Deut 28:34; 2 Kgs 9:20; and Zech 12:4. The Hebrew expression in 1 Sam 21:14 translated here as

Arabic and Assyrian that indicate various noises and this may suggest
that its sufferers were characterized by the production of animal sounds.[2]
Another instance of madness is that of Nebuchadnezzar in Daniel 4. The
king is driven out of human society to live like the wild animals and feed
on grass, his hair and nails growing very long, until his reason returns
(Dan 4:25–34).

The most important section of the Old Testament in relation to
madness, however, is the story of Saul in 1 Samuel 8–31, even though
the word *šag'a* is not used in connection with him. For this text both depicts a central character in the life of Israel suffering from a major form
of psychological disorder and also integrates the phenomenon into the
heart of the narrative in ways that have been insufficiently recognized in
existing scholarship. The madness of Saul in 1 Samuel 8–31 is central to
his character and to the movement of the plot. In addition, the text not
only provides details of the disorder, but it also offers a causal explanation and prescribes a form of therapy.[3]

In this chapter my aim is to propose an interpretation of the narrative of Saul in 1 Samuel 8–31, especially focusing on the madness that af-
flicts him, which (in line with the overall approach to this volume) offers
a view on how the narrative would have been understood by its ancient
Israelite audience in the broad cultural setting described in chapter 2. I
will also connect the narrative with the wider literary universe.

My focus will be how the development of the plot and of Saul's
character are related to what we moderns would call his abnormal
psychological state, his psychopathology. As in the other chapters in
this volume, so in this chapter I am not concerned with how what is
recounted in 1 Samuel 8–31 correlates with the historical facts of the
newly emergent Israelite monarchy. That is, I do not claim to be investigating a particular historical figure, Saul, but rather I seek to make sense
of his character as presented in a specific narrative that itself presupposes a particular cultural context. My focus is squarely on the narrative

---

"pretended to be mad" is a hithpael form of *hll*, a word of obscure etymology, which is
usually pejorative in meaning and denotes irrational, uncontrolled, feigned, or exaggerated behavior of various sorts, as at Jer 25:16; 46:9; 50:38; and 51:7, and not simply madness (Cazelles, "*hll*"). As a hithpael, its literal meaning is reflexive, "made himself mad."

2. Sussman, "Sickness and Disease."

3. Rosen, *Madness in Society*, 28.

as it would have made sense to its original audience, rather than on any actual historical circumstances that arguably "lie behind" the narrative.

To reiterate the point made more generally in chapter 2, my interpretation of 1 Samuel 8–31 takes seriously the fact that it is a product of an ancient Mediterranean culture very different from a North Atlantic modern or postmodern one. In this respect my reading differs from other types of readings.[4] Any attempt to situate a narrative in a cultural context distant from us in time, in this case by some three millennia, is necessarily historical—not in the sense of seeking to make out correlations between the narrative and the facts of the early Israelite monarchy, but rather in setting the text within the broad shape of ancient Israelite society, which at a certain level of abstraction shares many of the cultural features discussed in chapter 2. These include the orientation of social relations around the group (especially the family) rather than the individual, the importance of honor as a pivotal social value (together with related issues such as the extent to which those lacking honor feel envy toward those who possessed it, and the strength of the desire for vengeance where honor has been besmirched), and the fact that all goods were considered to exist only in finite quantities, the phenomenon referred to as the notion of "limited good."

When we come to situate the narrative of Saul with respect to other literary works from different cultures, we immediately encounter the fact that the notion that Saul's fate was tragic, that his experience represented a tragedy, is already well established.[5] Yet what do "tragic" and "tragedy" mean here? Cheryl Exum initially notes, in her fine book on the tragic vision in the Hebrew Bible, that the "idea that a work is tragic if it displays certain predetermined features, and not tragic if one of these features is missing, or even handled differently" is not supported in art or literary criticism. Soon afterwards, however, she claims that "all the essential tragic ingredients meet us in the story of Saul."[6] Rather than offering a precise formula for or definition of "tragic" or "tragedy," we will rely rather on a looser description, by focusing first on features that

4. See, for example, Humphreys, "Tragedy of King Saul"; Humphreys, "Rise and Fall of King Saul"; and Humphreys, "From Tragic Hero to Villain"; and Gunn, *Fate of King Saul*.

5. Exum, *Tragedy and Biblical Narrative*, 1 (and the works she cites). Also see the works by Humphreys and Gunn cited in the previous footnote.

6. Ibid., 2 and 16.

usually occur in works most people would regard as tragic,[7] and then by taking up the particular proposal made by Christopher Booker in relation to the "Tragedy" plot with the support of the specific texts he cites. As mentioned in chapter 1, Booker's *Seven Basic Plots* is utilized here in a phenomenological way (allowing connections to be made with the works he describes), and his proposal for the reasons underlying these plots is not taken up.

The heart of tragedy is to portray the movement of the protagonist, usually someone of high estate, from a happy and prosperous existence ("typically on top of the wheel of fortune"[8]) to his or her eventual wretched end, usually a violent death. In moving the protagonist from an exalted beginning to such an end, tragedy strikes a balance between attributing the outcome to some power external to him or her, on the one hand, and, on the other, to finding the cause in some fundamental flaw in the protagonist.[9] Exum refers to this as the combination of "fate and flaw," where those terms are of wide import: "The tragic protagonist is caught up in a situation not entirely of her or his own making. At the same time, she or he is also responsible, a guilty victim."[10]

Saul's experience is readily comparable with these views of tragedy, as we will see by summarizing the features of the narrative here, while deferring detailed consideration for later discussion. Israel wants a king like other peoples, who will be able to fight their battles, a warrior, therefore, even though Samuel warns them that a king will skim off their wealth and enlist many of them in his service. Yahweh grudgingly agrees (1 Samuel 8). So Saul, the tallest man in Israel, is anointed king (1 Samuel 9 and 10). Initially, Saul is successful in his warrior role: he defeats the Ammonites, who are threatening Jabesh-Gilead, and ends the grumbling against him in Israel (1 Samuel 11). But then things start to go wrong. He disobeys God through Samuel his prophet on two occasions (in 1 Samuel 13 and15), thereby incurring God's enmity towards him that takes the form, inter alia, of the dispatch of an evil spirit to terrify him. Abandoned by God, Saul seeks aid from a medium (1 Samuel 28), only to learn that on the next day he and his sons will die in battle

7. As Exum notes, "Although there is no formula for deciding what constitutes the tragic, most people have a general idea of what tragedy is about" (ibid, 4).

8. Frye, *Anatomy of Criticism*, 207.

9. Ibid, 209–10.

10. Exum, *Tragedy and Biblical Narrative*, 10.

with the Philistines, who will also defeat Israel. And so it comes about, with Saul dying on the battlefield by his own hand (1 Samuel 31). There is abundant evidence in the text for debate as to where the balance lies between "fate and flaw" in Saul's case.

Christopher Booker's analysis of the "Tragedy" plot is rather more elaborate. Based on an analysis of literary creations such as the myth of Icarus, the legend of Faust, Shakespeare's *Macbeth*, Robert Louis Stevenson's *Dr. Jekyll and Mr. Hyde,* and Nabokov's *Lolita,*[11] he discerns five stages in a tragic plot (although recognizing that not all may be present in any given work, and that a story may begin well into the five-stage sequence). First, in the "Anticipation Stage," some course of action or object of desire presents itself to the currently unfulfilled protagonist. Second, in the "Dream Stage," the protagonist commits to the course of action, and things are proceeding happily. Third comes the "Frustration Stage," when things begin to go wrong, and the hero or heroine has to undertake further "dark acts," while a threatening "shadow figure" sometimes appears. Fourth, in the "Nightmare Stage," things are slipping seriously out of control for the hero or heroine, with antipathetic forces closing in. Fifth is the "Destruction or Death Wish Stage," when the hero is killed or commits suicide.[12] It is unnecessary to repeat the summary of Saul's career given above to appreciate that it is closely comparable to these five stages, to which we will return in the conclusion to this Chapter.

THE NARRATIVE OF 1 SAMUEL 8–31 IN ITS CULTURAL CONTEXT

Saul's Early Career

Honor upon His House

In chapter 2 we considered how Samuel (acting on Yahweh's behalf) anoints Saul, the tallest Israelite, as the prince (*nagid*) over Israel: as the man who would defeat the enemies who were surrounding them (1 Sam 10:1). This had been the main reason that the people had asked for a king (1 Sam 8:19–20), a reason approved by Yahweh (1 Sam 9:16). First and foremost, Saul is to be a warrior-king and he makes a fair fist of succeeding in this part of his job description: "When Saul had taken

11. Booker, *Seven Basic Plots,* 154.

12. Ibid, 156.

the kingship over Israel, he fought against all his enemies on every side, against Moab, against the Ammonites, against Edom, against the kings of Zobah, and against the Philistines; wherever he turned he put them to the worse. And he did valiantly, and smote the Amalekites, and delivered Israel out of the hands of those who plundered them" (1 Sam 14:47–48, RSV).

But there is more to being king than this. After all, Samuel has already warned the Israelites of the onerous tithes and services that a king would demand from them (1 Sam 8:11–17) and had later given Saul himself a glimpse of this side of kingship before he anointed him: "And for whom is all that is desirable in Israel? Is it not for you and *for all your father's house?*" (1 Sam 9:20, RSV). Although Saul challenges this at the time: "And is not my family the humblest of all the families of the tribe of Benjamin. Why then have you spoken to me in this way?" (1 Sam 9:21, RSV), as Samuel had foretold, so it comes about. As chapter 2 noted, in a group-oriented society, a benefit gained by one member of a family is shared by all. Here we have a most egregious example of this process, where Saul sees his family lifted from the most humble in Israel to the most exalted.

Saul the Individual

But what of Saul the individual? As we have noted in chapter 2, although the individualism that has become characteristic of North Atlantic culture, especially in North America, during the last century or so was largely unknown in the ancient Mediterranean world, individuality most certainly was not. Great individuals did appear, and the prevalence of strong group bonds (especially within the family) and social immobility made their achievements all the more striking. Often outstanding individuals fell foul of the system, as the fates of Socrates and Jesus most graphically illustrate.

Prior to his anointing we do learn a little about Saul. In a culture that assessed persons primarily with respect to their group affiliation and group prestige, he enters the narrative (1 Sam 9:1) as a member of the tribe of Benjamin and the son of Kish, a *gibor ḥayil*, a man of honor and wealth.[13] Oddly, in view of instances such as 1 Sam 1:1 and Judg 13:2 and the general Mediterranean habit of assessing persons by their place

13. McCarter, *I Samuel*, 173.

of origin, the Masoretic Text does not mention where Saul lives in 1 Sam 9:1, and this induced Wellhausen (followed by many commentators[14]) to propose the plausible insertion of "from Gibeah" after "There was a man" at the start of 1 Sam 9:1, even though there is no textual warrant for this. We discover later, in any event, that Gibeah was Saul's home-town (1 Sam 10:26; 11:4; 15:34), probably the modern Tell el-Fûl.[15] We also learn something of Saul's appearance (as chapter 2 noted): that he was the most handsome and tallest man in Israel (1 Sam 9:2). Third, Saul is presented as a dutiful and obedient son, who obeys without question his father's direction that he and a servant go off and find some donkeys that have strayed. In so doing Saul dutifully honors his father and shows that he too is a man of honor. But Saul goes beyond this, in his concern that his father will begin to worry about them when they do not return (1 Sam 9:5). Here we gain a glimpse of the warmth and intimacy which characterizes the close relations among family members in the Mediterranean, a glimpse that is somewhat unusual in a culture that more commonly focuses on external, even stereotypical, features (such as those just mentioned) in describing persons. Even this feature, however, would have characterized most sons who loved their fathers in this culture, and it tells us very little that is unique about Saul as an individual. The manner in which he is described reveals how different were ancient Mediterranean ways of portraying persons, which tended to focus on the external and the stereotypical, especially in such areas as a person's family, place of origin, and other group affiliations,[16] com-pared with modern modes of description, where the aim is much more to bring out someone's unique identity, especially through the develop-ment of a sense of variegated psychological inwardness. This is not to say, however, that what was going on in a person's heart was not of inter-est to an ancient Israelite audience, as we will see especially in relation to David in chapter 6.[17]

14. See Smith, *Books of Samuel*, 59–60; Driver, *Notes on the Hebrew Text*, 68–69; and McCarter, *I Samuel*, 167.

15. Driver, *Notes on the Hebrew Text*, 69.

16. See Malina and Neyrey, *Portraits of Paul*, who offer an illuminating exposition of ancient Mediterranean ways of presenting personality in relation to texts concerning Paul, yet through insights capable of much wider application.

17. For a recent discussion of Bruce Malina's view that in the ancient Mediterranean world introspection was culturally unimportant, see Lawrence, *Ethnography*, 113–39.

Saul the Prophet

It is only after his anointing that a truly distinctive aspect of Saul's personality does emerge. Samuel foretells that he will go to Gibeah-of-God, a city with a Philistine garrison, and, as nearly all the versions translate, meet a group of *prophets* coming down from a high place, with harp, tambourine, pipe, and lyre; and they will be *prophesying* and "then the spirit of Yahweh will rush upon you, and you will *prophesy* with them and you will be turned into an another man" (1 Sam 10:6). The Hebrew word translated as "prophesy" in relation to the prophets and Saul is the hithpael of *nab'a*. The Hebrew Bible uses this root in a verbal sense only in the niphal and the hithpael, and it is often difficult (for example, at 1 Sam 19:20) to establish a semantic distinction between the two forms,[18] although the hithpael has traditionally been thought by Old Testament scholars to have a closer connection with ecstatic behavior.[19] Many years ago Driver proposed that the hithpael form functioned to denote playing or acting the prophet to the accompaniment of manifestations of physical excitement, like the dervishes of fairly recent times,[20] although this is only one example of the more general phenomenon of ecstatic behavior.

Wilson prefers a more nuanced approach, whereby the niphal means, "to prophesy," "to deliver a prophetic oracle" while the hithpael means "to act like a prophet," "to exhibit the behavior characteristic of a *nabi*" (a "prophet"), with the precise characteristics in question to be determined by an examination of the prophet in question.[21]

Yet Parker squarely poses a question of critical importance,[22] and noted by Wilson:[23] whether we should use the word "prophesy" at all with respect to the behavior that Samuel foretells (as well as in relation to the actual incident itself at 1 Sam 10:10–12 and a later occurrence of contagious "prophesying" at 1 Sam 19:20, where the niphal and the hithpael forms appear). Parker suggests that the reference here is to ecstatic behavior, or trance, to what those drawing on the research of Erika Bourguignon now call "altered states of consciousness," when the

18. Wilson, *Prophecy and Society*, 137.
19. Ibid, 138.
20. Driver, *Notes on the Hebrew Text*, 81.
21. Wilson, *Prophecy and Society*, 138.
22. Parker, "Possession Trance."
23. Wilson, *Prophecy and Society*, 138.

person concerned loses contact with everyday reality, often in association with startling kinetic effects and various types of utterance.[24] As Wilson points out, the behavior of the band Saul encounters is not specifically described, although the fact that those he meets are pictured as playing musical instruments suggests that trance may have been involved, since music is often used to induce trance.[25]

Bourguignon distinguishes two types of altered state of consciousness: the first, "possession trance," where the state is due to possession by spirits; and, second, trance not so interpreted, involving visions or hallucinations.[26] The instances just mentioned in 1 Samuel are of the former type. Moreover, possession trances may either be mediumistic, where they mediate a message from the spirit world to an audience, or personal to those involved. In the latter case they either provide subjective compensation for personal or social stress or an objective compensation through an enhancement of status that results from social recognition accorded the phenomenon. None of the three instances in 1 Samuel are mediumistic and this prompts Parker to suggest that it is inappropriate to employ the word "prophesy" in relation to the Hebrew root *nb'*. Parker argues that God does make his will known in 1 Samuel, through Samuel and with the use of lots, for example, but he never does so via forms of this root. The latter aspect of Parker's view runs aground on 1 Sam 28:6 and 15 where the *nebi'im* ("prophets") are viewed as one possible way for Saul to learn Yahweh's will. Nevertheless, Parker's argument is probably plausible as far as the experience of Saul is concerned, so that "fell into a possession trance" is a better translation than "prophesy," although it is probably worthwhile persisting with the use of "prophet" because of the possibility of a mediumistic role as in 1 Sam 28:6 and 15.

The phenomenon of possession trance in this case seems to function to extend subjective rather than objective compensation, since there is no sign that it produces increased status; indeed, the reverse is the case.[27] The first evidence for this comes in the statement at 1 Sam

24. See Bourguignon, "Introduction." For appropriations of Bourguignon's work in discussion of New Testament material, see Esler, "Glossolalia"; Pilch, "Visions"; and Pilch, "Transfiguration." Also see Lewis, *Religion in Context*; and Lewis, *Ecstatic Religion* for further discussion of ecstatic religion. For an older approach to this issue, without the benefit of recent social-scientific research, see Lindblom, *Prophecy*, 47–65.

25. Wilson, *Prophecy and Society*, 176; see also Lindblom, *Prophecy*, 59.

26. Bourguignon, "Introduction."

27. This is not to deny that the fact that someone has received the Spirit of God may

10:6 that Saul would be turned (= the niphal of *hafak*) into another man. Wilson considers that this is a positive experience for Saul, since it is a sign of divine election.[28] Yet there is reason to doubt this assessment. It is more likely that Saul's transformation would have been regarded as particularly ominous in a cultural context that (unlike modern Northern European and North American cultures) treasured social stability, as achieved through the maintenance of established roles and statuses, which is an aspect of the perspective of limited good. The verb used, *hafak*, is a particularly strong one, meaning "to overturn," "to destroy," "to transform radically." It is employed in relation to the destruction of Sodom and Gomorrah (Gen 19:21, 25, 29; Lam 4:6; Hos 11:8), the transformation of the rod into the serpent and water into blood in Exodus 7 (vv. 15, 17, 20), the transition from plague-affected or unclean flesh to healthy flesh (and vice versa) in Leviticus 13, and the alteration of a stream of water into pitch in Isa 34:9. These examples indicate how often the verb itself denotes change of a deleterious, even dangerous, type; and when it designates alteration in a person's social role and character, the effect is very negative indeed. Seybold comes reasonably close to this view in the following comment on the passage: "With reference to the ecstasy described in vv. 9ff., *hfk* in the niphal (like the qal in v. 9) is meant to represent the resulting change as a perversion of what is normal."[29]

If Saul is about to be transformed into another person, he is heading for a serious diminishment of the regard that those who know him have for him. Now this view can coexist with the position being quite different in Yahweh's eyes. Commentators, like Hertzberg,[30] who think the alteration fits Saul out to be God's instrument, miss the negative social implications of this development, against which the divine initiative is all the more striking. This irony is seen most graphically in the stately paraphernalia of drawing lots for the king, which ends with Saul, Yahweh's anointed, being pulled out of the baggage where he had hidden himself (1 Sam 10:23) and the fact that some in Israel still refuse to accept him (1 Sam 10:27).

---

result in their status and personal effectiveness being enhanced; such was the case, for example, with Gideon in Judg 6:34–35, where there are no other complicating factors. But Saul's experience is very different.

28. Wilson, *Prophecy and Society*, 176.

29. Seybold, "*hphk*," 426.

30. Hertzberg, *I & II Samuel*, 85.

The second indication that Saul's status is not promoted by his going into a trance comes at 1 Sam 10:7 where Samuel says that when Saul encounters these signs, of which the third and the last will be his experience with those in possession-trance at Gibeah, he should do whatever his hand finds to do, for God is with him. This type of reassurance implies a split between how such behavior might be viewed by observers, and what it really entails—the presence of God. Just as God can subvert the local social order by choosing someone from the lowest family of the lowest tribe to be his king, so too he can be present in exhibitions of exaggerated behavior that are susceptible of another explanation.

Third, since later in the narrative the hithpael form of the root *nb'* (used here at 1 Sam 10:6 of possession-trance) occurs in relation to one of the occasions when Saul is afflicted by the evil spirit of God (1 Sam 18:10), it is probably meant to be taken as personally dysfunctional; we are not just dealing with some status-enhancing eccentricity.

A Prophet in His Hometown

As Samuel predicts, so it comes to pass: "When they were going from there to Gibeah, a band of prophets met him; and the spirit of God possessed him, and he fell into a possession trance along with them. When all who knew him before saw how he fell into a trance with the prophets, the people said to one another, 'What has come over the son of Kish? Is Saul also among the prophets?' A man of the place answered, 'And who is their father?' Therefore it became a proverb, 'Is Saul also among the prophets?' (1 Sam 10:10–12, NRSV; slightly modified).

This incident is of critical importance in establishing Saul's character and in paving the way for the manner in which the plot will evolve. We must initially assume that Saul's behavior in this incident involves his transformation into a different person as predicted by Samuel, with the negative connotations just explored—an experience rendered even more problematic by the narrative's perspective on this type of experience as dysfunctional, which will emerge later. Yet the specific location of this event means that it has a far more precise significance within the narrative. This place, Gibeah-of-God, where Samuel had foretold that Saul would meet the prophets, is probably identical with the Gibeah mentioned as Saul's home in 1 Sam 11:4 and 15:34, and even at 9:1 if

Wellhausen's amendment is correct.[31] Saul encounters the prophets in his hometown, or at least in a town containing people who know him (10:11), which is all that is necessary for the argument here.

The extent to which scholars usually misinterpret the local reactions is a sign of their failure to read this text in its Mediterranean context. Thus we find some suggesting that the point of the story is to explain the unlikely fact that a well-placed person such as Saul would begin to prophesy,[32] or that it offers an etiology of the proverb "Is Saul also among the prophets?," or that it contradicts traditions that attributed the prophetic spirit to Saul.[33] Hertzberg at least recognizes that the observers are dubious about Saul, although his explanation of their attitude is anachronistic: "How does a reasonable man, well placed in civic life, come to be in this eccentric company?"[34] None of these explanations touches the meaning of the incident within Mediterranean culture or picks up the extent to which it is central to an understanding of Saul's character and the onward movement of the narrative.

It is important to realize that what we learn about Saul here does not resound to his credit; just the reverse. The sting of the account lies in the way local observers who know Saul interpret the possession-trance that comes upon him. The two questions they ask ("What has come over the son of Kish? Is Saul also among the prophets?") actually constitute a grievous insult; they do not reflect "amazement and wonder" at his transformation.[35] There is good evidence, some of which we noted in chapter 2, for the culture of ancient Israel's being one in which notions of limited good prevailed. One aspect of limited good is that people were expected to remain in the roles into which they were born; as Proverbs states, "Instruct a child in the way he should go, and when he grows old he will not leave it" (22:6; JB). Social mobility is a common feature in modern North Atlantic cultures but should not be anachronistically

---

31. Some commentators reject the identification, but the reasons for it are strong. The strongest is that 1 Sam 10:11 states that people who had known him previously were there (McCarter, *I Samuel*, 182). Moreover, as Smith notes (*Books of Samuel*, 68), Saul goes directly home after meeting the prophets. Third, the parenthetical expression at 10:5, "where there is a Philistine garrison" (or possibly prefect or pillar), seems to point ahead to 13:3, where the city is probably Gibeah of Benjamin.

32. Smith, *Books of Samuel*, 71; McCarter, *I Samuel*, 183–84.

33. See Klein, *1 Samuel*, 92–93.

34. Hertzberg, *I & II Samuel*, 86.

35. McCarter, *I Samuel*, 184; Klein, *1 Samuel*, 93.

and ethnocentrically imputed to the ancient Mediterranean world. In Mediterranean culture, after all, children were expected to follow the ways and adhere to the authority of their father and their mother. If they did not, both they and their families, their fathers above all, were gravely shamed: "A discerning son is he who keeps the Law; an associate of profligates brings shame on his father" (Prov 28:7, JB). This was a matter of great moment, given that honor was the preeminent social good: "A good name is more desirable than great wealth, the respect of others is better than silver or gold" (Prov 22:1).

It is in keeping with such views that Jesus's relatives think he is mad (Mark 3:20–21), presumably because they cannot conceive of another reason for the shameful way he was acting. In the present case, the local townsfolk are suggesting that Saul has stepped out of his usual role as the dutiful son of Kish, where he looked after affairs on the family estate, and this brings disgrace to Saul and his family, particularly to Kish, who has plainly not managed to control his son as a respectable father would.

This interpretation is confirmed by the next question: "And who is their father?" According to McCarter "this cryptic question has no obvious meaning," while Klein finds it "quite obscure."[36] Yet its meaning is hardly so opaque. One of the greatest insults that could (and can) be uttered to a person living in the Mediterranean region is to cast doubt on his lineage. Usually this suggestion implies that the mother of the person concerned was a prostitute, although sometimes it is a way of denigrating the son in relation to the father who is actually known (for which see John 8:31–59). In either case, the point of the remark is to convey that children of doubtful parentage are beyond the bounds of respectable society. In a similar vein, Nabal rejects David's request for food and drink for himself and his men because he does not know who he is, or where they come from (1 Sam 25:10–11). In the present case the text raises just such insinuations in relation to the prophets and also suggests that Saul has come to share in this grossly dishonorable condition by joining them. Hertzberg is a rare exception among recent commentators, who comes close to seeing the point, when he suggests that the question is meant as a contemptuous aside in reference to people who have no father, who come from anywhere, although some of the older scholarship came nearer the mark.[37]

36. McCarter, *1 Samuel*, 184; Klein, *1 Samuel*, 93.

37. See Hertzberg, *I & II Samuel*, 86; for an example from older scholarship, see

Eppstein rejects the suggestion that the question "who is their father?" is an expression of contempt, by reason of the description of events
later in the narrative when David has gone to the camps in Ramah with
Samuel to escape from Saul, where an alternative explanation is offered
for the saying, "Is Saul also among the prophets?":[38]

> Then Saul sent messengers to take David. When they saw the
> company of the prophets in a frenzy, with Samuel standing in
> charge of them, the spirit of God came upon the messengers of
> Saul, and they also fell into a prophetic frenzy. When Saul was
> told, he sent other messengers, and they also fell into a frenzy.
> Saul sent messengers again the third time, and they also fell into
> a frenzy. Then he himself went to Ramah. He came to the great
> well that is in Secu; he asked, "Where are Samuel and David?"
> And someone said, "They are at the camps in Ramah." He went
> there, toward the camps in Ramah; and the spirit of God came
> upon him. As he was going, he fell into a prophetic frenzy, until
> he came to the camps in Ramah. He too stripped off his clothes,
> and he too fell into a frenzy before Samuel. He lay naked all that
> day and all that night. Therefore it is said, "Is Saul also among the
> prophets?" (1 Sam. 19:20–24; NRSV, except "camps" for *naioth*)

Of the six references to "frenzy" or "prophetic frenzy" in this translation,
the first represents the niphal of *nb'* and the remaining five the hithpael
of that root.[39]

The passage reveals the highly contagious nature of the possession
states of the people in the camps.[40] Eppstein argues that since "so exalted
a personage" as Samuel himself is reported as being with, and in a position of authority over, the prophets (in 1 Sam 19:20 and 24), the earlier
question, "who is their father?" at 1 Sam 10:12 should not be treated

---

Budde, who said it implied that "no one knows to whom they belong; they are stray
vagabonds without name or pedigree" (*Religion of Israel*, 96).

38. Eppstein, "Was Saul," 298. See McCarter (*1 Samuel*, 328) for this translation of *naioth*. For a discussion of the groups of prophets in ancient Israel, see Lang,
Monotheism, 94–95.

39. *Targum Jonathan* alters the words *nb'ym* and the two forms of *nb'* to "scribes"
and "praising" (see Gordon, "Saul's Meningitis," 48) and this may suggest an unease with
the unruly picture these expressions convey. For the Aramaic text of this Targum, see
Sperber, *Bible in Aramaic*, and for an English translation, see Harrington and Saldarini,
Targum Jonathan.

40. See Lindblom (*Prophecy*, 47–65, especially 48), whose treatment, while thor-
ough for his time, looks rather dated now in view of recent advances in social-scientific
research on altered states of consciousness.

as contemptuous.[41] This objection is unconvincing. First, if one reads 1 Samuel as narrative, it is a long wait from the tenth to the nineteenth chapter to learn how one should interpret the issue concerning the parentage of the prophets. Second, Samuel does not himself take part in possession trance. His being in authority could be a way of keeping their behavior under some control; indeed, the location of the prophets apparently in camps away from permanent human habitations may emphasize that these people have thrown off the usual social conventions and domestic economy of village and town in a way that would not have been well received by those who had not. Third, the description of Saul's actions, including the shameful fact of his nakedness for a day and a night, is hard to reconcile with anything other than a very negative view of the cause of such a condition.[42]

Saul's situation bears a striking (although perhaps hitherto unnoticed) similarity to that of Jesus in the synagogue in Nazareth, especially in the Lucan version (Luke 4:16–30). Like Saul, Jesus abandons his traditional role in his hometown to take on a prophetic one, and as with Saul so with Jesus observers note that he is the son of a local man: "Is this not Joseph's son?" (Luke 4:22). As Richard Rohrbaugh has proposed in a convincing exposition of Luke 4:1–30, this question is an insult because in "antiquity persons were expected to act in accord with birth status and anyone who did not represented a troubling social anomaly";[43] to ask such a question was an effective way of ridiculing someone, as Cyril of Alexandria noted in relation to the Lucan passage long ago.[44] There is an interesting parallel in traditional Scottish society, where to say "Ah kent his feyther" ("I knew his father") is a derogatory way of referring to a man who presumes to act in a way out of keeping with the character of his father.[45] Exactly equivalent is the question asked of Saul by the people of Gibeah: "What has come over the son of Kish?" The extreme difficulty of escaping the force of the conventions that kept one tied to

41. Eppstein, "Was Saul," 298.

42. Targum Jonathan is sensitive to the embarrassment of Saul's nakedness and renders '*arom* ("naked") in v. 24 by *barsan*, which only occurs here in the Targums and which Gordon seeks ingeniously to interpret as meaning "afflicted by meningitis" ("Saul's Meningitis").

43. Rohrbaugh, "Legitimating Sonship," 186.

44. Ibid, 194.

45. I am indebted to Dr. Robin Salters, formerly of St Mary's College in the University of St Andrews, for alerting me to this usage.

the family and the role into which one was born provides the context for Jesus's remark, "Truly, I say to you that no prophet is acceptable in his hometown" (Luke 4:24), although the Marcan version of this saying puts it more completely: "A prophet is not without honor (*atimos*) except in his hometown, and among his relatives and in his own house" (Mark 6:4). Precisely the same sentiment could have fallen from the lips of Saul's contemporaries.

Considerations such as this help explain the next event in the narrative: "When his prophetic frenzy had ended, he went home. Saul's uncle said to him and to the boy, 'Where did you go?' And he replied, 'To seek the donkeys; and when we saw they were not to be found, we went to Samuel'" (1 Sam 10:13–14, NRSV, with one amendment).[46]

That it should be his uncle and not his father who speaks to Saul has been found almost inexplicable by commentators, at least by the ones who even notice the point as an issue.[47] One plausible explanation is based on the socially realistic scenario that the local gossip networks have swung into action and that Kish has soon learned of the disgraceful way his hitherto dutiful and considerate son has behaved in public. In such circumstances, a rupture between father and son would be a likely consequence. Kish would either have it out with Saul very dramatically or simply cut him off. That it is Saul's uncle who speaks to him on his return suggests that the former alternative may have come to pass; Kish is using his brother as an intermediary so as to avoid the explosion of anger that might occur if he went to his son himself. Given that it would be odd if the uncle had not heard that the son of Kish had disappeared while searching for donkeys, the question he asks Saul and his servant ("Where have you been?") should probably be read as an accusation: "What have you been up to?" and Saul's reply, focusing on the donkeys and Samuel, not on his activity with the prophets, is an exercise in prevarication, which he continues in reply to his uncle's equally blunt "Tell me what Samuel said to you" by restricting his answer to the issue of the donkeys (1 Sam 10:15–16).

46. The Masoretic Text has in v. 13, "he went to the high place (*hbmh*)," which makes no sense, and Wellhausen proposed the generally accepted amendment to *hbyth* ("to home"), followed here. Also see Josephus, *Judean Antiquities* 6.58.

47. "It is surprising to find Saul's uncle here instead of Kish, his father." McCarter, *I Samuel*, 184.

Accordingly, by the time that Saul's original and secret anointing as king is confirmed publicly following the drawing of lots at Mizpah (10:17–24), the reader knows that question marks hang over his character, for not only has he shown a dangerous lability of character by indulging in trance states, but he has done so publicly, to his family's shame.

Saul Sins before Yahweh

The doubts that surround Saul's character are strengthened later in the narrative by the two occasions on which he angers Yahweh. He knows that he has incurred Yahweh's displeasure, initially because he had not obeyed Samuel's command to wait for him at Gilgal until he would come there and give Saul further instructions (1 Sam 10:8). On this occasion Samuel gives Saul the grievously heavy news that his dynasty will not endure, and that Yahweh will seek out a man after his own heart and appoint him as leader over the people (1 Sam 13:13–14). This means that Saul has endangered his own authority and also the honor of his family that depends on it. Then Saul has compounded the offense by not obeying the order to put all of the Amalekites under the ban (1 Sam 15:3), in that he spares their king, Agag, and the best of their livestock (1 Sam 15:9). As a result, Yahweh explicitly tells Samuel that he has turned against Saul (1 Sam 15:10–11). So Samuel conveys the news to Saul that God has rejected him as king of Israel for his disobedience (1 Sam 15:22–23), and has taken the kingdom of Israel from him and will give it to a better man in his place (1 Sam 15:28). Saul acknowledges his sin but successfully seeks to have Samuel minimize the shame he must endure before Israel (1 Sam 15:30–31). These incidents set the scene for the first report of Saul's disorder, in the very next chapter of the text.

Saul's Evil Spirit and David's Lyre

As chapter 2 noted, anthropologists employ the idea of limited good to refer to the fact that all aspects of life in the Mediterranean are thought to exist in finite quantities, and there are unambiguous biblical examples of this outlook. The notion of limited good also forms an indispensable feature of the narrative concerning the onset of Saul's condition and the curative powers David's lyre playing has in relation to it.

First Samuel 16:1–13 recounts the way David comes to be anointed as king of Israel; beginning with Yahweh's asking Samuel how long he will go on mourning for Saul, whom Yahweh has rejected as king of Israel (16:1); continuing through the method of selection (16:6–12), which I will discuss in chapter 6; and concluding with the anointing itself: "So Samuel took the horn of oil and anointed him in the midst of his brothers; and the spirit of Yahweh fell upon David from that day onwards" (16:13).

The understanding of the finite nature of all aspects of life in the Mediterranean means that if David now has the spirit of Yahweh upon him then it can no longer be on Saul. This is precisely spelled out in the first clause of the next verse, when the narrator states: "The spirit of Yahweh left Saul."

This is not all, however; for the verse continues: "and an evil spirit from Yahweh repeatedly terrified (ba'at) him" (16:14). The primary meaning of ba'at is "to alarm," or "to terrify," although often this point is missed in the versions. The word occurs sixteen times in the Old Testament and always with this meaning.[48] Hertzberg plausibly suggests that the force of the consecutive perfect form of the verb used in v. 14 is to give the verb a sense of continual activity,[49] reflected in the translation just given. When this is combined with the picture in 16:16, which envisages that Saul will be afflicted on multiple occasions, it becomes clear that the attacks of the evil spirit are intermittent but persistent. This seems to be the dominant feature of Saul's condition from the perspective of the indigenous observer, although it is closely linked with the perceived cause of the problem. Within the emic perspective of the narrative, Saul has suffered a double catastrophe; not merely abandoned by Yahweh's spirit, he also repeatedly experiences the terror caused by an evil spirit actually sent by Yahweh. Saul's servants share the narrator's understanding of his problem: "An evil spirit of God is terrifying you," with the verb ba'at again appearing, as a piel participle (16:15). They recommend a form of treatment: that Saul should obtain a skilful lyre player so that when the evil spirit comes, he will play and Saul will get well (16:16).

48. Niphal: Esth 7:6; Dan 8:17; 1 Chr 21:30; piel: 1 Sam 16:14, 15; 2 Sam 22:5; Isa 21:4; Ps 18:5; Job 3:5; 7:14; 9:34; 13:11; 13:21; 15:24; 18:11; 33:7. The substantival form, meaning "terror," appears at Jer 8:15 and 33:7.

49. Hertzberg, I & II Samuel, 140.

Saul agrees, yet who should be chosen as lyre player? Few verses in the Bible are as poignant as the one that answers this question: "One of the young men replied, 'Look, I have seen a son of Jesse the Bethlehemite, who is skilful in playing, a brave man, a warrior, prudent in speech, and a man of good presence; and Yahweh is with him'" (16:18).

David Gunn has aptly noted that there is "no flabbiness in the narrative at this point," since the introduction of the spirit besetting Saul leads directly to David's entering Saul's life. Yet, writing at a time before Mediterranean anthropology had been brought to bear on biblical texts, Gunn misses the logic of the narrative: By the cruelest of fate's tricks, no sooner is David anointed and Saul unwell, "than his own servants are recommending David as the cure for his sickness."[50]

David's introduction is not a trick of fate but rather rests on the social reality of the limited good in circumstances known to the narrator and the readers of the text: the spirit of Yahweh that Saul has lost is now with David, and therefore in all of Israel only David will be able to help him. On the lips of the servant who recommends David, however, the recognition that "Yahweh is with him" is richly ironic; unlike the reader, the servant (treated here as a character in the narrative) has no idea of the precise accuracy of what he has said.

Yet the narrative develops this irony with an intensity that is almost painful, for when David is brought to the king, Saul loves him greatly (16:21). Does not Saul, his life accelerating on its long slide to ruin, see in David his old best self? Does he not sense in David a divine presence that has now forsaken him? No wonder that David can help Saul: "And whenever the evil spirit from God was upon Saul, David took the lyre and played it with his hand; so Saul was refreshed, and all was well, and the evil spirit departed from him" (16:23, RSV).

Saul Turns Against David

While the narrative of 1 Samuel after the defeat of Goliath in chapter 17 is largely propelled by the violent antipathy that Saul conceives for David, the intertwined dynamics of character and plot by which this is achieved give a central place to Saul's condition. To explore this issue, however, we must initially examine the way in which the narrator develops the theme of the king's madness in its narrative context.

50. Gunn, *Fate of King Saul*, 78.

David's effectiveness on the lyre is followed by the narrative that recounts his victory over Goliath (1 Sam 17), the subject matter of chapter 6 in this volume. In the Masoretic Text there are signs of clumsy blending of the tradition of David's lyre playing and his role as a warrior in Saul's need to ask the name of David's father at the conclusion of the Goliath episode (17:58), even though he had learned this earlier (16:18–22). Nevertheless, thereafter the narrator manages closely to integrate these strands and the continuing tale of Saul's decline. The deft and compressed way these themes are developed indicates a high degree of narrative artistry. Thus, after introducing the love between David and Saul's son Jonathan (18:1–4), the narrative proceeds in a sentence full of tragic potential: "David went out and was successful wherever Saul sent him; as a result, Saul set him over the army. And all the people, even the servants of Saul, approved" (1 Sam 18:5, NRSV).

There is something profoundly disordered in Saul appointing David to this post. One of the main reasons for which he had been made king was to lead Israel to war: "But the people refused to listen to the voice of Samuel; they said, 'No! but we are determined to have a king over us, so that we also may be like other nations, and that our king may govern us and go out before us and fight our battles'" (1 Sam 8:19–20, NRSV).

Yahweh himself had endorsed this rationale for kingship: "When Samuel had heard all the words of the people, he repeated them in the ears of the LORD. The LORD said to Samuel, 'Listen to their voice and set a king over them'" (1 Sam 8:21–22, NRSV).

By delegating military responsibility to David, Saul has eschewed a critical element in the responsibilities that had initially impelled Israel to seek a king. An ancient reader would understand that it is likely to lead Saul into trouble, just as surely as David later succumbed to disaster when he tarried in Jerusalem during the Ammonite war, "at the time of the year when kings go out to battle" (2 Sam 11:1, NRSV), with the consequences considered in chapter 9 of this volume.

Trouble does not take long to arrive. Saul has given David an arena where he will be able to win great honor for himself and in a culture where all goods, honor included, exist in finite quantities, it is inevitable that David will do so at Saul's expense. Later on Joab only manages to persuade David to leave Jerusalem and assume command of his army in capturing the Ammonite town of Rabbah by threatening to take the town and name it after himself (2 Sam 12:26–29). So it is not surprising that the ominous note of the universal approval for David's acquisition of command in 1 Sam 18:5 is immediately followed by events surrounding the return of David from slaying the Philistine: "As they were coming home, when David returned from killing the Philistine, the women came out of all the towns of Israel, singing and dancing, to meet King Saul, with tambourines, with songs of joy, and with musical instruments. And the women sang to one another as they made merry, 'Saul has killed his thousands, and David his ten thousands'" (1 Sam 18:6–7, NRSV).

In spite of Keith Bodner's suggestion that we should opt for "a happy reading of the song, a celebration of Saul and his armor bearer against all the odds,"[51] in the context of Mediterranean culture, where honor is both a claim to worth and the public concurrence in that claim, Saul has been grievously shamed. His social inferior has been very publicly awarded a much higher share of honor than he has. The usual response to such a process in the Mediterranean world is for the one shamed both to envy the person honored and also to seek vengeance against him. The activation of envy and the desire for vengeance is often associated with the phenomenon of the evil eye, a pervasive phenomenon in the Mediterranean area from at least the time of Hammurabi and even earlier, as Elliott has demonstrated in a number of important articles on the subject.[52] This is why victorious Roman generals enjoying their triumph carried amulets to ward off the consequence of the evil eye that the envy generated by their success was expected to arouse in onlookers.

For these reasons Saul's response is entirely expected: "Saul was very angry, and this saying displeased him; he said, 'They have ascribed to David ten thousands, and to me they have ascribed thousands; what more can he have but the kingdom?' And Saul eyed David from that day on" (1 Sam 18:8–9, RSV).

Some commentators note that Saul's eyeing David in v. 9 is a reference to the evil eye that is generated by envy.[53]

51. Bodner, *1 Samuel*, 194.

52. See Elliott, "Fear of the Leer"; Elliott, "Paul, Galatians, and the Evil Eye"; Elliott, "Evil Eye in the First Testament"; Elliott, "Matthew 20:1–15"; and Elliott, "Evil Eye and the Sermon on the Mount."

53. McCarter, *I Samuel*, 312–13, recognizes a possible evil-eye reference here, but wrongly excludes it. For the fundamental (although infrequently noticed) distinction in the biblical world between envy (meaning a negative disposition toward one who has a singular possession) and jealousy (meaning great attachment to and concern for what is exclusively one's own), see Malina and Seeman, "Envy."

Compounding the fact that he has won far less honor, moreover, is the additional risk, now perceived by Saul for the first time, that David represents a threat to his kingship. First Samuel 18–31 frequently emphasizes that David himself harbored no ambitions for the kingship or animosity toward Saul, but in the fiercely competitive world of the ancient Mediterranean Saul's fear, faced with a potential rival ranked so much higher than him in national esteem and where his loss of the kingship would impact on his family as well as himself, was not entirely an unexpected one.

More important than this, however, was the fact of Saul's distinctive personality that the narrator has been at pains to point out. Not only is he prone to the attacks of possession trance characteristic of prophets in this culture, but he is also afflicted by an evil spirit from Yahweh. These facts lay the foundation for the way the impact of the song sung by the women concerning David and Saul is so dramatically greater than what might have been expected: "The next day an evil spirit from God rushed upon Saul, and he raved (hithpael of *naba'*) within his house, while David was playing the lyre, as he did day by day. Saul had his spear in his hand; and Saul threw the spear, for he thought, 'I will pin David to the wall.' But David eluded him twice" (1 Sam 18:10–11, NRSV).

Reading 1 Samuel within its Mediterranean cultural context strongly suggests that the narrator of the Masoretic Text has deliberately created the impression that Saul has been so shaken by his public shaming on the previous day that he has now lost control completely, even to the extent of his trying to kill David with a spear! The two aspects of Saul's instability (the evil spirit that comes upon him bringing terror—although that particular element is not mentioned here—and his raving like one of the prophets at Gibeah—evoked by use of the hithpael of *naba'*) are now brought explicitly into conjunction. This is a point of major breakdown in Saul's life, triggered by the degradation of his status that he has just experienced. Yet for commentators like McCarter, writing before Mediterranean anthropology had made an impression on biblical criticism, the crucial role of this passage in the narrative is simply missed. McCarter's view on 1 Sam 18:10–11 is that this "duplicate of the incident in 19:9–10 seems out of place at this point"![54]

The presence of Yahweh with David, which had previously brought Saul relief, is not enough to keep at bay the violent anger that he now

54. McCarter, *I Samuel*, 305.

aims at David. Indeed, it features as its cause. For it must be at David that Saul's anger is directed, since in his torment of envy he has come to realize that the one person in Israel with the power to soothe his spirit has become the rival who might take his place as king. The full implication of what it meant for Yahweh's spirit to rest upon David, closely implicated in the notion of limited good, has become all too clear, as the text states: "Saul was afraid of David, because the LORD was with him but had departed from Saul" (1 Sam 18:12, NRSV).

Saul's Subsequent Career

Space is lacking within the compass of this volume to offer a detailed consideration of Saul's role in 1 Samuel until his death at Philistine hands (although the story of David in this period is the subject of chapter 7 in this volume). Nevertheless, it is worth noting a few features that indicate the extent to which his personality has been unhinged as a result of his condition, and the manner in which this fact propels the plot forward. From the time when Saul first raises his spear to David (1 Sam 18:10–11) his attitude toward him is essentially negative, indeed homicidal, with occasional remissions, as after the two opportunities David has to kill him but does not (1 Samuel 24 and 26:7–25). There is a further occasion when Saul attempts to kill David when he is playing his lyre for him at a time of affliction by the evil spirit (1 Sam 19:9–10), which is all the more dramatic since it occurs just after Saul has promised his son Jonathan not to seek to kill David (1 Sam 19:6). Again and again David tries to persuade Saul that he is not bent on treason, but Saul is unable to accept this, except on occasions of the sort just mentioned. The full extent of Saul's hostility emerges in the terrible slaughter of the priests of Nob, and every living thing in the town, in revenge for their having harbored David (1 Sam 22:18–19).

Yet nothing could more express the desolation of Saul toward the end of the narrative than his nighttime visit to the witch of Endor (1 Sam 28:7–25). Samuel is now dead and buried, and the sight of the Philistines, who have encamped against him at Shunem, has struck Saul with terror (1 Sam 28:4–5), somewhat reminiscent of the effect produced on him by the evil spirit, although different Hebrew expressions are used of his fear. The extent to which God has abandoned him is manifest in the fact that God will not answer Saul by dreams or by Urim or by prophets. To

whom can Saul turn? Only to the witch of Endor, a trafficker in spirits
and ghosts, of the very kind Saul himself had previously banished (1
Sam 28:3). He has her call up the ghost of Samuel, who has for Saul only
the worst of news: that Yahweh, who is now his adversary, will take the
kingdom away from him and give it to David; and that he and his sons
will die, and Israel will be defeated by the Philistines (1 Sam 28:16–19).
The message overpowers him with fear. But eventually he recovers
enough to eat and in due course engages the Philistines and meets his
fate with dignity and courage (1 Samuel 31).

SAUL'S MADNESS IN CROSS-CULTURAL PERSPECTIVE

Cross-Cultural Health Care

P. Kyle McCarter, writing in one of the main commentaries on 1 Samuel,
offers the following view of Saul's plight: "We may speak of mental illness if we want—Saul manifests some symptoms of paranoia, others of
manic-depressive illness—but surely Hertzberg is correct to stress the
fact that 'Saul's suffering is described theologically, not psychopatheti-
cally or psychologically.' The evil spirit is 'from Yahweh' and will play
its part in the working out of the divine plan."[55] McCarter seems to be
suggesting here that modern psychiatric accounts are largely irrelevant
to understanding Saul, and that what really matters in the narrative is
the divine origin of Saul's problem and the importance of Yahweh's spirit
in determining his fate. For this reason the appropriate designation for
Saul's suffering is "theological."

　　　Views such as these, hardly uncommon in biblical interpretation,
represent a high degree of theoretical confusion and misunderstanding
of the dynamics of plot and characterization in the narrative of 1 Samuel.
At the center of the fog lies a failure clearly to distinguish the various
perspectives with which one might view the phenomena of Saul's "madness," coupled with an attempt to give central place to one inadequately
formulated perspective over others. In the present instance, the approbation that Hertzberg and McCarter express toward a nondefined "theological" viewpoint seems transparently a function of their ascribing to
a particular approach to biblical interpretation rather than necessarily
telling us anything about 1 Samuel.

55. McCarter, *I Samuel*, 280–81.

In reading 1 Samuel 8–31, a product of a culture alien to ours, the disciplined investigation of foreign cultures conducted by modern anthropologists reveals that the fundamental distinction which must be drawn in such a case is that between the understanding of Saul's condition entertained by one of its original readers (which is the "native," "indigenous," or "emic" perspective), and that of a modern observer, trained in social and medical sciences and even in post-Enlightenment theology (the "etic" perspective).[56] Unless we outline both emic and etic positions, which involves doing justice, after all, to the *cultural* experience of both the ancient readers and of ourselves, it will be impossible to engage in *cross-cultural* comparison or to arrive at the next stage in the process, the development of genuinely *intercultural* insights and discernment, the importance of which I proposed in chapter 1.

We must always be aware of the difficulties inherent in an attempt to apply etic psychiatric perspectives to a narrative text from another historical epoch. Some of the problems emerged in the discussion that followed the publication in 1958 of Erik Erikson's *Young Man Luther: A Study in Psychoanalysis and History*. The principal problem is the lack of the abundant data that modern modes of psychiatric analysis utilize. Nevertheless, we should not overemphasize the difficulties. Just as nothing prevents someone today giving a very cautious diagnosis (no doubt hedged about with appropriate qualifications) on the strength of a brief written report of the condition of a patient in a non-Western context, so too there is no reason in principle why we cannot try to do the same in relation to the written record of the condition of a person from another age, even if we are dealing with a literary figure (who has presumably been portrayed in accordance with prevailing social scripts) rather than a historical personality. It is encouraging to see the approbation Roger Johnson gave to Erikson's attempt to do this for Luther, in spite of criticism Erikson had attracted.[57]

In dealing with Saul's condition, our primary point of reference will be the fairly new field of cross-cultural health care and medical anthropology. One of the early milestones in this area, *Patients and Healers in the Context of Culture*, was published in 1980 by Arthur Kleinman, a psychiatrist trained in anthropology, who did extensive fieldwork in Taiwan, where modern Western and a variety of types of

56. See Headland, *Emics and Etics*.

57. Johnson, *Psychohistory*.

traditional Chinese medicines and therapeutic practices exist cheek to
jowl. Although much subsequent research on cross-cultural medicine
and psychiatry has been published in the last few decades,[58] Kleinman's
work still stands out for the clarity with which he addresses the central
issues.[59]

According to Kleinman, the single most important notion for
cross-cultural studies of this kind is that in all societies health-care activities are closely interrelated. Each society has a health-care system,
which is a *cultural system* of symbolic meanings anchored in particular
arrangements of social institutions and patterns of interpersonal relations. Such a system, which is a conceptual model not an ontological
entity, encompasses descriptions of illness, beliefs about causation of
illness, norms governing choice and evaluation of treatment, socially
legitimated statuses, roles, power relationships, interaction settings, and
institutions. Patients and healers are the basic components, and they
are embedded in specific sets of cultural meanings and social relationships. The pronounced cultural orientation of the notion of a health-care
system radically distinguishes it from the biomedical model favored by
most health carers in North Atlantic contexts, in which biological processes alone constitute the reality addressed and are the central focus of
diagnosis and therapy.[60] Kleinman takes the view that the biomedical
model rests upon Western scientism and ethnocentrism.[61]

In a modern context it is possible to distinguish three broad sectors in a health-care system. The first is the popular sector, which comprises various levels such as the individual, family, social networks, and
community beliefs and behavior, and that around the world handles
most illness episodes. Normally disease is first encountered in the family, and then a number of steps are taken: symptoms are experienced
and perceived; the disease is labeled and evaluated; a particular kind
of sick role is sanctioned; decisions are taken as to what to do, even
to the extent of engaging in specific health-care-seeking behavior;

58. For a recent (2006) review of this field, see Kirmayer, "Beyond the 'New Cross-
cultural Psychiatry.'"

59. For research using non-Western health-care systems to understand features of
the New Testament, see the following by Pilch: "Healing in Mark," "Health Care System
in Matthew," "Interpreting Biblical Healing," and "Sickness and Healing in Luke-Acts,"
Healing in the New Testament, and "Jesus's Healing Activity."

60. Kleinman, *Patients and Healers*, 24–25.

61. Ibid, 32.

treatment is applied and evaluated; and other therapy may be sought from other sectors in the health-care system. The second sector is the professional one (usually meaning scientific medicine, although there are some premodern examples), and in some contexts this sector has been quite successful in driving out other types of health therapies, towards which it tends to have extremely negative views, labeling them as "irrational" and "unscientific." Third, there is the folk sector, comprising nonprofessional and nonbureaucratic specialists. In nearly all premodern societies the popular and folk sectors compose the entire health-care system. Folk healing can be sacred or secular, though this distinction is often difficult to maintain in practice. It covers phenomena such as shamanism, herbalism, and traditional surgical and manipulative treatments, such as bone setting.[62] Traditional Islamic medicine represents a mixture of the popular and folk sectors but also a movement toward a professional sector.[63]

A central feature of cross-cultural health care is the distinction between two aspects of sickness: disease and illness. *Disease* refers to a malfunctioning of biological or psychological processes, while *illness* refers to the psychosocial experience and meaning attached to the perceived disease. Illness includes secondary personal and social responses to a primary malfunction in the individual's physiological or psychological condition or both. But it also has significant social dimensions, involving communication and interaction within the ill person's family and social network. In this light, illness means the shaping of disease into behavior and experience. Health-care systems have a vital cultural function of creating illness from disease, and this, paradoxically, is actually the first stage of healing. Illness so understood is an adaptive response to disease.[64] It goes without saying that similar underlying diseases may be configured quite differently as illnesses in different cultural settings. A disease tends to have a typical course independent of setting, whereas an illness is always unique.[65] The Western biomedical model of health care tends to focus on the disease aspect, which its methodology is well adapted to diagnose and treat, whereas the health-care-system model sees both elements as essential.

62. Ibid, 49–60.
63. Ullmann, *Islamic Medicine*.
64. Kleinman, *Patients and Healers*, 72.
65. Ibid, 77.

As far as therapy is concerned, Western medicine is primarily interested in dealing with the underlying physiological cause of the disease, whereas in non-Western contexts therapeutic efficacy is sought through treatment of the psychosocial and cultural aspects of the illness.

Saul's Madness in the Context of Mediterranean Culture

These insights from cross-cultural health care provide a useful framework for examining Saul's condition and the way it was treated. We must face up to the initial hurdle—that we have only a tiny amount of evidence upon which to reach any view, as compared with the abundant empirical data available to researchers into similar phenomena in foreign cultures today.[66] Nevertheless, inspired by Kleinman, there are still interesting issues to pursue.

First of all, we must consider the health-care system in operation, which comes into view at 1 Sam 16:14–23. As usual a preindustrial agrarian society has no professional sector, yet rather more surprisingly no folk sector is in view either. The treatment of Saul's condition is left entirely to the popular sector. Here this is not composed of Saul's family, since neither his wife, Ahinoam; nor his sons, Jonathan, Ishyo and Malchishua; nor his daughters, Merab and Michal (1 Sam 14:49), play any part. Rather, the popular sector emerges from the social network consisting of his courtiers and soldiers (whom it would not be unreasonable to regard as his fictive kin) and one of his subjects, David, together with a body of beliefs and behavior thought to be efficacious. Furthermore, the process described above certainly takes place. Saul's symptoms, especially his terror, are noted and socially interpreted, with the problem being attributed to possession by an evil spirit, a particular role is envisaged for him—that he will receive therapy inside his house but will otherwise continue as king—and a decision is made to find a fine lyre-player who will be able to give him relief.

It is also possible to distinguish disease from illness in relation to Saul. The "disease" consists of some physiological or psychological malfunction that manifests itself in attacks of extreme dread. I will consider the possible nature of this disease from a modern psychiatric perspective

---

66. We also have more data available with respect to other historical periods. There is, for example, a reasonable amount of information available on the notion of "melancholia" in traditional Islamic society: see Ullmann, *Islamic Medicine*, 72–78.

further below. On the other hand, Saul's "illness" refers to the cultural complex which develops around this phenomenon, including the communication and interaction on the matter between himself and his servants, the interpretation attached to it as a visitation by a spirit and the behavior expected of Saul while he is receiving therapy.

Often it is possible to build up very full profiles of "illnesses" in contemporary foreign cultures because of the availability of informants who may be interviewed and examined. Three examples featuring anxiety states (chosen because they have some similarities to Saul's condition) are worth mentioning. In Chinese culture there is an illness known as *koro*, which is characterized by a fear of death. Its victims fear that their penis will retract into the abdomen and ultimately cause death, and the ill therefore take steps to prevent this happening. Belief of being afflicted by *koro* intensifies ordinary guilt over sexual excess and produces panic and depersonalization of the genitals. The illness occurs most frequently in immature, anxious persons who have been exposed to a sudden fright.[67] Second, *susto* (or *espanto*) is an anxiety illness that occurs in Spanish American culture and is believed to be caused by a sudden fright, the evil eye, black magic, or sorcery, all of which are thought to produce "soul loss." Associated with it are irritability, anorexia, insomnia, phobias, reduced libido, nightmares, trembling, sweating, tachycardia, diarrhea, and so on. Traditional cures are prescribed to coax the souls of those affected back to their bodies.[68] In both *koro* and *susto* the element of environmental stress is perceived as a significant causative factor. Third, there is "falling-out," a seizure-like disorder apparently connected with anxiety states that occurs among black Americans—Bahamians and Haitians who live in Miami—and that manifests itself as a state in which a person collapses without warning and for some time thereafter retains the capacity to hear and understand, while not being able to see or move.[69]

Quite possibly the malady that the ancient Israelite audience of 1 Samuel thought afflicted Saul was as well-known a phenomenon within their culture as *koro*, *susto*, and falling-out are within the modern cultures in which they occur. Unfortunately, there is simply insufficient

67. Kiev, *Transcultural Psychiatry*, 66.

68. Ibid., 69–70.

69. Weidman, "Falling-Out." I am indebted to Bruce Malina for drawing this condition to my attention.

information in the text to develop a profile of Saul's illness in anything like the detail possible with examples known to us from actual case studies. Nevertheless, an important feature distinguishing the Israelite condition is the centrality of possession by God's evil spirit to the analysis of the condition, and here we are able to consider comparative material. Murdock's useful worldwide survey of theories of illness points to a basic distinction between natural and supernatural theories of causation.[70] The phenomenon of spirit possession or spirit aggression, defined as "the attribution of illness to the direct, hostile, arbitrary, or punitive action of some malevolent or affronted supernatural being,"[71] and quite separate from magical causation where the supernatural being acts as the agent of a human aggressor, is actually the most common of all types of supernatural causation. Of 139 cultures surveyed by Murdock, spirit aggression was the most common cause of disease in seventy-eight and an important secondary cause in forty others.[72] Belief in spirit aggression as a cause of illness is almost universal.

Accordingly, there is nothing particularly surprising about the attribution of Saul's illness to possession by a spirit from Yahweh. There is controversy over whether the "evil spirit from Yahweh" had a status independent of God and was sent by him, or whether it was an aspect of his divinity.[73] Either way, the phenomenon is readily comprehended within the prevailing emic understanding of illness, which included a firm belief in the existence of a God who would deal with his human subjects in this way, just as in other cultures there is no doubt of the existence of spirits who cause illness. For this reason, it is submitted that we may regard Hertzberg's proposal, endorsed by McCarter, that the spirit's divine origin means Saul's suffering is described "theologically" as an anachronistic and ethnocentric imposition of a modern viewpoint on an ancient text.

Saul's Madness in a Modern Context

The cross-cultural approach also requires that we consider the phenomena under examination from a modern position informed by the social

70. Murdock, *Theories of Illness.*
71. Ibid, 20.
72. Ibid.
73. Kuemmerlin-McLean, "Demons (Old Testament)," 139.

and medical sciences. We need to ask how we (or most readers of this volume, at any rate), as post-industrial inhabitants of the North Atlantic culture zone, might conceptualize the full range of Saul's experience. This means that we must explore the nature of Saul's *disease* (since the notion of *illness* still sits more comfortably with the emic perspective we have just examined).

We lack sufficient evidence to make a firm diagnosis concerning Saul; all that we can do is to exclude conditions for which there is no support in the text and fix upon one that is at least reasonably plausible. If we had more symptoms described, other diagnoses would be possible. According to McCarter, as noted above, Saul exhibits some symptoms of paranoia, others of manic-depressive illness. Yet while Saul does in due course display arguably paranoid reactions toward David, to which we will return below, there is little support in the text for a manic-depressive diagnosis. Although depression is common to many cultures, Saul does not manifest its symptoms, such as sadness, hopelessness, lack of pleasure with the things of this world and with social relationships.[74] Moreover, the absence of thought disorders in the form of visual or auditory hallucinations seems to exclude schizophrenia as a diagnosis.

The dominant feature of Saul's condition to the extent that it is dysfunctional is the repeated incidence of terror, as shown in the use of the word *ba'at* in connection with it (16:14–15). As noted earlier, the use of the consecutive perfect form of this word at 16.14 suggests repetition of the experience. This is a very significant indicator of the nature of his problem and when Rosen falls into error by suggesting that "there is no direct information on his subjective condition when he was tormented,"[75] he may have been misled by versions that mistranslate the Hebrew verb without reference to terror. Within a psychiatric framework, one plausible diagnosis allowed by the evidence— and others might be available if we had more information—is that Saul suffers from an anxiety disorder featuring panic attacks. Psychiatrists report that these occur frequently, perhaps once weekly or more often; usually last minutes, rarely hours and are sometimes linked to specific situations.[76]

In Saul's case we are dealing with neurosis rather than psychosis, since psychosis involves a very serious disconnection with reality. In

74. Kleinman and Good, "Introduction: Culture and Depression," 3.

75. Rosen, *Madness in Society*, 29.

76. Davison and Neale, *Abnormal Psychology*, 146.

a panic disorder that is neurotic in nature there is a sudden and inexplicable attack of a host of jarring symptoms—labored breathing, heart
palpitations, chest pain, feelings of choking and smothering, dizziness,
sweating and trembling, and intense apprehension, terror and feelings of
impending doom. All of this is very different from the sadness and sense
of meaninglessness characteristic of depression. In other words, Saul is
too scared to be depressed! Where a panic attack occurs in the course of a
chronic anxiety neurosis, the acute anxiety is manifested in part by rapid
heart rate, and perception of the rapid heart rate is a feature of the illness
experience; the rapid heart rate exerts a positive feedback on the anxiety,
significantly worsening it.[77] In this context it is interesting that at Isa 21:4
the word ba‘at is used in connection with what may be pounding of the
heart. More compelling, however, is that the Septuagint, Josephus, and
Pseudo-Philo all interpret Saul's malady as choking or suffocation, and
thus seem to fix on one well-known feature of anxiety states.[78]

Some instances of panic disorder have physiological explanations.
In many cases it is caused by a cardiac malfunction in the form of a mi-
tral valve synapse, which can produce symptoms very similar to a panic
attack. The alarm of patients at the palpitations they experience for this
reason can cause their symptoms to escalate. Another possible physiological cause (disputed by some) is overactivity in the beta-adrenergic
nervous system, which controls the activity of many of the organs affected in a panic attack, and drugs that block the activity of this division
of the nervous system (beta-blockers) do reduce anxiety.[79]

Yet it has not been shown that physiological causes explain all
panic attacks. Environmental pressures seem to be of great significance
in some cases. Thus, the individual with an anxiety disorder of this type
is chronically and persistently anxious, and this is commonly linked to
life situations, for example chronic terror concerning a possible accident
to a child, or persistent worries about financial difficulties. Feelings of

77. Kleinman, *Patients and Healers*, 78.

78. See *pnigō* ("choke") in the Septuagint at 1 Sam 16:14, while Josephus uses *pnig-moi* ("choking") and *strangalai* ("suffocation") in this place of Saul's experience (*Judean Antiquities* 6.166) and Pseudo-Philo employs the word *prefocare* ("to choke," *Biblical Antiquities* 60.1).

79. Davison and Neale, *Abnormal Psychology*, 146.

not being in control and helplessness are common to those with anxiety disorders.[80]

It is important to note that an anxiety neurosis can be chronic and yet also have recurrent acute episodes, often as a result of psychosocial stress; indeed, in some cases the level of dysfunctionality manifested by the person may merit application of the term "decompensation," or breakdown. Kleinman came upon several such cases in Taiwan.[81] He cites, for example, the case of a Taiwanese man with an acute anxiety neurosis that was usually quiescent but at times became so severe as to suggest the diagnosis of "acute decompensation due to psychosocial stress."[82] In highlighting the significance of stress, such as that arising from financial or business concerns in a patient's life,[83] Kleinman is opting for one explanatory model among several offered by Western psychiatry. On the other hand, a behavioral model will stress current environmental and psychological contingencies reinforcing the deviant behavior, while a psychobiological one will fix upon neurobiological processes.[84]

Other psychological features can accompany an acute anxiety state, such as delusions of persecution and violent behavior in response, together with beliefs in spirit possession. All these were observed by Kleinman in a Taiwanese woman.[85]

As with the explanatory model selected, so too the treatment prescribed for persons with anxiety disorders largely depends on the conceptual framework of the therapist. Psychoanalysts view the disorder as resulting from unresolved conflicts and try to help their patients to confront the true sources of these conflicts. Behavioral clinicians adopt different approaches depending on how they construe the anxiety. If the anxiety can be resolved into a number of specific phobias, they might seek to employ desensitization treatment to them. However, where it is difficult to differentiate specific causes of anxiety, they might prescribe more generalized treatment, such as intensive relaxation training.[86]

---

80. Ibid, 148.
81. Kleinman, *Patients and Healers*, 123.
82. Ibid, 357.
83. Ibid, 343.
84. Ibid, 131.
85. Ibid, 167–68.
86. Davison and Neale, *Abnormal Psychology*, 150–52.

We will now consider Saul's condition within this framework, meaning the condition of a character in a narrative that presumably made cultural sense to the ancient Israelites for whom it was written, since I am not presuming to say anything whatever in relation to a possibly historical figure called Saul. His recent history was one of great stress. He knew that he had incurred Yahweh's displeasure, initially because he had not obeyed Samuel's command to wait for him at Gilgal and then by failing to put all of the Amalekites under the ban. He was threatened with the loss of the kingdom. Although it is uncertain whether Saul took these predictions with complete seriousness, we can assume that they would have caused him acute and ongoing concern. Although he is portrayed as primarily interested in his own position, that was not all that was at stake, for there was also the well-being of his whole family, whose wealth and honor it was his duty to maintain, as he makes clear later in the narrative (1 Sam 20:30–31). There can be little doubt, moreover, that Saul would have regarded himself as helpless before Yahweh and his prophet. The narrative makes psychological sense if we interpret the shock of these events—on a character whose propensity to possession states has already revealed a personality less tied to everyday reality than some—and the continuing apprehension that Yahweh was going to give his kingship to another as precipitating an anxiety disorder with associated panic attacks.

The first onset of the condition is recorded at 1 Sam 16:14–23. Its repeated nature, shown by David's being invited to play on repeated occasions, suggests the regularity typical of any panic disorder. The inexplicable nature of a panic attack would constitute a good reason for the emic interpreter to see in its presence a spirit from God. Extremely interesting, however, is that the therapy chosen, the skilful playing of the lyre, is recognizably similar to the intensive relaxation treatment recommended by behavioral clinicians in cases such as this, where we have a generalized anxiety syndrome.

The subsequent course of the disorder can also be accommodated to this diagnosis. Saul's first attack on David, at 1 Sam 18:10–11, which signals the beginning of the king's paranoid hostility toward him, correlates quite closely with the Taiwanese case cited by Kleinman, where delusions of persecution and outbreaks of hostility were associated with an anxiety condition. Yet the violence with which Saul turns against David justifies our referring to this incident as "decompensation," breakdown, in this instance triggered by the extreme stress of the day before when Saul had been publicly dishonored by the women's unfavorable comparison of him with David. Saul's sensitivity to his honor, which is quite typical of this culture, has already been established at 1 Sam 15:30–31. For this reason it is noteworthy, yet not surprising, that it should be the damage sustained to his honor that induces the psychosocial stress pushing an already chronic anxiety condition into a dangerously acute phase. Thereafter, although there are times when Saul is able to attend to the voice of reason of those around him or to relent of his hostility in the face of extraordinary displays of devotion by David, in general his anxiety condition is characterized by a paranoid and indeed homicidal attitude toward his erstwhile favorite.

One tragic consequence of this rejection of David is that the Israelite forces that would be available to wage war against the Philistines are hopelessly split. So it happens that at the last battle, when Israel is routed, Saul's sons are killed by the Philistine host on Mount Gilboa, and he kills himself (1 Samuel 31), David and his soldiers are campaigning against the Amalekites (1 Samuel 30), having previously offered their services to the Philistine king Achish against Israel (1 Sam 28:1–20), although perhaps hoping that circumstances would see them dispensed, as indeed they were (1 Samuel 29).

CONCLUSION

Making sense of how its original audience would have understood the story of Saul's rise and fall has entailed reading the narrative within the context of ancient Israel and paying particular attention to the issue of Saul's disordered mental state that influences him continually to pursue David with homicidal intent. We may now draw back a little to reflect upon Saul's progress in relation to other tragic heroes in line with Booker's "Tragedy" plot.

As for the first stage, "Anticipation," Saul is not initially presented as unfulfilled and looking towards the future. When Samuel reaches him to anoint him king, Saul is actually focused on the very immediate task of finding his father's asses (1 Sam 9:3–4) and is skeptical, naturally enough from a limited-good perspective, of Samuel's suggestion that he and his father's house will receive all that is desirable in Israel (1 Sam 9:20–21). Saul's reluctance to take on the kingship emerges in his hiding himself among the baggage (1 Sam 10.22). Saul does have a "Dream Stage," but it is fairly brief, consisting mainly of his victory over the Ammonites and acceptance as their king by the Israelites (1 Samuel 11). 1 Samuel 12 is largely occupied with a speech by Samuel asserting his own guiltlessness as a prophet of Yahweh and reminding the Israelites where they stand with their God now they have a king over them. But it also contains a foreboding of trouble in the people's request to Samuel: "Pray for your servants to the Lord your God, that we may not die; for we have added to all our sins this evil, to ask for ourselves a king" (1 Sam 12:19, RSV). During the course of 1 Samuel 13 and 14 there is some intermixing of the "Dream" and "Frustration" Stages, which contributes to the complexity of this narrative. Whereas 1 Samuel 13 begins with Saul's severe announcement that because Saul has disobeyed the commandment to await his arrival, he has lost the kingdom and God will choose another in his place (1 Sam 13:14), 1 Samuel 14 sees him heavily defeating the Philistines, and records his defeat of many other peoples (1 Sam 14:47–48). With 1 Samuel 15, however, comes Saul's failure to put Agag (king of the Amalekites) and the best of their animals to the ban. This can be interpreted as a further "dark act" that locks Saul in to his fate, since it elicits from Samuel a second renewed prophecy that Yahweh had torn the kingdom from Saul and will give it to another (1 Sam 15:28), Saul's "Dream Stage" is well and truly over. And now the "shadow figure," someone to replace Saul whom Samuel has mentioned twice, finally appears in 1 Samuel 16 in the form of David. Initially Saul does not recognize David for what he is and is delighted with his securing victory over the Philistines by beheading Goliath (1 Samuel 17). Saul's turning against David in 1 Sam 18 represents his entry into the "Nightmare Stage" that lasts until 1 Samuel 28, when he "has a mounting sense of threat and despair,"[87] in that he is rejected by God and unable to rid himself of David, a period that culminates in his reaching the limits of desolation during his visit to the medium of Endor (1 Sam 28:20). After a brief interlude dealing with David and the Philistines (1 Sam 29–30), Saul encounters the "Destruction Stage, when the Philistines rout Israel and pursue him and his sons to Mount Gilboah. Badly wounded by Philistine archers, Saul falls upon his own sword. Later the Philistines dishonor his corpse. The ease with which Saul represents a pattern that

---

87. Booker, *Seven Basic Plots*, 156.

finds similarities at every stage with the tragedy of Macbeth,[88] reveals the extent to which we have in 1 Samuel 8–31 a narrative—with a structure and experience of its tragic protagonist—that resonates across cultures widely separated in space and time.

88. Ibid., 156–57.

6

David and Goliath (1 Samuel 17:1—18:5)[1]

In Israelite tradition the figure who achieved the greatest individual feat of arms was a young shepherd named David, when he defeated and killed Goliath, the giant champion of an invading Philistine army, beheading him with his own sword, a result that was followed by Israel routing the Philistines. David's victory and its immediate aftermath are told in Hebrew Scripture in 1 Sam 17:1–18:5, with his anointing by Samuel as king and his appointment to play his lyre therapeutically to Saul appearing in 1 Samuel 16. Before defeating Goliath David was a mere shepherd who had killed wild beasts that threatened his flock; after he had done so, however, he was a warrior, the greatest in Israel. We have seen in the previous chapter how Saul's bouts of madness were aggravated by the envy he felt toward David because of his sudden rise to military pre-eminence in Israel: "Saul has slain his thousands," the women of Israel would sing, "and David his tens of thousands" (1 Sam 18:7). The story of David and Goliath is etched into Jewish and Christian imaginations and has been subject to repeated retellings.[2] Over the centuries many great artists have painted or sculpted the scene.[3]

There is another, much shorter version of the story of David and Goliath that survives in the Old Greek version represented in Codex

---

1. I am grateful to professor John H. Elliott and to other members of the Context Group for their comments on an earlier version of the material in this chapter.

2. See Nitsche, *David gegen Goliath*, for an excellent treatment.

3. To cite only a few examples from a large number of representations, the scene has been painted by Caravaggio (several times), Bernini, William Blake, Burne-Jones, Gustave Doré, and Chagall and sculpted by Bernini and Donatello.

Vaticanus (LXX^B). I have recently published an essay on this version of the David and Goliath story understood in relation to the phenomenon of *monomachia* ("single combat") in the ancient Mediterranean world, comparing it with the remarkably similar story Livy tells of a single combat between a small Roman and a large Gaul (*History of Rome* 7.9.6—10.14).[4] In chapter 8 of this volume I will compare and contrast this shorter version in the Greek Old Testament with the story of Judith, the Israelite woman who slays Holofernes, leader of an army invading Israel.

In this chapter, however, I am solely concerned with the different and distinctive Hebrew version, which is the one with which nearly everyone is familiar (from translations of the Bible, especially). The sections of the narrative, comprising twenty-six and a half extra verses in fact, that appear in the Masoretic Text but not in the Old Greek version include: 1 Sam 17:12–31, 41, 48b, 50, 55–58; and 18:1–5. The additional material in 1 Sam 17:12–31 is particularly noteworthy, and I will consider it in detail below: it relates how David is sent by his father to bring food to his brothers in Saul's army, hears Goliath challenging Israel, asks what shall be done to the Philistine, and is rebuked by his eldest brother.

The Masoretic Text probably represents an expansion of a shorter, original version now seen in the Old Greek.[5] That a shorter text has been subsequently expanded is more probable than that the longer version we find in the Masoretic Text has been reduced to produce a version like the Old Greek. Emanuel Tov has demonstrated through a meticulous examination of the translation techniques evident in the Septuagint of 1 Samuel how unlikely it is that the Septuagintal translators would have deleted such large chunks of a text akin to the Masoretic Text either intentionally or in error.[6] In addition, substantial fragments of a scroll of Samuel in Hebrew were found in Cave 4 at Qumran (4QSam^a) and have now been published in the official edition.[7] This version is close in many

---

4. Esler, "*Monomachia* in the Ancient Mediterranean."

5. Supporters of this view include Tov, "Nature of the Differences"; Lust, "Story of David and Goliath" and "David," Auld, "Making"; and Hutzli, "Mögliche Retuschen." Scholars who do not regard Codex Vaticanus as an earlier text include Gooding, "An Approach"; Nitsche, "David gegen Goliath"; and Aurelius, "Wie David."

6. Tov, "Nature of the Differences."

7. Cross, *Qumran Cave 4.*

ways to the Old Greek, as pointed out long ago by Frank Moore Cross.[8] Nevertheless, the existence of a fragment of 4QSam[a] that probably contains part of 1 Sam 18:4–5[9] (that is, one of the additional passages that exist in the Masoretic Text), warns us against assuming too complete a similarity to the Old Greek version.

A scholarly discussion exists on what historical circumstances, if any, lie behind the story of David and Goliath. Two significant approaches that have been applied to the text are, first, that it is historically accurate and represents the realities of eleventh-century Israel, and, second, that it is a work of fiction or royal propaganda from a much later period.[10] Although I do not need to delve into the precise reasons for the additional passages in 1 Samuel 17, since I am concerned with how an ancient audience would have understood that version as it stood, Johan Lust has reasonably argued that this additional material should be attributed to the desire of a redactor to tell his audience more about David as a young man.[11] This is a more plausible view than that of Auld and Ho to the effect that the redactor was trying to offer a picture of David that in certain respects showed a figure superior to Saul.[12]

My aim in this chapter, as with the others in this volume, is to seek to read and understand the narrative with its original audience in ancient Israel. Although I am not concerned here with the question of whether any actual events in Israelite history inspired the earliest phase of this tradition,[13] my analysis is still historical in that it focuses on the

8. Cross, "A New Qumran Biblical Fragment."

9. See Cross, *Qumran Cave 4*, 80 (reconstructed text of the fragment) and Plate XIIa (photo of the fragment). This fragment is not mentioned in Ulrich, *The Samuel Text*, or Finke, *The Samuel Scroll*.

10. Representatives of the first view include Azzan Yadin, N. Bierling, and J. E. Miller, and of the second include Israel Finkelstein, John Van Seters, and Baruch Halpern—see Yadin, "Goliath's Armor" for details. One textual feature calling doubt upon the historicity of the account of David and Goliath in 1 Samuel 17 is this statement in 2 Sam 21:19: "And there was again war with the Philistines at Gob; and Elhanan the son of Jaareoregim, the Bethlehemite, slew Goliath of Gath, the shaft of whose spear was like a weaver's beam" (RSV).

11. Lust, "Story of David and Goliath."

12. Auld and Ho, "Making of David and Goliath."

13. On this subject, however, see Isser, *Sword of Goliath*, where he usefully surveys scholarship on the use of 1 and 2 Samuel and part of 1 Kings to get to the historical David, before mounting a very different argument: that David actually functioned as a heroic image, like Achilles or King Arthur, a model of *aretē*.

way the narratives would have been interpreted by those who heard or read them at the time of their publication in the past.

As far as the question of the cross-cultural appeal of the story of David and Goliath is concerned, Robert Couffignal has analyzed the narrative using the folktale analysis of Vladimir Propp and the structural analysis of A. J. Greimas.[14] In this chapter, however, I will consider the strong similarities that the narrative of David and Golath has to the plot Christopher Booker describes as "Overcoming the Monster," and interesting similarities that the picture of David in 1 Samuel 16, combined with the narrative concerning Goliath, has with "Rags to Riches." We have already focused on the "Rags to Riches" plot in relation to Tamar in Genesis 38 (chapter 3) and Hannah in 1 Samuel 1–12 (chapter 4), and the relevant area here is the way in which David, as the youngest son of an undistinguished family working in the lowly occupation of shepherd, rises to become king of Israel. In describing his "Overcoming the Monster" plot, Booker covers works like the Sumerian *Epic of Gilgamesh* (which he shows bears striking structural similarities to the James Bond film *Dr No*); fairytales such as "Little Red Riding Hood," "Jack and the Beanstalk," and "Hansel and Gretel"; myths like Theseus and the Minotaur and Saint George and the Dragon; and literary works like *Beowulf*, Bram Stoker's *Dracula*, and H. G. Wells's *The War of the Worlds*. The essence of this plot concerns some powerful embodiment of evil (animal or human) threatening destruction, sometimes to a whole community. It is confronted by a hero, often armed with magical weapons and usually in some lair or some other deep and enclosed place, where battle ensues, so that, against all the odds and often in a surprising escape from death, the hero wins and slays the monster, thus liberating his or her people from the threat hanging over their survival.[15] Booker himself mentions David and Goliath as an example of this plot.[16]

I will return to a further consideration of these cross-cultural literary structures in the conclusion to this chapter. The primary task, however, is to undertake an examination of the narrative of David and Goliath within its ancient context, beginning with the feature of the greatest relevance (challenge-and-response in a group-oriented culture) and return to other significant contextual aspects necessary to appreciate the longer version of the story preserved in Hebrew

14. See Couffignal, "David et Goliath."

15. See Booker, *Seven Basic Plots*, 21–29, especially 23.

16. Ibid, 22–23, 220.

Scripture (family conflict and the dishonorable role of the shepherd) at the appropriate point in the discussion.

CONTEXTUAL FEATURE 1: CHALLENGE-AND-RESPONSE IN A GROUP-ORIENTED CULTURE

The principal contextual feature that helps us to understand the narrative of David and Goliath is the pattern of challenge-and-response, as explained in detail in chapter two. Originally observed by Pierre Bourdieu among the Kabyle tribe of North Africa and then modeled by Bruce Malina for use in biblical interpretation,[17] this social dynamic is at home in a culture where people value their honor and take every opportunity to maximize their possession of it at the expense of others, and where its gain or loss affects not just the two persons involved in the interchange but also the groups from which they both come. The David and Goliath narrative is usefully interpreted as such an *agōn*, a contest, but of the type characterized by maximum violence, that of the battle. By situating the contest between David and Goliath within the pattern of challenge-and-response we have an interpretative framework within which to understand how the narrative unfolds much closer to the way an ancient Israelite audience would have understood it than if we rely on taken-for-granted views of social relations formed in North America or northern Europe.

To recapitulate briefly, the process begins with a challenge, which is a claim to enter the social space of another by deed or word, sometimes positive in nature but usually negative. Second, there is an assessment by the person challenged as to whether his or her honor is engaged by the challenge: rough equality of status is needed. The third stage is the receiver's response: an intentional refusal to act (accompanied by disdain or scorn), an acceptance of the challenge manifested in word or action, or a failure to respond, which is likely to produce dishonor. The fourth stage is the public verdict, the determination of who won the exchange, of who gained the honor to be won from the interaction, both in relation to the actual participants and the groups to which they belong. This pattern provides a theoretical framework that allows us to align ourselves with the ancient audience of the story of David and Goliath. It does not add any extra data but allows us to shed modern North Atlantic understand-

17. Bourdieu, "Sentiment of Honour"; Malina, *New Testament World*, 3rd ed., 33–36.

ings of such an exchange and to interpret the existing data in a historically more plausible way, to "draw the lines between the dots" in a manner much closer to how its original audience would have drawn those lines.

The Philistine Challenge to Israel and the Israelite Response

The initial challenge in this narrative was delivered by the Philistines to Israel, from one people to another, when the Philistines gathered their armies for battle at Socoh, which belonged to Judah, one of the Israelite tribes (1 Sam 17:1). This was a negative challenge by deed, the most significant imaginable in this culture, since the Philistines actually entered the physical space of Israel with the intention of reducing them to vassalage (1 Sam 17:9). John Beck, applying a narrative-geographical approach to the text, has recently emphasized the significance of the geographical references in 1 Sam 17:1–4, placing the Philistine army in the eastern portion of the Elah valley, an area with both economic and military importance since it possessed natural resources and also served as a buffer zone between the Philistines and the Israelites.[18] By this invasion the Philistines were imperiling not just the honor of Israel and (as we will see) of Israel's God, but the survival of the people under their own rule. One of the reasons that the Israelites had called on Samuel to anoint a king over them was so that he could lead them in battles (1 Sam 8:20), thus providing the necessary leadership in just such an emergency as that presented by the arrival of the Philistine army at Socoh.

The Philistine challenge required a response, in terms of both Israelite group honor and group survival, and the Israelites duly provided it, with Saul's mustering their army and drawing it up in line of battle against the Philistines (1 Sam 17:2). So far, so good. That this was a confrontation between combatant armies of equal status as required for one of them to win the honor from the exchange emerges in the imagery of the Philistines and Israelites each standing on a mountain on opposites sides of the valley of Elah (1 Sam 17:3).

The Challenge by Goliath

At this point, however, we have a challenge within a challenge, when a giant warrior, Goliath of Gath, emerges from the Philistine ranks of-

---

18. Beck, "David and Goliath," 324–26.

fering single combat against an Israelite, with the fate of the battle to
depend on the outcome: either the Philistines will become servants of
the Israelites or vice versa (1 Sam 17:4–10). It is important to note, even
if most commentators do not, that such a combat indicates a strongly
group-oriented culture, where the triumph or failure of a group could
be allowed to turn on the performance of one of its members. Just as a
family could be honored or disgraced by the actions of one member, so it
was considered appropriate, in certain circumstances, for a whole people
to rise or fall depending on the outcome of a contest involving just one
of its representatives. There are many examples of *monomachia* ("single combat") known from various parts of the ancient Mediterranean
(including a large number from Republican Rome), both in historical
and literary texts. Occasionally, as with David and Goliath, they were
intended to decide the issue between the two armies,[19] while in most
other instances they were occasions where, although this result would
not ensue, individual and group honor was put on the line. So it was
with the combat between Hector and Ajax in the *Iliad*, book 7.[20]

We must suppose that Goliath has sought and obtained authoriza-
tion from the Philistine commanders to make the offer he does, since
he thus puts at hazard the freedom of his people, just as David will later
seek such permission from Saul to fight Goliath (1 Sam 17:32–37). In
Republican Rome (even though the fate of battles was not allowed to
turn on the result of such a contest) any soldier who broke ranks to fight
an enemy needed the prior permission of his commanding officer and
risked execution if he did not have it.[21]

Before considering the details of Goliath's challenge, we should
dwell for a moment, as the original audience of this narrative most certainly did, on how Goliath is described. First of all, he is said to be six
cubits and a span in height (1 Sam 17:4). On the basis that a cubit is

19. Another example, according to Hoffner, occurs in the Hittite text, *The Apology
of Hattusilis III* (see "Hittite Analogue").

20. I have recently considered the question of *monomachia* in the ancient
Mediterranean with assistance from cultural anthropology (Esler, "*Monomachia*").

21. Two Romans who did seek such permission were Titius Manlius, to fight a Gaul
in the 360s BCE (Livy 7.9.7—10.14), and Claudius Asellus in 215 BCE (Livy 23.47.1).
Two Romans who failed to get the requisite consent and were then executed (even
though their fathers were in command of the army and ordered the execution) were
A. Postumius Tubertus in 431 BCE (Diodorus Siculus 12.64) and the son of T. Manlius
Torquatus in 340 BCE (Livy 8.7).

eighteen inches and a span nine inches, this equates to nine feet and nine inches.[22] In many other versions, including the Old Greek and 4QSamᵃ, Goliath's height is given as four cubits and a span, equating to six feet and nine inches. J. Daniel Hays has recently argued for the smaller height being the original and better reading.[23] In spite of criticism from Clyde Billingham,[24] Hays is probably correct, both by virtue of his analysis of the manuscript tradition and because he has shown how a scribal error could have led to "six" being read for "four" in v. 4.[25] Alternatively, the reading in the Masoretic Text makes good sense as a subsequent exaggeration of the original figure aimed at magnifying the honor of David and his God when the Philistine is ultimately defeated. This could either be an independent alteration to an earlier Hebrew text, or it could have been introduced at the same stage as the additions to be discussed below. Nevertheless, not a great deal turns on the correct reading since at a time when, according to Victor Matthews,[26] the average height of male adults in Israel was about five feet, Goliath would have been a giant of a man on either possibility.

As to the details of Goliath's arms and armor, he wore a bronze helmet, a bronze coat of mail weighing 5000 shekels, or about 126 pounds,[27] and bronze greaves.[28] He had a bronze sword slung between his shoulders,[29] and a huge spear with a shaft like a weaver's beam and an iron head weighing 600 shekels of iron, or about 15 pounds (his sword is also mentioned at 1 Sam 17:45 and 51).[30] He has a shield bearer

---

22. McCarter, *I Samuel*, 291. It is, however, wrong to regard these feet and inch equivalents to cubits and spans as invariable in ancient Israel (Billingham, "Goliath").

23. Hays, "Reconsidering."

24. Billingham, "Goliath," to whom Hays has replied ("Height of Goliath").

25. Hays "Reconsidering," 706.

26. Matthews, *Manners and Customs*, 3.

27. McCarter, *I Samuel*, 292.

28. This is the only place in the Old Testament where greaves are mentioned, although they were commonplace around the Aegean, so their mention may indicate an awareness of Greek warfare—see Yadin, "Goliath's Armor"; and Bodner, *1 Samuel*, 178.

29. The Hebrew word for "sword" is *kidon*, which McCarter explains was curved, hence "scimitar" (*I Samuel*, 292). Some critics interpret the word to mean a javelin, but it would be odd if in enumerating Goliath's armor and weaponry the author failed to mention the very weapon that David would later use to decapitate the Philistine. Goliath's sword is also mentioned later in the account (1 Sam 17:45, 51).

30. McCarter, *I Samuel*, 293.

carrying his shield before him (1 Sam 17:5–7). The reference to iron is significant, because at this time the Philistines enjoyed a monopoly in the production of this metal, so that they had a military advantage over the Israelites, who were reliant on the softer bronze.

Goliath's address to Israel plunges us straight into the dynamic of challenge-and-response: "Why have you come out to draw up for battle? Am I not a Philistine, and are you not servants of Saul? Choose a man (*'iš*) for yourselves, and let him come down to me" (1 Sam 17:8: RSV). This statement constitutes an unambiguous challenge. Goliath is seeking a worthy opponent, an *'iš*, which (like the Latin *vir*) here means a man in the sense of a warrior, someone at least roughly equal to him in status, even if it is unlikely that the Israelites will be able to proffer anyone who matches him in physique, armor or weaponry. Having said this, Goliath has put Israel's honor on the line; the model suggests (and the subsequent course of the narrative confirms) that Israel must either respond with a warrior to fight Goliath or be shamed.

In the (earlier) Greek version, there is nothing particularly offensive in Goliath's words themselves. Goliath asks the Israelites, in a fairly neutral way, if they are not "Hebrews of Saul." The Hebrew version is different, since it sharpens the edge of the challenge by having Goliath ask if they are not servants (*'ebadim*) of Saul. It is probable that underlying these two variants is confusion between the Hebrew words *'ebed* ("servant") and *'ibri* ("Hebrew"), which have the first two consonants in common and have as their third consonant, respectively, the easily confused *dalet* and *resh*. Nevertheless, I am seeking to interpret the narratives as we have them, and the existence of "servants" in the Masoretic Text rather than "Hebrews" greatly sharpens the insult of the challenge. For Samuel had warned Israel when they asked for a king that he would tax and oppress them (1 Sam 8:10–18), thus reducing them to the condition of servants (*'ebadim*; 1 Sam 8:17), but they did not listen. They said they wanted to be like other nations, who had kings to fight their battles (1 Sam 8:20). Ironically, however, their most dangerous neighbors, the Philistines, did not have kings. The Philistines had an oligarchic, not a monarchical, system of political organization, so that they were an exception among the nations having kings referred to in 1 Sam 8:5. They seem to have been led by a military aristocracy consisting of the individual rulers, or governors, of each of their towns.[31] For this reason Goliath is able to reproach the Israelites with their servile status.

Having proposed that the outcome of their contest determine that of the battle (1 Sam 17:9), Goliath continues: "Today I have challenged the ranks of Israel. Give me a man and we will fight one another" (1 Sam 17:10). The word I have translated here as "I have challenged" is *haraf*, a verb that occurs thirty-nine times in the Hebrew Bible, mostly as a piel (as here), but on four occasions as a qal. It is regularly translated in the LXX by *oneidizein*, for example in 1 Sam 17:10, 36, and 45. While Liddel, Scott, and Jones give "reproach" as the core meaning of this word,[32] in many of the instances they cite there is a strong dimension of dishonor. In translating *haraf* as "challenged," I am using "challenge" in the sense set out above for this culture, where the very fact of the challenge produces dishonor. The related noun *herepah*, which appears at 1 Sam 17:26, carries the sense of the "disgrace" that results when nothing is done speedily to rectify the initial insult.

In his detailed discussion of *haraf*, E. Kutsch prefers to see its core meanings as "to abuse (verbally)," "to blaspheme," and "to scoff," although he does note that Goliath "defies" the ranks of Israel by challenging them to send forth a representative to engage in single combat.[33] When one considers the various instances of this word in the Hebrew Bible, however, it seems necessary to pay more attention than Kutsch does to the use of *haraf* in relation to the act of challenging someone, itself as insulting as a slap on the face, that is, an invasion of someone's social space—which calls for an appropriate response. Thus Kutsch, although he notes that if "the subject of the taunts is mightier, they incite him to action; he will take vengeance on those who would humiliate him; he will punish them,"[34] this view only covers one of three possible situations, namely, where a challenger is lower down the social scale than the person "challenged." Kutsch omits the other two cases: first, where challenger and challenged are roughly equal in status and strength, and, secondly, where the challenger is (at least superficially) stronger than the challenged.

31. Bright, *A History of Israel*, 185.
32. Liddel et al., *Greek-English Lexicon*, 1230.
33. Kutsch. "*hrf*," 211–12.
34. Ibid., 212.

The type of challenge Kutsch refers to is present in the story of Sennacherib's ill-fated challenge to Yahweh in 2 Chronicles 32, which was discussed in chapter 2. The word appears in 2 Chr 32:17, but also occurs a further seven times in the other versions of these events in 2 Kings 19 (vv. 4, 16, 22, and 23) and in the matching passage in Isaiah 37 (vv. 4, 17, and 24). Yet there are many other examples of the word where it has the sense of a "challenge" to God, or at least impudence or breach of a duty to him of a type he will punish, even though it cannot be said that his honor is on the line: Pss 74:10, 18; 79:12; 89:51; Isa 65:7. The second category, consisting of challenges, involving participants who are roughly equal in status, is also well represented: Pss 42:11; 44:17; 55:12–13; Zeph 2:8, 10 (where the issue of social equality is raised); Prov 14:21 and Neh 6:13. In the third category we should perhaps include the five instances of the verb in the narrative of David and Goliath (1 Sam 17:10, 25, 26, 36, and 45) and the three other cases in other passages referring to a challenge by a giant of Gath (2 Sam 21:21; 1 Chr 20:7) or the Philistines (2 Sam 23:9). For although the challenge uttered by Goliath is initially aimed at securing a worthy and therefore roughly equal opponent, it is accepted by someone who, at least to the audience and certainly to Goliath, is very much inferior to the challenger. The evidence just cited indicates the extent to which the use of *haraf* five times in 1 Samuel 17 very explicitly in the context of a challenge is in accordance with the wider patterns of usage of this verb in the Hebrew Bible.

The Israelite Response to Goliath's Challenge

The response of the Israelites to this challenge is grossly dishonorable. We do not find brave Israelites jostling to fight Goliath; instead, the text explains that "When Saul and all Israel heard these words of the Philistine, they were dismayed and greatly afraid" (1 Sam 17:11, RSV). A failure of courage in the face of such a challenge brings their manliness into question. Goliath has asked for an *'iš*, a man to fight with him, yet none such exists in Israel, not Saul their king nor anyone else in the Israelite army. There is an instructive comparison to this in Book 7 of the *Iliad*. When none of the Greeks is willing to accept Hector's challenge to combat, Menelaus attempts to do so, accusing them of being Greek women not Greek men (v. 96). Cowardly failure to accept the challenge means their very manhood is in doubt. When Agamemnon restrains Menelaus from fighting Hector, old Nestor shames the Greeks into action by saying if he was young he would fight Hector, since he once killed a giant of a man himself. Yet there is, at least initially, no one in Saul's army like Menelaus or Nestor who is willing to face Goliath. Until an Israelite can be found who will do so, Israel's honor is besmirched.

It is worth saying a little more about Saul, specifically mentioned in v. 11, in addition to all Israel as being dismayed and greatly afraid. J. Daniel Hays has astutely pointed to the important role of Saul in this narrative (it is not just about David and Goliath) and has highlighted two factors that mean the king's failure to fight Goliath represents a far greater dereliction of courage on Saul's part than for the members of his army.[35] First, when Saul is introduced we are told that he is a head taller than anyone else in Israel. This was clearly a useful factor in the man to be king, who was to "go out before us and fight our battles" (1 Sam 8:20); yet in spite of this unique height advantage, when faced with the giant Goliath Saul cowers in the camp like the rest of Israel. Second, Saul has armor, in the form of a bronze helmet and a coat of mail (1 Sam 17:38). Even if the other Israelite soldiers did not have such armor (and most of them could not have the resources to acquire it), Saul their king did. Yet still his courage deserts him.[36]

Precisely at this point in the Old Greek version, David tells Saul he is willing to fight Goliath (that is, the Old Greek jumps straight from v. 11 to v. 32.), so the honor of Israel and Saul is only under a shadow for a brief time. One could imagine king and people being nonplussed by Goliath but perhaps capable of summoning their courage fairly soon after the initial shock, a development rendered unnecessary by David's speedy intervention. The Hebrew text, on the other hand, is very different. It here inserts a passage fully twenty verses long, occupying vv. 12–31, before we reach David's offer to fight Goliath in v. 32, a passage that includes the remarkable feature that Goliath went on repeating his challenge—enacting, in effect, a ritual of status degradation on Israel and on Israel's king—for forty days (1 Sam 17:16). This period entirely excludes the possibility that Saul or one of his soldiers might have found the courage to fight Goliath in due time. The Hebrew version makes

35. Hays, "Reconsidering," 710–12.

36. For another approach to the narrative of David and Goliath that sees this as an antimonarchical text, see Jobling "David and the Philistines."

clear that this was simply never going to happen. It presents their honor as utterly tarnished.

So let us now turn our attention to the material in 1 Sam 17:12–31, which describes what happens when Jesse his father sends David with provisions to his three brothers who are in Saul's army facing the Philistines. In line with our general approach in this volume we will leave to others discussion of the sources of this passage, focusing instead on the question of its function within the narrative of David and Goliath as the Hebrew text presents it. What would ancient Israelite readers or listeners have made of it? What is its literary function within the story and within the wider context of ancient Israelite culture that we must always bear in mind if we are to arrive at a socially appropriate interpretation of how the story would have worked for its original audience? What would it have told them about the God they worshiped? But before considering the text we need to consider further details of the context.

CONTEXTUAL FEATURES 2 AND 3: CONFLICT IN FAMILIES AND THE DISHONORABLE ROLE OF SHEPHERD

Family Conflict

We noted in chapter 2 that families possess a collective honor rating as far as non-kin were concerned, so that honor enjoyed or shame suffered by one family member affects all. Nevertheless, tensions and disputes still arise within families. As already noted, the fact that parental regard is understood as finite makes sibling rivalries likely. J. K. Campbell nicely elucidates some of the possibilities when, writing of the Sarakatsani, a tribe of transhumant shepherds in Greece, he notes that "precisely because siblings are conceived by one another and by outsiders as occupying in many respects similar status roles, their performances may be compared and evaluated, and the resulting rivalry may lead to envy, and at a further remove, to open enmity."[37] If a brother has the opportunity of winning the applause of outsiders or some other benefit from them, even though at his brother's expense, he may be very tempted to take the opportunity. George Foster cites the example of a Mexican peasant who did not involve his brother in an invitation to Foster's house because he was experiencing a coveted "good" and did not want to dilute the satisfaction he was experiencing by sharing

37. Campbell, *Honour, Family and Patronage*, 174.

it with another, even with his own brother.[38] Campbell notes that the "danger is greatest in situations where individual skills or qualities, for instance abilities as a shepherd or as a dancer, the proof of courage or the possession of a fine physique, may become the basis for judging differences between brothers."[39]

The possibility for disputes among brothers is lessened by auto-matically allocating certain rights depending on priority of birth order. We have already noted in chapter 2, accepting the argument of Frederick Greenspahn,[40] that primogeniture, in the sense that the eldest son in-herits the whole estate, was not a feature of Israelite inheritance law, since each son received a share of the estate. Nevertheless, there was a presumption that seniority would prevail in many areas.[41] Among the Sarakatsani the eldest brother normally becomes head of the family after the death or retirement of the father, and provision is likely to be made that siblings of the same sex will marry strictly in order of seniority.[42] The latter phenomenon is visible in Genesis 38, when Judah first has Er, his oldest son, and then (on Er's death) Onan marry Tamar, and (falsely) undertakes that his youngest son, Shelah, will marry her in due course.

It follows, however, that where such rules exist, their abrogation in favor of younger siblings, which turns out to be a common pattern in the Old Testament, as Frederick Greenspahn has pointed out,[43] will cause disputes. Similarly, anything that upsets the usual order of seniority and hence precedence within a family will lead to tension. A good example from the Old Testament is found in the story of Joseph in Genesis 37. Not only did Jacob love Joseph, a son of his old age, most, thus giving Joseph more than his fair share of a limited good and thereby arousing the hatred of his brothers (Gen 37:3–4), but Joseph had dreams inti-mating his superiority over them, dreams that annoyed even his father and made his brothers envy and hate him all the more (Gen 37:5–11). Cultural features like these must be taken into account in interpreting the interaction between David and his brothers in 1 Samuel 17, as we will see below.

38. Foster, "Peasant Society," 307.
39. Campbell, *Honour, Family and Patronage*, 174.
40. Greenspahn, *When Brothers Dwell Together*, 36–59.
41. Ibid, 15.
42. Campbell, *Honour, Family and Patronage*, 176.
43. Greenspahn, *When Brothers Dwell Together*.

Nevertheless, we must also note that there are many instances in the Old Testament of younger brothers being favored by God or becoming preeminent over their older siblings, such as with Abel over Cain (Genesis 4), Isaac over Ishmael (Genesis 21), Jacob over Esau (Genesis 25–27), Perez over Zerah (Genesis 38), Ephraim over Manasseh (Genesis 48), and, particularly relevant here, David over his elder brothers and Solomon over his. That these elevations represent a divergence from the usual social norm of priority to the firstborn is shown by the way that special explanations are usually given in the text explaining how this unexpected result could occur.[44] Writing independently of one another in the 1990s Everett Fox and Frederick Greenspahn offered explanations for this biblical pattern of the firstborn being passed over in favor of his younger brother.[45] Much can be said for Everett Fox's suggestion that this pattern reflects the larger experience of Israel as a small and comparatively young people facing larger, more powerful and older neighbors and yet continually having God's support in times of trouble.[46] Israel's checkered history may well have prompted a sense of anxiety or even mystery about God's choice of them as his people.[47] While Fox identifies two historical periods when this experience would have been particular apposite—during the time of the exile in the sixth century BCE or, somewhat earlier, after the fall of the united monarchy and the rise of Assyria in the eighth century BCE—it is not necessary to reach a decided view on this point to see the power behind the idea of relating the motif of the preeminent younger son to the changing historical fate of Israel.

Dishonor and the Shepherd

As I discussed in chapter 2, honor may be acquired by one's one effort or ascribed, that is enjoyed simply by virtue of who one is, because of one's family, birthplace, position, or occupation. The occupation relevant to what follows is that of shepherd. Being a shepherd in Palestine is, and always has been, a hard life, since it means continually moving the flocks

44. Ibid, 13.

45. Fox, "Stalking the Younger Brother"; and Greenspahn, *When Brothers Dwell Together*.

46. Fox, "Stalking the Younger Brother," esp. 59–67.

47. Ibid, 60.

of sheep and goats about during the dry summer in search of available grass and thus often spending time in areas a long way from home.[48] It also involves sleeping outside at night with one's flocks,[49] especially to protect them against dangerous wild animals and thieves, while the other members of the family are sleeping far more comfortably inside a house. Since shepherding carried these disadvantages, we would expect it to be allocated to junior siblings in the family, while the father and senior siblings attended to crop raising closer to home, where they could enjoy the domestic comforts. This is what we find in Gen 4:1–2, where the older brother, Cain, works the land and the younger brother, Abel, tends the flocks. Shimoff presents altogether too rosy a view of shepherding in the Patriarchal period,[50] missing, for example, the fact that although it was Abel's sacrifice that God accepted, Abel (as younger brother) had the worse job. Vancil also overlooks the negative dimensions to being a shepherd in the Old Testament.[51]

In rabbinic tradition shepherding features among the despised occupations which involved thieving and cheating, presumably because the independence of shepherds, especially during the summer when they were often on the move with little supervision, offered them numerous opportunities for theft,[52] either by taking objects or grazing their flocks on other people's land. A shepherd who left his women at home with no adult male to protect them could also be regarded as dishonorable for that reason.[53] One rabbi actually asked in amazement how God could be called "my shepherd" in Psalm 23 when shepherds were so despicable.[54] Given the way such attitudes are rooted in the cultural features of Mediterranean society in existence long before the rabbis, there is no reason why we should not assume their existence at the earliest stages of Israelite tradition. These attitudes toward shepherds and shepherding

48. Jeremias, "*Poimen*," 486.

49. See Luke 2:8 for this phenomenon, which has persisted into contemporary Palestine, as seen in a recent account of a day in the life of Ahmed Abyyiat, a shepherd outside Bethlehem (see Dunn, "Ahmed Abyyiat").

50. Shimoff "Shepherds."

51. Vancil, "Sheep, Shepherd," 1189–90.

52. Jeremias, "*Poimen*," 488–89.

53. Malina and Rohrbaugh, *Social-Science Commentary*, 232.

54. R. Jose ben Chanina (c. 270 CE) in Midr. Ps. 23 §2, cited by Jeremias, "*Poimen*," 489.

form part of the context within which David would have been perceived by an ancient Israelite audience.

With these features of the cultural context in mind (conflict among brothers and the dishonorable character of shepherding) we may now proceed to read the story of David and Goliath in a manner closer to that of an ancient Israelite. But before we proceed to 1 Samuel 17 it is necessary to consider certain events in the preceding chapter that will weigh heavily on what transpires when David arrives at the Israelite camp.

THE ANOINTING OF DAVID IN 1 SAMUEL 16:1–13

Both these contextual elements (family conflict and the dishonor attached to being a shepherd) come into play in the story of David shortly before his arrival at the Israelite army, in the account of his anointing by Samuel in 1 Sam 16:1–13. The Lord tells Samuel that he has rejected Saul as king of Israel and that he is sending Samuel to Jesse the Bethlehemite, from whose sons he has provided for himself a king (1 Sam 16:1). Since Samuel is concerned that Saul will kill him if finds out what he is up to, the Lord suggests he conduct a sacrifice as a ruse, and invite Jesse (with his sons) along to it (1 Sam 16:2–5). This necessarily implies that when Samuel comes to the actual anointing, he does not tell Jesse and his sons its precise purpose as relating to the kingship, even if he does reveal that it involves selection by God (1 Sam 16:10). In addition, just to be anointed by so great a prophet was a huge honor, a very pure form of ascribed honor in fact, whatever it meant. Since it will soon become apparent that Samuel only has one anointing to bestow, this whole process is a finite-sum game, with the winner to take all. This is one of those exceptions to the limited good world of peasant, of the sort described by George Foster,[55] where an outside intervention will suddenly, unexpectedly and legitimately bring about an accretion of honor for a particular individual. It is also one of those dangerous situations mentioned by Campbell where an attribute or quality possessed by one brother may become the basis for judging between them.

Imagine the scene, therefore, when Jesse first presents Eliab, his eldest son (he is specified as the first-born in 1 Sam 17:13), to Samuel (1 Sam 16:6). The prevailing cultural norms suggested that, as the eldest, Eliab was the one likely to be chosen by Samuel. Jesse and Eliab must

---

55. Foster, "Peasant Society," 315–16.

have thought so, and so did Samuel, since the Lord specifically tells him to disregard Eliab's appearance and height (and he scores strongly on both counts), for the Lord does not judge by external appearance but looks into the heart (1 Sam 16:7). So Samuel considers Eliab, listening to what the Lord is telling him, and then communicates in some way (by word or gesture) to Eliab and his father that he is not the one. This would have been deeply humiliating to Eliab: was he not the eldest son, his father's firstborn? How could he be rejected? Perhaps these feelings would have been mitigated somewhat when Samuel also failed to anoint his six brothers who were present, starting with Abinadab and Shammah, Jesse's second and third sons (1 Sam 17:13), as Jesse made them pass before Samuel one at a time (1 Sam 16:8–10). If none was to be anointed, Eliab's distress would have been lessened or removed entirely, since there would be no one among the seven brothers, living at home and with roughly similar roles, whom he could thenceforward regard as a rival who had bested him on the occasion of the anointing by Samuel, and envy in consequence, envy that might have led to open conflict at some stage. But there is an eighth brother, the youngest and therefore (especially to Eliab) the most insignificant, who is off working as a shepherd, a lowly role that befits his position at the bottom of the sibling hierarchy. Samuel calls for him, and he is brought in, "ruddy" ('*admoni*), with "beautiful eyes ('*im yepheh 'eynayim*)" and "good to look at (*tob ro'i*)" (1 Sam 16:11–12). Greenspahn, in responding to the puzzlement that many commentators express at a favorable description of David's physical appearance coming so soon after a statement that he did not look like a king, has accurately noted that David is described in terms normally associated with female beauty.[56] Thus, being "good" (*tob*) or "beautiful" (*yepheh*) in appearance is predicated of Sarah (Gen 12:11), Rebecca (Gen 24:16 and 26:7), Rachel (Gen 29:17), Abigail (1 Sam 25:3), Bathsheba (2 Sam 11:2), Tamar (2 Sam 14:27), and Esther (Esther 1:11). Also the word '*admoni* is applied to the newly born infant Esau in Gen 25:25), where the usual translation "ruddy" should probably be "pink," or at least a color associated with the skin of a new baby. While we will return to this description in discussing Goliath's response to David, one can imagine the look of disdain on the faces of his brothers as David is presented to Samuel looking, in fact, like a pretty girl. As Walter Brueggemann has rightly observed, "The young David is one

---

56. Greenspahn, *When Brothers Dwell Together*, 87.

the marginal people. He is uncredentialed and has no social claim to make."[57] "How could it be him?", David's seven brothers must have been asking themselves. Yet David is indeed the Lord's choice, and Samuel takes the horn of oil and anoints him "in the midst of his brothers" (1 Sam 16:13). For Eliab, Abinadab, Shammah and the other four unnamed brothers, there is no escape: David's status elevation occurs right in their midst, an elevation indicated not only by the anointing with oil but by a onrush of the Spirit of the Lord upon him, the arrival of which was possibly accompanied by ecstatic phenomena.[58] He who was least among them has now been singled out for special honor by God himself. If Joseph's brothers were envious of him merely because he had a dream of being their superior (Gen 37:11), what pitch of envy and dislike must David's brothers have felt for him as a result of his anointing by Samuel and receipt of the Spirit!

One of the problems with the expanded Masoretic Text version of the events in 1 Samuel 17 is that the text provides information about David in a way that may seem to sit a little uneasily with the fact that we already know a great deal about him, especially this anointing by Samuel (as king over Israel) in 1 Sam 16:1–13 and the fact that Saul has already engaged him as his armor bearer and to play the lyre to him when he is suffering from one of his bouts of mental disturbance in 1 Sam 16:14–23 (as discussed in chapter 5 in this volume). Thus David is introduced in 1 Sam 17:12 in a fashion typical for this culture—by situating individuals with respect to significant groups—as "the son an Ephrathite of Bethlehem in Judah, named Jesse" (1 Sam 17:12), a description that might suggest we had not hitherto heard of him. So we learn David's father, hence family, his district (Ephrath), town (Bethlehem), and tribe (Judah). For ancient Mediterranean readers, who judged people more by external and stereotypical features than we do,[59] especially those related to the groups to which the person in question belonged, these details supplied

---

57. Brueggemann, *First and Second Samuel*, 123–24.

58. First Samuel has earlier described how the Spirit of the Lord "rushed upon" (*ṣalaḥ 'al*) Saul a little after his anointing by Samuel when he met a band of prophets and he prophesied or went into an ecstatic trance among them (1 Sam 10:6, 10); and the same expression, "come mightily upon" (*ṣalaḥ 'al*) is used in relation to the Spirit's impact on David in 1 Sam 16:13.

59. See Malina, *New Testament World*, 3rd ed., 58–67; Malina and Neyrey, *Portraits of Paul*, 10–18.

essential information for "knowing" David, that is for being able to place him within an established social framework. We next learn (in the same verse) that Jesse had eight sons, and that he was already old. This feature would have suggested to an Israelite audience that Jesse was approaching death, at which time the oldest son would assume the mantle of authority in the family. Jesse's three eldest sons had followed Saul (1 Sam 17:13–14), while David, the youngest son, "went back and forth from Saul to feed his father's sheep at Bethlehem" (1 Sam 17:15, RSV).

Some existing interpretation regards 1 Sam 17:15 as a clumsy harmonizing verse in the narrative,[60] and certainly the manner in which it connects David with both the domestic scene (which is all important in the interpretation of vv. 12–31) and Saul's army is rather artificial. Nevertheless, it still serves two important literary functions. First, it represents the vital link that relates the activities of David in 1 Samuel 16 and 17, for otherwise the only reason that David would have been going to Saul was to serve as his armor bearer and to play the lyre to him when we was disturbed by an evil spirit as recounted in 1 Sam 16:14–23. This link suggests that the original audience of this narrative was also meant to recall that they have already encountered Eliab, Abinadab, and Shammah before: when Samuel rejected each of them in turn, starting with Eliab, as the son of Jesse whom the Lord wanted to anoint as king over Israel (1 Sam 16:6–9). Second, the link between chapters 16 and 17 would certainly have reminded an ancient audience that things were not proceeding in the usual way in the family of Jesse. Within the customs of ancient Israelite society David, as the youngest son at the end of a long line of sons with Eliab at their head, could not have expected any preeminence in the house of Jesse or among Israel at large.[61] As we have seen, the responsibility he had been allotted (of shepherd) was a difficult and dishonorable one. Yet this narrative is unfolding in a larger framework in which shortly before the events being described here David has been anointed by Samuel as king of Israel (1 Sam 16:1–13) and has been with more ascribed honor by becoming lyre-player and armor-bearer for Saul (1 Sam 16:14–23)! The social anomaly is visible here in the juxtaposition of David's two roles: the youngest son with the worst job at home also has important duties in the service of the king, no less. Plainly, David has already been selected for great things and there may be more surprises

60. Klein, *1 Samuel*, 177.

61. See Greenspahn, *When Brothers Dwell Together*.

in store! The reader is being warned to expect further subversion of customary familial patterns. As Keith Bodner has noted, David is similar to one of the poor and the needy whom Hannah had sung would be lifted up to sit with princes (1 Sam 2:8).[62] The next verse (1 Sam 17:16), which specifies that Goliath came out, challenging Israel morning and evening, for forty days draws the reader's attention to the likely arena for any action by David, as well as underlining how grossly Israel is shamed by a challenge not taken up for such a long period. The flow of the narrative in the Hebrew version, moreover, demands that David not hear Goliath's words until the end of this period. David is too busy shuttling backwards and forwards between Saul and his sheep.

DAVID VISITS THE ISRAELITE CAMP

At this point Jesse tells his son to take supplies to his brothers and their commander at the front and to bring back news of them, thus sharply exposing his paternal care for his three oldest sons who are on the brink of battle with a formidable enemy (1 Sam 17:17–19). Jesse's gift to his sons' commander (of ten cheeses) is probably directed to having the commander not order them to do anything too conspicuously dangerous. This reason for getting David to the front on this occasion may have been inspired by the circumstance that in the original and shorter version (now represented by the Old Greek) David had first come to Saul's camp bearing bread, wine and a kid for the king (1 Sam. 16.20). The itemized description of the supplies that Jesse tells David to bring to his brothers and their commanding officer—parched grain, bread and goats' cheeses—reveals how intimately David is insinuated into the daily routines of domestic life and paints a scene in relation to which his subsequent elevation will be all the more spectacular.

The next morning David, an obedient son, sets off to do as his father has directed, but also shows a sense of responsibility by delegating someone else to look after the sheep, even though his father had said nothing of this (1 Sam 17:20). On arriving at the camp, he leaves the provisions with the quartermaster and, showing the excitement of youth toward war, runs to his brothers in the ranks (1 Sam 17:21–22). While he is talking to them, Goliath repeats his challenge, and David hears him (1 Sam 17:23). This is apparently the first time David has witnessed

62. Bodner, 1 Samuel, 171.

Goliath's challenge. There is no necessary inconsistency in the narrative here, because on the previous occasions when David visited Saul it is possible that the Philistines had not invaded, meaning that Saul was probably at his hometown of Gibeah in Benjamin (1 Sam 9:1; 10:26).

The shame of Israel is compounded when the Philistine's words produce flight and fear among "every man" (*'iš*), meaning every warrior, of Israel (1 Sam 17:24), a description that must include Saul himself. This note establishes the context within which David will act; while all the warriors of Israel may tremble with fear, one youth is about to act courageously. An Israelite tells David that Goliath is coming up to challenge (*leharef*) Israel and that the king will reward whoever kills the Philistine with riches, presumably from the taxes and levies Israelites became subject to when they made Saul king, the gift of his daughter, and freedom for his father's house (1 Sam 17:25).

David is greatly affronted by Goliath and asks, "What shall be done for the man who kills this Philistine, and takes away the reproach (*herepah*) from Israel? For who is this uncircumcised Philistine that he should challenge (*haraf*) the armies of the living God?" (1 Sam 17:26, RSV).

This is the first time that God has been mentioned in 1 Samuel 17, and it is significant that it is David who mentions God.[63] It is clear that David sees Goliath's insult extending from the armies of Israel to the God to whom those armies belong. David is sensitive to God's honor in a way the rest of Israel is not; or, to express this more traditionally, he understands the theological dimensions of what is happening. David comes across as someone strongly moved by love for and loyalty to his God, the God of Israel, in a way that is unique among all the Israelites encamped with Saul. Is it so surprising then, that it was David whom the Lord instructed Samuel to anoint? That some aspect of David's character had attracted God's attention?[64] In so directing Samuel, God had ignored the external appearance of David and looked into his heart (1 Sam 16:7). We now see what strong allegiance to God that heart contained. At the same time, Samuel had previously told Saul that his kingdom would not

63. Campbell (*1 Samuel*, 173) has also noticed that David is sensitive to the theological dimension in a way the other Israelites are not.

64. This would make David an exception to the fact, as Fox ("Stalking the Younger Brother," 60) points out: "Younger brothers do not appear to be selected for their merit, at least initially."

continue and that God had sought out a man "after his own heart" to be prince over this people (1 Sam 13:14). Keith Bodner has recently sought to play down the clear reference to David here as the person whom God regards as "after his own heart" because of certain qualities David possessed by suggesting (in line with other commentators, such as John Goldingay) that the burden of the expression is actually God's freedom in matters of election.[65] Yet two factors make this view ring somewhat hollow: first, David does indeed have special qualities that would have made him attractive to God (he alone sees Goliath's challenge as an insult to the living God); and, second, we have the use of "heart" by God in connection with David only three chapters after 1 Sam 13:14, in 1 Sam 16:7, so that the narrator is establishing a link between God's heart and David. David lives in God's heart and God in David's; it is very much a case of *Cor ad cor loquitur* ("Heart speaks to heart"), the motto of Cardinal John Henry Newman.[66]

At this juncture, however, the everyday world of family relationships intrudes upon the action, again setting the scene for what is about to unfold. Eliab (Jesse's oldest son) hears David talking with the men and becomes angry. "Why have you come down?" he asks. "With whom have you left those few sheep in the wilderness? I know your presumption (*zadon*) and the evil of your heart (*ro'a lebabeka*); for you have come down just to see the battle" (1 Sam 17:28).

The most revealing aspect of what Eliab says is his attribution to David of *zadon*, "presumption," "pride," or "arrogance."[67] The word primarily refers to a person going beyond acceptable social limits. There is a cognate verb *zod* or *zid* and a cognate adjective, *zed*. The original meaning of the root in connection with the seething or bubbling up of boiling water,[68] as in Gen 25:28, well conveys the sense of going beyond normal boundaries. In a limited good culture, this meaning fuelled a semantic shift in the direction of pride, impudence and presumptuous-

65. Bodner, *1 Samuel*, 123.

66. The motto of the visit of His Holiness, Pope Benedict XVI, to the UK from the 16th to the 19th of September 2010, culminating in Cardinal Newman's beatification on 19th September in Birmingham, was "Heart speaks unto Heart." The Pope inscribed the words *Cor ad cor loquitur* on a brief memorial of his visit that he left at St Mary's University College, Twickenham, on Friday 17th September 2010.

67. The word appears in ten other places in the Old Testament (Deut 17:12; 18:22; Jer 49:16; 50:31, 32; Prov 11:2; 13:10; 21:24; Ezek 7:10 and Obad 3).

68. Bertram, "*hubris*," 300.

ness. In such a society, moreover, people are all the more sensitive to any transgression of accepted boundaries. Thus the word is used of someone who does not obey a priest (Deut 17:12), of a prophet who says he is speaking in the name of the Lord when he is not (Deut 18:22), of wrongful pride (Jer 50:32) and even, so it seems, of actual aggression (Prov 11:2 and 13:10).[69] When Eliab applies this word to David, therefore, he is suggesting that his youngest brother is someone who wickedly refuses to keep within his station, who will not adhere to his customary role as the youngest and most insignificant son with the lowliest occupation and who therefore represents a threat to the usual order, especially to his brothers in the immediate context of the family. What is a mere shepherd boy doing here at the front, a place only appropriate for the most senior of Jesse's sons? He must be someone with an evil heart. This is a clear example of the notion of limited good being worked out in the sphere of intra-familial relations in the manner already discussed. The attitude taken to Joseph by his brothers when they thought he was getting beyond himself offers a useful comparison (Genesis 37).

At one level, then, Eliab is simply behaving like any elder son in this culture who will soon be taking over the leadership of the family on his father's death and who is ever on the alert to restrain any attempts by a younger sibling to trespass on his prerogatives. That Eliab's remarks are typical of what David has come to expect from his brother is implied in the first part of David's response, "What have I done now?" (1 Sam 17:29). As a contrast to my attempt to situate Eliab's attitude to David within the cultural dynamics of ancient Israel, reference may be had to J. P. Fokkelman's invocation of "psychology from ordinary emotional life" (he does not specify where) to observe how children seek to project their failings onto others as a form of self-protection.[70] It is hard to see what knowledge of this ancient text is gained by laying so modern an interpretation upon it. It is also very likely that there is an additional factor that is derived from the recent history of this family, namely, that Eliab is still smarting from seeing David anointed by Samuel in the presence of all the sons of Jesse (1 Sam 16:13), as discussed above.[71]

---

69. The Septuagint translates the word by *huperēphania* at Deut 17:12, by *asebeia* at Deut 18:22 and by *hubris* at Prov 11:2 and 13:10, where *hubris* means an act that invades the sphere of another to his detriment (Bertram, "*hubris*," 295).

70. Fokkelman, *Narrative Art*, 163.

71. Fokkelman does make a point very similar to this one (*Narrative Art*, 163).

Keith Bodner has recently maintained that it is wrong to take too negative a view of Eliab, since when he says that he knows the evil of David's heart (1 Sam 17:28) he is actually injecting a note of caution about David and foreshadowing flaws in his character that will emerge later, especially in his adultery with Bathsheba and his murder of her husband, Uriah.[72] This view is very difficult to accept. In 1 Sam 16:7 God had told Samuel that he looked into a person's heart. Since he later instructed Samuel to anoint David, it follows that he had looked into the young man's heart and liked what he saw. In spite of the evil that David will much later commit, on no other occasion is he described in 1 Samuel, 2 Samuel, or 1 Kings as having an evil heart.[73] A second problem with Bodner's suggestion is that Eliab's allegation that David has an evil heart is tied to three specific accusations, all of which are false. First, he suggests David has been remiss in his responsibility to look after the family sheep; as we have already been informed, however, David made arrangements for their safety even though his father had not asked him to do so (1 Sam 17:20). Second, Eliab accuses David of presumption, when David is guilty of nothing of the kind: he did not seek anointing by Samuel or the appointment as armor bearer and lyre player to the king. These honors befell him without any presumptuous actions on his part. In truth, Eliab simply cannot abide his youngest brother being preferred in these extraordinary ways. Thirdly, Eliab asserts that David has just come down to see the battle; this also is entirely false, since David is there at his father's command in ways that will help his brothers. Accordingly, it is not possible to take seriously Eliab's suggestion that David has an evil heart when the other three charges that accompany this one are patently untrue.

DAVID, SAUL, AND GOLIATH

Eventually what David has been saying comes to Saul's ears and the king sends for him (1 Sam 17:31). The meeting is rich in irony, since here we have Saul, the one-time anointed of the Lord but now rejected by him (1 Sam 16:1), in conversation with David, the Lord's new anointed. Whereas Saul is failing to do the very thing for which he had been anointed king—to go before Israel and fight its battles (1 Sam 8:20)—that

---

72. Bodner, "Eliab."

73. See Lisowsky, *Konkordanz*, 708–12.

is exactly what David is about to do. Thus David confidently offers to go and fight the Philistine (1 Sam 17:32). The text does not say whether Saul recognized that this was his armor bearer and lyre player before him, but nothing the king says at this point is actually inconsistent with such a recognition (although the case is stronger in the Old Greek version, since. v. 32 is where that text resumes after 1 Sam 17:11, and David's proximity to Saul to fulfill his official duties allows him to speak up so quickly). David's confidence meets Saul's unsurprising response that he is just a youth (*na'ar*), whereas Goliath has been a warrior (literally: "man of war," *'iš-milḥamah*) from the time of his youth (1 Sam 17:33). Has Saul forgotten that he had previously been told that David was "a man of valor" and, in a surprising statement that seems to represent a slip by the author or editor of this passage, "a man of war" (*'iš-milḥamah*; 1 Sam 16:18).[74] Or is the point that Goliath is an experienced warrior whereas David is only now old enough to become a warrior? Because of his youth and inexperience David was an unlikely candidate to be able to respond successfully to Goliath's challenge, and in offering to do so he must have given the appearance of making an honor claim without foundation. The only way David can dislodge such skepticism is to describe his skill in combat against large and fierce beasts, in particular, lions or bears which came to seize his sheep (1 Sam 17:34–35). In similar fashion he would take on and defeat the Philistine, who he said, repeating his earlier statement, "had challenged the armies of the living God" (1 Sam 17:36, RSV). Yet David does not simply attribute his victories over lion and bear to his natural abilities, he also acknowledges that God was with him: "The Lord who delivered me out of the paw of the lion and from the paw of the bear, he will deliver me from the hand of this Philistine" (1 Sam 17:37, RSV). Once again it is David alone among the Israelites who reminds them of the presence of God in human affairs and of his care for his people.

Saul is persuaded by what David tells him and gives him permission to fight Goliath with the words, richly ironic in the extent of their aptness for David (but not for Saul himself): "Go, and the Lord be with you"(1 Sam 17:37). As noted above, however, an ancient audience

---

74. Brueggemann suggests that the courtier's description of David, including as a warrior, represents an "overnomination" for the position of Saul's lyre player, thus indicating that the narrator "is obviously presenting David's credentials for more than court musician" (*First and Second Samuel*, 125–26).

would have probably thought less of Saul, a man taller than any in his army and equipped with armor, for not answering Goliath's challenge himself. That Saul does not fully understand the extent to which the Lord really is with David surfaces in his having David put on his armor, which David, discovering it impedes his progress, eschews in favor of his shepherd's sling (1 Sam 17:38–40). David Halpern has argued that, so equipped, David had, in his nimbleness and agility, a decisive advantage over the very heavily armored Philistine.[75] Yet this rationalizing explanation for David's success is alien to the text itself, since the analogy drawn between Goliath and lions and bears, which are large and can move quickly (lions especially), does not imply that the Philistine was necessarily slow moving.

The story of David and Goliath features something of a deliberate contradiction of the element in "Overcoming the Monster" plots where the hero is provided with superior or even magical means to help him defeat the monster, just as Gilgamesh is provided by armorers with special weapons (a great bow and a huge axe) to kill Humbaba.[76] Here David rejects such assistance in the form of Saul's armor and opts to rely simply on his own sling.

The clash between David and Goliath begins with a verbal exchange; this represents the early stages of the challenge-and-response dynamic that rapidly escalates to violence. Patrick Miller has recognized the extent to which what he calls "verbal feuding" in the Hebrew Bible derives from the role of honor in the culture of ancient Israel.[77] The moment of Goliath's realization that David has come out to fight him is richly illustrative of the honor-and-shame culture in which the contest would be fought. Seeing a youth (na'ar) before him, "pink ('admoni) and beautiful in appearance (yepheh-mar'eh)," "he despised (bazah) him" (v. 42): "Am I a dog that you come to me with sticks?" And the Philistine cursed[78] him by his gods (v. 43, RSV).

---

75. Halpern, David's Secret Demons, 10–13.

76. As noted in Booker, Seven Basic Plots, 21.

77. Miller, "Verbal Feud," in relation to Judg 3:12–30 and chaps. 19–21. It is surprising that in an article published in 1996 that ranges widely and creatively through social-scientific and biblical secondary literature, Miller, even though at one point he discusses "parry" and "riposte" (111–12), has missed both Bourdieu, "The Sentiment of Honour"; and the first edition of Malina's New Testament World, published in 1981.

78. Piel of qalal.

From Goliath's point of view, he is being treated like a dog, a dis-honorable animal. As Firmage has noted, although we today may regard the dog as "man's best friend," in the Bible "the dog is always spoken of in contempt," a contempt partly explicable on the basis of packs of feral dogs roaming the outskirts of towns where refuse was plentiful.[79] Thus Goliath has been denied the opportunity of fighting a worthy opponent from whom honor could be won by victory. The word "despised" expresses Goliath's recognition of the (apparent) difference in military ability be-tween him and David: the frequency with which the Hebrew verb is used with a non-personal object (for example, Gen 25:34; Num 15:31; 2 Sam 6:16; 12:9; Ezek 16:59; Mal 1:6) suggests that that it carries the connota-tion of "hold of little or no account." Challenge-and-response requires reasonable equality between the competitors; someone in a greatly supe-rior position may, as it were, flatten his opponent as one would a fly, but no honor can accrue from such an encounter. The reason for Goliath's contempt is that David, as discussed above, has the complexion and looks of a pretty girl. That is why he cursed David by his gods. In addition, this reference to Goliath's gods (including, no doubt, Dagon, an important Philistine deity,[80] and Baal) reminds the reader of the two dimensions to this combat, the human and the divine, with David's God and Goliath's gods in view, and with their honor on the line too.

Goliath then transits from curse to threat: "Come to me, and I will give your flesh to the birds of the air and to the beasts of the field" (v. 44, RSV). This was probably a worse fate than Goliath would have meted out to a worthy opponent, in that it means the corpse could never be buried (and was thus worse than what the Philistines did later to the bodies of Saul and his three sons [1 Sam 31:8–13]). The extremity of what he has in mind for David's body registers his disgust at the prospect of killing a boy armed only with a sling.

Goliath's words constitute a negative verbal challenge, and David provides a lengthy riposte in which he outdoes his experienced oppo-nent (vv. 45–47), thus confirming the earlier description of David as "intelligent with words" (*nebon dabar*; 1 Sam 16:18). Central to David's reply is the way he situates the combat within a theological framework in

79. Firmage, "Zoology," 1143.

80. Handy, "Dagon," 2. It is interesting that in 1 Sam 5:3–4 the statue of Dagon falls before the ark of the covenant.

which the dynamics of honor and shame are still very much in evidence. The important elements of vv. 45–47 are these:

a. Whereas Goliath relies on sword and spear and javelin, David relies on the name of the Lord, God of the Israelite armies, whom Goliath has "challenged" (*haraf*);

b. God will give David victory over Goliath;

c. he will go beyond what Goliath has threatened to do to his corpse, both by cutting off the Philistine's head and also by giving the dead bodies of the Philistines (not just his opponent) to the birds and beasts; and

d. everyone present (meaning Israelite and Philistine) will know that the God of Israel needs neither sword nor spear and will determine the outcome of the battle. It would not have been lost on the ancient audience of this narrative that the same word *haraf* is used by Goliath when he "insults"—that is, offers a negative challenge to— the army of Israel (vv. 10) and also by David when stating that Goliath has "insulted" God himself (v. 46), even though Goliath has never mentioned Israel's God. In a group-oriented context such as this one, to challenge a people or its army was also to challenge their God.

Once the battle actually begins it is again Goliath who takes the initiative, but David quickly runs towards him (v. 48). While there is no doubt that David then executed a successful attack on Goliath with his slingshot, there is a question as to precisely how this was achieved. The Hebrew text states that David slung his stone and struck Goliath on, in the usual interpretation, his *meṣaḥ* ("forehead"), and the stone sank into (*ṭabaʿ*) his *meṣaḥ* and he fell on his face on the ground. There is, however, another possibility that involves repointing the relevant word to produce *miṣḥah*, "greave," so that Goliath was knee-capped.[81] The former meaning, which entails that Goliath is dead with a stone in his brain when he hits the ground, is by far the more likely interpretation (and appears in the Septuagint and the Vulgate). For how could an ancient audience have understood that David "prevailed" over Goliath (v. 50) if he were merely on the ground with an injured knee, or that David simply slipped the Philistine's sword from its sheath and cut off his head (v. 51).

81. Deem, "And the Stone."

In any event cut off Goliath's head he does, thus making good on his threat and dishonoring his opponent's corpse to magnify the glory of his victory, just as the Philistines later decapitate the bodies of Saul and his three sons (1 Sam 31:8–10). At this the Philistines flee, with the Israelites in pursuit and attacking them as they go, before returning to plunder their camp. Presumably, we must understand David to have taken part in this chase, so as to make good his threat in v. 46. In stating that David took the head of the Philistine and brought it to Jerusalem, the text falls into "obvious anachronism,"[82] since Jerusalem was at that time a Jebusite city and was not captured by David until much later (2 Sam 5:6–10).[83] Less awkwardly, David puts Goliath's armor into this tent, although Hertzberg detects a difficulty here, in that David had no tent.[84] Curiously, however, shortly afterwards Goliath's sword is located in the temple at Nob (1 Sam 21:9). We never find out in what circumstances it got there. Although it is temping to presume David dedicated the weapon to Yahweh in thanks for this victory (similar to the action of the Hittite commander Hattusilis III who dedicated to the goddess Ishtar the weapon with which he had succeeded in single combat),[85] this is hard to reconcile with the fact that David seems to have forgotten having done so when he visits the temple at Nob later in the narrative (1 Sam 21:8–9).

The final section of the David and Goliath story, which has been added to an earlier version that is now represented in the Septuagint, comprises vv. 55–58. Also missing from the Old Greek version is the passage 1 Sam 18:1–5, in which Jonathan comes to love David and enters into a covenant with him, Saul takes him into his house and he is successful as a military leader. I have noted earlier how David's oldest brother, Eliab, wanted to confine his youngest brother to his usual lowly place in the familial and social hierarchy (1 Sam 17:28–30). While his

82. Driver, *Notes on the Hebrew Text*, 147.

83. Bodner, on the other hand, suggests (*1 Samuel*, 188) that the narrative means that David took the sword to Jerusalem, then controlled by the Jebusites, which he was even then thinking of a "neutral" capital for his kingdom.

84. Hertzberg, *I & II Samuel*, 154. Hertzberg repoints the Hebrew of "his tent" to mean "Yahweh's tent," thus producing a reference to the tent-sanctuary of Yahweh at Nob in 1 Samuel 21, where David will later get back the sword. This is ingenious but probably over-interpretation: surely an ancient audience would have assumed that someone who had just caused Israel to defeat a Philistine army would be given a tent in the Israelite camp.

85. For this see Hoffner, "A Hittite Analogue," 222.

victory over Goliath would probably have been enough to allow David escape such conventional stricture, the extra material in the Masoretic text of 1 Sam 17:55–58 serves to confirm in very visual terms the full extent of the culturally anomalous rise of David to pre-eminence.

According to 1 Sam 17:55 Saul does not even know the identity of David's father, which also entails that neither Saul nor Abner know where he has come from, even though for some time he has been serving as the king's armor-bearer and lyre-player. This is one of the major anomalies in this narrative. Nevertheless, if we take 1 Sam 17:55 as we find it, within the canons of local culture, Saul's not knowing David's father meant that David was a nobody. David is left to inform the king of his undistinguished lineage and place of origin as he stands before him holding the head of Goliath (1 Sam. 17.58)! His humble origins and stunning achievement are brought into stark juxtaposition. Eliab and his brothers, on the other hand, sink entirely from view, even to the extent that David has no subsequent use for them, his own family, in helping win control over or later rule Israel.[86] David proves to be the great fighter even though they had been the first sons of Jesse to join Saul's army.

CONCLUSION: CULTURAL CONTEXT, NARRATIVE STRUCTURE, AND THEOLOGY

The Story of David in 1 Samuel 17:1—18:5 in Its Cultural Context

Although the textual data on the contest between David and Goliath is understood in socially realistic terms within the culture of ancient Israel using the pattern of challenge-and-response, the version of the story in the Masoretic Text distinctively diverges from a probably older version (now represented in the Old Greek of Codex Vaticanus), especially by the addition of 1 Sam 17:12–31 and 55–58. At the heart of these passages lies an intense interest in how traditional patterns of kinship as they function within the domestic economy are overturned in the case of David. The usual customs of ancient Israelite family life are subverted in God's elevation of David far above his brothers. It is most helpful to

---

86. Thus, the later conflict is between David and the house of Saul (2 Sam 3:1), not between David's house and Saul's. None of David's relatives figures in the list of his heroes in 2 Sam 23:8–39. Another sign of the striking estrangement between David and his family is that a son of one of his brothers suggests to his son Amnon the device whereby Amnon will be able to rape his half sister Tamar, an action which leads to such tragedy (2 Sam 13:3–5), a narrative discussed in chapter 10 of this volume.

see these verses, not as attributing to David enhanced features of the narrative already related of Saul in 1 Samuel 9–10, as argued by Auld and Ho,[87] but as amplifying the theme introduced in connection with David's anointing as king (1 Sam 16:1–13), that God does not judge by appearances but by reference to a man's heart (1 Sam 16:7), even where the man in question is the youngest of eight brothers and charged with the uncomfortable and dishonorable job of shepherd over the family's flocks. Indeed Jesse is described as presenting his "seven sons" without reference to David (1 Sam 16:10), as if David was not his son, and only mentions his youngest son, almost as an afterthought, when prompted by Samuel, who is no doubt becoming rather exasperated with the way the affair is proceeding: "Are these all the sons you have" (1 Sam 16:11)? So David's place in the family is plainly the most insignificant one, yet in the result his father and brothers have to look on while Samuel anoints David and the Spirit of the Lord falls on him, even if they receive no explanation for these events (1 Sam 16:13). In the narrative of David's visit to the front, the same three brothers who are named in this incident are mentioned and much the same point is made, although the antipathy that Eliab at least bears towards David is highlighted. How the three brothers reacted to David's defeat of Goliath is not recorded, but the text assumes that they would have witnessed it along with all the other Israelites, drawn up on their side of the valley of Elah. At the end, indeed, it is David—carrying Saul's head in his hand—who is brought to the king in triumph.

Narrative Structure in the Broader Literary Landscape

The story of David in 1 Sam 17:1—18:5, in which a young shepherd, of little consequence to his own family, is quietly anointed king of Israel, becomes lyre-player to the king, causes victory for his people over a Philistine invasion force by slaying their huge champion, and is then put in charge of Israel's army to universal approbation, represents a fusion of the plots that Christopher Booker calls "Rags to Riches" and "Overcoming the Monster." The five stages of the "Rags to Riches" plot can be seen,[88] admittedly with some variations, in the story of David. First, there is the initial lowly state at home, where he is overshadowed

---

87. Auld and Ho, "The Making of David and Goliath."

88. Booker, *Seven Basic Plots*, 65–66.

by at least one "dark" figure in the form of his eldest brother, Eliab, even if there is no sign that David is particularly unhappy. This phase ends, as in other such tales, with his being called out into the wider world, both through his anointing by Samuel and through his commission to play his lyre to Saul. The second phase, where the hero goes out into the world and has some initial success, comes when David finds favor with Saul, "who loved him greatly," and successfully plays his lyre to the king, so that the evil spirit leaves him (1 Sam 16:19–23). The third stage is the "central crisis." That this stage is very attenuated in the case of David represents the major point of contrast between this plot and the biblical narrative. He is not "overwhelmed with despair" like many heroes in stories with this type of plot. Yet he does encounter opposition from his elder brother, even if he puts little stock in this. That it is David's elder brother who alone among Israel expresses hostility towards David chimes with the similarly negative role played by somewhat similar "dark figures" in two other "Rags to Riches" tales: Joseph's brothers in Genesis 37 and, indeed, Cinderella's vain and unpleasant stepsisters in the fairytale of that name.[89] His worst moment is probably when Goliath draws near him with his shield-bearer (1 Sam 17:41), but there is no sign that David's faith in his God or in his own skill with the sling ever wavered. The *fourth* stage, when we come to see the hero in a new light, does occur but in a greatly compressed form: one minute David is a shepherd with his sling standing in front of the huge Philistine warrior, and the next he is standing over his corpse that he has just decapitated. The *fifth* stage, of completion and fulfillment, takes the form not of matrimony or the succession to a kingdom, but the love of Jonathan, the leadership of Saul's army and the high regard of all the people (1 Sam 18:1–5). Turning to the other plot, like many heroes in "Overcoming the Monster" plots David grows in stature as the narrative proceeds,[90] with his defeat of Goliath activating his divinely-sanctioned potential for an even greater role as a the leader of his people. There is one distinctive variation from this plot worth noting, especially as Booker himself has got this wrong in David's case. Sometimes the hero's reward for defeating the monster is the hand in marriage of the princess. Prior to his fighting Goliath, Saul's Israelite soldiers had actually said to David that Saul would give his daughter to the man who killed the Philistine. Yet Saul does not

89. For these "dark figures," see ibid., 54.
90. Ibid, 220.

give David the hand of one of his daughters for killing Goliath, so that Booker goes astray when he states, "For being the saviour of his country, he is given the hand in marriage of King Saul's daughter, the Princess Michal."[91] Saul only gives Michal to David later, for a quite separate act, the slaying of two hundred Philistines and the delivery of their foreskins to the king, and only then when he has previously promised David another daughter, Merab, and then married her off to someone else. In both cases, moreover, Saul hoped that David would die at Philistine hands in seeking victory against them to win the hand of a princess. Accordingly, we witness a striking variation of the theme of winning the hand of the princess that serves to underline Saul's murderous hostility towards David and lay the foundations for the future development of the plot.

Theology

Finally, we must ask if the type of analysis undertaken in this Chapter is inconsistent with a theological understanding of the narrative? Far from it! In contrast with the extensive Roman material on single combat,[92] for example, the Israelite tradition of David and Goliath throws up profound theological issues. The first Israelite readers of/listeners to this narrative did not merely derive aesthetic satisfaction from it, but learned about the God whom they worshipped and upon whom they rested their identity as a people.

But to comprehend the way in which God deals with humanity in this text, we must be attuned to the context in which the events in question unfold. Only by setting the narrative of David and Goliath in its original setting can we appreciate its theological dimensions, for to grasp the magnitude of God's choosing David and giving him victory over Goliath, we must first appreciate his initial insignificance within his own family and the wider culture of Israel and the extent to which God inverts the customary life of Israel for his sake.

The Israelite God acts by the countercultural uplifting of the lowly, a tradition going back to the prophets of the eighth century BCE, but announced at the start of 1 Samuel too, in 1 Sam 2:7–8 (and alluded to in Mary's Magnificat in Luke 1:51–53):

91. Ibid, 25.
92. See Oakley, "Single Combat."

> The Lord makes poor and makes rich;
>   he brings low, he also exalts.
> He raises up the poor from the dust;
>   he lifts the needy from the ash heap,
> to make them sit with princes
>   and inherit a seat of honor. (RSV)

In telling the story the author provides a narrative enactment of one of the most notable interactions of God with his people of this type. The core of the message is that God will not be restrained by established social roles and institutions in effecting his purposes, especially to the extent that he means to raise the lowly (whether in warfare or domestic life) to positions of preeminence.

It is also probable that the story of David in this narrative was regarded as homologous to the story of Israel itself within a setting where it was a small nation among much bigger and more powerful ones. While in this setting Israel might seem small, inferior and despised, facing huge odds, it nevertheless had a unique advantage, for the living God was on its side, unseen but powerful and coming to its aid in various dangers, rescuing it for a continuing role in history. This theme begins with Abraham and the patriarchs and continues throughout the history of Israel that the Bible records.[93]

Yet to understand the nature of the divine initiative as far as David was concerned, we must set it against the usual and everyday patterns of ancient Mediterranean social life that bring out its radical nature. Indeed, unless we make a real effort to appreciate the power of the social conventions at work in this culture, we cannot begin to understand what an ancient Israelite reader would have made of the God who so thoroughly overturned them for his purposes.

In this perspective, theology emerges in a way intrinsic to the text. In seeking to assess how the tradition of the David and Goliath story represented in the Masoretic text would have been assessed by the original audience within their cultural context, part of the culture shock one experiences is the integration of views about God into the distinctive way the narrative unfolds. The central theological dimen-

---

93. I am grateful to John H. Elliott, in commenting on an earlier version of this chapter, for suggesting the importance of the matters in this paragraph as part of the wider theological dimensions of the narrative.

sion is the close relationship between God and David, a lowly shepherd. By following the path of understanding the narrative within its ancient context we encounter new ways of experiencing the theological dimension of the texts that may pose an interesting alternative to extrinsic theologies as in the older biblical-theology approach or the newer forms of canonical criticism.

7

David, Banditry, and Kingship
(1 Samuel 19:1—2 Samuel 5:5)

HOW DAVID SURVIVED SAUL TO BECOME KING

An ancient audience encountering the ending of 1 Samuel 18, with its unequivocal expression of Saul's fear of and enmity for David, prompted by his recognition that the Lord was with David and that Israel loved him (1 Sam 18:28–29), would surely have wondered, "How then did David ever survive Saul's hostility and become king?" The narrative stretching from 1 Sam 19:1 to 2 Sam 5:5 provides an answer to that question. 2 Samuel 5 marks the conclusion of the longer narrative of the rise of David that began in 1 Samuel 16, the earlier course of which was considered in chapters 5 and 6 of this volume. I prefer to see this narrative having its terminus at 2 Sam 5:5, with its summary of David's regnal years, so that vv. 6–10, with their account of his capture of Jerusalem for his capital, mark a new narrative unit. Many critics, on the other hand, regard this latter section as the conclusion of the story of David's ascension to power.[1] Not a great deal, however, turns on whether we consider the narrative of David's rise to kingship ends at v. 5 or v. 10 of 2 Samuel 5.

The narrative in 1 Samuel 19 to 2 Samuel 5:5 contains two sections, of very unequal length. The first, the thirteen chapters comprising 1 Samuel 19–31, deals with the period in David's life when he had to remove himself from Saul's presence because of his fear that Saul would

---

1. Brueggemann, *First and Second Samuel*, 236.

kill him and ends with the death of Saul and three of his sons during a battle with the Philistines. This section is the major focus of the present chapter. The second section of this narrative, comprising just over four chapters (2 Sam. 1:1–5:5), relates how David came to establish his claim to be the legitimate successor to Saul as the king of Israel. I will deal with this section briefly toward the end of this chapter.

The investigation of 1 Samuel 19 to 2 Samuel 5:5 set out in this chapter will continually relate the narrative to the recurrent contextual features of ancient Israel set out in Chapter 2 of this volume, in addition to a more specific focus on issues of banditry and social banditry (soon to be described). At the same time, however, this narrative offers numerous points of comparison with the plot Christopher Booker describes as "the Quest,"[2] while also presenting significant areas of contrast that help us appreciate the distinctiveness of the portrayal of David's survival and eventual succession to the kingship of Israel in 1 and 2 Samuel.

Here is Booker's initial explanation of the "Quest" plot: "Far away, we learn, there is some priceless goal, worth any effort to achieve: a treasure; a promised land; something of infinite value. From the moment the hero learns of this prize, the need to set out on the long hazardous journey to reach it becomes the most important thing to him in the world. Whatever perils and diversions lie in wait on the way, the story is shaped by that one overriding imperative; and the story remains unresolved until the objective has been finally, triumphantly secured."[3]

Examples of the "Quest" plot include Homer's *Odyssey*, Virgil's *Aeneid, Jason and the Argonauts*, Dante's *Divine Comedy*, John Bunyan's *Pilgrim's Progress*, Rider Haggard's *King Solomon's Mines*, J. R. R. Tolkien's *The Lord of the Rings*, Richard Adams's *Watership Down*, and Steven Spielberg's *Raiders of the Lost Ark*. Very often the gaining or establishing of a kingdom is the goal toward which the quest is aimed.[4]

The first feature of this plot is "the Call": The "Quest" usually begins on a note of the most urgent compulsion. For the hero to remain quietly "at home" (or wherever he happens to be) has become impossible. Some fearful threat has arisen. The "times are out of joint." Something has gone seriously and terrifyingly wrong.

2. Booker, *Seven Basic Plots*, 69–86.

3. Ibid, 69.

4. Ibid, 82 (examples include the *Odyssey*, the *Aeneid, Jason and the Argonauts* and *Watership Down*).

In these dire straits, someone often warns the hero of the danger and alerts him or her to the solution: the ghost of Aeneas's wife, Creusa, tells him among the flames of Troy that he will find a new home in the West; in *Pilgrim's Progress* Christian meets Evangelist, who urges him to head for the distant "shining light"; and in *Watership Down* one rabbit warns some of the others of grave danger threatening their warren and of the need to escape.[5] The similarities and dissimilarities with the story of David in 1 Samuel 19 are highly instructive. Certainly David must leave Saul's court if he is to stay alive, as Jonathan warns him (1 Sam 19:2). Yet no one tells him that he should do so if he is to become king, or offers the kingship as the solution to his problem. Throughout the course of 1 Samuel 19–31 David does nothing that will bring an end to Saul's kingship or secure his own position as his successor as king. As McCarter accurately notes, the narrator wants "to absolve David from any suspicion of wrongdoing in the course of his ascent to royal office. To this end he has presented David throughout as a man innocent of overweening ambition, whose extraordinary successes result less often from self-interested undertakings of his own than from the willing deeds of others."[6]

This means that the "Quest" in 1–2 Samuel will be very unusual one, where the hero refuses even to acknowledge that he is interested in the goal in sight, let alone to take any deliberate step that will allow him achieve that goal. This presentation of David as a reluctant hero is all the more strange given that anyone listening to or reading the story in ancient Israel would be aware that the he was now the Lord's anointed and that the Spirit of the Lord had abandoned Saul.

Other features of the "Quest" plot do figure less ambiguously than the *call* in the story of David. One of them is "the extent to which, more than in any other kind of story, the hero is not alone in his adventures."[7] Although initially a solitary fugitive, David eventually acquires a band of *companions*. In addition to the call and the hero's companions there is the *journey*: the hero and his companions must proceed on a journey where they encounter a succession of dangerous ordeals, followed by periods of respite where they receive help from people who then send them on their way. They might encounter monsters, or temptations, or other

---

5. Ibid, 70–71.

6. McCarter, *II Samuel*, 133.

7. Booker, *Seven Basic Plots*, 71.

terrible dangers.[8] We will see that David and his men journey across Judea pursued by Saul and that David experiences a temptation to do serious wrong from which he is narrowly averted. Distinctive to the narrative of David and his men on the run, however, as we will see below, is the extent to which the behavior of the hero and his companions can be assimilated to that of a gang of bandits. The *helpers* who assist the hero tend to be wise old men and beautiful young women (like Virgil and Beatrice, who lead Dante in the *Divine Comedy*; or Gandalf and Galadriel in *The Lord of the Rings*): "Their role is not so much to intervene in the action as to act as guides and advisers, drawing on supernatural wisdom and prescience."[9] We will see how Abigail fulfils a comparable function for David in 1 Samuel 25. The "Quest" usually culminates in severe "final ordeals" which, once overcome, allow the attainment of the *goal*.[10] The closing chapters of 1 Samuel and in 2 Samuel 1–5 contain events that can be interpreted as such *final ordeals*.

DAVID, BANDITRY, AND SOCIAL BANDITRY (1 SAMUEL 19–31)

First Samuel 19 begins with Saul's command to Jonathan his son and all his servants that they should kill David (v. 1), and it is only Saul's death in 1 Samuel 31 that lifts this threat from him. To avoid death at the hand of Saul and his men David withdraws to various parts of Judea and the Philistine territory, often to the wilderness, gathering a group of men around him as he does (1 Sam 22:2). In an essay on Jesus and the "social bandits" (an expression popularized by E. J. Hobsbawm to which we will return below), K. C. Hanson has suggested in passing that David and his band as described in this section of 1 Samuel constitutes "one of the most startling cases of social banditry in the Old Testament."[11]

My aim in this section is to explore 1 Samuel 19–31 through the lenses of banditry and social banditry. Initially I will set out what is meant by these expressions and the critiques that have been leveled against Hobsbawm's formulation of "social banditry." In line with the method adopted throughout this volume, I will then proceed through the events of the narrative in the order in which they appear in the

---

8. Ibid, 73–77.

9. Ibid, 77–78.

10. Ibid, 78–83 (although Gandalf is not adverse to "mixing it" with his foes!).

11. Hanson, "Jesus and the Social Bandits," 284.

Hebrew text using the discussion of banditry and social banditry as a social-science perspective. This process will allow me to put questions to this magnificent narrative not normally posed by other commentators and to organize the answers produced and the textual data highlighted in a way that makes more sense than if we were reliant on our instinctive modern assumptions and prejudgments about such phenomena. In so doing I will also draw upon other areas of ancient Mediterranean culture dealt with at greater length elsewhere in this volume. Even if Hobsbawm's "social banditry" idea will ultimately not prove applicable to David and his band, it is still is a provocative suggestion worthy of investigation and I am indebted to K. C. Hanson for having stimulated this enquiry by suggesting its relevance.

The Nature of Banditry and Social Banditry

Banditry

We will begin with banditry. This topic has attracted far less attention in recent discussion, which is somewhat surprising: given that social banditry is a benign form of banditry, how can one understand the former activity without first saying something about the latter? In fact, as we will see below, much recent research on bandits and banditry has been driven by the aim of disproving the social banditry thesis of Eric Hobsbawm rather than from scholars' intrinsic interest in the theory.

In contemporary English usage a "bandit" is someone who takes property from others by force or the threat of force, usually in an isolated or remote place and often operating in concert with others. An instance of a bandit in this sense in the New Testament is to found in Luke 10:30–37, in the account of the man traveling down on the road from Jerusalem to Jericho, who is set upon by bandits (*lēstai*, v. 30), stripped naked, beaten, and left for dead.

During the nineteenth and earlier twentieth centuries gangs of bandits were particularly common in certain parts of the world, such as Mexico and China. At certain times in during this period bandit gangs managed to capture whole towns. On October 28, 1902, for example, the *New York Times* carried a report received in St Petersburg on October 27 from Kharbin, a new Russian town on the Manchurian Railroad, and titled "Manchurian Bandits Capture a Town" to the effect that the town of Bodune, Manchuria, had been captured by bandits, and that Russian troops had been sent to its relief.

During the early 1930s southern China was the scene of an explosion of banditry, due to factors such as weak central government, a civil war in the north, the effects of the world-wide depression, and famine in the south. This phenomenon was widely covered by the Western press, such as by numerous stories in the *New York Times* (with the reports now available online),[12] especially as missionaries from Europe and the USA were often captured and ransomed or killed by the bandits. Some of these bands were associated with the Communist Party, so that they had an ideological dimension to their activities (with a view to their party and movement ultimately gaining power in China), but some were simply criminal bands with no aims beyond the acquisition of resources by violence from others, driven either by choice or the harsh economic and political conditions then prevailing in China. I will refer later to a specific example of banditry from China in the 1930s.

Banditry has still not disappeared. During 2008 and 2009 humanitarian assistance in Chad, for example, was repeatedly subject to interruption by bandit attacks. On November 13, 2009, the United Nations News Center reported that "humanitarian assistance to tens of thousands of people in Chad is under threat from banditry, which has led several aid agencies to temporarily halt their operations in the face of attacks, the United Nations relief wing reported today . . . Since the beginning of 2009 about 190 banditry attacks affecting humanitarians had been reported in eastern Chad, nearly double the 110 in 2008."[13]

The violent proclivities of bandits probably explain the dearth of scholarly literature into their actual activities and forms of organization as opposed to how they were *perceived* or *depicted* by outsiders. Even a recent work like Chris Frazer's *Bandit Nation: A History of Outlaws and Cultural Struggle in Mexico, 1810–1920*, although it does include valuable references to primary data in administrative archives and legal records, nevertheless focuses more on the nature and role of foreign-travel accounts, novels, and popular ballads (*corridos*) to investigate how and why Mexicans and visitors to the country from the USA, Great Britain,

12. Some of this *New York Times* material is helpfully summarized in McEndarfer, "The Chinese Bandit Menace in 1930."

13. See UN News Centre, "Banditry Jeopardizing Humanitarian Work in Eastern Chad." Online: http://www.un.org/apps/news/story.asp?NewsID=32949&Cr=chad&Cr1.

and elsewhere created and used images of banditry to influence Mexico's
state formation, hegemony, and national identity.[14] Even further away
from the actual practices of bandits is Juan Pablo Dabove's *Nightmare of
the Lettered City: Banditry and Literature in Latin America, 1816–1929*,
which analyzes the common theme of banditry in literary works, essays,
poetry, and drama from the early nineteenth century to the 1920s, and
the pivotal role of banditry during the conceptualization and formation
of the Latin American nation-state. In the course of addressing (for the
first time) the *depiction* of banditry in Latin America as a whole, Dabove
focuses on Argentina, Mexico, Brazil, and Venezuela.

Social Banditry

Eric J. Hobsbawm first published his "social bandit" idea in 1959, in his
book *Primitive Rebels: Studies in Archaic Forms of Social Movement in
the 19th and 20th Centuries*, in chapter 2, titled, "The Social Bandit."[15]
A year later a U.S. reprint of this work appeared under the title *Social
Bandits and Primitive Rebels*.[16] A fuller development of the idea appeared in his book *Bandits* in 1969, with a summary form published in
1974.[17] The central notion in "social banditry" was that some bandits
had an essentially positive relationship with the local peasantry and represented a form of social protest. Here is how Hobsbawm summarized
social banditry in 1974:

> It consists essentially of relatively small groups of men living
> on the margins of peasant society, and whose activities are con-
> sidered criminal by the prevailing official power-structure and
> value-system, but not (or not without strong qualifications) by
> the peasantry. It is this special relation between peasant and ban-
> dit which makes banditry 'social': the social bandit is a hero, a
> champion, a man whose enemies are the same as the peasants',
> whose activities correct injustice, control oppression and exploi-
> tation, and perhaps even maintain alive the ideal of emancipa-
> tion and independence. Hence, in the extreme—and historically
> almost certainly exceptional—case of the genuine Robin Hood,
> the social bandit is the very opposite of a criminal, in the public

14. Frazer, *Bandit Nation*; but also see Joseph, "On the Trail."
15. Hobsbawm, *Primitive Rebels*.
16. Hobsbawm, *Social Bandits and Primitive Rebels*.
17. Hobsbawm, *Bandits* and Hobsbawm, "Social Banditry."

mind. He represents morality: Jesse James, in popular anecdote and romance was a devout Baptist and Sunday school teacher.[18]

Hobsbawm's formulation of the social bandit proved to be a big idea that provoked a large body of research into bandits and banditry around the world and was fairly quickly applied by specialists in a number of fields to help them understand textual and material data. By 1984 Roman historian Brent Shaw was able to write an essay on bandits in the Roman empire that began by critically reflecting on the social banditry idea and the powerful impact it had made on scholarship.[19] In 1985 Richard Horsley and John Hanson made extensive use of Hobsbawm's ideas to help them explore popular movements in the time of Jesus.[20] Since then social banditry has been employed by several other biblical interpreters.[21]

Yet Hobsbawm's formulation of the social-banditry idea soon ran into opposition. First, Anton Blok argued strongly against the notion central to *social* banditry, namely, the positive relation between bandits and peasants. In Blok's view, these allegedly "good" thieves were actually violent men who preyed on the peasants rather than defending them against elite oppression.[22] Although Hobsbawm has rejected this criticism by insisting that some real social bandits have indeed existed,[23] convincing evidence for them has proved hard to find.

This leads to a second and related problem with social banditry: the sort of evidence upon which Hobsbawm had relied. By and large this consisted of folklore and fictional literature. This meant it was hard to distinguish social reality from the creations of popular or literary imaginations, both of which were more than capable of generating highly colorful bandits having little necessary correspondence with historical fact. Many early critics of Hobsbawm argued that his social bandits

18. Hobsbawm, "Social Banditry," 143.

19. Shaw, "Bandits in the Roman Empire." Shaw updated this essay in 2004. Also see Isaac, "Bandits."

20. Horsley and Hanson, *Bandits, Prophets, and Messiahs.*

21. Horsley, "Josephus and the Bandits"; and Horsley, "Ancient Jewish Social Banditry"; Freyne, "Bandits in Galilee"; Hanson and Oakman, *Palestine in the Time of Jesus*, 80–85 and passim (and note the summary of the idea in Hanson, "Jesus and the Social Bandits," 290).

22. Blok, "The Peasant and the Brigand," 496, 499.

23. Hobsbawm, "Social Bandits: Reply."

were romanticized and largely fictional productions.[24] Thus, researchers working on primary sources from various parts of the world, including Latin America, found major differences between the kind of bandits Hobsbawm had envisaged and what data to be found in administrative and legal archives indicated that they had actually been like.[25]

Intriguing light is thrown on this question by the administrative archives of ancient Egypt. There is an Egyptian edict from 210 to 214 CE, to which K. C. Hanson has drawn our attention, in which a high official orders the *stratēgoi* in two nomes to search out bandits (*lēstai*), offering rewards to those who cooperate and punishment for those who disobey. Hanson suggests that "this edict may indicate the symbiotic relationship between local villagers and the social bandits, as articulated in Hobsbawm's definition."[26] Yet this is unlikely. In the third century CE the *stratēgoi* were the local leaders of the nomes;[27] they were people of considerable wealth. Against these sort of people, Hobsbawm saw bandits aligning themselves with peasants. The edict is really directed at these people because of slackness in doing their duty, not because they have any positive relationships with the bandits, on which matter the edict is silent.

Third, Brent Shaw has pointed to the frequency with which Hobsbawm was often talking about the *perception* of these men as other than common criminals. How do we know if a particular perception is matched to reality and what if perceptions about a particular bandit differ? Thus he cites a story mentioned in Galen of a bandit who had been killed by a traveler repelling his attack and to whom the local inhabitants would not give a proper burial, so great was their hatred of him.[28] Was this attitude to the man exceptional or the local norm? I would suggest, probably the latter, since otherwise someone would surely have slipped out one night to gather the remains and bury them. Was he a social bandit or just a bandit? Again, I would suggest probably the latter.

24. See Slatta, "Eric J. Hobsbawm's Social Bandit," 23–24. Also see Slatta, *Bandidos*.

25. See Blok "The Peasant and the Brigand"; Chandler, *The Bandit King*; Lewin, "Social Banditry in Brazil"; and O'Malley, "Social Bandits."

26. Hanson, "Jesus and the Social Bandits," 287, citing *Oxyrhynchus Papyri*, 1408 and Hunt and Edgar, *Select Papyri*, 114–17.

27. Bowman, *The Town Councils of Roman Egypt*, 76.

28. Shaw, "Bandits in the Roman Empire," (2004 version), 328–29.

Yet while the Egyptian edict and the case from Galen both probably push against Hobsbawm's social banditry thesis, this still leaves open the possibility that particular cases of this type of bandit could be found. Hobsbawm has helpfully alerted us to a possible pattern of relationship between bandits and peasantry that throws up a set of questions for consideration in any particular case, including that of David and his band. Various aspects of the material he cites, and also data to contrary effect referred to by his critics (such as Anton Blok), often suggest very interesting issues to put to narratives such as 1 Samuel 19–31. The same applies to the very perceptive observations Hobsbawm frequently makes on contextual details of his examples, since these generally have a more secure historical foundation than the particular ways (possibly reflecting imagination rather than historicity) in which bandits are portrayed. In addition, Shaw's negative view of "perceptions" misses an important point, namely, that while the differing responses to bandits may make reaching a decided view on the actual nature of their actions very difficult (and often beyond historical reach), the perceptions they generate are themselves valuable evidence for the experience and views of the people who express them. We will see that the differing perceptions various characters entertain towards David are very important in understanding the narrative of 1 Samuel 25.

Reading 1 Samuel 19–31 from the Perspective of Banditry and Social Banditry

Saul as King of Israel

The nature and power of the prevailing political authority inevitably have a great significance for anyone engaged in activities that involve or even merely threaten violent attacks or robbery against the population. In particular, those who maintain and benefit from the current political order will necessarily seek to eliminate any threat to it. The political authority relevant to David was Saul, king of Israel, and 1 Samuel provides considerable illumination into the character of his rule, which we have already considered in detail in chapter 2. The nature of Saul's kingship, beginning with his anointing by the Lord and characterized especially by its dependence on patron-client relationships with fellow-members of the tribe of Benjamin, provides the context within which we must explore the interactions between himself and David.

Saul's Attitude and Behavior towards David and their Interactions

For Hobsbawm the social bandit ("a noble robber") "begins his career of outlawry not by crime but as the victim of injustice, or through being persecuted by the authorities."[29] First Samuel certainly presents David as an innocent victim of Saul's murderous hostility who nevertheless on two occasions (in chapters 24 and 26) notably fails to kill Saul even though he could easily have done so. To that extent David bears a prima facie similarity to the "social bandit." Stimulated by this initial resemblance, by looking more closely at how 1 Samuel 19–31 explains Saul's attitude and behavior toward David, the interactions between the two men, and how David and his men behave, we will be able to test Hobsbawm's theory against data in the text relevant to this issue in a manner that will show the usefulness of the theory in raising fresh questions. This discussion will also lay the foundation for the later consideration of incidents where other Israelites and non-Israelites respond to David in ways relevant to his possible status as "social bandit."

The Motivation and Rationale for Saul's Antipathy towards David

On numerous occasions, as we will soon see, Saul tries to have David killed. While I considered the way the text portrays the genesis of this animosity in detail in chapter 5, it will be useful here to review the main data on Saul's view of David. His attitude toward David first sours when the women sing a song celebrating David as a greater military commander than Saul: "Saul has slain his thousands, and David his tens of thousands" (1 Sam 18:7). This makes Saul very angry, for he fears that David may replace him (1 Sam 18:8). In addition, Saul also becomes envious of David. His reputation among the people has been diminished because of the greater military successes of David. He "eyes" David from then on (1 Sam 18:9)—the Hebrew verb conveys envy[30]—and tries to kill him with a spear the next time David plays the lyre to him to assuage the evil spirit by which Saul was occasionally beset (1 Sam 18:10–11). When Saul's hopes that the Philistines will kill David (1 Sam 18:17, 21) are dashed, and he sees that the Lord is with David and that all Israel loves him (1 Sam 18:28), he becomes even more afraid of him and is his enemy ('oyeb) continually (1 Sam 18:29). He also regards David as

---

29. Hobsbawm, *Bandits*, 35.

30. See chapter 5 this volume, and also McCarter, *I Samuel*, 312–13.

his enemy (*'oyeb*; 1 Sam 19:17), a charge David is later at pains to prove false.

Saul does not regard David as merely a threat to himself, however, for he is greatly concerned that his descendants are at risk of losing their position in Israel because of David. Thus at one point Saul rebukes Jonathan: "For as long as the son of Jesse lives upon the earth, neither you nor your kingdom shall be established" (1 Sam 20:31, RSV). Later, when David has failed to kill Saul when he had the chance, thus showing he is not Saul's enemy (1 Sam 24:1–19), Saul tells David that he knows David will be king (v. 20), but then adds, "Swear to me therefore by the Lord that you will not cut off my descendants after me, and that you will not destroy my name out of my father's house" (v. 21). David so swears (v. 22). Jonathan, on the other hand, is concerned to secure David's loyalty towards his father's house in the event that the Lord should take vengeance on David's enemies (1 Sam 20:15); Jonathan's vision of the future is that David will be king and he will be beside him (1 Sam 23:17).

The Course of Saul's Antipathy towards David

It is worth noting at the outset that Saul's hometown and capital once he became king was the city of Gibeah, in the territory of Benjamin, Jerusalem not becoming the capital till later, under David (2 Sam 5:6– 10). This ancient city, also known as "Gibeah of Saul" (1 Sam 11:4; 15:34) was situated on a prominent height (the word probably means "hill") on the north-south ridge of hills between Ramah and Jerusalem, with Jerusalem located three miles to the south, and has been identified with Tell el-Fûl.[31] The fact that Gibeah was Saul's hometown appears explicitly at 1 Sam 10:26 (cf. 1 Sam 11:4), but (as noted in Chapter 5) some critics, beginning with Wellhausen, have amended the text of 1 Sam 9:1, so that it starts "There was a man of Benjamin *from Gibeah*."[32]

At the start of 1 Samuel 19 Saul instructs his son Jonathan and his men to kill David. Although Saul had previously entertained the wish that David would be killed (1 Sam 18:10–11, 17, 21, 25), this is the first time that he communicates this wish to Jonathan and his servants, let alone instructs them to kill David. Indeed, not long before he had told

31. See McCarter, *I Samuel*, 172 (citing Lapp, "Tell el-Fûl").

32. See Smith, *The Books of Samuel*, 59–60; Driver, *Notes on the Hebrew Text*, 68–69; and McCarter, *I Samuel*, 167.

his servants that he was delighted with David (1 Sam 18:22). Jonathan, however, who loves David and is bound to him by a covenant (1 Sam 18:1–4), immediately alerts him to this threat and instructs him to hide somewhere until he can see if he can dissuade his father from this course (1 Sam 19:1–3). Initially Jonathan's mediation efforts are successful and David returns to Saul's presence (1 Sam 19:4–7). With the onset of another war with the Philistines and David's military success against them, however, the evil spirit again comes upon Saul while David is playing his lyre to him and the Saul makes a further attempt to spear him, prompting David to flee (1 Sam 19:9–10). David goes home and although Saul sends his men to watch the house and kill him in the morning, David's wife Michal, Saul's own daughter, assists him to escape by a cunning ruse (1 Sam 19:11–17).

Saul is the father of a family that is quite dysfunctional in terms of its local context, since his son and daughter have such love for his enemy that they defy their father's will and even, in Michal's case, lie to him to assist David to avoid death. The cultural context of this narrative, where there was a close connection between the honor of a family and the conduct of its members, suggests that Saul would interpret his children's preference for David over him as a cause of shame that reverberated through his family. That such is the case emerges a little later in the text when Saul insults Jonathan for choosing David by saying he has done so to his (Jonathan's) shame (*bošeth*) and to the shame (*bošeth*) of his mother (1 Sam 20:30). We will see below in discussing 1 Sam 22:6–8 that Saul also has considers that the members of his tribe have also failed to fulfill the personal obligations they owe to him in consequence of his having distributed to them the resources he is receiving as king, which was discussed in Chapter 2.

It is clear that throughout the course of events described after David's flight, Saul is receiving reports from various parts of the country concerning his enemy's whereabouts. This reflects the intelligence-gathering function to which the kingdoms of the ancient Near East paid considerable attention.[33] Rather than dispatching paid spies to various locales in Israel, however, Saul seems to have been able to rely upon information being supplied to him by servants and retainers or by people in the population who wished to keep on the good side of the king.

33. See Sheldon, *Espionage*; and Sheldon, *Spies*; and Dubovsky, *Hezekiah and the Assyrian Spies*.

David flees to Samuel, and the two of them go off and dwell at Naioth in Ramah, which lies only a few miles north of Gibeah. Saul duly receives intelligence of this ("And it was told [*wayyugad*] to Saul" [1 Sam 19:19]), but his attempts to capture David there are frustrated by the fact that the men Saul sends and then the king himself fall into fits of prophesying when they come near Samuel and his company (1 Sam 19:18–24). Saul's behavior on this occasion is said to explain the proverbial question: "Is Saul also among the prophets?" (1 Sam 19:24).[34]

With Naioth, nevertheless, apparently becoming too dangerous for David, he flees to Jonathan (apparently in Gibeah), protesting his innocence of any sin in relation to Saul (1 Sam 20.1). Jonathan and David now devise a stratagem to test whether Saul really intends to kill him (with David thinking he does and Jonathan thinking he does not). The stratagem involves David absenting himself from the king's table on the pretence he has gone to Bethlehem to a family feast with his brothers. When Jonathan learns that the king does intend David's death, he passes on this message by an arranged device with David, and the two meet and part on good terms, with David again fleeing (1 Sam 20:2–42).

David next comes to Nob, only about a mile and a half from Gibeah, to the south. Here he converses with Ahimelech the priest (1 Samuel 21). Asked why he is alone, David pretends he is on a mission for Saul and, needing food, persuades the priest to give him bread for the young men he is allegedly about to meet. Actually, he is on his own, not having yet acquired a band of followers. The only available bread is the holy bread being offered to the Lord (cf. Lev 24:5–9), but David assures Ahimelech that his men are pure, surely a comic touch at this point in the narrative. David—who in his fugitive state lacks weapons—also asks the priest whether he has a sword or spear he can give him, and Ahimelech hands over Goliath's sword, which had been left in the temple. Unfortunately for Ahimelech, all this is being witnessed by Doeg, an Edomite, one of Saul's men, the chief of his herdsmen (1 Sam 21:1–9), who will in due course report what has transpired there to Saul. Keith Bodner, following a suggestion of Pamela Reiss, has argued that David does not mislead Ahimelech during their conversation, but that they are in league with one another in view of the presence of Doeg.[35] While this is a significant

---

34. An alternative explanation for the saying is found at 1 Sam 10:10–12.

35. See Bodner, *1 Samuel*, 223–27; and Reis, "Collusion at Nob."

fresh interpretation, it is not easy to reconcile with David's asking the priest for a weapon.

From Nob David flees (still alone presumably, but now at least with a sword) to Achish, the (Philistine) king of Gath. This would have involved a journey of over twenty miles west-southwest.[36] When the servants of Achish remind him of David's military successes in the past (by implication, against fellow Philistines), David sees the danger and feigns madness, causing Achish to ask why he should have a madman in his house (1 Sam 21:10–15). No longer welcome in Gath, David flees again to the fortress (or possibly the "cave") of Adullam, which was a Judahite city ten miles east-southeast of Gath and sixteen miles southwest of Jerusalem.[37]

We now witness the beginnings of his band, a matter of great significance for the attitude Saul takes towards him and for the future course of the narrative. As noted above, bandits often operate in groups, and the fact that David acquires a band of followers raises the possibility of his future actions being recognizable as banditry or social banditry. The people joining him fall within two broad categories.

The first category consists of "his brothers and all his father's house" (1 Sam 22:1). In a group-oriented culture where family was the dominant group, it is not surprising that David's brothers and relatives rally around him. An ancient audience would have understood their motivation as the desire to defend their family (its members, resources, and honor) by defending its representative who was in trouble. In addition, this same desire to preserve the family means that it is very likely that David's relatives joined him for *their* protection. Hertzberg aptly notes that Bethlehem (the hometown of the family) was dangerously close to Saul;[38] Gibeah was only some eight miles north. This possibility is confirmed by David's soon installing his parents in Mizpeh of Moab until he might find out what God would do for him (1 Sam 22:3–4). Ruth 1:1 describes another instance of Israelites from Bethlehem going to live in Moab (although there because of famine, not from fear of violent attack). This Moabite arrangement also saved David's parents from the privations to be expected in a life on the run from the authorities.[39] Apart

---

36. See McCarter, *I Samuel*, 356.

37. Ibid., 357.

38. Herzberg, *I & II Samuel*, 184.

39. Herzberg, ibid., notes that David's parents "could hardly be expected to lead an

from questions of their security, it is also probable that David's family gathered to him in order to share in any material rewards that would flow from his becoming king of Israel. This certainly seems to be a factor explaining the second category of people who join him (1 Sam 22:2).

This category consists of "everyone who was in straits, and every one who was in debt, and every one who was discontented." Let us look at the three types of person mentioned a little more closely.

"Every one who was in straits." The Hebrew is *kol 'iš maṣoq*. The word *maṣoq* means a condition of severe distress that is caused by severe constraint, by being "squeezed." It is not particularly common in the Hebrew Bible, occurring only seven times in all. Its most prominent usage comes in the terrible passage in Deut 28:52–57 where it refers to the starvation caused by a siege that induces townspeople to eat their own children (vv. 53, 55 and 57). It has the same meaning in Jer 19.9, which alludes to Deut 28:52–57. In the remaining instance, Ps 119:143, it has the meaning of "distress" in a general sense. Given the prominent connection of *maṣoq* with starvation in Deuteronomy 28 and Jeremiah 19, and the fact that indebtedness is mentioned immediately afterwards, in 1 Sam 22:2 the word probably refers to a person whose "distress" consists of starvation.

"Every one who was in debt" (lit. "who had a creditor").[40] The Hebrew is *kol 'iš 'ašer-lo noše'*.

"Every one who was embittered." The Hebrew is *kol 'iš mar-nepeš*. The expression *mar-nepeš* literally means "bitterness of soul." While Driver notes that the expression "implies a state of mental embitterment, i. e. disappointment, dissatisfaction, discontent," McCarter more accurately comments that it suggests "embitterment and discontent, *especially as occasioned by some kind of deprivation* (emphasis added)."[41] He justifies his view with reference to the application of the phrase to the homeless Danites (Judg 18:25), to Hannah because of her barrenness (1 Sam 1:10), to the men of Ziklag who are said to be *marah-nepeš* from the loss of their children (1 Sam 30:6), and to David and his followers fleeing from Absalom, who are "bitter of spirit like a bear bereaved (*šakul*) of its

---

outlaw's life permanently."

40. Driver, *Notes on the Hebrew Text*, 179.

41. Driver, *Notes on the Hebrew Text*, 12; McCarter, *I Samuel*, 357 (emphasis added).

cubs" (2 Sam 17:8). To reasonable similar effect are the instances of the expression at Job 3:20 and Prov 31:6.

McCarter suggests that all these men "have suffered some kind of loss or deprivation that has left them embittered" and that David becomes "the champion of the discontented, the disenchanted, and the mistreated."[42] This is correct but does not really bring out the material deprivation of those who gathered to David, some of whom were probably starving. By paying due weight to the their material conditions, especially their hunger and their indebtedness, we inevitably identify these people as the typical casualties among the non-elite from an advanced agrarian society such as this one, as described in chapter 2. Two factors suggest that the narrator probably intends some, if not most, of these people to be seen as victims of actions by Saul himself. First, they have attached themselves to David, probably because they share with him some form of alienation from Saul, and, secondly, because of what Samuel had warned the Israelites to expect from their king: "He will take the best of your fields and vineyards and olive orchards and give them to his servants" (1 Sam 8:14). We know Saul had done exactly this, acting as a patron to his fellow Benjaminites by giving them all fields and vineyards (1 Sam 22:7). So we have royal confiscation of land from some and royal distribution to others who were members of the king's tribal ingroup. That some were fortunate enough to receive such land presupposes other Israelites who had been deprived of it, and who must have been impoverished, possibly reduced to quite desperate straits as a result. Israelites such as these fell within the first and third types just mentioned. They would have seen in David not simply someone who might assist them in their misfortune, but who would do so by injuring Saul, the very person who was responsible for their reduced condition. The debtors referred to in the second type were probably indebted to other, rich Israelites (but Saul may also have been a major creditor). Why would they flee from their creditors to David? One reason would be to avoid having to sell themselves in debt bondage to their creditors (Lev 25:39–42; Deut 15:12–15).

Over all these people, who numbered about four hundred men, David becomes captain (śar) (1 Sam 22:2). On its surface the description of the people who collect around David appears to support Hobsbawm's social-banditry thesis. This band looks like it has arisen as a form of

42. McCarter, I Samuel, 357.

social protest from the ranks of the Israelite peasantry, and that David will be at odds with Saul and on the side of the peasants. To test this hypothesis we must now see how David and his men behave towards and are treated by other Israelites. To anticipate the discussion, the pattern that emerges will veer towards banditry rather than social banditry.

The formation of a band of around David also represents the creation of a group of companions who accompany the hero on his quest in the plot type of that name identified by Booker. The scene is now set for the journey during which the hero and his companions will encounter various ordeals before attaining the goal that David himself never mentions, kinship over Israel. Yet it is only by bearing in mind the type of people who accompany David, casualties of ancient Israelite agrarian society, that we can appreciate the meaning carried by this particular group of companions in this particular context. As chapter 1 noted, this provides an answer to the problem of the decontextualization that otherwise tends to beset any form of structural comparison of a range of stories (like Booker's).

The next step in the narrative (after David's installation of his family with Mizpeh of Moab, in vv. 3–4, discussed above) is that on the advice of Gad, a prophet, David abandons the stronghold (of Adullam) and moves into the forest of Hereth, in Judah (1 Sam 22:5), a forest not mentioned anywhere else and the whereabouts of which are unknown. These developments at Adullam and in the forest of Hereth do not escape Saul's attention. He hears that David has been discovered (*noda^c*) "and men who were with him" (1 Sam 22:6), although we are not told the source of this intelligence. Whereas previously David had been a lone fugitive on the run, initially even without any weapons of his own, now he has a band of followers. An ancient audience of this text would have understood that this made David all the more dangerous a threat to Saul and to his children after him. The narrative has David gathering around him the disaffected of Israel and implies that many of these probably had grudges to settle against Saul himself. As far as Saul was concerned, there was now a possibility that David would stage an armed revolt against his rule.[43] The fact that debtors were fleeing to David as well would have threatened Saul's position and reputation among his richer subjects (people like Nabal perhaps, whom we will encounter in 1 Samuel 25).

43. Herzberg, *I and II Samuel*, 186.

The action that Saul takes upon receiving this news confirms how seriously he regards it. In a vignette that illustrates many aspects of ancient Near Eastern kingship (1 Sam 22:6–8), he addresses his fellow Benjaminite "servants," probably meaning his inner group of military leaders and officials—that is, his "court"—drawn from his family and tribe. Saul assembles his advisors while he is at Gibeah, seated under a tamarisk tree on the height, spear in hand, and they are standing around him. Saul's opening remark sets out a home truth concerning his patronage, in that he asks whether "the son of Jesse" would give them fields and vineyards or make them military commanders (of thousands and hundreds, not fifties, since Saul is addressing more senior officers) as he obviously has done. Saul is implying that this question must be answered in the negative, since David would bestow such patronage on members of his own family and his own tribe, Judah, if he were to become king. The question serves to introduce Saul's real grievance with his servants (1 Sam 22:8): he believes the men of Benjamin (rather than responding positively to such generosity) have all conspired (*qašar*) against him by failing to tell him that Jonathan is in league with David and is stirring up (*heqim*) David against him to lie in wait (or "set an ambush"; *'oreb*), and by not being sorry for him (the latter being a generally accepted emendation of the Hebrew, which reads "sick" here).[44] This is the language of a patron complaining of a breach in the personal relationship his clients should have with him (they are not "sorry" for him); they should have been loyal to him in return for his benefits to them by telling him about David and Jonathan, but they have let him down by failing to do so. The complaint that God makes to David via the prophet Nathan in 2 Sam 12:7–9 is very similar. In this earlier event, it is not a Benjaminite but the Edomite, Doeg, who merely "stood by the servants of Saul," who conveys information about David to the king (1 Sam 22:9–10).

From Saul's point of view, David and his band represent more a threat than do the type of raiding gangs mentioned in Judges 9.4 and 11:3 since he regards David as lying in wait for him (1 Sam 22:8), which means he interprets David's gathering a band as motivated by hostile intent toward him. Later Saul will accuse Ahimelech, the priest of Nob, of aiding David against him in the same language here applied to Jonathan (1 Sam 22:13). Saul has apparently discovered something of the arrangements made between Jonathan and David (beginning with 1 Sam

44. Driver, *Notes on the Hebrew Text*, 180.

19:1–7); we do not learn how, but Saul clearly has informants (even if not among his "servants"). That Saul can accuse his fellow Benjaminites of not being sorry for him brings out quite graphically the powerfully personal and affective aspect of their patron-client relationship.

It is unclear from the narrative whether Saul's senior commanders actually do know about Jonathan and David and do not tell him, or simply do not know. The former option would need some explanation: why would they not honor their obligations to their fellow Benjaminite and patron, Saul, and tell him what they know about David? The answer might be that if David was so attractive a character that even Saul's own family members (Jonathan and Michal) sought to protect him against the wishes of their father, perhaps the men of Benjamin felt much the same way. Or perhaps they wished to distance themselves a little from Saul in case David eventually took his place. There is no warrant in the text, however, for the view that Saul's servants had a favorable attitude toward David as a valiant defender of the peasantry in accord with Hobsbawm's social bandit notion. At this stage in the narrative, David has not actually done anything to further the interests of the peasantry, other than to accept some hundreds of them into his band.

At this point Doeg the Edomite intervenes to tell Saul what has happened between David and Ahimelech at Nob. As a result, Saul summons the priest and all his male relatives, also priests, to him and has Doeg slay all eighty-five of them, before putting Nob to the ban (1 Sam 22:9–19). Yet one of the priests, Abiathar, escapes to David and stays in his protection (1 Sam 22:20–23).

In 1 Samuel 23 we see the first action by David and his band, when, at God's direction, they defeat and slaughter the Philistines attacking and robbing the inhabitants of Keilah, a Judahite town (Josh 15:44), capture the Philistine cattle, and save the town's inhabitants (1 Sam 23:1–5). The continuation of these events provides interesting data relevant to Hobsbawm's social-bandit thesis. Saul is informed that David is in Keilah and, thinking that the town's gates and bars will trap David, summons his men "to besiege David and his band" (1 Sam 23:7–8). Using the ephod provided by Abiathar, David consults God and discovers (1 Sam 23:9–12), first, that Saul will come down to besiege the city; and, second, that if he does, the inhabitants of Keilah will hand David over to Saul (in order, the text implies, to prevent the destruction of their city). This prompts David and his men, now numbering six hundred, to flee the town and to retire to the wilderness of Ziph, where Saul unsuccessfully seeks them (1 Sam 23:13–14). So here we have a recognition that even though David and his men had saved Keilah from the Philistines, and even though he and its inhabitants were from the same tribe (Judah),[45] the people of Keilah would still hand him over to Saul. While this runs counter to the good relationship between a bandit and the local population that is central to the social-bandit thesis, it is highly probable that the townsfolk did have a positive attitude towards David because he had saved them from the Philistines. Nevertheless, this factor simply did not weigh as heavily in the balance as the thought of what Saul and his army would do to the town of Keilah if they failed to hand David over.

After another meeting between David and Jonathan, and another covenant between them, (some) Ziphites[46] inform Saul that David is hiding at Horesh and if the king comes they will hand him over (1 Sam 23:16–21). This incident is difficult to reconcile with the social-bandit thesis. Whereas the willingness of the people of Keilah to hand David over to Saul was motivated by fear of the destruction of their town that would have trumped any warm feelings they felt towards David, the Ziphites have no such motivation. Nevertheless, it is possible, as Fokkelman suggests, the Ziphites may have regarded themselves as being in a similar situation to the population of Keilah: either remain loyal to Saul as the established authority or transfer allegiance to David, "the new warlord," and they chose the former option.[47] They have alerted Saul to David's whereabouts (and here we have a good example of how Saul could have kept track of David from informants in a particular region), either because they wanted to curry favor with the king generally (so Fokkelman), or because they were unhappy at a powerful band of men camped out in their territory. They aid Saul in spite of the fact that Ziph is a town in Judah (Josh 15:24), so in telling Saul where David is hiding the Ziphites are taking a definite step to put their relationship with the king ahead of their tribal bond with David. Saul's statement that these Ziphites have shown compassion to him indicates the fact that their personal relationship has been promoted by their coming to

45. McCarter, *I Samuel*, 370–71 proposes that the willingness of the lords of Keilah to hand David over suggests that the city was not Judahite at this time. This seems unlikely.

46. Whereas the Masoretic Text has "(some) Ziphites," the LXX has "the Ziphites."

47. Fokkelman, *Narrative Art and Poetry*, 2:475.

him with news of David. But acting as good clients is unlikely to have
been their only motivation. For it is very difficult to imagine how a
fairly remote town like Ziph could in any way benefit from having six
hundred armed men bivouacked nearby, especially given the resources
they would require merely for their subsistence (a factor to which I will
return below); this is another likely explanation for the Ziphites' providing information to Saul.

Saul sends the Ziphites off to get more information. Meanwhile,
David and his men are in the wilderness of Maon, and Saul and his
men seek him there but call off their attempt to capture him when word
comes of a Philistine raid, prompting David to move to the strongholds
of En-gedi (1 Sam 23:22–29).

In 1 Samuel 24, having finished with the Philistines, Saul takes
three thousand men to capture David in the region of En-gedi. Here
David passes over the chance to kill Saul when the king comes to relieve
himself in a cave where David and his men are hiding and swears to Saul
not to wipe out his name or descendants after his death.

David, Abigail, and Nabal (1 Samuel 25)

The events recounted in 1 Samuel 25 provide the most detailed picture
in the text of David and his band interacting with the Israelite population of Judea. Walter Brueggemann aptly observes that in this chapter
we see a different David, one who is not dealing with Yahweh's anointed
king (whom he is loath to kill even when he has the chance) but with
someone else: "The consequence is that David lives much closer to the
practice of violence. Indeed, David's potential violence seems to evoke
and require the shrewd intervention of Abigail."[48]

The chapter begins by relating the death of Samuel, which leads to
"all Israel" gathering to mourn and bury him. This raises the intriguing possibility that David and his band and Saul and his forces were
all there, with Saul temporarily suspending his pursuit because of the
solemnity of the occasion. In any case, the next information we receive
is that David (and surely his men) then rose and went down to the
wilderness (*midbar*), either of Paran (MT) or Maon (LXX). Certainly
the action occurs in and around Maon (modern Tell Maʿin, circa eight

48. Brueggemann, *I and II Samuel*, 174–75.

miles south of Hebron,)[49] and Carmel. David's band still number six hundred men (1 Sam 25:13).

David and his men have gone off to the wilderness of Paran after the death of Samuel (1 Sam 25:1). The unspoken issue is how are they going to live, from where will they obtain the food to support the band. The text is extremely reticent as to how David and his six hundred men were able to survive in the wilderness (at least until they moved into the employ of the Philistine Achish, king of Gath, and embarked on a campaign of successful raiding on the pre-Israelite peoples of the land, as described in 1 Samuel 27). Moreover, the description of the second part of his band provided in 1 Sam 22:2, as explained above, suggests considerable indigence. People like this are most unlikely to have brought the necessary supplies with them. The reality of their position is clear and explains the silence of the text, for, as Hobsbawm notes, "there is no other way for an outlaw to earn his living except by appropriating the surplus of someone else's labour."[50] There is a good example of this in Judges 11. When Jephthah, the son of Gilead and a harlot, was thrust out of his house by the legitimate sons of Gilead, he fled from them "and dwelt in the land of Tob; and worthless fellows (*'anashim reqim*) collected around Jephthah, and went raiding with him" (v. 3, RSV, where "went raiding with him" appropriately translates "and they went out with him"). In the dealings between David on the one hand and Nabal and Abigail on the other we have a fine vignette of another way a person on the run with a sizeable band of followers could appropriate the surplus of someone else's labor.

This question is immediately answered by mention of a man in Maon, who is described as being "very great" (*gadol me'od*), meaning very wealthy. He possesses three thousand sheep and one thousand goats and is shearing his sheep in the nearby village of Carmel (1 Sam 25:2). Both Maon and Carmel were towns in Judah (Josh 15:55), and Saul had erected a monument at Carmel after his defeat of the Amalekites (1 Sam 15:12). The magnitude of the numbers of the man's livestock can be appreciated by comparing him to Job, who before catastrophe struck, owned seven thousand sheep, three thousand camels, five hundred yoke of oxen and five hundred she asses and was "the greatest of all the people of the east" (*gadol mi-kol beney-qerem*; Job

49. McCarter, *I Samuel*, 24.

50. Hobsbawm, "Social Banditry," 145.

1:3). Both Nabal and Job fall within the same category in that they were "great" (*gadol*), that is, wealthy: Nabal very wealthy and Job the wealthiest man in the east. The scene is set for a drama in which the man's abundance will meet David's need.

The narrator then mentions the man's name, Nabal, and also that he had a wife called Abigail, before offering a thumbnail sketch of the two of them that will be reflected in the story that follows. Whereas Abigail is of good understanding (*tobat-śekel*) and beautiful (*yiphat toar*), Nabal is rough (*qaśeh*) and "evil in his practices" (*ra'ma'alalim*), a Calebite after all (1 Sam 25:3). The Calebites were a people of non-Israelite origins (Num 32:12; Josh 14:6, 14), subsequently incorporated into Israel (Josh 14:14; 15:13).[51] Abigail, on the other hand, is probably an Israelite (as we gather from her references to the Lord when she is speaking to David), from the tribe of Judah.

Unfortunately, we are not told the nature of Nabal's evil practices. Fokkelman douses him with immorality, speaking of his "evil deeds," his "harsh egoism," and his "debauchery," the last word being Fokkelman's unjustified description of his intoxication at a feast (v. 36).[52] Brueggemann, on the other hand, suggests he is "not bad but stupid,"[53] which does not seem to do justice to his description as "evil in his practices." It is tempting to see in Nabal one of the elite who have become or stayed rich by exploiting those beneath them, for example, by driving the peasantry into debt. Although he becomes intoxicated at the feast he lays out, presumably for his family and richer friends (a feast like the feast of a king; v. 36), he provides only meat, bread, and water (not wine) for his shearers (v. 11).

The trigger for the action is that David hears "in the wilderness" that Nabal is shearing his sheep. For the flock owner, the occasion of shearing sheep was like a harvest festival and was a cause for celebration and feasting and drinking, as can be seen from the description in 2 Samuel 13:23–29.[54] With six hundred mouths to feed and clearly expecting a considerable gift from Nabal, David sends off ten young men. Although Hertzberg suggests that at times like this a man might be expected to give something to "needy neighbors," David does not intend to make

51. McCarter, *I Samuel*, 396.

52. Fokkelman, *Narrative Art and Poetry*, 2:482.

53. Brueggemann, *First and Second Samuel*, 175.

54. Hertzberg, *I & II Samuel*, 202.

a claim on Nabal on the basis of his indigence (even if that accurately reflected the position of his band).[55] David's sense of honor would have ruled out anything that looked like begging. The instructions he gives his men reveal a very different motivation for his request:

> Go up to Carmel, and go to Nabal, and greet him in my name. And thus you shall salute him: "Peace be to you, and peace be to your house, and peace be to all that you have. I hear that you have shearers; now your shepherds have been with us, and we did them no harm, and they missed nothing, all the time they were in Carmel. Ask your young men, and they will tell you. Therefore let my young men find favor in your eyes; for we come on a feast day. Pray, give whatever you have at hand to your servants and to your son David." (vv. 5–8, RSV)

For present purposes, the critical words here are "we did them no harm" (lo' heklamnum) in v. 7. The verb here is the hiphil of kalam, a verb that appears thirty-eight times in all its forms in the Hebrew Bible, of which ten instances are in the hiphil.[56] The word, which forms part of the abundantly rich language of honor and shame in the Hebrew Bible, actually means "to humiliate, disgrace or insult": "A person to whom klm is applied is degraded both subjectively and objectively. That person is isolated within his previous world, and his own sense of worth is impugned. He becomes subject to scorn, insult and mockery, and is cut off from communication."[57]

There are two substantival forms: kelimma (31 instances) and kelimmut (one instance), both meaning "disgrace." How would David's men have humiliated Nabal's shepherds? There are three possibilities: by verbal abuse, by physical violence, or by demanding by force or stealing some of the sheep Nabal's shepherds were tending. The last of these is by far the most probable, since these words are immediately followed by a reference to their having missed nothing, meaning none of their sheep was lost.[58] This explains why the RSV translation of "we did them no harm" is acceptable, even if it fails to convey the precise shame-related flavor of that harm in the Hebrew. At this point the Septuagint makes

55. Ibid.

56. Judg 18:7; Ruth 2:15; 1 Sam 20:34; 1 Sam 25:7; Job 11:3 and 19:3; Ps 44:10; Prov 25:8; 28:7; and Jer 6:15.

57. Wagner, "klm," 186.

58. To similar effect, see ibid.,187.

explicit what is certainly implied in the Masoretic text, "we did not hinder them (*ouk apekōlusamen autous*), and we did not demand anything from them" (*ouk eneteilametha autois outhen*). The Vulgate, on the other hand, closely follows the Masoretic Text, except that it clarifies that it was sheep that failed to go missing: *Nunquam eis molesti fuimus, nec aliquando defuit quidquam eis de grege* ("Nor were we ever troublesome to them, nor did anything ever going missing from their flock").

We must face up to the hard edge to what David is saying. He is not suggesting that his men protected Nabal's shepherds from other thieves or raiders; David makes no mention of such people. Instead, David's men *themselves* forbore from injuring the shepherds or taking sheep from their flocks by force. David is saying in effect, "We had your men and your sheep in our power, but we did nothing to them. Now please reward us for our forbearance." This dimension is regularly missed by some commentators. J. P. Fokkelman, for example, uses the expression "guard duties" in relation to the position of David's men vis-à-vis Nabal's shepherds and sheep, as if they were protecting them from marauding third parties.[59] He suggests that "services . . . were provided" for the shepherds, although such services had not been asked for.[60] By failing to attend to the words *lo' heklamnum*, Fokkelman misses the dark side of David's position and blackens Nabal. Closer to the truth of the situation, and yet still excessively favoring David over Nabal, are the views of H. W. Hertzberg. In an interesting observation, if inconsistent with his explanation that Nabal might have been inclined to give support to the needy, Hertzberg explains that in this region wandering groups of men represent a danger to herdsmen and their animals. Yet, if these men are friendly to the herdsmen and leave their flocks unmolested, they expect some sort of tribute, "and this is regarded by the herdsmen, as we learn now, as being completely justifiable." He observes that David has not exaggerated in the reasons he gives for his request, and that one of Nabal's servants states that David's men were a "wall" for them, "in other words that he has kept off dangers from other quarters." Thus, what transpires is "all completely grounded in the relationships of the open wilderness."[61] This is, however, too benign a view of the situation,

59. For "guard duties," see Fokkelman, *Narrative Art and Poetry*, 2:475, 485, 486.
60. Ibid, 489.
61. Hertzberg, *I & II Samuel*, 202.

and not simply because Hertzberg overlooks the fact that David himself has indicated his men were potential predators.

Walter Brueggemann, on the other hand, sees the social realities in the text very clearly. David, he suggests, sends a message not of peace but "of intimidation and confiscation." David's greeting is, in fact, a warning: "David appears to be making a subtle but unmistakable request for protection money." David and his band pose a threat to those "who benefit from, value, and maintain a settled pastoral economy."[62] Brueggemann's remarks are entirely apposite and raise issues that require further exploration with respect to banditry and social banditry.

E. J. Hobsbawm has well described the social context for the type of interaction that occurred between David's men and Nabal's shepherds. He notes that

> "Few except returned ex-soldiers are entirely if temporarily outside the village economy, though still part of peasant society . . ." But exceptions are "the herdsmen, alone or with others of their kind—a special, sometimes secretive group—on the high pastures during the season of summer pasture, or roving as semi-nomads across the wide plains . . . But there are others as well, including "the armed men and field guards, whose job is not to labour, the drovers, carters and smugglers, bards and others of the kind . . . Indeed as often as not mountains provide their common world, into which landlords and ploughmen do not enter, and where men do not talk much about what they see and do. Here bandits meet shepherds, and shepherds consider whether to become bandits themselves."[63]

Certainly David's men met the shepherds; yet the text is silent both as to whether any of the latter wished to join David, or as to any act that could be characterized as banditry; indeed, there is a strong denial that anything of that kind happened to Nabal's flocks.

How should we characterize the approach David has taken to Nabal? It is possible to expand upon Brueggemann's suggestion that David wanted protection money by considering for comparative purposes protection racket phenomena from rural Sicily in the nineteenth

---

62. Brueggemann, *First and Second Samuel*, 176. I do not agree, however, with Brueggemann's categorization of David's men as "unsettled, greedy, malcontents" (176), since I prefer to see them as casualties of the social system or relatives of David (as discussed above).

63. Hobsbawm, *Bandits*, 28.

and early twentieth centuries as described by Anton Blok. The dominant pattern of agriculture was one in which peasant workers leased
fragmented fields from wealthy landlords, to whom they owed a large
proportion of their crops, and had continually to walk between them
to get to their plots: "This itinerant character of labor, moreover, given
the situation of endemic insecurity and the inability of the State to guarantee public order in the countryside, rendered the peasant vulnerable
to assault and hence dependent on private power holders capable of
providing 'protection' in exchange for tribute— all in addition to the
burdens of direct exploitation, which in certain periods left the peasant
sharecropper with but a quarter of his product."[64]

In addition, and even more relevantly, "natural pastures and their
relative scarcity entailed a migratory orientation of animal husbandry,
and this ruled out fixed boundaries and fenced places where the herds
could be kept under adequate surveillance."[65] So the animals were frequently kept roaming over desolate and distant places, in a manner not
dissimilar to what the ancient Israelite audience of this text must have
imagined was the case with the herders of Nabal's sheep outside Maon.

The peasants also had to give gifts to the people who employed
them. "These gifts werein fact tributes the peasant paid for protection."[66]
Very often it was to the Mafia that the peasants or landlord paid money
for protection against animal rustling and theft. During the early 1920s,
for example, one manager of a large estate faced rampant rustling of
their cattle. They kept enormous bloodhounds to prevent incursions and
thefts but they were robbed all the same. They then employed a Mafioso
and the robberies stopped. They paid him a yearly salary.[67]

So what happened to people who did not wish to pay money to
have their livestock and crops protected against theft?

> Persons who refused to pay or were unwilling to come to terms
> with the *mafiosi* who controlled the area suffered damage to crops
> and animals, and even risked their lives. Punishments involved
> theft, arson, and destruction: crops were set on fire or stolen;
> trees and vines were cut down; and animals either disappeared,
> or were wounded or killed on the spot. Sometimes cattle owners

64. Blok, *The Mafia of a Sicilian Village*, 46.

65. Ibid, 148.

66. Ibid, 55.

67. Ibid, 146.

succeeded in recovering part of their stolen flocks for a ransom. Such protection was always a racket: it was forced upon people by violence and intimidation.[68]

The question that arises from this comparative material is, just how close is David to running a "protection racket" like that of the Mafia in rural Sicily? Although he has not reached any agreement with Nabal to offer such protection in advance of doing so, he has a strong sense of entitlement to a reward after the event nevertheless. We need to ask, what would David have done if Nabal had politely refused his request. Probably he would have responded very adversely, perhaps with not quite the degree of hostility with which he reacted to Nabal's inept response to his request, but certainly in a way that reflected Nabal's failure to provide a reciprocal benefit to David's "protection." There would have been trouble. David was in a position to act just as the Mafia did, with violence and intimidation, and it is difficult to see what would have stopped him from doing so. Unfortunately, we will never have an answer to this question because politeness was not in Nabal's nature.

Nabal replies to David's men this way: "Who is David? Who is the son of Jesse? There are many servants nowadays who are breaking away from their masters. Shall I take my bread and my water and my meat that I have killed for my shearers, and give it to men who come from I do not know where?" (vv. 10–11, RSV).

Nabal's reply is offensive to David (when reported back to him by his men) in at least two respects. First, he has gone out of his way to insult David both by suggesting he is like a runaway slave from his master (that is, from Saul) but also by disparaging his lineage, by denying it the honor that comes from being connected with a known place. Nabal is also traducing the reputations of David's men in the same way. Second, Nabal counts David's claim to a reward for "protection" as nothing compared with his desire to provide food and drink to his shearers. Nabal's refusal to succumb to David's implied threat by giving his men provisions is understandable; he probably thinks that the threat is not real, or that he could handle it on his own.[69] Yet he is still foolish. He was clearly courting trouble by replying in a high-handed manner that would surely provoke David to anger and a consequent desire for revenge, and a man

68. Ibid, 151.

69. So Brueggemann, *First and Second Samuel*, 177.

with ten men probably has many more, even if Nabal does not know that behind David's request are six hundred swords waiting to punish refusal. *Nabal* means "foolishness" in Hebrew (as Abigail will later remind David; 1 Sam 25:25), and here we have it exemplified in Nabal's words to David's men. Although the game is a brutal one, failure to play by its rules risks disaster. As we will now see, Abigail, already introduced as someone with a good understanding, immediately realizes what has to be done.

So David's messengers return to him, and on learning of Nabal's answer, David says nothing to his men except "Gird on your swords" before leading four hundred of them out (1 Sam 25:12–13). Later we learn his intention is to slaughter Nabal and all his men (1 Sam 25:34). Meanwhile, however, one of Nabal's men has told Abigail what had happened: "Behold, David sent messengers out of the wilderness to salute (*lebarek*) our master; and he railed (*wayya'at*) at them" (v. 14, RSV).

The infinitive *lebarak* here conveys a greeting plus a blessing, a reference to the peace (*šalom*) David invokes upon Nabal, his house, and all that he has (1 Sam 25:6). The Hebrew translated as "railed at" is the qal imperfect of *'it*, a rare word meaning "to scream or shriek." This gives us a useful insight into the manner with which Nabal replied to David's men, something that is not apparent from the text of vv. 10–11. The man then continues, saying to Abigail, "Yet the men were very good to us, and we suffered no harm, and we did not miss anything when we were with them in the fields, as long as we went with them; they were a wall (*homah*) to us both by night and by day, all the while we were with them keeping the sheep" (vv. 15–16, RSV).

This is a rather sanitized view of the situation. Although the Hebrew verb translated "we suffered no harm" is again *kalam*, only here in the hophal ("we were not humiliated"), the man does not tell Abigail that the only people who were actually a threat to the shearers were David's own men. Probably he did not know; he has just assumed that David's men meant them no harm, and while they were there no one else could attack them; so they were a "wall." Maybe David's own men did not realize that throughout this period he fully understood the realities of the arrangement and was open to the possibility of commanding them to humiliate the shepherds by demanding that they hand over some of their sheep.

In any event, the young man wisely advises Abigail to consider what she should do, "for evil is determined against our master and against all his house, and he is so ill-natured (translating the Hebrew *ben-beliyya'al*, "a son of worthlessness," an expression used of the worthless sons of Eli in 1 Sam 2:12) that one cannot speak to him" (v. 17, RSV). Not only is this a remarkable thing for a servant to say to his master's wife about her husband,[70] but Jon Levenson has pointed to the irony involved in Nabal's having observed just previously that there are many servants nowadays "who are breaking away from their masters" when he himself has a servant of this type.[71] Abigail's subsequent actions indicate that she accepts the servant's view as an accurate assessment of her husband's character. Now we will see that Abigail knows the rules of the game even though her husband does not.

E. J. Hobsbawm makes an observation in relation to nineteenth-century rural Mexico that is highly relevant to the situation of Nabal and Abigail vis-à-vis David: "Isolated estates in such regions have long learned how to establish diplomatic relations with brigands. Ladies of good birth recall in their memoirs how, when still children, they were hustled out of the way as some troop of armed men arrived at the hacienda at nightfall, to be welcomed politely and with offers of hospitality by the head of the house, and to be sent on its mysterious way with equal politeness and assurances of mutual respect. What else could he be expected to do?"[72]

David clearly expected Nabal to act in this way; his expectation shows how closely his behavior aligns to that of bandits. The anticipated mutual expressions of respect cloak the reality of the violence that the visitors will unleash if they do not get what they want; the politeness they offer (in this case David's thrice repeated *šalom* and his describing his men as Nabal's "servants" and himself as Nabal's "son," in v. 8) is really just a salve to the honor of the person whom they are about to separate from some of his possessions. Whereas her husband failed to understand what was required, Abigail grasps the point perfectly, and she also knows that it will now take more than just supplies to deflect David from exacting murderous revenge. Without telling Nabal, she loads up an ass with food and wine, and intercepts David and his men (1 Sam 25:18–20).

70. So Fokkelman, *Narrative Art and Poetry*, 2:492; and Brueggemann, *First and Second Samuel*, 177.

71. Levenson, "1 Samuel 25," 16.

72. Hobsbawm, *Bandits*, 78.

In a very fine piece of characterization, as Abigail heads towards David, the narrator has him musing on the thought, "Surely in vain have I guarded all that this fellow has in the wilderness, so that nothing was missed of all that belonged to him; and he has returned me evil for good" (v. 21, RSV). The brilliance of this lies in the presentation of David as someone who has conveniently forgotten, in his anger, that the only threat that Nabal's shepherds and sheep ever needed guarding against was that posed by David himself.

In a long and remarkably astute performance,[73] Abigail wins David over by abasing herself before him, by asking him to blame her and not her clod of a husband, by her gift and by her praising David for having foregone incurring blood guilt by taking vengeance in the light of his important role from the Lord in the future of Israel (1 Sam 25:23–31). David grants her petition (1 Sam 25:32–35), which means in context that she saves him from committing the act of violence that he had actually sworn an oath to God he would commit (1 Sam 25:22). This potential act of bloodshed brings out the brutal realities involved in feeding six hundred men on the run and in the wilderness.

Keith Bodner has rejected the idea that David was running the ancient Near Eastern equivalent of a protection racket, both because such operations have "a peculiarly mafia-like aroma" and also because this would not "envelop David in a positive fragrance."[74] Yet the answer to the first objection is that the Mafia protection activities were really just manifestations of older patterns of behavior on grazing land remote from legal or political authority and to the second that this is a text that does show a darker side to David's character, both in his first approach to Nabal and in the effort needed by Abigail to stop him doing evil when his wishes are thwarted.

David's interaction with Abigail closely corresponds with two aspects of the "Quest" plot identified by Booker that were mentioned earlier in this chapter: temptations to which the hero is subject and helpers who offer him positive assistance. In David's case this is not just material aid (such as King Alcinous and his daughter, Princess Nausicaa, offer Odysseus when he is washed up on their island after being shipwrecked, in books 6–13 of the *Odyssey*), but also crucial advice, such as the warnings of danger which the old man Infadoo gives Alan Quatermain and

---

73. See Matthews, "Female Voices," 10, on David and Abigail.

74. Bodner, *1 Samuel*, 261.

his friends in *King Solomon's Mines*).[75] In book 6 of Malory's *Morte d'Arthur*, Sir Galahad, Sir Bors and Sir Percival meet Sir Percival's sister, a beautiful maiden, who guides them onto the ship that will carry them across the sea to begin the closing stages of their quest for the Grail and who, when they find another vessel, warns Galahad not to enter it unless he is sinless. A large chunk of Abigail's address to David (six out of eight verses: 1 Sam 25:26–31) concerns the need for David to avoid shedding blood without cause because of his destiny to be appointed prince over Israel (v. 30). Although this material serves Abigail's immediate purpose of deterring David and his men from slaughtering every male in her household and no doubt David was delighted to hear this woman's confident statement of his future leadership over Israel, these elements do not detract from the truth of what she was saying: to kill without cause was inconsistent with and, by necessary implication, probably destructive of, his future as the Lord's appointed ruler over Israel. Such killing, Abigail is saying, is simply inconsistent with this role. Killing Nabal and the other men in her house represents a serious temptation that could be fatal to his destiny (and to the quest that he refuses to acknowledge he is even engaged upon). The extent to which David takes seriously this view of his position before God emerges initially in his response to her: "Blessed be your discretion, and blessed be you, who have kept me this day from bloodguilt and from avenging myself with my own hand!" (1 Sam 25:33 RSV). But we also see it later in his disavowal of responsibility for the murder of Abner and his ordering the death of those involved in the deaths of Saul and his son, Ishbosheth, discussed below.

On her return home after her meeting with David, Abigail does not tell her husband what she has done because she finds him very drunk at the feast he is holding. A man who was not so stupid would no doubt have been very sober and moving around his estate setting armed guards to counter any revenge attack by David. So she waits till morning to tell him, at which moment "his heart died within him and he became as a stone" (1 Sam 25:37, RSV). About ten days later "the Lord smote Nabal; and he died" (1 Sam 25:38, RSV). Why does Nabal die? This is an important question, although some commentators do not bother to ask it.[76] We must consider the two stages. First, the initial occurrence, when his heart died within him and he became like stone, and then,

75. For these examples see Booker, *Seven Basic Plots*, 77.
76. For example, McCarter, *I Samuel*.

secondly, God, as it were, finishing him off. According to Fokkelman, Nabal dies because Abigail's report to him of her intervention in 1 Sam 25:37 entails his sudden discovery "of how completely isolated he has become morally. This sharing of knowledge in v. 37b petrifies him and finally leads to his death."[77] Moral isolation is a suspiciously modern explanation for the first stage. According to Jon Levenson, the cause lies in his loss of the provisions his wife has given to David, a tiny amount in comparison to his total resources, so that he "suffers a fatal stroke over a negligible loss."[78] Yet this seems a highly unlikely explanation; Nabal may not want to feed David and his men but he is not presented as a miser. The cause far more probably lies in the shame that has enveloped him by reason of his servants and his wife plotting to subvert his will in a manner that was entirely necessary given his patently ludicrous mishandling of the danger that David represented. Not only have his wife and servants taken control of his affairs, their very survival depends on their doing so. How could a man as haughty as this face any of them again? As for God's killing him after ten days, that may well represent, as Brueggemann suggests,[79] the consequence of Nabal's standing against the Lord's anointed king, even if such opposition was inadvertent. David interprets his death, less plausibly but not surprisingly, as God's repaying Nabal for the insult and the evil-doing he had offered him (1 Sam 25:39). On Nabal's death, David woos and marries Abigail (1 Sam 25:39–42).

David the Bandit: 1 Samuel 26–31.

The remaining chapters of 1 Samuel provide graphic evidence for how David and his band survived in the period that remained up to the deaths of Saul and his sons in battle with the Philistines. The most accurate word for their activity is "banditry."

First Samuel 26 recounts how Saul, with three thousand men once again goes off after David in the wilderness of Ziph, where David again refrains from killing him when he could easily have done so. Nevertheless, ever fearing for his life at Saul's hands, David escapes (for a second time) to Achish, the Philistine king of Gath, with his six hundred men and every man with his household, including David with his two

---

77. Fokkelman, *Narrative Art and Poetry*, 2:480.

78. Levenson, "1 Samuel 25," 17.

79. Brueggemann, *First and Second Samuel*, 180.

wives, Ahinoam of Jezreel and Abigail of Carmel. At David's request, Achish allows him to settle in Ziklag (1 Sam 27:1–7).

David now initiates a series of raids (*pašat*) upon the original inhabitants of the land, on the Geshurites, the Girzites, and the Amalekites, as far as Shur, to the land of Egypt (1 Sam 27:8). Here was what he and his men did: "And David smote the land, and left neither man nor woman alive, but took away the sheep, the oxen, the asses, the camels, and the garments, and came back to Achish" (1 Sam 27:9, RSV).

David is pretending to Achish that he is attacking Judah and her allies, whereas in fact he is attacking the old enemies of Judah. He kills every man and woman in the towns he sacks so that there will be no one to contradict his account (1 Sam 27:10–11). As a result, Achish thinks David has alienated Israel and become his servant (1 Sam 27:12).

Now compare this with the account of an act of banditry in 1930s China, as reported in the *Free-Lance Star* (a newspaper published in Fredericksburg, Virginia) on April 28, 1930. The newspaper (and others in the United States for this date, such as the *New York Times*) reported that bandits had looted and burned the town of Kingsuchén, which lay on the northern border of Kiangsi and Anhwei provinces, about one hundred miles from Nanking, the nationalist-government capital of China. The bandits had killed one thousand men, women, and children, and captured another thousand. They were reported to have displayed a ferocity that had no parallel in the annals of Chinese banditry, which was then occurring on a gigantic scale. One hundred bandits, arriving on horses, had set up thirty machine guns and raked the streets, mowing the villagers down. As the bandits departed, they forced their captives to carry the loot.

What David did was essentially identical to this, except that the Chinese bandits at least left some of the townsfolk alive so they could carry the loot. David was also attacking old enemies of Judah and the other Israelites, but there was no current threat from these peoples. The fact that David may have been settling old scores would not have mattered much to those he slaughtered, and his band clearly kept all the booty for themselves. David was acting as the leader of a powerful bandit gang with an interesting pretext for his actions. The narrator appears to see no evil in David's actions, probably because this was a culture where moral duties were owed to members of one's ingroup, and the outgroups were fair game for insult and attack.

Ironically, David is soon on the receiving end of attention from a marauding gang similar to what he is dealing out to the towns in southern Canaan. We can pass over the events described in 1 Samuel 28 and 29 briefly. First Samuel 28 begins with the Philistines preparing for war against Israel, and Achish telling David he and his men will fight with him (1 Sam 28:1–2). At this point Saul makes a nocturnal visit to a woman at Endor, a medium, who summons forth the soul of Samuel with the news that the morrow will bring Philistine victory over Israel and the death of Saul and his sons (1 Sam 28:3–25). As the armies are mustering—the Philistines at Aphek and the Israelites at Jezreel—at the insistence of the Philistine leaders who do not want David and his men at their back during the battle, Achish dismisses him and his men from the field and they leave early in the morning to return to Philistine territory (1 Samuel 29). Thus is David saved from raising his arm in violence against an Israelite.

By the time they get to Ziklag, however, a few days later, they find that "the Amalekites had made a raid (*pašeṭu*) upon the Negeb and upon Ziklag. They had overcome Ziklag, and burned it with fire, and taken captive the women and all who were in it, both small and great; they killed no one, but carried them off, and went their way" (1 Sam 30:1–2, RSV).

While David and his men were away at Aphek, the Amalekites had captured their wives and children, including David's wives Ahinoam and Abigail; so angry were his men at this that they spoke of stoning David (1 Sam 30:3–6). Later we learn that the Amalekites had also, as we would expect, taken spoil, especially their flocks and herds (1 Sam 30:20). So the Amalekites had meted out to David's town what he had meted out to them, except he had killed every man and woman he captured, whereas the Amalekites had killed no one. The same verb—*pašaṭ*, "to make a raid" against (*'al*) or upon (*'el*)—is used of David's attacks on the Geshurites, Girzites and Amalekites in 1 Sam 27:8 and 10 and of the Amalekites raid on Ziklag in 1 Sam 30:1 and 14 (as also of that by the Philistines in 1 Sam 23:27). After enquiring of the Lord through the priest Abiathar's highly useful ephod (1 Sam 30:7–9), David pursues the Amalekites. Having located them with the help of the a sick Egyptian slave they had left to die in the desert (1 Sam 30:10–16), he falls upon them as they are celebrating their success. His men kill all of them (except for 400 who escape on camels) and recover their wives, children and booty the Amalekites had carried off from Ziklag, but also other spoil they had taken from the Philistines and from Judah (1 Sam 30:17–20).

On four occasions in 1 Samuel 30 the Amalekites are referred to as "a marauding band" (*gedud*) of men (vv. 8, 15 [bis], 23). This word is also employed of Rezon the son of Eliada and his "marauding band" (*gedud*) in 1 Kgs 11:23–25. The word would have had equal applicability to David's band, given their behavior,[80] but the text does not employ it in relation to them. Indeed at the end of chapter 30 the narrator records an aspect of David's conduct that clearly aims to distinguish him from the nasty *gedud* of the Amalekites, namely, that on his return to Ziklag "he sent part of the spoil to his friends, the elders of Judah, saying, 'Here is a present for you from the spoil of the enemies of the Lord'" (1 Sam 30:26). The narrator then mentions a number of towns and ends by noting that these were "all the places where David and his men had roamed" (1 Sam 30:27–31). This is interesting in two respects. First, David is suggesting that he has not been about enriching himself and his men, but doing the Lord's business. Second, his gift may represent payback for support the towns in Judah have provided him, or compensation for any damage they may have done. There is, however, no evidence of either phenomenon in the text, and the earlier textual data considered above about Keilah and Ziph indicates a marked disinclination on the part of the towns of Judah at any rate to help David and his men. More likely, this is a gift from David to elders of Israel extending beyond the people of his own tribe of Judah to curry favor with them in the general context of his struggle with Saul.

First Samuel 31 initially recounts, as Samuel had predicted, the victory of the Philistines over the Israelites on Mount Gilboa; their killing of Saul's sons—Jonathan, Abinadab, and Malchishua, Saul's wounding with arrows (1 Sam 31:1–3). In this sorry state, Saul unsuccessfully tries to have his armor bearer kill him and then falls on his own sword, as does his armor bearer. As a result, the Israelites flee from their cities, and the Philistines occupy them (1 Sam 31:4–7). The Philistines dishonor the bodies of Saul and his three sons, but the inhabitants of Jabesh-Gilead remove them by night and give them a proper burial (1 Sam 31:8–13).

---

80. As noted in Hanson, "Jesus and the Social Bandits," 284.

Conclusion: David and Banditry

To summarize this discussion, the narrative's portrayal of David and his band is recognizably similar to banditry, although the narrator takes great pains to ensure that David never actually treats an Israelite with violence. But it is very difficult to square the textual data with Hobsbawm's notion of a social bandit. David is not shown as having a positive relationship with the Judean peasantry, nor is he engaged in some form of social protest. The whole operation is really about protecting him and preserving his position vis-à-vis Saul. David knows that the kingship is at stake in his relations with Saul, not least because Abigail makes this clear in 1 Sam 25:30. David also has a band that eventually numbers 600. The scale of David's band can be gauged by the fact that Saul was only able to muster 3,000 men to take on David's 600 (1 Sam 24:2 and 26:2). All this means that we have a picture fairly far removed from Hobsbawm's "social bandit." As he himself says, "The kind of social protest which banditry represents is therefore normally neither very conscious nor highly organized. Nor are its objectives very ambitious."[81] Saul would have considered he was facing the threat of what we would call a revolution, not a problem of a reasonably small bandit gang preying on wayfarers and those living in isolated regions.

DAVID BECOMES KING (2 SAM 1:1—5:5)

Saul had been tortured by the thought that David and not his descendants would rule as king of Israel. Second Samuel 1:1—5:5 sees those fears realized, yet not for several years after the death of himself and three of his sons, Jonathan, Abinadab and Malchishua on Mount Gilboa. For Saul had another son, Ishbosheth, whom Abner, commander of Saul's army, made king of Israel. Ishbosheth reigned for two years (2 Sam 2:8). In the meantime, the tribe of Judah has anointed David king over them (2 Sam 2:4, 7). The narrator informs us that David established his court at Hebron and reigned over Judah for seven years and six months (2 Sam 2:11).

An ancient Israelite reader of the narrative no doubt would have wondered how Yahweh's purpose in having Samuel anoint David would finally be fulfilled, how this complication of two kings in Israel reigning in Israel simultaneously would be resolved. 2 Samuel provides an early

81. Hobsbawm, "Social Banditry," 145.

intimation of David's right to kingship when the Amalekite who comes
to David with news of Saul's death brings him the king's crown (*nezer*)
and armlet (*eṣ'adah*; 2 Sam 1:10). Just as Abigail assumes that the Lord
would one day appoint David as prince (*nagid*) over Israel (1 Sam 25:30),
the Amalekite is in no doubt that David is Saul's successor. Following the
pattern of 1 Samuel, however, David himself expresses no interest in the
kingship and is punctilious in honoring Saul's memory. He has his men
slay the Amalekite who claimed (probably falsely)[82] to have killed Saul,
"the Lord's anointed" (2 Sam 1:13–16). After his magnificent lament for
Saul and Jonathan (2 Samuel 1: 19–27), David moves his headquarters to
Hebron at the Lord's direction, where the men of Judah anoint him king
over the house of Judah. That he does have an interest in the rest of Israel,
to the north, surfaces in his commending the men of Jabesh-Gilead and
offering them his good services for their honorable burial of Saul (2 Sam
2:4–7). Yet even here he does not claim to be king over Israel.

When the inevitable hostilities break out between the supporters
of David and those of Ishbosheth, they do so without any apparent in-
volvement by David, since the initial conflict is arranged by proxies of
the two kings, by Abner and Joab, David's senior military leader (2 Sam
2:12–31). Although David's side get the better of that day's fighting (2
Sam 2:17, 30–31), this proves only the start of what proves to be a "long
war" between the house of Saul and the house of David (2 Sam 3:1).

The war only comes to end because Abner turns against Ishbosheth
at the Ishbosheth's negative reaction to his taking Saul's concubine for
himself (2 Sam 3:6–11). Abner offers to deliver the rest of Israel over to
David (2 Sam 3:20–21), and although he is killed by Joab, an act of which
David washes his hands (2 Sam 3:28–30), the tribes of Israel do indeed
anoint David as their king (2 Sam 5:1–5). In the meantime, Ishbosheth,
who is nothing without Abner's support, has been murdered (2 Sam

---

82. Scholars have grappled with the inconsistency between 1 Samuel 31, where
Saul kills himself (v. 4), and 2 Samuel 1, where the Amalekite claims he killed Saul (v.
10). Whereas most commentators take the view that the Amalekite is lying to secure
himself an advantage from David, and that 1 Samuel 31 is closer to historical reality,
Brueggemann suggests that "we do not have any firm data by which to sort out and assess the two reports" (*First and Second Samuel*, 213). Whatever the underlying historical facts, however, which is not a focus of interest in this volume, the narrative certainly
conveys the impression that the Amalekite must be lying, since in 1 Samuel 31 it is the
narrator who describes Saul's suicide, and this text gives us no reason to believe that we
have an unreliable narrator. But Brueggemann (ibid.) is certainly correct to say that the
David had to assume the Amalekite was telling the truth about killing Saul.

4:5–7) and David has his killers slain (1 Sam 4:8–12), just has he had ordered the death of the Amalekite who claimed to have killed Saul.

All of this reveals the extreme lengths to which the narrator goes to rebut any charge that David had seized the kingdom or had shed blood dishonorably in the process of gaining it. As Brueggemann notes, "When David finally arrives at full power, he is innocent and unsullied."[83] Although anointed by Samuel as the Lord's anointed long before, David is presented as standing by for years while circumstance and the actions of others propel him towards the kingship he is loath to grasp with his own two hands, even though various characters foretell he will be king: Jonathan (1 Sam 23:17); Saul (24:20); Abigail (25:28); the Amalekite, by his actions (2 Sam 1:10). At the same time, his closeness to God, that deep reality in his heart that God so valued (as discussed in chapter 6 of this volume), appears repeatedly: in this refusal to kill Saul when he had the chance, in his sentence of death on the Amalekite who had killed the Lord's anointed, and in his settling at Hebron at the direction of the Lord.

The years of war between the supporters of David and Saul and the problem posed to David by Joab's murder of Abner are comparable to the final ordeals that characterize many stories that Booker classifies as having the "Quest" plot.

CONCLUSION: DAVID AND THE QUEST

We have now considered the manner in which 1 Samuel 19 to 2 Sam 5:5 provides an answer to the question: "How then did David ever survive Saul's hostility and become king?" While Saul lived, the pattern of life pursued by David and his band cannot be aligned with Hobsbawm's notion of the social bandit. The main reason for this is that there is little evidence that David had a positive relationship with the local peasantry or that this actions represented a form of social protest against the prevailing power structures. While he certainly attracted the typical victims of an agrarian society, he is not shown as having a positive relationship with the peasantry, nor is defending them against Saul. Rather, he is maintaining a power base that would allow him to survive Saul's attempts to capture him and, eventually, to take Saul's place. David's band and its activities were what would enable him to become king of Israel himself

83. Ibid., 224.

and thereafter benefit from the same system that Saul had enjoyed. His trajectory is towards joining the elite, not challenging it on behalf of the non-elite.

David's career is, however, closely comparable with banditry. The nature of his activity would not have troubled an ancient Israelite audience, however, since the text presents the victims of David's banditry as uniformly non-Israelite. Fairly early in his career Abigail dissuades David from shedding the blood of anyone in her household (1 Samuel 25) and in his active career as leader of a bandit gang while under the patronage of Achish, the king of Gath, the towns he takes and the people he kills are non-Israelite (1 Sam 27:8–12). He is prevented from going into battle against Saul's army by the suspicions of Philistine commanders who persuade Achish that David is not to be trusted in such a conflict (1 Sam 28:1–2; 29:1–11). The ethics reflected in the text are not universal in nature but are confined to the responsibilities owed to fellow-members of Israel as an ethnic group and to Yahweh, Israel's God.

Once Saul has died, much remains to be done before the kingship passes from the Saulides to David (2 Sam 1:1—5:5). Nevertheless, the result is never in doubt. The obstacles posed to David's fulfilling the promise of his anointing by Samuel, initially by Saul and later by his general Abner and his son Ishbosheth are progressively removed, although not by direct action on David's part, and certainly not by his shedding of Israelite blood.

Finally, the whole narrative from 1 Samuel 19 to 2 Samuel 5:5 is recognizably similar to, and usefully comparable with, Christopher Booker's "Quest" plot type. The major difference from other examples, such as the *Odyssey*, Dante's *Inferno*, the *Morte d'Arthur*, and *King Solomon's Mines*, lies in the reluctance of David even to admit that he is involved on a quest for the kingship of Israel or to take any violent action that would further that end. This distinctive feature brings out the extent to which the narrative presents David as extremely sensitive to the reality of Yahweh as Israel's God and close to him. Nevertheless, other features of the "Quest," such as the Call, beginning on a note of urgent compulsion, the hero's band of followers, the long and hazardous journey, the perils on the way and the assistance offered to the hero to help negotiate them by helpers, and the final ordeals before achievement of the goal, are all present. These features are all contextualized in the particular context of ancient Israel and the particular phenomenon of banditry that David and his men engage upon to see them through the most dangerous phase of their quest, when David is being hotly pursued by Saul. Thus the story of David, one-time bandit and then king of Israel, takes its place as a particular type of the "Quest" plot that has struck a chord in various manifestations with millions of readers across the borders of time and culture.

8

"By the Hand of a Woman":
Judith the Female Warrior

ADDRESSING THE DILEMMA OF JUDITH

The book of Judith poses a short and sharp dilemma. What are we to make of a biblical text[1] which, although originating in a notably androcentric culture, tells of a *woman* who acts as God's agent to save her people, and does so by first deceiving and then decapitating the leader of the enemy host? The shock of this text lies in the fact that it describes how Israel is saved when God strikes down the foe "by the hand of a woman" (*en cheiri thēleias*), a phrase used on three occasions in the work: in Judith's prayer for success (9:10); when she informs the Bethulians she has slain Holofernes (13:15); and in the concluding prayer (16:6).

Not surprisingly a book as provocative as this has attracted considerable attention from scholars. Older interest on the part of Catholic critics lay especially in the question of possible historical foundations for

---

1. In line with the approach set out in chapter 1 (pp. 2–3), I will refer to the book of Judith as "biblical" on the basis of its deuterocanonical status from the time of Jerome onwards, a status it still enjoys among Roman Catholic and Greek Orthodox Christians, even though it was never accepted into the Hebrew canon (indeed not a fragment of the ancient Hebrew text usually supposed to lie behind the Greek versions extant from antiquity has survived) and is, accordingly, an apocryphal text for Protestants. The fact that it was included in Christian Bibles from the time of Jerome onwards justified the enormous interest shown in the text by Western artists and writers. See Moore, "Why Wasn't the Book of Judith," for a discussion of why this text was not included in the canon.

Judith and her actions,[2] although that interest now seems misplaced and has largely disappeared in favor of the view (accepted here) that Judith is a fictional character. In recent years we observe a concern with the inherent literary qualities of the book,[3] its intertextual links to Israelite[4] or even Greek writings,[5] its portrayal of its central character,[6] its influence on later Jewish and Christian tradition,[7] its potential for feminist interpretations,[8] and its huge impact on the European visual arts tradition.[9] Essays in the last three of these areas frequently take up the ethical dimensions of Judith's actions.

In the present chapter, in line with the general approach taken in this volume, I have a rather different aim. My aim is to read the story of Judith within the framework of a Mediterranean culture.[10] That is to say, although I concur with the central point of narrative criticism that we should always be alive to the total literary form of a biblical text, I am concerned to see how the story would have worked *as a story*, but within a Mediterranean cultural context quite alien to our own.[11] This was a culture with a strong group orientation that is very remote from Northern European and North American individualism.[12] I hope to

2. See Brown et al., *Jerome Biblical Commentary*, xvii, for a discussion of this perspective, which largely disappeared under the influence of the papal encyclical *Divino afflante Spiritu* (30 September 1943), although in the 1950s Bruns ("Judith or Jael?" and "The Genealogy of Judith") continued to argue that Judith was a real person.

3. See Alonso-Schökel, "Narrative Structures"; and Craven, "Artistry and Faith."

4. See Skehan, "The Hand of Judith"; Merideth, "Desire and Danger"; and White, "In the Steps."

5. See Caponigro, "Judith."

6. See Hellmann, *Judith*.

7. See Dubarle. "La Mention de Judith."

8. Levine. "Sacrifice and Salvation"; and van Henten, "Judith as Alternative Leader."

9. See Hellmann, *Judith*; Bal, "Head Hunting."

10. The original version of this chapter appeared as an essay in the Festschrift in honor of Bruce J. Malina (*Social Scientific Models for Interpreting the Bible*, edited by John J. Pilch). I first encountered Malina's short but seminal work, *The New Testament World*, originally published in 1981, while a doctoral student at Oxford in the early 1980s, and it persuaded me of the importance of taking seriously Mediterranean ethnography and anthropology in order to undertake historical exegesis of biblical texts.

11. In speaking of "Mediterranean culture" I am admittedly speaking at a fairly high level of abstraction, and I do not deny that there was a great amount of variety in the ancient Mediterranean region, both regionally and diachronically. See the discussion in chapter 2.

12. I do not deny that individuality existed in the ancient Mediterranean world,

show how many features of the text, especially some of those that have troubled commentators for one reason or another, can be interpreted afresh using this perspective.

At the same time, however, we cannot avoid the frequent notices in the text that Judith was working God's purposes in her mission, so that we must consider how the way the story is told in its context carried a theological message for its original audience. Indeed, I will seek to go further and suggest that it is difficult to get the theological point of the book without undertaking this process. To this extent, I hope that the present chapter will illustrate how social-scientific approaches to biblical texts are not inimical to theological ones (which is a common misunderstanding) but can actually facilitate a new appreciation of the theological point of biblical works.[13] While I would certainly not claim that this approach exhausts the dilemma posed by the book of Judith with which I began, I hope it might be regarded as at least throwing some light on it.

In terms of Christopher Booker's seven basic plots, the Book of Judith seems reasonably comparable with the plot he calls "Overcoming the Monster," which was also evident in relation to David's defeat of Goliath (see chapter 6). Some superhuman embodiment of evil appears on the scene (either human or animal) threatening an entire community. Eventually the hero, often armed with some magic weapons, confronts this figure (usually in or near its lair) and kills it, thus overthrowing its dark power. The hero liberates the community from this threat to its survival and wins great honor as a result.[14] So Gilgamesh kills the monster Humbaba in its lair, Theseus kills the Minotaur in its maze, Beowulf kills Grendel and his mother (the latter in an underwater battle), St George slays the dragon, and James Bond kills Dr No. We will have cause to see how this type of plot is comparable to that of the book of Judith further below. For the moment, however, it is worth noting that only rarely is the role of monster slayer in such a story played by a woman. Booker notes an interesting example in the 1979 science fiction film *Alien*, in which Ripley, the female officer who is second-in-command of a spacecraft in-

---

only that individualism did not. For the meaning of individualism in this context, see Hofstede, *Culture's Consequences*; and Hofstede, *Cultures and Organizations*; and Esler, *Galatians*, 13–14.

13. For a similar approach to a New Testament text, see Esler and Piper, *Lazarus, Mary and Martha*.

14. Booker, *Seven Basic Plots*, 23.

vaded by a powerful alien, alone of the crew members on her spacecraft survives its attacks and kills it.[15]

Although the issue of the date of composition of the Book of Judith will not feature much in what follows, I agree with commentators who consider that the work was written in the Hasmonean period.[16] Apart from the signs in the text of Hellenistic provenance,[17] a particular reason for this dating is the similarity between the presentation of the Israelite government in the text, by a high priest and council of Israelite elders (*gerousia*, 4:8; 15:8), and the epigraphs on Hasmonean coinage, probably first minted about 103 BCE by Alexander Jannaeus (who reigned 103–76 BCE),[18] which regularly refer to a (named) high priest and a *ḥeber* of *yehudim*, a council of Judeans.[19] There is a good case to be made for a date in the first half of the first century BCE, rather than in the secondary century BCE in the time of Hyrcanus, but nothing much turns on that issue here.[20]

CHALLENGE-AND-RESPONSE IN THE STRUCTURE OF JUDITH

Encountering the Book of Judith as an Ancient Mediterranean Story

There are sixteen chapters in the book of Judith, and Judith herself does not appear until chapter 8. To some critics this feature represents a problem with the structure of the work. Thus A. E. Cowley, having suggested that the work fell naturally into two parts, "the introduction" (chapters 1–7) and "the story of Judith" (chapters 8–16), went on to observe: "The book is thus almost equally divided between the introduction and the story proper. The former is no doubt somewhat out of proportion, and the author dwells at rather unnecessary length on the military details."[21]

---

15. Ibid, 45.

16. Cowley, "Book of Judith," 245; Moore, *Judith*, 67–70; Moore, "Judith," 1123.

17. Delcor, "Le livre de Judith."

18. Meshorer (*Ancient Jewish Coinage*, 75) argues against suggestions that John Hyrcanus 1 (reigned 135–104 BCE) minted his own coinage.

19. See Kindler, *Coins of the Land of Israel*, 9–21; Hendin, *Guide to Ancient Jewish Coins*, 13–17; Meshorer, *Ancient Jewish Coinage*, 74–87.

20. See Moore, "Judith," 1123.

21. Cowley, "Book of Judith," 242–43.

Other critics share this estimation.[22] More recently, however, commentators, including Craven, Moore and van Henten, have asserted the unity of the work and have tended to reject the notion that it is unbalanced.[23]

Craven, who has been especially influential, has argued that chapters 1–7 serve as a foil for chapters 8–16 in a number of ways, such as in developing a detailed contrast between Nebuchadnezzar and Holofernes with their huge military force on the one hand and Judith, with her beauty, faith and astuteness on the other. She describes the focus of her interest as "the compositional architecture of the text,"[24] or its "structure," by which she means "something akin to a narrative x-ray of the architectural or compositional pattern that undergirds the story."[25] In practice, inspired by Robert Lowth's pioneering explorations into the nature of Hebrew poetry in the eighteen century and Muilenburg's call to critics to attend to the structure of Hebrew texts,[26] Craven seeks out and finds patterns of parallels and antitheses in the work, both at the level of features of the plot and also of linguistic expression. For example, she argues that chapters 1–7 and 8–16 form two balanced sets of chiastic structures,[27] a phenomenon she describes, rather oddly, as "the *external* (my emphasis) design" of the text, meaning that the pattern she has discovered should be susceptible of "external verification."[28]

Although Craven finds these patterns aesthetically pleasing, it is clear that this judgment would not be shared by everyone today who agreed that they were to be found in the text, since some of us might wish to suggest that this level of symmetry (and contrived asymmetry) in a literary text is simply monotonous.[29] In any event, Craven's interpretation is certainly a specialist one, born of long and patient work on the book's architecture, and seems rather a long way from the response of a

22. Alonso-Schökel, "Narrative Structures," 3; Dancy, *Shorter Books*, 67.

23. See Craven ("Artistry and Faith" and *Artistry and Faith*), Moore (*Judith* and "Judith"), and van Henten ("Judith as Alternative Leader").

24. Craven, *Artistry and Faith*, 45.

25. Ibid., 20.

26. Muilenburg, "Form Criticism."

27. Craven, *Artistry and Faith*, 47–64.

28. Ibid, 45.

29. If, for example, the world is divided into those who find chiastic structures noteworthy and significant and those who do not, I confess to finding myself in the latter group.

non-specialist reader, whose experience of how the text works *as a story* will depend more on an encounter with its overt features in their narrative order as the text unfolds than with any sense of what an "x-ray" of its structure might reveal. In other words, ordinary readers encounter literary texts, just like persons, with respect to their external presentation and movement, not their bone-structure, so that radiography seems an inappropriate metaphor for a non-specialist reading. This brings us to a criticism of Craven's approach somewhat similar to that made against the structuralism of Lévi-Strauss in chapter 1.

The same considerations apply *à fortiori* to ancient readers, although now we need to bring their very different cultural context into the picture. I wish to propose that an *ancient Israelite audience,* engaging with the overt features of the text as the narrative unfolded (probably by hearing it read aloud than by reading it), would have found the work a satisfying and socially engrossing artistic unity for the particular reason that it embodies a central social dynamic of ancient Mediterranean culture—the pattern of challenge-and-response. First formulated by Pierre Bourdieu in 1965 from his ethnographic work among the Kabyle of North Africa and developed for biblical criticism by Bruce Malina in 1981, challenge-and-response refers to the myriad examples of social interaction, in cultures oriented around achieving honor, where one person "challenges" another, that is, makes a claim to enter his (rarely her)[30] social space and this claim is met by a vigorous response, frequently eliciting a counter-challenge from the original challenger, then another response and so on until some final resolution is reached, often the disgrace and sometimes even the death of one of the parties. Since I have discussed this social dynamic in chapter 2, I will not rehearse the details here, but will refer to appropriate aspects where relevant below.

I am proposing, then, that ancient readers (or listeners) would have derived a sense of the work operating as an effective story, carrying them along briskly from its beginning through its middle to its end, not so much from the factors to which Craven has valuably drawn our attention, nor indeed from others which van Henten has argued render

---

30. Since the focus in ancient texts is most commonly on interactions between males, with the book of Judith constituting a rare exception, usually both the challenger and the person challenged are males. However, one interesting arena of the pattern involving women occurs in households where the dominant male has two wives, or a wife and another woman, in competition with one another. A good instance is that of Hannah and Peninnah in 1 Samuel 1–2, discussed in chapter 4.

Judith 7–13 cohesive,[31] but from experiencing the exciting succession of challenge and counter-challenge, which flows remorselessly from Nebuchadnezzar's initial attack on Arphaxad (1:5) and his request for help from the western countries (1:7–10) to Israel's final expression of victory and self-exultation (16:1–24).

CHALLENGE-AND-RESPONSE IN THE BOOK OF JUDITH

The Initial Stages

The work begins with the (historically impossible)[32] reference to the twelfth year of Nebuchadnezzar's reign over the Assyrians in Nineveh (1:1), before immediately mentioning that Arphaxad was then reigning over the Medes in Ecbatana, a city that he had surrounded with huge stone walls (seventy cubits in height), towers and gates (1:2–4). This description of the huge fortifications of Ecbatana serves to set the scene for the scale of Nebuchadnezzar's daring in initiating war against Arphaxad and the scale of his ultimate triumph, but it is also the first challenge in the work, since fortifications on this scale enter the social space of other kings in the region, such as Nebuchadnezzar, both simply through the virtuosity of their architecture ("No-one can build more magnificently than I!") but more importantly as a military threat ("With these fortifications no-one can defeat me!").

An ancient reader, accordingly, would not be surprised by the very next action described in the text: "At this time King Nebuchadnezzar joined battle with King Arphaxad in the great plain that lies in the territory of Ragae" (1:5).[33] This constitutes a likely response by a neighboring king, with the initial focus on the military aspect of the challenge, although the eventual (and necessary) destruction of Arphaxad's capital was presumably a goal of the campaign.

All the peoples from adjacent regions (in the east) came to the aid of Nebuchadnezzar (1:6). Yet the result was very different when Nebuchadnezzar sent to all the inhabitants (*pantas tous katoikountas*)

31. Van Henten, "Judith as Alternative Leader," 225–32.

32. The extraordinary, indeed ludic, treatment of history in the work is an important feature that is beyond the scope of this chapter, but which I have discussed elsewhere— see Esler, "Ludic History."

33. In this chapter, translations from the Greek text of Judith or other sections of the Septuagint (such as 1 Samuel 17) are mine unless otherwise stated.

of Persia and the western lands, (that is) to those inhabiting (*tous ka-toikountas*) Cilicia, Damascus, Lebanon, and Anti-Lebanon and to all those along the coast, Carmel, Gilead, Upper Galilee and the great plain of Esdraelon, to all those in Samaria and its cities, to those beyond the Jordan as far as Jerusalem, Bethany, Chelous, Kadesh, and even as far as Egypt (1:7–10), In terms of challenge-and-response, his message (presumably a request that they come to his assistance) constituted a positive challenge, to which a positive response would have been to march quickly to his side.

One can sense the gasp of horror that would have been voiced among an ancient audience listening to this story by the actual response of these peoples (1:11): "All those who dwelled in all the land derided (*ephaulisan*)[34] the message of Nebuchadnezzar king of the Assyrians and they did not rally to him for the purpose of war, because they were not afraid of him and as far as they were concerned he was a single man. So they sent his ambassadors home empty, with their faces covered in shame" (*en atimia pro prosōpou autōn*).

The uniformity of the response is worth noting. The peoples in this list of those who scorned Nebuchadnezzar, someone with the status of "a single man" (presumably meaning a person without allies) and therefore liable to be destroyed easily (6:3), and shamed his ambassadors includes several whom the text will later identity as Israelites inhabiting Judea (1:12; 4:1, 13; 8:21; 11:19),[35] from Galilee in the north, through Samaria and as least as far as Jerusalem in the south. In other words, the Judeans engage in prevailing cultural patterns relating to honor and shame just as surely as do the other peoples mentioned. As the story develops, the extent to which the Israelites are deeply embedded in the ambient culture and, at least in some quarters, highly adept at playing its central game of challenge-and-response will emerge as important themes.

In this culture such a negative response to Nebuchadnezzar's positive challenge inevitably leads to the sort of reaction the king exhibits: "Nebuchadnezzar was grievously angry with all this land and swore by his throne and his kingdom to take revenge on all the regions of

34. Note that the point of the verb, that the recipients consciously dishonor the message, is missed in the JB translation that has "ignored."

35. The word *Ioudaios*, "Judean," does not appear in the book of Judith although it is very common in other literature from the Maccabean period, including 1 and 2 Maccabees.

Cilicia, Damascene and Syria and to destroy with his sword all those who dwelled in Moab, the children of Ammon, all those of Judea and all those in Egypt as far as the regions of the two seas" (1:12).

This is the typical reaction in this culture if a request for help is rejected, since such a response shames him who sought the help. The desire for vengeance to restore one's besmirched honor (which the Judith and the Israelites will themselves express later) motivates each of the latter stages of challenge-and-response. There are other cases in the Old Testament very similar to Nebuchadnezzar's reaction. Gideon, for example, asks the towns Succoth and Penuel to help him, but they refuse since he has not yet defeated his enemies, and when he is victorious he wreaks a harsh vengeance upon them (Judg 8:4–17). Secondly, when David's messengers are refused provisions from Nabal, he is only prevented from taking vengeance in the form of killing every male in Nabal's household by the timely intervention of Abigail (1 Sam 25:2–35). Thirdly, when the envoys David sends to greet the new king of Ammon are sent home in complete disgrace, the insult leads to war (2 Sam 10:1–7).

In due course, when Nebuchadnezzar and his forces have defeated Arphaxad's army, captured Ecbatana, effectively responded to the original challenge by turning its magnificence (*kosmos*) into a disgrace (*oneidos*), killed Arphaxad himself and then feasted for 120 days (1:13–16), Nebuchadnezzar plans "to take vengeance on the whole land, just as he had threatened" (2:1). An ancient reader, probably expecting something rather special from Nebuchadnezzar at this point, would not be disappointed with his counter-challenge to those who scorned him. The king informs a council of his staff that he wants everyone who did not answer his appeal to be destroyed (2:2–3). He chooses the leader of his armies, Holofernes, as his agent for this plan, aided by one hundred twenty thousand infantry and twelve thousand cavalry. They are to conquer the region, holding those who surrender to await the arrival of the king and killing all those who resist (2:4–13). Holofernes then begins the campaign, putting the counter-challenge into effect, as directed (2:14–20).

Further Developments

The rest of the book, including the actions of Judith and Israelites right through to chapter 16, is naturally interpreted as consisting of various types of responses to the challenge posed to the western nations by

Holofernes's invasion. The dynamic of challenge-and-response provides the unifying structure for the work. After his initial successes (2:21–27), the terror-stricken coastal towns such as Sidon and Tyre, Jamnia, Azotus and Ascelon, send envoys to sue for peace, laying themselves open to his advance (2:28—3:5). They welcome him with garlands and dancing (3:7), yet he demolishes their shrines, destroys all local gods and compels the people to worship Nebuchadnezzar alone and to hail him as god (3:8). This is, in fact, the first time that this dimension of Holofernes's campaign has been mentioned and it considerably augments the nature of the challenge to the peoples of the west, especially, as will soon emerge, to monotheistic Israel.

At this point Holofernes stops for a month to muster supplies, camping on the edge of Esdraelon, near Dothan, a village facing the great ridge of Judea. Thus is Nebuchadnezzar's counter-challenge brought home to the sons of Israel living in Judea" (*hoi huioi Israēl hoi katoikountes en tē Ioudaia*, 4:1). They tremble for the threat posed to their own recently rebuilt temple (no doubt because Holofernes has just destroyed the shrines of neighboring peoples), alert the people in various parts of the country, occupy the summits and prepare for war (4:1–5). Joakim the high priest in Jerusalem orders the inhabitants of Bethulia and another village facing Esdraelon to occupy the mountain passes and prevent an enemy advance (4:6–7), which they do (4:8). Thus the counter-challenge of Holofernes on behalf of his master Nebuchadnezzar is met with a courageous response, not a capitulation as with the coastal towns. With prayer and fasting all the children of Israel beseech God to save them and their temple from profanation and ridicule (chapter 4). An early sign that God will rescue them comes at 4:13: "The Lord heard their voice and looked with favor upon their affliction."

In chapter 5 Holofernes seeks intelligence concerning the Israelites who alone of all the western peoples are opposing him and receives from Achior, leader of the Ammonites, a brief history of the Israelites and a warning that if their God is against them Holofernes should attack, but that if their God is with them, they are best left well alone: "But if there is no lawlessness (*anomia*) among their nation, let my lord leave them alone, lest their lord and their God shield them and we become a laughing-stock (*oneidismos*) before all the earth (5:21).

Within the context of challenge-and-response Achior's words constitute a warning to the Assyrians only to respond to the initial insult to

Nebuchadnezzar on the condition that Israel's God is against the Israelites. In quite predictable fashion Holofernes's men take these words as a challenge to their honor—why should they be frightened of a puny people like the sons of Israel? After threatening to tear Achior apart, they urge Holofernes into battle so as to remove this slur on their valor: "Therefore, we will go up, and they will become provisions for your whole army, Lord Holofernes" (5:22–24).[36]

In chapter 6 Holofernes continues rebuking Achior, but goes beyond merely criticizing him for his views on when and when not to fight the people of Israel (*genos Israēl*) to utter what will prove to be *verba mortifera*: "(You say) that their God will protect them. But who is their God if not Nebuchadnezzar? He will send forth his power and wipe them from the face of the earth, and their God will not save them" (6:2).

In terms of the model, Holofernes has made the terrible mistake of directly challenging Israel's God. He has insulted him, both by suggesting that he will not protect his people, but also by asserting that he is not really their God at all, for that role is filled by Nebuchadnezzar. Although invading Judea and threatening Israel had also constituted a challenge, now we have Holofernes putting God's honor directly on the line. Although the pattern of challenge-and-response was played between social equals, in the present case Holofernes is really speaking as the agent of Nebuchadnezzar, so that one (purported) god is challenging another God. Ancient Israelite readers of this story would have surely expected that Holofernes would come to a terrible end by reason of such hubris and folly. From this point on, the expectation of the divine vengeance that will inevitably flow from this effrontery will form part of the dynamic of the narrative. In chapter 2 of this volume we considered a close parallel to Holofernes's challenge and its consequences in the in the narrative of 2 Chronicles 32 that sets out what happens when Sennacherib insults Israel's God.

Holofernes, having predicted complete victory against Israel, then arranges for Achior to be handed over to the Israelites of Bethulia, to die with them in due course (6:10–13). The Bethulians take him to their town, where he tells them what transpired before Holofernes (6:14–17). Not surprisingly, Achior interprets what Holofernes had to say as "boasting ('talking big') over the house of Israel" (6:17) and at this the people (*laos*) fall on their faces in worship and ask God to "look upon their ar-

---

36. On the role of Achior in the text, see Roitman, "Achior."

rogance (*hyperēphania*) and take pity upon the humiliation (*tapeinōsis*) of our people (*genos*) (6:19)." This expression unequivocally reveals the honor/shame dimension to the challenge and the Israelite desire for God to bring about an appropriate response.

On the following day, Holofernes orders his army to begin the campaign against the Israelites (7:1–5). On the next day they take the wells at the foot of Bethulia, to force the town to succumb through thirst, rather than taking it by force, which could result in a loss of considerable numbers of their own men (7:6–18). After thirty-four more days the Bethulians have run out of water and beseech Uzziah (previously identified as belonging to the tribe of Simeon, 6:15) and the chief men of the town to surrender (7:19–29). Uzziah suggests giving God five more days to save them and sends them home (7:30–32). Within the framework of the model, their imminent capitulation (after a robust start to their resistance) constitutes a very feeble response to the Assyrian challenge. The people are in favor of complete surrender and the abject and utter dishonor that would involve; they would be enslaved but at least they would live. Yet a little later Judith points out that the consequences would be worse than that: "If indeed they capture us, as you expect, then all Judaea will be captured too, and our holy places plundered, and we shall answer with our blood for their profanation" (8:21, JB).

The fact that Holofernes and his army represent a threat to the very survival of Israel brings the book of Judith into line with examples of what Booker calls the "Overcoming the Monster." The monster "is always deadly, threatening destruction to those who cross its path or fall into its clutches. Often it is threatening an entire community or kingdom."[37] Because the stakes are so high, as with other heroes in such plots, the actions that Judith takes and result she achieves gain added significance. She is engaged not just in some petty skirmish on the frontier but in a contest on which hangs the survival of her people.

At this juncture Judith enters the narrative. The extent to which patterns of challenge-and-response figure in the course of chapters 8–16 will appear in the next section of this chapter, where they are given a particular character by virtue of intertextual linkages with other parts of Israelite tradition. To round off the current section of this chapter, however, it is enough to say that by the end of the work the challenge

---

37. Booker, *Seven Basic Plots*, 23.

thrown down by Holofernes and the Assyrians to Israel and Israel's God will have been subjected to a decisive, indeed triumphant response.

JUDITH AS A NEW DAVID?

Intertextual Approaches to the Book of Judith

There have been many attempts to relate the Book of Judith to other parts of the Old Testament. These are based on what van Henten has plausibly described as "the intricate palette of intertextual relations" that exists between Judith and (other) biblical writings, a factor he reasonably cites against any tendency to interpret the text only in relation to one other Old Testament tradition.[38]

Several intertextual explorations have related Judith to decisive female characters. One comparison often cited is to Jael, the wife of Heber the Kenite who slew the Canaanite Sisera, as described in Judges 4:17–22 and 5:24–27. Thus J. Edgar Bruns argued in 1954 (and 1956) that the book of Judith was composed by one of the Jews of Elephantine on the model of Jael (whom he regarded as historical) when his people were facing a threat from the growing independence of their Egyptian neighbors.[39] "In both cases a heroine slays a national enemy singlehandedly, and in both cases she does so by attacking the victim's head."[40] On this thesis, which seems too implausibly localized to have won support, Judith becomes "a symbol of Jewish resistance to foreign tyranny based on the truly historical character of Jael, whose memory lived among the Jews of the dispersion in this way."[41]

A more plausible use of the Jael story has been offered recently by Sidnie Ann White. Her thesis is not historical but literary in nature: she argues that "the author of Judith had the story of Jael and Deborah in the front of his mind as he wrote his story."[42] She sets out a number of parallels, beginning with two fairly general observations.

---

38. Van Henten, "Judith as Alternative Leader," 224.

39. See Bruns, "Judith or Jael" and "The Genealogy of Judith."

40. Bruns, "Judith or Jael," 12.

41. Ibid, 2.

42. See White, "In the Steps," 5. White notes (Ibid, 14 fn. 2) that in spite of this way of putting it, she does not assume the author is male. Van Henten ("Judith as Alternative Leader," 225, 245–52) squarely raises the intriguing (and, for many reasons, attractive) possibility of a female author for the book of Judith but also the presence of "female voices" within the text.

First, in each story "a heroine slays an enemy of Israel singlehandedly, by attacking his head."[43] This is similar to Bruns, whom she does not cite. Secondly, as far as the structure of the two stories is concerned, each starts with a political struggle (which has religious implications) between the Israelites and a foreign power, moves to a climax in a private scene between the heroine and the male opponent that ends in his death, and culminates in a victory song. White next sets out a number of similarities at the level of plot and character, the most significant of which are as follows:

a. Both Judith and Jael enter the story at a late point in the plot. Once they have entered (that is, been mentioned), they are identified in relation to husbands who are, although for different reasons, absent. Both are childless. Since Judith is a widow, and Jael a member of a non-Israelite clan, so both are somewhat anomalous in relation to Israelite society.

b. Both Judith and Jael deceive the men they kill.

c. In both cases the scene of the action is a tent.

d. Both men are encouraged to drink something that lulls them to sleep, milk in Sisera's case and wine for Holofernes.

e. The heads of both men are the target of the attacks.

f. Judith pulls down Holofernes's bed canopy and takes it with her and Jael covers Sisera with something like a rug.

Other points of comparison she proposes, however, are not nearly as noteworthy as these.[44] In addition, a number of factors not taken into

---

43. White, "In the Steps," 5.

44. (a) Although, as she notes, both Judith and Deborah (not Jael) regard themselves as knowing God's will and give men orders accordingly, this is inherent in the situation of a woman who acts decisively.

(b) While there are two references to the hand of Jael (Judg 4:21 and 5:26) and Judith says the Lord will deliver Israel by her hand (8:33) and deliverance "by a woman's hand" (9:10; 13:15; 16:6) is an important motif, the hand is such a common theme in Israelite literature (see Skehan, "The Hand of Judith") that this feature does not create an obvious link between the two stories.

(c) Following Mieke Bal, she suggests that just as there is a sexual theme in the encounter of Judith and Holofernes, is it also possible to imply one between Jael and Sisera. But this is rather far fetched.

(d) To claim that Achior is a foil for Judith as Barak is for Deborah produces a rather strained comparison.

account by White weigh against her thesis. First of all, the scale of the action is very different. Israel is threatened by Holofernes and his host, but not by Sisera, whose army has already been annihilated to the last man by Barak (4:12–16) before Jael kills him. While the issue of the campaign actually turns on what Judith does, Jael is engaged in little more than a handy mopping-up operation. Thus, Judith is a heroine who saves Israel, Jael is not. Second, Judith's intervention is planned by her in advance and authorized by the local representatives of Israel, whereas Jael's action is a piece of *post eventum* opportunism. Thirdly, Judith's conquest occurs in a situation where her victim had been seeking to get the better of her; it was a contest, a further pattern of challenge-and-response, a version of single combat in fact, which she won. There was no contest between Jael and Sisera; she simply offered a fugitive hospitality and then slew him.

We are left then in the position that although it is possible to agree, on the basis of the more persuasive points of similarity proposed in White's careful comparison, that there might be allusions to the story of Jael and Sisera and that ancient readers or listeners might have derived a sense of some intertextual affinity to Jael in Judith's actions (thus supporting van Henten's insistence on the intertextual richness of the Book of Judith), there are good reasons for proposing that significant disparities between the two narratives prevent us regarding Jael as a central model for Judith. I will argue in the next section of this chapter that there is a far more persuasive comparison available, but before doing so I will note two other commentators who have sought to compare Judith with male figures in Israelite tradition.

(e) Just as there is a victory hymn in the book of Judith (chapter 16), a victory hymn is featured in Judges 5. Yet even White notes that Judith's hymn is also indebted to Miriam's in Exodus 15, and this case has been powerfully argued by Skehan ("The Hand of Judith"), whom she cites.

(f) Judith displays the head of Holofernes after she has killed him, just as Jael shows the body of Sisera to Barak. "These events confirm Yahweh's use of a weak, marginalized member of society in order to save it" (White, "In the Steps," 10). Yet this is a standard method of dishonoring an enemy in ancient Israel (it happened to Saul—1 Sam 31:9), and while Judith is a widow, she is also a person of property, honor, and influence.

(g) Although White proposes that both Jael and Judith bring peace to the land for a generation, Barak had already slain Sisera's army to the last man (Judg 4:12–16) before Jael killed the fleeing Sisera in what was really just a mopping-up operation.

(h) Her suggestions that both texts seem to share a Deuteronomistic theology, or that Jabin stands behind Sisera just as Nebuchadnezzar stands behind Holofernes, are too generalized to be convincing. Moreover, there are unmistakable Isaianic elements in the book of Judith.

First, Toni Craven has suggested a resemblance to 1 Kings 18, which records the contest between Elijah and the prophets of Baal on Mount Carmel, since "the Book of Judith tells a story in which the enemy of Israel takes the lead in the contest."[45] More particularly, she notes, one character stands against the many, Elijah stands against 450 prophets of Baal and the mute community of Israel; Judith stands against the hoard of Nebuchadnezzar, and the cowardice of her community (saying in her prayer that she knows Yahweh's power does not depend on numbers (9:11); both stories contain "delightful mocking scenes" (1 Kgs 18:27–29; and Jdt 10:11—13:10a); and in both stories the aim is to ensure all know that Yahweh is God.[46] On the other hand, the facts that 1 Kings 18 does not involve a military confrontation between Israel and a powerful and threatening external enemy and that the outcome of the contest does not result in any immediate improvement in the position of Israel (which retains Ahab as its king) and Elijah (who must soon flee to the wilderness) both count against seeing this narrative as particularly close to that concerning Judith.

Second, van Henten has proposed that the narratives concerning Moses in Exodus 17, Numbers 20 and Deut 33:8–11 have served as a model for important features of Judith 7–13.[47] Van Henten points to features in the book of Judith such as thirst (of which the Bethulians complain to their leaders) and drinking, a forty-day framework for the predicament and salvation of Bethulia and several other features. Van Henten's reading of the text "focuses on the testing of the leader in a situation of an impending catastrophe for the people; and suggests a comparison of the role of Judith, granddaughter of Levi according to Jdt. 8.1 (sic), with that of Moses, another descendant of Levi (Exod. 2.1)."[48]

While it is reasonable to discover such allusions in a work as rich as the Book of Judith, it is submitted that certain fundamental differences between the position of Moses and that of Judith prevent us seeing in any connection between the traditions the principal intertextual resonance. The main differences are the fact that in the Book of Judith Israel faces a powerful, external military threat, that the people remain faithful

---

45. Craven, *Artistry and Faith*, 47.

46. Ibid, 47–48.

47. Van Henten, "Judith as Alternative Leader."

48. Ibid, 240. Judith's ancestor was Simeon (9:2), not Levi his brother (Gen 34:25).

to Yahweh (even if tempted to surrender) and that the Israelite leader saves the people by killing the leader of their foes.

Nevertheless, while there are difficulties with according a privileged place to either of their proposals, both Craven and van Henten have taken an important step in putting forward male models for Judith. As such, they have established a precedent for the proposal which I will now develop, that it is actually in the story of David and Goliath in 1 Samuel 17 that we have the most extensive material available for intertextual comparison with the Book of Judith in the Israelite tradition.

THE CONNECTION WITH DAVID AND GOLIATH IN 1 SAMUEL 17 (LXX)

As far as I am aware, this is the first extended attempt in the field of biblical scholarship to relate Judith to David, although on rare occasions commentators have pointed out some aspects of comparison.[49] Yet the connection between the two narratives has long been made by artists and civic leaders in the West. Thus, Judith is portrayed on Ghiberti's Gates of the Garden of Eden in Florence (constructed in 1450) with a sword in her right hand next to a panel describing David's war against the Philistines.[50] After the expulsion of the Medicis from Florence, Donatello's statue of Judith and another he had done of David with Goliath's head at his feet were moved to the main square of the city as symbols of Florentine independence and freedom.[51] The killings of Goliath and Holofernes are depicted together on a fresco on the ceiling of the San Ignazio church in Rome.[52]

During my discussion in chapter 6 of this volume of the very distinctive version of the story of David and Goliath that appears in the Hebrew Bible, I mentioned that there exists a much shorter version, which is probably older,[53] in the Old Greek form of the Septuagint of

49. Thus van Henten cites 1 Sam 17:16 as a case where biblical salvation comes after forty days, but without developing the comparison between David and Judith ("Judith as Alternative Leader," 230).

50. Stone, "Judith and Holofernes," 81.

51. Ibid, 81–82.

52. Van Henten, "Judith as an Alternative Leader," 230. It is interesting that this valuable observation did not prompt van Henten to develop the comparison himself (see footnote 47).

53. I am unable to set out the reasons for this view within the ambit of the present chapter, but see the reasons offered by Tov ("Composition of 1 Samuel 16–18" and

1 Samuel 17. In an investigation into that very different Septuagintal version of the David and Goliath story that I have published elsewhere recently,[54] I have isolated twenty-two distinct elements in the Old Greek version of the encounter between David and Goliath in 1 Samuel 17. While there may be other ways to subdivide this narrative, the use of these elements, here slightly modified to twenty separate aspects, in the order in which they appear in the LXX of 1 Samuel 17, will facilitate a detailed comparison between the David and Goliath story and Judith.

1. The Setting: Between Two Armies

The Septuagint describes the setting as follows: "The Philistines (*allophyloi*) gathered their armies for battle, and gathered together at Soccoth of Judea, and encamped between Soccoth and Azeca in Ephermen. And Saul and the warriors of Israel gathered together, and they encamped in the valley, and arranged themselves for battle against the foreigners. The Philistines stood on the mountain (*oros*) on one side, and Israel stood on the mountain (*oros*) on the other side, and the valley (*aulōn*) was between them" (17:1–3).

Bethulia was located in the mountains (*ta orea*) and the Assyrians occupied the slopes (*anabaseis*) leading up to the town (Jdt 7:7, 10–11), then took control of the valley (*aulōn*) and its wells on which the Bethulians relied for water (7:17) and camped in the plain (*pedion*) (7:18). Thus, we have recognizably similar topography, although the rough parity of forces and position which characterized Philistines and Israelites is not replicated in the Book of Judith, where the Bethulians face a huge opposing force which has compelled them to rely on the safety of their town walls and the mountainous terrain. The situation is also different in that Judith will go right into the enemy camp for her confrontation with Holofernes, and not like David to a space between the two armies.

2. A Huge Enemy Comes Forward

Goliath was physically huge and a champion, although he was not the leader of the Philistines: "And there came forth a mighty warrior out of

"Nature of the Differences").

54. Esler, "*Monomachia* in the Ancient Mediterranean."

the Philistine army, Goliath by name, of Geth; his height was four cubits and a span" (1 Sam 17:4).

Yet we learn nothing of Holofernes's physique and he *is* the leader of the enemy. Nevertheless, both accounts have in common that the Israelite engages with the most prominent member of the enemy host. Each contest represents a form of single combat, *monomachia*, which was a phenomenon known in the eastern and western Mediterranean.[55]

3. His Armor and Weapons

Goliath had fearsome equipment: "And he had a helmet upon his head, and he wore a breastplate of chain armor; and the weight of his breastplate was five thousand shekels of brass and iron. Greaves of brass were upon his legs, and a brazen shield was between his shoulders. The staff of his spear was like a weaver's beam, and the spear's head weighed six hundred shekels of iron; and his armor-bearer went before him" (1 Sam 17:5–7).

There is no description of Holofernes to match these details of Goliath's armor and weapons. On the other hand, there are several references, before and after the actions of Judith, to the huge size and power of the Assyrian army which, in effect, she defeats (2:5–17; 7:2, 18; 9:7; 16:3), acting with the agreement of the leaders of only one town in Israel. In both cases victory is achieved against highly unfavorable odds. Bagoas (the eunuch in charge of his personal affairs; 12:11) may be regarded as fulfilling a role analogous to Goliath's armor-bearer.

4. Challenge

The challenge of Goliath is of the negative type, that is, an insult (in contrast to a positive challenge which takes the form of a gift, praise or a request for help): "He stood and cried to the army of Israel, and said to them, 'Why are you coming out to arrange yourselves for battle against us? Am not I a Philistine, and are you not Hebrews of Saul? Choose a warrior for yourselves, and let him come down to me'" (1 Sam 17:8).

The (negative) challenge posed by Holofernes comes most immediately from his having brought up his forces against the Bethulians with

55. For the eastern Mediterranean, see de Vaux, "Single Combat"; for *monomachia* among the Romans in the west, see Oakley, "Single Combat"; for a comparison of *monomachia* in the Old Greek of 1 Samuel 17 and in a story in Livy of a clash between a Roman and a very large Gaul, see Esler, "Ancient Mediterranean *Monomachia*."

hostile intent and cut off their access to water. In addition, however, there is the challenge offered to Israel's God at Jdt 6:2–3, as previously discussed.

5. Proposed Result of the Combat for the Rival Peoples

There is nothing in the Book of Judith to match the direct arrangement that Goliath offers Saul's Israelites: "And if he will be able to fight against me and to defeat me, then will we be your servants: but if I should prevail and defeat him, you will be our servants and serve us." (1 Sam 17:9).

Nevertheless, Judith certainly regards what she is about to do (which will only involve Holofernes) as leading to complete victory for her people, as she tells Uzziah, "Listen to me. I intend to do something, the memory of which will be handed down to the children of our people from age to age . . . Before the time fixed by you for surrendering the town to our enemies, the Lord will make use of me to rescue Israel" (Jdt 8:33).

6. Repetition of Challenge

There is nothing in the book of Judith directly parallel to Goliath's repeated challenge, the word for which (*ōneidisa*) underlines that he has dishonored Israel: "And the Philistine said, 'Behold, today, this very day, I have challenged (*ōneidisa*) the army of Israel: give me a warrior, and we will both fight in single combat" (17:10).

On the other hand, as just noted, Holofernes does make two challenges, one to God and one to Israel in the form of his assault on Bethulia.

7. Shameful Response by Challenged Army

The response of the Israelites to Holofernes is very similar to the response of Israel to Goliath: "Saul and all Israel heard these words of the Philistine, and they were dismayed, and greatly terrified" (17:11).

The Bethulians are described as fainthearted or dispirited (*oligopsychēsen to pneuma autōn*) as soon as the Assyrians have surrounded them (Jdt 7:19). After a siege of thirty-four days that leaves them without water, they are in favor of complete capitulation even though that will mean enslavement; at least that way they and their wives and children will live (7:26–29). Uzziah persuades them to wait five more days before taking this step. Within the local cultural norms, their imminent surrender entails gross dishonor for the Bethulians—as stated in the text, the people in the city were in a state of great humiliation (*tapeinōsis pollē*, 7:32). While Saul's Israelites did not go so far as to contemplate capitulation, just like the Bethulians they had no response to the enemy other than the dishonorable one of inaction.

8. The Hero Steps Forward

It is at this critical juncture that the one man of honor among Saul's Israelites steps forward: "And David said to Saul, 'Let not the heart of my lord sink within him: your servant will go and he will fight with this Philistine.' And Saul said to David, 'You will not be able to go against this Philistine to fight with him, since you are a mere youth, and he is a warrior adept at war from his youth'" (17:32–33).

But whereas readers of 1 Sam 17:32 are already familiar with David from his anointing as king of Israel by the prophet Samuel in 1 Samuel 16, the author of the book of Judith needs to introduce her before describing the very similar way in which she offered herself to assist Israel out of its dilemma. Accordingly, we learn details of her very long (and therefore honorable) lineage, always of major interest in the group-oriented culture of Israel (Jdt 8:1), her husband and the circumstances of his death (8:2–3), the seriousness of her widowhood (8:4–6), her beauty and resources (8:7) and, last but certainly not least, her good repute and devotion to God (8:8). This last feature is very significant in view of the devotion that David shows towards God in the account of his rise to kingship (1 Sam 16:1 to 2 Sam 5:5). Having heard that the townsfolk have become dispirited (*ōligopsychēsan*) with lack of water and wish to surrender to the Assyrians, Judith steps forward just like David. She summons two of the elders and, in a rather long speech (which contrasts with David's few words to Saul), Judith rebukes them for having, in effect, put God to the test, when the proper attitude is simply to pray to him for help (Jdt 8:9–20). She is extremely sensitive to the shame that will result from their surrender, and the inevitable defeat of the rest of Israel thereafter (8:21–23): "our new masters will look down on us as an outrage (*proskomma*) and a disgrace (*oneidos*); for our surrender will not reinstate us in their favor; no, the Lord our God will establish it as something shameful (*atimia*)."

She urges them to be steadfast and pray to God (8:24–27). Since up to this point, Judith has not actually offered to do anything herself in relation to the Assyrians, it is not surprising that Uzziah should assume something of Saul's mantle by suggesting that although she is a wise and a devout woman the best thing would be for her to go off and pray for rain (8:28–31)! Perhaps provoked by this courteous dismissal, Judith now at last steps forth, like David, to offer herself as the agent of salvation for Israel: "Listen to me. I intend to do something, the memory of which will be handed down to the children of our race from age to age . . . Before the time fixed by you for surrendering the town to our enemies, the Lord will make use of me to rescue Israel. You must not ask what I intend to do; I will not tell you until I have done it" (8:32–34, JB).

9. The Hero Makes an Honor Claim to Establish His Credentials to Fight

David needs to convince Saul he is adequate for the task and does so like this:

> And David said to Saul, "Your servant was tending the flock for his father; and when a lion came and a she-bear, and took a sheep out of the flock, then I went out after him and defeated him, and snatched it out of his mouth: and as he rose up against me, I caught hold of his throat, and defeated him, and slew him. Your servant smote both the lion and the bear, and the uncircumcised Philistine shall be as one of them; shall I not go and defeat him, and remove this day this insult from Israel? For who is this uncircumcised one, who has challenged the army of the living God? The LORD who delivered me out of the paw of the lion and out of the paw of the bear, he will deliver me out of the hand of this uncircumcised Philistine." (1 Sam 17:34–37)

Judith makes no honor claims of this sort, but the issue of her credentials does arise, since Uzziah has already conceded she is wise and devout before she announces she herself will take the initiative (8:28–31). Moreover, just as in 1 Sam 17:36 David reveals how greatly he resents the shame Goliath has inflicted upon Israel, so too does Judith exhibit a strong sense of affront.

10. The Leader Gives Permission, Invoking Divine Help

Saul's next statement to David, "Go, and the Lord will be with you"
(1 Sam 17:37), is closely matched by Uzziah's words to Judith: "Go in
peace. May the Lord show you a way to take revenge (*ekdikēsis*) on our
enemies" (Jdt 8:35). Both men have the wit (or inspiration) to realize
that God is at work in the improbable warrior before them. In addition,
Uzziah's indication that revenge is necessary at a time when not a single
Israelite has died at Assyrian hands indicates the extent to which in this
culture the mere suffering of a challenge incites the need for vengeance
to redeem the honor of those who have been challenged.

11. Arming of the Hero

In 1 Samuel the traditional motif of arming of the hero takes an almost
comic term when David at first unsuccessfully tries on Saul's armor before settling on his usual (and humble) shepherd's weaponry:

> Saul clothed David with a military coat, and put his brazen hel-
> met on his head. And he equipped David with his sword over his
> coat: and David was exhausted having walked about with them
> once or twice and said to Saul, "I will not be able to go forward
> with these, for I am not experienced with them." So they took
> them off him. And he took his staff in his hand, and he chose for
> himself five smooth stones out of the wadi, and put them in the
> shepherd's bag which he used for his supplies, and his sling was
> in his hand . . . (1 Sam 17:38–40)

Judith also prepares herself to "fight." She begins by repeating the
rituals of mourning, throwing herself to the ground, scattering ashes on
her head and uncovering the sackcloth she was wearing (Jdt 9:1), before
saying a long prayer to God at the same time as the afternoon sacrifice
was being offered in the Temple in Jerusalem (9:2–14). Although I will
return to the terms of her prayer below, it is useful to note that it climaxes
in her imprecation that God would give her deceptive speech (*logos mou
kai apatē*) to wound and kill those who have plotted evil against his covenant in order to show that Israel has him as its sole protector (9:13–14).
At the conclusion of this prayer, Judith "arms" herself for the mission. At
this point ancient readers would have encountered a comic dimension
to the story, analogous to the comedy surrounding David's arming to
meet Goliath, in the fact that Judith prepares for her contest by making as

beautiful as possible. She washes, anoints herself, arranges her hair, puts on a turban and her best dress, and then dons sandals, necklaces, bracelets, rings, earrings and all her jewellery. "She made herself very beautiful to catch (*eis apantēsis*) the eyes of the men who saw her" (10:4).

12. The Hero Approaches Challenger

Just as David "advanced against the Philistine warrior" (1 Sam 17:40), so too Judith, accompanied by her maid, went down the mountain and across the valley (Jdt 10:10), seeking Holofernes (10:12–13) and eventually being brought to him in his tent (10:20–23).

13. Verbal Exchange between Challenger and Israelite

Prior to the physical contest between David and Goliath, they engage in an exchange of insults. Goliath begins this rather ritualized interaction (called "flyting" in medieval European contexts) that forms part of their total pattern of challenge-and-response by disdaining David as an unworthy opponent: "Goliath saw David, and despised him; for he was a lad, and ruddy, with attractive features. And the Philistine said to David, 'Am I as a dog, that you come against me with a staff and stones?' David responds briefly, 'No, but worse than a dog'" (17:42–43).

This elicits a curse and a threat from Goliath: "And the Philistine cursed David by his gods. The Philistine said to David, 'Come to me, and I will give your flesh to the birds of heaven, and to the beasts of the earth'" (17:44).

Which elicits this reply:

> And David said to the Philistine, "You come against me with sword and with spear and with shield; but I come against you in the name of the Lord God of hosts of the army of Israel, which you have challenged this day. And today the Lord will deliver you into my hand; and I will kill you, I will cut off your head and I will give your limbs and the limbs of the army of the Philistines this day to the birds of heaven, and to the wild beasts of the earth. Then all the earth shall know that there is a God in Israel. And all this assembly shall know that the Lord delivers not by sword or spear, for war is the Lord's, and the Lord will deliver you into our hands." (17:45–47)

David's is a much more involved insult, so that he might be regarded as having bested Goliath in this area before defeating him in physical combat. David matches the invocation by Goliath of his gods by drawing the Israelite God into his response. He makes clear, for example, that Goliath has challenged God in challenging the Israelite army.

The extensive material in the book of Judith detailing the conversations between Judith and Holofernes that precede his death provides a reasonably close parallel to this trading of insults. Since, Judith needs to win her way into his confidence, she does not insult him so much as deceive him with flattery (Jdt 11:8) and with lies about how the Israelites are sinning and will incur God's wrath at Holofernes's hand (11:9–19). At the same time, he greatly flatters her (11:20–23) and wants to seduce her, since not to do so would sound to the Assyrians' dishonor in a culture where the men of one group are honor-bound to have sex with the women of other groups: "He said to Bagoas, the eunuch in charge of his personal affairs, 'Go and persuade that Hebrew woman you are looking after to come and join us and eat and drink in our company. We shall be disgraced (*aischron tō prosōpō hēmōn*) if we let a woman like this go without knowing her better. If we do not seduce her (*epispasōmetha*) everyone will laugh at us!'" (12:11–12, JB).

Each is trying to get the better of the other by the arts of discourse; indeed Judith's use of the word "deceive" (*ēpatēsen*, 13:16) in relation to her having gulled Holofernes is also used to describe how he had hoped to get the better of her (*apatēsai*, 12:16). In other words, we have here an oral contest that precedes the physical one which, *mutatis mutandis*, is similar to that of David and Goliath.

14. Combat Begun by Challenger

The fact that it is Goliath who initiates the combat—"And the Philistine arose and went to meet David" (1 Sam 17:48)—finds an echo in Holofernes's invitation to Judith (via Bagoas) to come and occupy the seat of honor opposite him in a drinking party (Jdt 12:13). Judith readily agrees, adding that doing so will give her joy to her dying day (12:14)!

15. Hero Kills Challenger by Superior Technique

David is successful against Goliath by means of his superior military technique, even though the fact he has God with him is suggested by the improbable feature that his stone actually penetrates the Philistine's helmet into his forehead: "And David stretched out his hand to his bag, and took out a stone, and slung it, and struck the Philistine on his forehead, and the stone penetrated through the helmet into his forehead, and he fell on his face upon the ground . . . And David ran, and stood over him, and took his sword, and killed him" (1 Sam 17:49, 51).

Judith also manifests a superior technique, first by making herself beautiful ("dressing to kill," as it were) in a way which incites in Holofernes a powerful desire to sleep with her and then to drink more than he had ever drunk before, so that he passes out on his bed, leaving no-one in the tent except Judith (Jdt 12:15—13:3). Although the scene is not played out before the rival armies, there is a congruence of situations in that what will prove the fatal space is shared only by the contestants in the *monomachia*.[56] Thus, Judith, like David with his sling, manages to render her enemy prostrate and defenseless. And just like David, Judith uses Holofernes's own sword to cut off his head.

16. Treatment of Challenger's Body

The fact that Judith employs decapitation, as David had (1 Sam 17:51), is a noteworthy detail common to the two narratives. Both these Israelites could have applied the sword to their opponent's body in some other fashion to deliver the quietus. That they both chose to decapitate their foe testifies to the status of the head as the most honorable part of the body in this culture and the importance of grossly mistreating it in this way to maximize the disgrace inflicted on the enemy. This consideration explains why the Philistines cut Saul's head from his corpse (1 Sam 31:9) and why John the Baptist would later suffer death by beheading (Mark 6:17–29).

17. Response by the Enemy Army

Since the combat between David and Goliath is played out before the two armies, the reaction of the Philistines is immediate: "The Philistines saw that their champion was dead, and they fled" (1 Sam 17:51).

The secrecy with which Judith effects her defeat of Holofernes results in the narrative developing in a somewhat different direction, to

56. Although Goliath's shield bearer is mentioned at 1 Sam 17:7, he is not mentioned in the confrontation, just as Judith's maid stays outside the tent (Jdt 13:3).

the extent that the Philistines learn immediately of their hero's death, while Holofernes's men only learn later. Judith and her maid must first return to Bethulia (Jdt 13:10–15), where she displays Holofernes's head triumphantly to the townsfolk and emphasizes that she dishonored Holofernes, not he her: "My face deceived (*ēpatēsen*) him to his own destruction; he committed no sin with me to pollute and disgrace (*eis miasma kai aischynēn*) me" (13:16).

In accordance with Judith's instructions, the next morning the Bethulians hang Holofernes's head on the town walls and charge down upon the Assyrians (14:1–4, 11). At this point Bagoas discovers what has happened to his master, accurately summing up the situation as follows: "One Hebrew woman has brought dishonor (*aischynēn*) on the house of king Nebuchadnezzar. Look, Holofernes is lying dead on the ground and his head is not on him" (14:18).

The result is that consternation strikes the Assyrian army (14:19). Just like the Philistines, they too flee when they see their hero has been decapitated (15:1–3).

18. Response by the Hero's Army

Saul's army pursued the Philistines: And the warriors of Israel and Judah arose, and shouted and pursued them as far as the entrance to Geth, and as far as the gate of Ascalon: and the slain among the Philistines fell in the way of the gates, both to Geth, and to Accaron" (1 Sam 17:52).

So too did the Israelites set off after the Assyrians: "As soon as the Israelites heard the news, they fell on them as one man and massacred them all the way to Choba" (Jdt 15:5). In due course, moreover, "the warriors of Israel returned from pursuing the Philistines and they destroyed their camp" (1 Sam 17:53). The same fate befell the Assyrians' camp in the book of Judith: "The rest, who had stayed in Bethulia, fell upon the Assyrian camp and looted it to their great profit. The Israelites returning from the slaughter seized what was left" (Jdt 15:6–7).

19. Further Dishonor of the Challenger

In 1 Samuel 17 David compounds the dishonor he metes out to Goliath in this way: "And David took the head of the Philistine, and brought it to Jerusalem; but he put his armor in his tent" (1 Sam 17:54).

In the book of Judith Holofernes's head has already been subjected to public ridicule by being hung on the battlements of Bethulia; thus, the element is common to both narratives but in a slightly different order. Nevertheless, one other point of similarity to David's bringing Goliath's head to Jerusalem is that Judith dedicates her share of the booty as an offering in the temple (16:19).

20. Praise for Hero

The next section in the Septuagintal version of the story[57] is the description of women coming out with dancing and musical instruments to greet David (1 Sam 18:6), and saying, "Saul has struck his thousands, but David his tens of thousands" (v. 7). This public response to David's contest with Goliath and other Philistines (not hitherto mentioned in the text) makes Saul very angry (vv. 6–7).

In the book of Judith there are two expressions of praise for the heroine. The first enunciated by Uzziah when she has returned with Holofernes's head (Jdt 13:18–20) and the second one, after the total defeat of the Assyrians, by the high priest Joakim and the council of the elders of Israel (15:9–10). Both statements refer to Judith's honor and invoke God's blessings on her. Uzziah prays that she may be blessed beyond all women on earth (13:19) and Joakim and the council assert that she is the great foundation for the honor (*mega kauchēma*) of their people (15:9).

Yet there is one particular feature of the praise which Judith receives which is very reminiscent of David. For just as the women came out from all the towns on Israel to meet David and Saul, singing and dancing to the sound of the tambourine and lyre and singing the song just cited, so too in the book of Judith, "all the women of Israel, hurrying to see her, formed choirs of dancers in her honor" (Jdt 15:12). She then led the women as they danced.[58]

---

57. The Masoretic Text contains the additional details of Saul's inquiry about David's identity (1 Sam 17:55–58), the friendship between David and Jonathan (1 Sam 18:1–4), and the fact that Saul gave David command of the army (1 Sam 18:5).

58. It should be noted that in chapter 16 there is a long hymn of praise to God, sung by Judith with all Israel around her, which goes beyond anything in 1 Samuel 17–18 at this point, and which has echoes of the song of triumph in Exodus 15 (Skehan, "Hand of Judith"). This is a sign of the intertextual richness of this work, which has been mentioned already.

THE POINT OF THE COMPARISON WITH DAVID

I have argued in chapter 6, in relation to the longer Hebrew Bible version, that lying at the heart of the story of David and Goliath is the profound social upheaval involved in David's emerging as victor and I will now reiterate a few of the factors (also present in the Old Greek version of the story under consideration in this chapter) that would have made his victory surprising to an ancient Israelite audience. First, David does not enjoy the ascribed honor that comes from belonging to an aristocratic family. In fact, he tells Saul's servants that he is a man who is humble (*tapeinos*) and not honorable (*endoxos*, 1 Sam 18:23). Secondly, in a culture that honors age, David is a mere youth (*paidarion*, 1 Sam 17:33), inexperienced in war. Thirdly, he is the youngest member of his family in a culture which tended to give precedence to elder sons over younger, so that it was a sign of social disorder for youths to be pre-eminent (Isa 3:4). On this basis, if any of the sons of Jesse was to volunteer to fight Goliath it should have been the oldest one. Fourthly, David was a shepherd, a difficult and despised occupation, associated with various forms of dishonor (such as thievery), and naturally relegated to the male in the family of lowest status. On the other hand, David does enjoy the ascribed honor of being Saul's lyre-player and armor-bearer and also has something of a reputation for being intelligent, a fighter, prudent in speech, handsome and of having the Lord with him (1 Sam 16:18), although the extent of his fighting abilities is not specified and the real significance of the last feature was not appreciated until he had defeated Goliath. Thus we have the youngest brother, a lowly shepherd in fact, from a non-elite family, yet secretly anointed by God to be his king (16:1–13) and destined to become a famous warrior. It is this juxtaposition of David's very different status with respect to the divine and human levels that would have struck ancient Israelites as perhaps the most arresting aspect of the narrative and of the facts of Israel's past that they would have thought it represented. In choosing someone like David as his anointed, a person of lowly status and little honor, God had overturned central cultural norms in Israel. Even Samuel himself had to learn this lesson, since when he went out to anoint one of the sons of Jesse as king he naturally assumed it would be the eldest, Eliab, but soon discovered that God judges not by appearance, but looks into the heart (16:6–13).

The portrayal of Judith is readily explicable in the light of such a presentation of David. For Judith, too, is an utterly improbable savior of

Israel, not because of the features just mentioned in relation to David, but simply because in a society that assigned most public roles to men, especially those of waging warfare, she is a woman. For although she is a woman of wealth and respected in the community in a way David was not (even if being an attractive widow outside male control rendered her somewhat anomalous),[59] it is her status as woman and the active role she takes in the male world of war, even to the extent of cutting off Holofernes's head, that renders her achievements as surprising as those of David. That her victory even involves the extremely violent and usually male act of lifting a sword and decapitating a prostrate foe means that she has fully entered the realm of warrior. Thus her victory is noteworthy for the same reason as David's, since it is only the nature of their initial apparent inability to succeed which differs. Her story is really David's played in a different key.

Fully to assess the significance of the similarity between these two Israelites requires a consideration of the theology operative in the two texts and this will be taken up in the last section of this chapter. Prior to doing so, however, we must consider one last aspect of the text in its cultural context, namely, the role of deceit in Judith's victory, since this feature is important in reading the story and in understanding the nature of its theological significance.

THE FUNCTION AND VALUE OF JUDITH'S DECEIT

The Issue

It is by deception that Judith contrives the situation that she is left alone with a dead drunk Holofernes and is thereby able to remove his head. This deception, as we will see in a moment, covers two forms: first, Judith's outright lies and cleverly ambiguous statements and, secondly, the allure of her physical appearance. Both features contribute to her success and the text openly celebrates them.

Our overall aim of seeking to understand the dynamics of the story within its original cultural framework requires that we pay some attention to the function and value of Judith's deceit as it emerges in the text. This is especially important given that many commentators in modern times have expressed unfavorable views of Judith in precisely this area. H. M. Hughes is a good example from early in the twentieth century:

59. See Malina, *Windows*, 50.

"The writer is at pains to make clear that Judith violated none of the ceremonial laws of diet . . . This scrupulous regard for ceremonial purity stands in striking contrast with the deliberate pursuit of lying and deceit (Jdt 12:1–4). The end is held to justify the means. Judith even prays that her deceit may be used as a weapon of divine chastisement of the enemies of Israel (9:10, 13). In the very act of her deceit she protests the truth of her utterances (9:5). The moral standard is low."[60]

The point is a critical one and brings out very sharply the issue of the cultural difference between modern values, which usually recognize a duty to be honest to everyone, not just to members of one's ingroup, and those of ancient Mediterranean cultures, such as Israel's. In Chapter 2 of this volume I have set out at some length how research by anthropologists, such as Juliet DuBoulay and Michael Gilsenan, into the role of the deceit in contemporary Mediterranean cultures has been fruitfully developed and applied to biblical interpretation by critics such as Bruce Malina and John Pilch. In summary, Malina argues that in the first-century CE context "there was no such thing as universal, social commitment . . . Lying and deception are or can be honorable and legitimate. To lie in order to deceive an outsider, one who has no right to the truth, is honorable."[61] We will see that this position is reflected in the Book of Judith.

Deceit in the Book of Judith

The Story of Dinah (Genesis 34)

The theme of deceit enters the text in way that is both unexpected and provocative. Once the elders of Bethulia have departed, having heard Judith's announcement that the Lord will use her to rescue Israel and avenge themselves on their enemies, she begins her prayer like this, by summarizing the events of Genesis 34:

---

60. Hughes, *The Ethics*, 85–86. Hughes continues this passage by saying, "and an unfavorable light is cast by the book upon the moral (as distinct from ceremonial) standard of Pharisaism" (ibid., 86). The idea that Judith represents a Pharisaic position is a fairly common one. Like some others (including Craven, *Artistry and Faith*, 120–21), I consider this suggestion erroneous, but the focus of the present chapter renders a detailed consideration of the issue inappropriate.

61. Malina, *New Testament World*, 3rd ed., 41.

Lord, God of my father Simeon,
you armed him with a sword to take vengeance (*edikēsis*) on the foreigners
who loosed a virgin's womb (*mētra*)[62] to defile her (*eis miasma*),
stripped her thigh to her disgrace (*aischynē*),
polluted her womb (*mētra*) to her dishonor (*oneidos*),
since you said, "This shall not be," yet they did it.
For this you delivered their leaders to slaughter,
and in relation to their bed, which was ashamed by their deceit (*apatē*),
they were deceived (*apatētheisan*) into the shedding of blood. (Jdt 9:2–3)

She then recounts how they struck down the slaves with the masters, carried off their wives and children, and shared out their spoils "among the sons you loved, who had been so zealous for you, had loathed the stain put on their blood and called on you for help" (9:4).

Genesis 34 recounts how Shechem, the son of Hamor the Hivite took Dinah, the daughter of Jacob and Leah, lay with her, and, the Septuagint adds, humiliated (*etapeinōsen*) her. But Shechem, whom we discover later had actually carried Dinah off to his house (34:26), loved her and asked his father to arrange a marriage. Jacob heard that his daughter had been defiled (*emianen*) when his sons were away and kept silent until they returned. They were deeply disturbed when they found out. Faced with a marriage proposal from Shechem, Jacob's sons agreed on the basis that all the Hivites first be circumcised. But this was an arrangement made falsely (*meta dolou*), since their sister had been defiled. The Hivites were circumcised and two days later, while they were still in pain, two of Jacob's sons, Simeon and Levi, full brothers of Dinah, armed themselves with swords, broke into the town and killed every male. They retrieved their sister, and carried off all the Hivites' women, children and possessions. When Jacob remonstrated with them for the danger into which they had brought him by these actions, they replied, "Is our sister to be treated as a prostitute?"

Judith celebrates this bloody incident at the start of her prayer, which begins with an invocation to God revealing that Simeon was actually her ancestor, whose trickery and homicide she completely endorses. Judith's version is fairly close to the Genesis narrative, except for the mention of "their deceit," that is, the deceit of the Hivites. This is noteworthy, since there is no deceit in the source, merely Shechem's forcible ravishing and

---

62. This word is frequently translated as "girdle."

abduction of Dinah. The author of the book of Judith has interpreted these actions as "deceit" (*apatē*, 9:3) to provide a balance, or rather a contrast, to the successful deception of Simeon and Levi. The idea is sharpened by the role of a bed (Shechem's) both in experiencing shame at the violation of Dinah and also in playing a role in the bloody act of revenge, presumably because Shechem was in bed recovering from circumcision when Simeon and Levi killed him.

That Judith should begin her prayer with this incident immediately brings us into the group-oriented ethics described by Malina. What matters is not adherence to some absolute standards of truth such as those familiar to modern readers, but rather the tactical use of lying and deception to advance the interests of a particular group—in the case of Simeon and Levi, those of their immediate family, and in Judith's case, the interests of Israel vis-à-vis those of the Assyrians.

This means that there is, in effect, an institutionalized form of double standard in this context presupposed in the text. It is perfectly acceptable to rail against the lies and deceit of other people, even while you do exactly the same thing yourself. The point is to be the final winner, to promote the honor of oneself and one's group by obtaining revenge (*edikēsis*) in the action which brings the exchange to its close, thus conclusively settling the score for previous dishonors suffered, such as those of Dinah (*aischynē*; *oneidos*; *miasma*) or of the Israelites before Judith's intervention. Thus, the detailed description of the vengeance of Simeon and Levi in Jdt 9:2–4 sets the tone for all the many subsequent references to deception in the text. Moreover, to condemn Judith's actions with reference to modern canons of morality misses this aspect of their contextualization in ancient Mediterranean culture.

There is other data that falls to be understood within this framework. When Judith says in this same prayer, "by the deception of my lips (*ek cheileōn apatēs*) strike slave down with master" (Jdt 9:10) and "give me a deceitful discourse (*logos mou kai apatē*) to wound and kill" (9:13), she is speaking from this moral universe where the abiding responsibility is to defend one's group and its honor.

Judith's Lies, Charms, and Ambiguities

This attitude is then manifested in thirteen direct lies that Judith tells to Holofernes and other Assyrians and five cleverly ambiguous statements that further promote her scheme. I will now run through both categories.

First, the lies. She tells the Assyrian scouts that she is fleeing from the Hebrews, since they will soon be their prey (10:12), that she has trustworthy information (*hrēmata alētheias!*) for Holofernes and that she will show him the road to take if he wants to capture all the highlands without losing a single life (10:13). She offers a wish for long life to Nebuchadnezzar (11:7). She says that death is about to fall on her people (11:11), offering the imaginative fiction that this will happen since they are about to eat animals, corn, wine and oil dedicated to God (11:12–15). Her seventh lie is that she fled from the Bethulians when she heard of this plan (11:16). She seeks permission to go out each evening to pray to God to let her know when they have committed their sin (11:17), whereas she actually intends going out to bathe. Her ninth lie is that she will tell Holofernes when God has so informed her, so he can march out against them (11:18). She foretells that she will enthrone him in the middle of Jerusalem (11:19), that he will lead the Israelites like sheep (11:19) and that she has foreknowledge of all these events for the purpose of telling him (11:19). Her thirteenth lie is to Bagoas prior to joining Holofernes in his tent, that she will be going out to her prayers (13:3).

Next there are her cleverly ambiguous statements. She tells Holofernes that she will speak no lie (*pseudos*) in "to my lord tonight" (11:5), where he would think she was referring to him, whereas she means the Lord God. She further informs him that God will bring his work to a successful conclusion (11:6), which is similar to the Pythian oracle telling Croesus of Lydia that if he invaded Persian he would destroy a great kingdom (Herodotus, *Histories* 1.53). God has sent her to do things with Holofernes that the world will marvel to hear (11:16). Before she has run out of her own provisions, the Lord will have used her to accomplish his plan (12:4). Lastly, she is happy to drink with Holofernes since she had never felt her life more worthwhile than on this day (12:18).

The second broad aspect to Judith's deception, in addition to her discourse, is her beauty. After her success she states that her face deceived (*ēpatēsen*) Holofernes leading to his destruction, although he committed no sin with her to defile (*eis miasma*) or disgrace (*eis aischynēn*) her (13:16), thus avoiding the fate (described in the same terms) which had befallen Dinah (cf. 9:2). In the hymn at the end it is said that "she disarmed him with the beauty of her face" (*en kallei prosōpou autēs parelusen auton*, 16:6). Finally, the same hymn contains a section describing how various aspects of her appearance helped to fool Holofernes:

> She anointed her face with perfume,
> bound her hair under a turban,
>
> put on a linen gown to deceive him (*eis apatēn autou*).
> Her sandal seized (*hērpasen*) his eye,
> her beauty captured (*ēchmalōtisen*) his life,
> and the scimitar ran though this neck. (16:8–9)

There is grim humor here in military language (*hērpasen*, *ēchmalōtisen*) being applied metaphorically to the effect of "weapons," which consist of women's clothing and cosmetics, but in a passage that climaxes with the woman so clothed and perfumed using an actual weapon to achieve a very literal result.

If we compare Judith's preparations for her encounter with Holofernes with other examples of "Overcoming the Monster" tales, it is apparent that we are dealing with the common feature of arming the hero, often with magical or at least unusual weapons. In *Beowulf*, for example, the hero wears chain mail that will prevent any enemy crushing his rib-cage and is lent a sword that was tempered in blood and had never failed anyone in battle.[63] In the James Bond movies, the hero obtains special vehicles and weapons from Q. Judith, on the other hand, will conquer with her looks, perfume, turban, gown and jewels.

Irony in Context

According to C. A. Moore, while a number of biblical books make effective use of irony, "few, if any, are as quintessentially ironic as Judith."[64] Basing himself on a dictionary definition of irony (rather than, say, the understandings of irony to be found in ancient rhetoric and in modern literary theory) and on E. M. Good's *Irony in the Old Testament*, Moore sets out a large amount of data in the text which he finds "ironic." Some of this data includes features discussed above in connection with the lies and ambiguities crafted by Judith to gull Holofernes, for example her

---

63. See *Beowulf*, lines 1443–47 (chain-mail) and 1455–64.
64. Moore, *Judith*, 78.

statement that she would say nothing false to her lord this night (11:5) or that God has sent her to accomplish with him things that would astonish the whole world (11:16).

There is no doubt that these, and many other features of this type, are ironic as suggested by Moore (and by Good before him), since they do illustrate in various ways how characters in the narrative, Holofernes and his Assyrians, are ignorant of what is well known to the audience. Israel's enemies are excluded from knowledge of the actual state of affairs until it is too late. Through most of the narrative they exist in a dangerous fog of incomprehension. I will add to Moore's discussion that this type of irony had been brought to a high pitch of perfection in the ancient Mediterranean world long before the book of Judith was written, in Athenian tragedy, in plays such as Aeschylus's *Agamemnon* and Sophocles's *Oedipus Rex*.[65]

The difficulty with Moore's approach to irony is that it is essentially a pigeon-holing exercise; he is concerned to establish certain categories of irony and then to show that data capable of inclusion within each can be found in the text: "The total effect of all the preceding passages . . . is to create a work which contains Good's three categories: punctual, episodic, and thematic irony. Thus, the book is a perfect example of what Northrop Frye (*Anatomy of Criticism*, p. 162) has characterized as the last of the four categories of narrative literature, namely, the tragic, the comic, the romantic, and the ironic."[66]

Although it is of some help to have textual data classified in this way, it is difficult to see how simply lining the text up against a conceptual grid like this contributes significantly to understanding how it works as a story, in particular a story told in an ancient Mediterranean context. We need to move beyond merely *describing* instances of irony in order to offer an *explanation* of what function they serve in the narrative. To achieve this result we must ask what role the irony stemming from the persistent ignorance of the Assyrians on matters understood in quite another sense by the audience plays in the unfolding narrative, but always in the light of group-orientation and honor focused in the pattern of

---

65. Note the very poignant irony in *Agamemnon* that consists in the fact that the Trojan prophetess Cassandra prophesies truly to the chorus the slaying of Agamemnon by Clytemnestra, but nothing is done to save him.

66. Moore, *Judith*, 83–84.

challenge-and-response which, as we have already seen, structures the text from beginning to end.

In this perspective the critical feature of the text comes immediately after Bagoas has discovered the headless corpse of Holofernes:

> He gave a great shout, wept, sobbed, shrieked and rent his clothes. He then went into the tent which Judith had occupied and could not find her either. Then, rushing out to the men, he shouted, "Those slaves have duped us! One Hebrew woman has brought shame on the House of Nebuchadnezzar. Holofernes is lying dead on the ground, with his head cut off!" When they heard this, the leaders of the Assyrian army tore their tunics in consternation, and the camp rang with their wild cries and their shouting. When the men who were still in their tents heard the news they were appalled. They were so gripped with panic and dread that no two men could keep together; the rout was complete. They fled along every track across the plain or through the mountains. (14:16—15:2, JB)

In the terms of ancient rhetoric these events constitute an *anagnorisis*, a sudden recognition, when the scales fall from the eyes of some of the characters.[67] Here the author has depicted in sharp relief the moment when the Assyrians discover that they have been defeated and that all is lost. This is the very point at which the veil of ignorance is torn away, when at last they see the whole situation in the bitter light of reality and react in the usual fashion in an honor-culture like this. We might compare this with the scene in Sophocles's *Oedipus Rex* when Oedipus at last discovers as an undeniable fact that he has killed his father and married his mother (1182–85), an *anagnorisis* to which the play has been pressing with remorseless insistence, or with the moment in Aeschylus's *Agamemnon* when Agamemnon cries out in death at the hand of his wife Clytemnestra (1343–45), a death ironically hinted at earlier by Clytemnestra herself (906–13)[68] and which Cassandra had predicted to the chorus but to no effect (1246). In the book of Judith, however, the tone is very different, being mordantly comic rather than tragic.

---

67. See Aristotle, *Ars Poetica*, 11; and Esler, "Introduction," 1, for *anagnorisis* in the Emmaus story (Luke 24:30–32).

68. Especially note lines 910–911, where Clytemnestra gives this direction to her attendants as Agamemnon alights from his chariot on returning from Troy, with their veiled prophecy of Agamemnon's death: "Immediately strew his path with purple, so justice (*dikē*) may receive him into a house he never hoped to see."

Triggering the Assyrians' collapse leading to their total defeat is the realization that slaves (*douloi*) have duped (*ēthetēsan*) them, that one Hebrew woman (*mia gynē tōn Hebraiōn*) has brought shame (*aischynē*) upon the House of Nebuchadnezzar. This is the significance of the death of the Holofernes—that all of them have been disgraced by decisively losing the contest. In a context where individual selves were closely aligned with significant groups, the shameful death of the group leader is the death of their honor as well.

How an ancient Israelite audience must have savored this picture, with its imaginative evocation of the greatest success in a challenge-and-response interaction possible in their experience! Yet we can go further than this, for throughout the course of the narrative to this point such an audience would have appreciated every reference to Judith's successfully lying to the Assyrians, or employing cunning ambiguity, or flaunting her many charms at him, as part of her stratagem of drawing the enemy deeper and deeper into a state of compliant ignorance until she had finally reduced Holofernes (and his army) to utter helplessness. Thus, the extensive irony in the text, that is the way in which the Assyrians operate on one, very defective level of knowledge, to their cost, while (Israelite) readers have access to the full picture, operates within the challenge-and-response structure of the work both to underline the brilliant way in which Judith takes control of the situation as soon as she encounters her first Assyrians and also to enhance Israelite appreciation of the scene when the Assyrians recognize to their horror and utter shame how they have been tricked.

THE THEOLOGY OF THE BOOK OF JUDITH[69]

As suggested at the start of this chapter, we cannot read the Book of Judith without noting its high level of theological seriousness. That is to say, although Judith is a fictional character, her story conveys a profound message concerning how the God of the ancient Israelites dealt with his people. We may be confident that the first Israelite readers of the Book of Judith (just like the readers of 1 Samuel 16–18 before them) did not merely regard it as a fine tale, but learned from it about the God whom

69. I gratefully acknowledge my debt to John H. Elliott in this section, in stimulating my reflections in this area in relation to an earlier essay of mine on David and Goliath (which is not to say that he should be held responsible for the views here expressed).

they worshipped and on whom they rested their identity as a people. At the core of that lesson was the dilemma posed by the entire book, that was mentioned at the start of this chapter: that it is a woman who saves Israel. In the improbability of its hero (and in many other respects) the author of the story of Judith provides a fictional parallel to the story of David and Goliath by recounting one of the most stunning interactions of God with his people, and one of the most momentous instances of challenge-and-response, which could possibly be imagined. With Judith, as with David, the core of the message is that God will not be restrained by established social roles and institutions in effecting his purposes, especially in that he means to raise the lowly to positions of pre-eminence and to bring down the mighty.

Yet to understand the nature of the divine initiative as far as Judith and David were concerned, to comprehend their truly radical nature, we must contextualize their stories within the usual and everyday patterns of ancient Israelite social life. Indeed, unless we make a real effort to appreciate the power of the social conventions at work in these narratives, we cannot begin to understand what an ancient Israelite reader would have made of the God who so thoroughly overturned them for his purposes.

Both Judith and David represent Israel as a whole in being small, inferior and frequently despised compared with surrounding nations, and often facing apparently insuperable odds, but nevertheless with God on their side, a God who comes to the aid of the weak and socially marginal and rescues them from dangerous predicaments. This is a storyline that in Israelite tradition reaches from Abraham to the Maccabees.

Throughout the Bible, Israel's God exalts the lowly and crushes the arrogant who oppress them. He leads the Israelites from slavery in Egypt to the promised land. He helps them to conquer the powerful peoples of Canaan. He brings them home from exile. He takes the side of the widow and orphan against rich and corrupt judges and merchants. He reverses the shame of initially barren women (like Sarah, Rebekah and Hannah). He regularly prefers younger sons over their brothers (Abel over Cain, Isaac over Ishmael, Joseph and his son Ephraim over their brothers, Jacob over Esau, and Moses and David over their elder brothers and so on). He even gives victory to women (like Deborah, Jael, Esther and Susanna), an unusual phenomenon in the ancient Mediterranean. One of the great expressions of this theme is the song of Hannah (1 Sam

2:1–10), which is echoed in Mary's Magnificat (Luke 1:46–55). It is fair to say that the Book of Judith is a powerful expression of a characteristically Israelite theology that is central to the meaning of the Bible, in both its Testaments.[70]

There is one notably unambiguous expression of this theology in the work. In the prayer she makes before departing for the Assyrian camp, after referring to the actions of Simeon and Levi (9:2–4) and expatiating upon the need to smite the arrogant Assyrians, to break their pride with a woman's hand (9:7–11), Judith says:

> For your strength does not lie in numbers,
> nor your might in strong men;
> but you are the God of the humble (*tapeinōn*),
> the help of the lowly (*elattonōn*),
> the support of the weak (*asthenountōn*),
> the refuge of the despairing (*apegnōsmenōn*),
> the savior of those who have lost hope (*apēlpismenōn*).

Yet a similar message emerges elsewhere, for example in the long passage in the concluding hymn which describes how apparently all-powerful Assyria—sweeping down from the mountains in the north, to burn the land, kill the young men and children and carry off the women—was improbably thwarted by a woman:

> For their hero did not fall at the young men's hands,
> it was not the sons of Titans who struck him down,
> no proud giants made that attack,
> but Judith, the daughter of Merari,
> who disarmed him with the beauty of her face (16:6, JB).

After a description of how Judith deceived him (16:7–9), discussed above, the hymn continues with an account of the humble (described in a way that echoes the language of 9:11) overthrowing the mighty:

> The Persians trembled at her boldness,
> the Medes were daunted by her daring.
> These were struck with fear when my humble ones (*hoi tapeinoi*) shouted,
> these were seized with terror when my weak ones (*hoi asthenountes*) shouted louder,
> and when they shouted loudest, these gave ground.
> The children of mere girls ran them through,
> pierced them like the offspring of deserters.

70. Also see Walsh, *Mighty from Their Thrones.*

They perished in the battle of my Lord. (16:10–12, JB, slightly modified)

Yet even here the celebration of Judith's deceit (16:7–9), by which, with God's complete blessing, she secures a victory for her people, serves to reinforce the extent to which this message comes to us embedded in a cultural perspective which is quite alien to our modern sensibilities. For we have moved far away from the profound group-orientation of this text, with its adamant insistent on God's partiality for a lowly and humble Israel and opposition to her enemies, and the accompanying ethic that virtually anything is permissible to defeat them.

Accordingly, we must face up to this cultural distance if we wish to continue to find in the story of Judith resources for the enrichment of contemporary Christian identity, thought and action. This is not an unreasonable goal when we consider how the understanding of God as the protector and liberator of the humble of the earth has fuelled various liberation theologies in the last few decades.

THE LITERARY APPEAL OF THE BOOK OF JUDITH

Yet the Book of Judith is, finally, a narrative for everyone, of religious faith or none. Its storyline shares the appeal of numerous other narratives where the plot concerns a hero who overcomes a "monster" threatening death and destruction to a community. To take but one example, *Beowulf* describes the arrival of the monster Grendel who, from his lair in a nearby lake, begins night-time attacks on the warriors sleeping in the hall of Heorot. To save these men, Beowulf must battle with the monster and kill not just Grendel but his even more fearsome mother, the latter in a battle beneath the water of a lake. With both monsters slain and the threat to its survival lifted, the community celebrates and begins its customary life, while Beowulf is richly rewarded.[71] Holofernes poses a threat to the survival of the people of Bethulia and to Israel as well; after a siege has brought the Bethulians to the point of capitulation through lack of water, they know that surrender will mean slavery for all of them (Jdt 7:26–29) and even the extinction of Israel (8:21). At this point, enter Judith, not, like *Beowulf*, a mighty hero newly arrived from across the sea, but a widow from their own town, yet someone equally willing to take on the monster in his lair, in this case his tent in the en-

71. Booker begins *Seven Basic Plots* with a discussion of the close similarities between the plots of *Beowulf* and the movie *Jaws* (1–2).

emies' camp. Like many heroes in these stories, she too arms herself with special weapons, but very different from the usual sort: her good looks, augmented with fine clothes, jewels and perfume. She bravely enters the enemy camp, fools and decapitates Holofernes and makes her escape. His army is defeated and Israel rejoices. Unlike many heroes in these stories, however, Judith neither receives nor desires any special reward for her service. She returns to the quiet normality of her life as a widow, refusing offers of marriage, and eventually dies and is buried with her husband, mourned by Israel for seven days. Her story has the universal appeal of tales where a hero or heroine overcomes some monster and allows the community to live in peace. It is one of the most enduring and universal of all literary plots.

PART 3

Sex

The narratives considered in the next two chapters of this volume both concern situations in which a man's sexual desire for a woman leads to catastrophe. Chapter 9 deals with David's desire for Bathsheba, the wife of Uriah (a soldier in his army), and what happens when he acts upon that desire at a time when Israel is engaged in war with the Ammonites (2 Samuel 10–12). Chapter 10 has as its focus the lust David's son Amnon has for his half sister Tamar, which, when acted upon, leads to Tamar's violation and loss of all happiness in life and to Amnon's own death at the command of Tamar's full brother Absalom (2 Samuel 13).

As if the sheer collocation of these stories is not striking enough, with the second following immediately after the other in 2 Samuel, the text itself offers strong cause for regarding them as closely related. One aspect of the David's narrative in 2 Samuel 10–12 is that the prophet Nathan foretells that as a result of his having had Uriah killed and taken Bathsheba as his wife, "the sword shall never depart from your house" (2 Sam 12:10). That prophecy finds its first fulfillment in Absalom's having Amnon killed, in the very next chapter of the book, probably by sword thrusts (2 Sam 13:28–29). Does this connection make Tamar "collateral damage" in the unrolling of God's anger towards David for his murder of Uriah? Or is it more that Nathan merely predicts that what will happen when David's sons, starting with Amnon, begin to emulate the sinfulness of their father?

Whatever the answer to these questions, the two narratives in view here continually require to be set within the context of ancient Israel, with aid from modern Mediterranean ethnography for their compre-

300

hension. They are narratives embedded in a particular time, place, and culture, and the meanings they communicated to their original audience emerge best when that setting is carefully taken into account. At the same time, both stories resonate with literary works from other contexts, David's story being comparable to what Christopher Booker calls the "Voyage and Return" plot; and the interactions of Amnon, Tamar, and Absalom with the "Tragedy" plot.

9

David, Bathsheba, and the Ammonite War
(2 Samuel 10–12)

AN ISRAELITE STORY AND ITS LITERARY COUSINS

Following the same broad approach to reading Old Testament texts with their ancient Israelite audience by use of social-scientific ideas and insights adopted elsewhere in this volume, I will focus in the current chapter upon the narrative in 2 Samuel 10–12, which describes what happens when, in the midst of a war with Ammon, David engages in an illicit sexual liaison with Bathsheba. How would this story have functioned as a narrative within the ancient Mediterranean culture in which it appeared? How would its first audience, listeners rather than readers, have understood and related to it?

An interpretative method best justifies itself if it produces insights into a biblical text that go beyond the yield from existing scholarship. It will be submitted that using social-scientific insights to investigate 1 Samuel 10–12 as a narrative embedded in the peculiar culture of the ancient Mediterranean world does lead to results of this kind, not least the fact that this section of the text comes alive as a tight artistic unity that integrates the war with the Ammonites and David's interactions with Bathsheba and Uriah more strongly than in existing discussion.

As with my discussion of the other Old Testament narratives in this volume, I am not assuming the historicity of any element of this narrative, nor am I denying it. My point is to explore how an ancient audience would have perceived what was happening. When I refer to "David" or any of the other persons mentioned, I am treating them as characters in the narrative, whether they existed or not and whether what is described actually happened or not. I am also concerned with the how this narrative works in its final form, not with its composition history.[1]

There is no need for present purposes to propose too precise a date for the final form of the Masoretic Text of this story. While the text seems to contain pre-exilic materials that received a final editing in the exilic or post-exilic period, possibly in Deuteronomistic hands,[2] the two issues of the context on which I will concentrate are applicable across the entirety of this period; they are in no way tied to the specific features of any particular period.

If we ask whether the story told in 2 Samuel 10–12 bear similarities to other narratives in world literature, the plot that Christopher Booker describes as "Voyage and Return" provides intriguing comparative possibilities,[3] even if, like most models, it requires some modifications to be most fruitfully used in relation to this biblical text. The essence of the Voyage and Return story, according to Booker, is that the hero or heroine travel out of their familiar and everyday world into another world, which seems strange and abnormal. At first this new world is exhilarating but then a shadow intrudes. The hero or heroine feels trapped but eventually escapes from this abnormal world back into the familiar one from which they set out.[4] Rather light-hearted exercises in this plot include Lewis Carroll's *Alice in Wonderland*, Frank Baum's *The Wizard of Oz*, J. M. Barrie's *Peter Pan* and Beatrix Potter's *The Tale of Peter Rabbit*. Darker examples include Apuleius's *The Golden Ass*, Evelyn Waugh's *Brideshead Revisited* and H. G. Wells's *The Time Machine*. But some of these stories have a high moral seriousness, in that the hero or hero not only goes off to a foreign land but in that place engages with evil from which he or she is restored at the end: examples include Luke's parable of the Prodigal Son, Samuel Taylor Coleridge's *The Rime of the Ancient Mariner*, and in its own unique way, C. S. Lewis's *The Lion, the Witch and the Wardrobe*.[5] Although these stories normally entail a voyage to

1. But for a provocative attempt to discover history beneath the account of the Ammonite War in 2 Samuel 10–12, see Halpern, *David's Secret Demons*, 345–53.

2. See McCarter, *II Samuel*, 4–8. We are now witnessing, it is worth noting, a resistance to "pan-Deuteronomism," that is, the tendency to see the work of Deuteronomistic editing across vast sweeps of the Old Testament—see the essays in Schearing and McKenzie, *Three Elusive Deuteronomists*.

3. Booker, *Seven Basic Plots*, 87–106.

4. Ibid, 87.

5. All these works are mentioned by Booker (*Seven Basic Plots*, 87–106).

a different place, some take the hero out of his familiar world to a different time (Wells's *Time Machine*, for example) or to a different social milieu (as with Waugh's *Brideshead Revisited*).[6] Whereas the heroes of the "Quest" plot feel a compulsion toward some far-off goal, heroes in Voyage and Return stories tend to stumble into something totally unexpected, typically by being in a state of mind—through boredom, or a craving for something different or exciting—which has prepared them for adventure.[7] As their dream turns into a nightmare, the experience means that the heroes are taken away from some "crucial defining point of their sense of reality and identity."[8] These characters often start off as quite selfish, "not really recognizing anything in the world outside themselves," but in the end they achieve salvation of some sort, their eyes are opened and they have gone through a fundamental change of heart. So it is with the Prodigal Son and the Ancient Mariner: the real victory has been not over the dark forces of the outside world but over "the same dark forces within themselves."[9]

Second Samuel 10–12 centers on the character of David and his story becomes closely comparable to Booker's Voyage and Return as soon as we modify that pattern in one respect: to extend the new realm the hero enters from a different place, or time, or social milieu to a new moral (or, in David's case, immoral) state. Indeed, one of the ironies of the story, as we will see, is that if David had made a particular journey, the short one across the Jordan river to lead his army in the war against Ammon and not lingered in Jerusalem, he would not have seen or desired Bathsheba, nor got himself into a position where he needed to have her husband, Uriah, murdered to avoid exposure of his sinfulness. It is because of his initial state of idleness, and even boredom, as he remains in Jerusalem while his army invests the walls of the Ammonite capital, that he is able to journey off into state of immorality away from his core identity of faithfulness to the Lord. While he will repent of the explosion of dark forces released within him, in the short and long term he will pay a heavy price for this voyage away from this true self, both in the death of the first child Bathsheba bears to him and in the homicidal violence that will thereafter beset his house.

6. Ibid, 92–93.
7. Ibid, 95–96.
8. Ibid, 97.
9. Ibid, 102.

As we have seen with the other narratives in this volume, however, the particular way in which a biblical story that reflects a broad plot form known in other literary embodiments unfolds depends on its being embedded in the particular culture of ancient Israel. This brings us to exploring how 2 Samuel 10–12 would have made sense within this context.

TWO SOCIAL-SCIENTIFIC PERSPECTIVES: CHALLENGE-AND-RESPONSE AND THE PATRON/CLIENT RELATIONSHIP

In exploring 2 Samuel 10–12 I will rely on two perspectives that derive from anthropological research conducted into the Mediterranean region in the last four decades which, since I have set them out in some detail in chapter 2, I need only briefly sketch them out here.[10]

The first is the social dynamic of challenge and response, first analyzed by French anthropologist Pierre Bourdieu in relation to the Kabyle, an Arab people from North Africa and given prominence by Malina.[11] In a world where honor is the primary social good and exists in finite quantities, every social occasion offers one participant the chance to enhance his or her honor at the expense of someone else, so long as that someone is roughly equal in social status. This social dynamic begins with a challenge, which is a claim to enter someone's social space. Most commonly this happens in a negative way, by an insult or a physical assault. But is can also be positive in nature, as when one person gives another a gift, or praises him or sends a message of goodwill. The person then challenged must consider how to respond, fully aware that there is an audience that will rapidly view a failure to respond or a weak response as a victory for the challenger, and hence award him or her honor at the challenged person's expense. There are three broad modes of response: positive rejection, usually with scorn and contempt, acceptance coupled with a counter-challenge, and the dishonorable course of no response. We have already considered this model in the light of David's combat with Goliath in 1 Samuel 17 (chapter 6) and Judith's interaction with Holofernes (chapter 8).

---

10. See pp. 61–4 for challenge-and-response, and pp. 68–9 for patron-client relations.

11. Bourdieu, "The Sentiment of Honour"; and Malina, *New Testament World*, 3rd ed., 33–36.

The second perspective is that of the relationship between patron and client, a relationship often mediated by a broker. In the Old Testament field the importance of the patron/client relationship has been proposed by Niels Lemche in 1995 and 1996, by Raymond Hobbs in 1997 and by Ronald Simkins in 1999.[12] Zeba Crook, on the other hand, has usefully pointed out that patron and client relationships are really a sub-species of what he calls "asymmetrical reciprocity" (otherwise, less helpfully, known as "generalized reciprocity").[13] Other examples of relationships where there is a marked inequality of power and resources between the parties, such as vassal treaties, are probably best viewed as another instance of this general pattern of asymmetrical reciprocity, rather than as being assimilated to the patron/client relationship (as sometimes occurs in the field at present). But in cases of vassal treaties and other covenants, as Crook notes, there is a high degree of formality, with explicit promises and threats, oaths, witnesses, and, above all, solemnization of the relationship in writing. Patron and client relationships, on the other hand, although a form of asymmetrical reciprocity, are far more informal and lack these features.

Although I follow the broad lines of Crook's proposal here, many of the ideas of Lemche, Hobbs, and Simkins remain useful. Thus Lemche is correct to argue that *ḥesed* expresses the loyalty that binds together patron and client and the parties to other relationships such as covenant and treaty (even if the latter should now not simply be regarded as particular cases of patron/client relationships).[14] We can use the notion of higher level of generalization or of abstraction to relate phenomena such as covenant and the patron/client relationship to the more general category of asymmetrical reciprocity.

A patron is a person in an elevated socioeconomic position in possession of material goods, such as land and other wealth, and immaterial goods, such as honor and power in a particular urban or rural setting. In a world of limited goods, a patron is able to share access to some of these benefits with a limited number of clients. In return the clients honor

12. See Lemche, "Kings and Clients" and "Patronage Society;" Hobbs, "Reflections on Honor"; and Simkins, "Patronage."

13. See Crook, "Reciprocity."

14. See Lemche, "Kings and Clients"; and Hobbs, "Reflections on Honor," expressing the same view in relation to covenants and treaties. On *ḥesed*, see Clark, *The Word Hesed*.

the patron with their attention and provide services when required. The relationship is an asymmetrical, but mutually beneficial one. These relationships are informal, that is to say, they are not solemnized in written form, as are, for example, vassal treaties. At times a broker will mediate between a patron and a client. Often a broker will function as a client to the ultimate patron and as a patron to the clients.[15] Patron/client relations take on aspects of relationships between kin. Patron and clients are bound together by mutual commitment, solidarity and loyalty, as seen in the asymmetrical reciprocity that marks their dealings with one another.[16]

The relationship between patron and client appears well suited to interpreting a number of biblical phenomena, especially the relationship between God and his people, as mediated by the prophets in the Old Testament and Jesus in the New. Some work along these lines already exists. In 1988 Bruce Malina published an essay titled "Patron and Client: The Analogy Behind Synoptic Theology,"[17] which suggests a model for understanding the relationship between God, Jesus the Messiah, and his people along the lines of patron, broker and clients which is also applicable to the Old Testament understanding of God.

APPLICATION OF THE MODEL

Current Explanations of the Structure of 2 Samuel 10–12

Most critics, especially because they are driven by interests in source criticism or composition history, fail to discern the extent to which 2 Samuel 10–12 is a tightly integrated and unified narrative. Often the war with Ammon is seen merely as the "background" for the David-Bathsheba-Uriah story. According to A. A. Anderson, for example, it "seems that chapters 10–12 comprise *a more or less unitary* (emphasis added) account of three consecutive events during David's Ammonite-Aramean wars, namely, the defeat of the Ammonite-Aramean coalition (10:6–14), the defeat of the reinforced Aramean alliance (10:15–19), and, finally, the siege and capture of Rabbah, the Ammonite capital (11:1 + 12:26–31)." Anderson considers that the description of the

---

15. See Moxnes, "Patron-Client Relations" for an illuminating discussion of patron-broker-client in relation to Luke 7:2–10.

16. Malina, *New Testament World*, 3rd ed., 95–96.

17. Reprinted in Malina, *Social World*, 143–75.

Ammonite-Syrian wars was probably derived from annalistic sources and reworked. "In the present context," he adds, "it provided the setting and background (emphasis added) for the David-Bathsheba-Uriah story."[18] Similarly, McCarter observes, "The resolution of the Ammonite conflict is deferred in the narrative as our attention is directed away from public affairs to the private life of the king."[19] This comment makes a distinction between "public" and "private" in relation to David that we will soon see is unsustainable and generally overlooks the tight connection between the course of the Ammonite war and the king's behavior in Jerusalem. Even a scholar such as Fokkelman, who insists on what he calls the "organic unity" of this section of 2 Samuel with respect to how the war with the Ammonites and David's affair with Bathsheba are interwoven, misses the real character of their integration, which, as we will see, centers around David's culpable delay in taking vengeance on Ammon.[20] Applying the social-scientific perspectives set out above, on the other hand, will bring out the unity of 2 Samuel 10–12 within the culture of the ancient Mediterranean world. It will also allow us to discern how an audience in such a context would have appreciated this section of 2 Samuel as a coherent narrative.

Ammon's Challenge to Israel: The Casus Belli

The narrative begins with the death of the king of Ammon and the accession of his son Hanun in his stead (1 Sam 10:1). Since the deceased king Nahash had expressed (ḥesed) toward David, a word that carries the connotation of reciprocity marked by loyalty,[21] probably in this case by providing him with assistance when he was being hounded by Saul,[22] David decides to extend such loyalty (here with a strong connotation

18. Anderson, 2 Samuel, 145–46.

19. McCarter, II Samuel, 288.

20. Fokkelman, Narrative Art 1:41–96: at one point he speaks of David's reaction being discharged only gradually, but this is the lull before the storm of 12:26–31 (45). The real problem is that David does not react as a king should until the very end, when Joab forces him to it.

21. On the reciprocal dimension of ḥesed, see Clark, The Word Hesed. The LXX translates ḥesed as eleos.

22. The text does not tell us precisely how, but since Saul had previously inflicted a major defeat on Nahash (1 Samuel 11), Nahash may have offered David assistance on the principle of "my enemy's enemy is my friend." For a similar view, see Hertzberg, I & II Samuel, 303.

of kindness) to his son. He does this by sending ambassadors to Hanun with a message of consolation concerning his father. The message probably included a rehearsal of the great deeds and high honor of Nahash, a view confirmed in v. 3. Within the dynamic of challenge and response, this initiative represented a challenge, that is, a claim to enter the social space, and indeed here the physical space, of Hanun. As far as the David was concerned, it was what we are calling a positive challenge, made with friendly intentions. Nevertheless, a challenge it was and it necessitated that Hanun consider it and determine how he should respond in such a way as to preserve his self-respect. Presumably David assumed that the new king would simply take up the relationship that his father had enjoyed with David.

Yet David reckoned without the princes of the Ammonites who are advising the new king and the possibility that they would put a different interpretation on his embassy. In a statement that brings to the surface the honor code in which the scene is being played out, they ask Hanun, "Do you think that because David has sent comforters to you, he is honoring your father?" (1 Sam 10:3). No, they insist, David's real aim is to use his ambassadors to reconnoiter the city and overthrow it. It is not clear why the princes offered Hanun this advice.[23] In any event, they interpret David's gesture as a negative challenge, here one that takes the form of a surreptitious threat and an attempt at fulfilling it, and persuade Hanun that their view is correct.

That David should fail to foresee this particular interpretation that the princes of Ammon would put on his actions indicates a certain naiveté on his part within the storyline of 2 Samuel. On a previous occasion, after all, when he was willing to trust Abner (who wanted to be reconciled to him), Joab warned David that Abner really came to deceive him, to learn about his movements and dispositions (2 Sam 3:25).

Of the three options available in responding to a challenge noted above, only the second—acceptance and counterchallenge— was likely

---

23. Perhaps they had private motives, just as Joab killed Abner (2 Sam 3:27) not because of the threat he represented to David but to avenge Abner's murder of his brother Asahel (2 Sam. 2:22–23). Yet within the narrative logic of 2 Samuel a basis for their suspicions (even if unfounded) exists in the fact that two of David's opponents, Abner and Ishbaal, had been murdered (2 Sam. 3:22–23 and 4:1–12), even though David disavowed responsibility for their deaths. Note Hertzberg's comment: "The unnatural deaths of Abner and Ishbaal will certainly not have gone unnoticed round about" (*I & II Samuel*, 303).

to satisfy Hanun and those advising him. From their perspective, David's ambassadors posed an actual threat to Ammon and a strong riposte to meet it was necessary.

The action taken by Hanun brings out once again the social script of honor and shame in which this narrative is written. The king apprehends the ambassadors, shaves half their beards[24] and cuts off their garments around their waste so that their buttocks are exposed. This particular humiliation may have been administered with mordant humor aimed at the purported basis for the embassy, since it was perhaps a parody of the shaving that accompanied conventional rites of mourning (Isa 15:2).[25] We can imagine Hanun saying, "You come to mourn my father? I'll help you mourn!"

We have evidence from other contexts of the damage done to a person's honor produced by being shaved (Isa 7:20) and having one's buttocks exposed (Isa 20:4). The text summarizes the effect of such indignities within the honor and shame code of operating in this setting when it says that David went to meet his ambassadors, because they were greatly ashamed (2 Sam 10:5). Their shame prevented them traveling to Jerusalem lest their condition be exposed to public gaze. So he told them to stay at Jericho until their beards had grown.

From David's perspective, the insult that had been inflicted on his embassy by the Ammonites constituted a deadly affront. For clearly implied in the text is that by insulting his ambassadors they had also grievously insulted him and, indeed, Israel itself. Honor earned or received by one member of a group is enjoyed by all, while the shame suffered by one touches all. For we learn in the very next verse (2 Sam 10:6) that the Ammonites saw that "they had become odious to David" (nibᵓašu bedawid).

The expression nibᵓašu bedawid deserves close attention. The qal baᵓaš means "to stink." It is used of the Nile stinking with dead and rotting fish (Exod 7:18, 21), of stinking manna (Exod 16:20) and of fish stinking in dried-up rivers (Isa 50:2). It is thus employed of a very powerful and unpleasant smell. In the niphal (as here), occurring only three times in the Hebrew Bible (1 Sam 13:4; 2 Sam 10:6; 16:21), it means "to be/become stinking (to someone)."

---

24. MT; in the LXX they lose all their beards.

25. So Gordon, *1 & 2 Samuel*, 250.

Yet we need to be aware of the force of *ba'aš* and the context in which it appears. Firstly, since the niphal carries the connotation that someone has become as offensive to another as rotting fish, it conveys that an extreme pitch of detestation has been reached. Secondly, the niphal belongs exclusively to the social dynamic of challenge and response. It refers to the condition of someone who has grievously shamed another, and who has thereby incurred the enmity of that person and expects a robust response. Consider the example in 1 Samuel 13, which bears close similarities to the incident of David's ambassadors to Hanun. For here Jonathan had defeated the Philistines, and Saul then trumpeted the news throughout the land (1 Sam 13:3). So all Israel heard that Saul had destroyed the Philistine garrison (the actions of Jonathan being attributed to his king), and Israel considered that they had "become odious" to the Philistines (1 Sam 13:4). Thus the whole collectivity of Israel, typically for this culture, incurs responsibility for the actions of some of its members. In fact, Israel's realization of this is followed immediately by Saul's summoning the people and their being threatened by the Philistine host (1 Sam 13:5).

At 2 Sam 16:21 the niphal of *ba'aš* is used to describe the consequence of one of the most heinous insults offered anyone in the Old Testament, when Absalom has sexual intercourse with his father's concubines (as Nathan had predicted in 2 Sam 12:11). By so doing, Absalom "became odious" to his father, meaning that he had injured him grievously and desecrated his honor to such an extent that a severe reaction from David was to be expected. Indeed, Ahitophel had urged Absalom to do this, since the ire it would stir up in David would strengthen the resolve of Absalom's group (2 Sam 16:21).

The meaning of the niphal of *ba'aš* at 2 Sam 10:6 is essentially the same as in these two other instances. This interpretation of *ba'aš* within framework of challenge-and-response receives ancient confirmation in the way the Septuagint translates it—by use of *kataischynein* ("put to shame") or *aischynomai* ("be put to shame") in each case.[26]

---

26. In 2 Sam 10:6 the Septuagint translates precisely in line with the explanation here: "And the sons of Ammon saw that the people of David had been put to shame (*ho laos Dauid katēischynthēsan*). It must be noted, however, that at 1 Sam 13:3–4 LXX there are considerable differences from the Masoretic text. Now Saul does not proclaim the victory, but says throughout the land "The slaves (i. e. the Philistines) have despised us" (1 Sam 10:3). In the next verse the Septuagint follows up on this theme by including the sentence: "Israel has been put to shame (*ēschynthēsan*) before the foreigners."

The Ammonites not only realized the enormity of what they done in insulting David's ambassadors, but also foresaw the likely reaction—a military response from David. The model suggests that the grievous challenge offered to David's ambassadors—and hence to him—demands a response. David needs to take decisive action to restore his honor and that of Israel. The original audience of this text would have been itching to learn what steps David took to this end. The obvious one was for him to lead an army of Israelites out to crush the Ammonites and capture and sack their city. This is what an honorable man would have done within the social script forming the context of this narrative. We can be certain this is an accurate interpretation of the situation because this was exactly what the Ammonites themselves were expecting. The Ammonites appreciate that David has been so enraged by what they have done to his ambassadors that he will inevitably attack them in force. Accordingly, they begin to augment their own army by hiring thousands of extra soldiers, namely, the Syrians, the army of the king of Maacah and the men of Tob (2 Sam 10:6). No doubt they were expecting that David would soon appear at the head of a huge host to confront them.

David's Response: The Beginnings of the Ammonite War

Yet the original audience must have received a big shock when they learned what David does upon discovering that Ammon was mustering its own forces and those it had hired: "he sent Joab and all the host of mighty men." Joab? Why did David not lead the army himself? Although Peter Ackroyd considers it "normal procedure" for David to entrust this mission to Joab,[27] that is not the message the text conveys. This will emerge clearly later, at the start of chapter 11, but even here the point is implied from the fact that it was David's ambassadors whom Hanun had insulted and he, as Israel's king, had been insulted with them. The Ammonites saw that "they stank before David" (2 Sam 10:6). So why does he delegate leadership of his army to Joab? David was, after all, the

---

While in the Hebrew version, it is the Philistines who have been shamed, this change makes sense as a reflection of the different point made in the previous verse and still retains the honor/shame dimension of the social dynamic in play between Israel and the Philistines. In the case of Absalom, the Septuagint is closer to the Masoretic text since it reads: "All Israel will hear that you have dishonored (*katēischynai*) your father" (2 Sam 16:21).

27. Ackroyd, *Second Book*, 100.

man who, at an earlier point in his career, had been the only Israelite brave enough to redeem the honor of Israel from the arrogant reproaches of Goliath (1 Sam 17:26). Thus begins a theme that will not only be prominent until the very end of this narrative in 2 Samuel 12, but will also constitute the prime factor in the plot, namely, David's inexplicable and dishonorable failure to take to the field against Ammon.

In the event, Joab and his brother Abishai are successful against both the Ammonites and the Syrians, with the Ammonites withdrawing to their city, an important element in the plot as it unfolds (2 Sam 10:9–14). Yet compounding the sense in the text that David is behaving in a way that is culturally disordered is that he does now lead Israel out to war, yet not against the Ammonites who had insulted him, but against the Syrians whom they had hired and other Syrians who came to their aid from beyond the Euphrates. David defeated them and they feared to help the Ammonites thereafter (2 Sam 10:15–19). But none of these actions constitute an appropriate response to the insult offered by the Ammonites. They have fled to the protection of their city and David himself has not taken a single step against them, being content to leave the campaign in the hands of Joab.

David, Bathsheba, and Uriah

The implicit unease with David's behavior in the text bursts to the surface at the start of the next chapter: "And it came to pass, in the spring of the year, when kings go forth (sc. to battle), that David sent Joab and his servants with him, and all Israel, and they ravaged the Ammonites and they besieged Rabbah. But David remained in Jerusalem" (2 Sam. 11:1).

Here "kings" is read in the first line with virtually every ancient witness (including 1 Chr 20:1) except the Masoretic Text (which reads "messengers").[28] The reading in the Masoretic text seems an obvious attempt to salvage David's reputation. This campaign against Ammon is a continuation of the previous year's war with the Ammonites, in spite of Peter Ackroyd's surprising view to the contrary.[29] The siege of Rabbah

28. Other witnesses reading "kings" include the LXX, Old Latin, Targum, and the Vulgate.

29. Ackroyd, *Second Book*, 100. Gordon also misses the criticism of David present in the text (*1 & 2 Samuel*, 252), since in offering 2 Sam 10:7–14 as an occasion when David did stay behind in Jerusalem, he fails to realize how greatly David's personal presence was demanded then as well.

mentioned here reflects the fact that in the previous year the Ammonites had fled to the protection of their capital (2 Sam 10:14). The siege of Rabbah will be a crucial feature of the narrative as it develops.

The text offers no reason why David now repeats his failure of the previous year to lead the assault on Ammon. It merely asserts in the bluntest terms his breach of social convention applicable to kings by his remaining in Jerusalem, a breach which, in this narrative, entails his failure to respond appropriately to the shame heaped on his ambassadors by the Ammonites. David's disregard of the responsibility of kings to take to the field, especially when they have an egregious insult to avenge, proves to be the causal factor for the whole shape of his life thereafter, a life into which tragedy intrudes—beginning with his adultery with Bathsheba, the death of her husband Uriah and the sword that will never thereafter depart from his house, a sword most visible in the rebellion of Absalom. Put bluntly, if he had done the right thing and led his men to war, he would never have got into the trouble he did.

The account of his liaison with Bathsheba is remarkable for its brevity and its androcentric character. From his rooftop David sees a beautiful woman washing herself, he finds out that she is Bathsheba, the wife of Uriah the Hittite (whom he apparently knows is off fighting the Ammonites with Joab),[30] he sends messengers to bring her, he has intercourse with her (which is possible for her, ironically, because her rooftop bathing has purified her of her monthly uncleanness), she returns to her house, she conceives, and then sends David the news that she is pregnant. All of these details are compressed into two verses. The emphasis is upon David as the agent in all this; Bathsheba is passive, and speculation as to whether she counted on the possibility that David would see her while she was bathing seems wide of the mark.[31]

The main interest in this part of the narrative falls on the interaction between David and Uriah, about whose character we learn important details. Although Uriah is described as a Hittite, the "Yah" element in his name (which means "Yahweh is my light"), suggests a connection with Israel. Perhaps "Hittite" indicates his ancestry.[32] It emerges later in the text that Uriah was one of David's thirty heroes, some of whom are

---

30. As revealed by 1 Sam 11:6.

31. Hertzberg raises this possibility (*I & II Samuel*, 309).

32. Ibid., 310.

non-Israelite (2 Sam 23:39). David sends to Joab to have Uriah sent to him (2 Sam 11:6)

When Uriah arrives, David goes through the charade of asking him about the campaign, as if that had been the purpose for his presence (2 Sam 11:7). David then tells Uriah to go home and sends food after him (2 Sam 11:8), no doubt to encourage a festival atmosphere in Uriah's house. David wants Uriah to sleep with Bathsheba so it can be claimed the baby is his. Instead of going home, Uriah sleeps at the door of the royal palace with David's men (2 Sam 11:9). On learning of this puzzling event, David asks Uriah for an explanation (2 Sam 11:10).

Uriah's answer deserves quotation in full: "The ark and Israel and Judah dwell in booths; and my lord Joab and the servants of my lord are camping in the open field; shall I then go to my house, to eat and to drink, and to lie with my wife. As you live, and as your soul lives, I will not do this thing" (2 Sam 11:11).

There is one emic expression, admittedly not used here, that describes the motivation for Uriah's actions: it is *ḥesed*. What Uriah manifests is loyalty—loyalty to his God, his divine patron (who is represented by the ark, which is the visible sign of his presence [1 Sam 4:3–9]); to his people (Israel and Judah), also dwelling in tents; to his commander Joab (his patron in the military sphere) and to his fellow soldiers, who are camping in the open field. For Uriah loyalty entails that, as far as possible, he shares the privations that they are experiencing. In short, Uriah exemplifies *ḥesed*. David exemplifies its opposite. It is sometimes suggested that Uriah sees through David and realizes he has slept with Bathsheba;[33] but this would mean he is playing games with David just as David is with him and such a similarity would damage the stark contrast the author is drawing between the characters of two men: the dutiful Uriah and the manipulative David.

After this, David tries to soften Uriah's will by having him stay a few days in Jerusalem and plying him with food and wine. All to no avail; he does not go home (2 Sam 11:12–13). As Ackroyd nicely puts it: "Uriah drunk is more pious than David sober."[34] From David's perspective, this means that there is no alternative but to have Uriah killed. He achieves this end with Joab's help, through orders that Uriah is to be placed in the most dangerous place in the battle (2 Sam 11:14–26). When Bathsheba

33. So Barton, *Ethics*, 26.

34. Ackroyd, *Second Book*, 102.

hears that Uriah was dead, she mourns for him, probably for seven days (1 Sam 31:13). Immediately thereafter, David sends for her to become his (latest) wife and she bares him a son, who passes unnamed in the text. Yet this section of the text ends with the ominous statement that prepares the audience for what is about to occur: "The thing which David had done was evil in the sight of the Lord" (2 Sam 11:27).

David and Nathan

This divine displeasure with David manifests itself as the next episode in the narrative, when God sends Nathan to him. The details of the account make good sense within the framework of God as patron, Nathan his prophet as broker and David as client.

Nathan begins with the tale of two men in one city, a rich man, with many flocks and herds, and a poor man, with only one ewe lamb, to which he was greatly attached. Having heard how the rich man spared his own flocks and took the poor man's lamb to feed a visitor, David explodes with "As the Lord lives, the man who has done this deserves to die; and he shall restore the lamb fourfold, because he did this thing, and because he had no pity" (2 Sam 12:5–6). Then Nathan springs his trap: "You are the man! (*'atah ha-'iš*)" (2 Sam 12:7). David has condemned himself by his own mouth. What David wrongly thought were the facts of a real case, turn out to be a parable about his own behavior.

We should note how Nathan categorizes David's wrong. The story does not refer expressly to some provision of Israelite law, but rather focuses upon the situation of a poor man robbed of the creature he loved. Nathan responds to David in a manner that brilliantly illuminates the patron-client relationship that existed between God and the king: "Thus says the Lord, the God of Israel, 'I anointed you king over Israel, and I delivered you out of the hand of Saul; and I gave you your master's house, and your master's wives into you bosom, and gave you the house of Israel and of Judah; and if this were too little, I would add to you as much more'" (2 Sam 12:7–8, RSV).

The primary function of a patron, as far as his clients are concerned, is to provide them with goods, material and immaterial, in a society where all goods are thought to exist in finite quantities. Nathan is reminding David that God has given no one as many goods as him. No one has had a more generous patron; indeed God substituted David for

Saul as king of Israel. If David had wanted more wives, God would have provided them. By taking Bathsheba in this way, David has scorned the generosity of his divine patron. He had not done what was expected of a client in his culture.

Yet there is more. "Why have you despised the word of the Lord,"[35] Nathan continues (2 Sam 12:9), "to do what is evil in his sight?" We should not interpret despising God's word too narrowly as meaning contravening this or that provision of his law. Despising God's word is essentially equivalent to despising God, a charge explicitly leveled against David in the next verse (2 Sam 12:10). The context here is that of a patron/client relationship, where the gifts of one should find reciprocation in the loyalty and obedience of the other. This is an honor/shame culture where to despise means to treat someone with disrespect, to dishonor him or her. Having given David so much, the implied subtext here is that all God wanted in return was loyalty (*ḥesed*). Instead, David dishonored God by doing what was evil in his sight. David has proved himself a disloyal client and his scorned patron will now act to punish him.

Although by taxing David with having despised the word of the Lord, Nathan thus underlines the relational and honor-based nature of the king's offence, the prophet then proceeds in the remainder of 2 Sam 12:9 to give content to this insult in terms of David's treatment of Uriah. "You have smitten Uriah the Hittite with the sword, and have taken his wife to be your wife, and have slain him with the sword of the Ammonites." This element in the narrative discloses something fundamentally important about this divine patron—he has an abiding concern for justice.

To interpret the offense in David's liaison with Bathsheba in terms of this or that provision of the Pentateuch applicable to all Israelites forbidding murder and adultery would not be wrong in a technical sense but would miss the real point of David's wrong—that not only had be breached his obligations to his patron but he had murdered a man and stolen his wife. David's wrong is, indeed, far worse than that of the rich man in the parable who did not, at least, have the poor man murdered to conceal the theft of his lamb. Thus the text focuses upon the devastation David has wrought both in his personal relationship with God and in its

---

35. "The word of the Lord" occurs in the Masoretic Text; the versions have "the Lord."

effect on Uriah rather than on his infringement of any specific provision of Israelite law.

With bitter irony, Nathan proceeds to announce that since David (acting through the Ammonites of 2 Sam 11:17) slew Uriah with a sword, "now therefore the sword shall never depart from your house, because you have despised me, and have taken the wife of Uriah the Hittite to be your wife (2 Sam 12:10, RSV).

The sorry course of David's life and reign henceforward is then intimated in the details Nathan next provides, which again refer to punishment for David in a form that ironically replicates upon him what he perpetrated on Uriah: "Thus says the Lord, 'Behold, I will raise up evil against you out of your own house; and I will take your wives before your eyes, and give them to your neighbor, and he shall lie with your wives in the sight of this sun. For you did it secretly; but I will do this thing before all Israel, and before the sun'" (2 Sam 12:11–12, RSV).

Sharpening the force of this penalty is the added factor that David will be harmed in relation to the wives that he himself had inherited from Saul as part of the blessings that God had showered upon him. God, speaking through Nathan, at least spares David the news that the "neighbor" will actually be his son Absalom (2 Sam 16:21–22). There is an ironic narrative logic to David's being punished in the same way that he had injured Uriah. Whereas Uriah exemplifies loyalty, David, in this instance, has exemplified disloyalty, so it is appropriate in narrative terms that the sword David inflicted on the loyal man he in turn should suffer as the disloyal man.

Having heard Nathan, David acknowledges that he has sinned against the Lord; in our terms, he recognizes that he has offended his patron. With some dignity, David does not ask for mercy. Nathan tells him, however, that the Lord has put away his sin and he shall not die (this is in spite of the fact that David had adjudged the rich man worthy of death). But this is not the end. Because by his deed David "has caused the enemies of the Lord to blaspheme,"[36] the child of his adulterous union with Bathsheba will die (2 Sam 12:13–14). This soon happens. After Nathan's departure, the child falls ill and David begins a period of fasting and prayers for his recovery that went on for seven days. David clearly hopes that, in spite of his sin and Nathan's prophecy that the child would die,

---

36. The phrase "enemies of" is often omitted in translations, yet it occurs in all the ancient witnesses and there the piel can have a causative sense (so Hertzberg, *I & II Samuel*, 315).

his heavenly patron might yet extend another benefit to him in the form of the child's life (2 Sam 12:22). Yet the child dies. So David comforts Bathsheba for the death of their son and she conceives and gives birth to another son, Solomon, whom God loves (2 Sam 12:24). Then comes the curious episode in the story when God sends Nathan to give Solomon another name, Jedidiah, meaning "Beloved of the Lord," even though this name is not used of Solomon thereafter (2 Sam 12:25).

At this point in the narrative the scene has been set for the second half of 2 Samuel and the beginning of 1 Kings, especially the terrible events that will engulf David's family as the sword ravages his house (2 Samuel 13–24). Yet, at the same time, a son has been born to him who has particular favor with the Lord. Solomon will be the focus of the much happier story in 1 Kings 2–11. Yet all that lies in the future and David still has unfinished business to attend to in the present.

The Defeat of the Ammonites and Capture of Rabbah

The last six verses of 2 Samuel 12 bring the ancient Israelite audience back to the Ammonite war. Enculturated into the honor-laden dynamics of challenge and response, they will have been waiting to hear that David, his lesson learnt, had now taken the field at the head of his army to smite the Ammonites and to avenge their treatment of his ambassadors. Yet such an audience would have been amazed to learn that even now David was not performing in accordance with local cultural values. For in spite of the Ammonites' insult and the trouble he got into when he stayed behind in Jerusalem, David has still not taken command of the campaign himself but continues to entrust that responsibility to Joab. His general is actually doing rather well, having captured part of Rabbah (2 Sam 12:26).

At this point in the narrative the ancient audience would have well understood the exasperation felt by Joab at David's failure to take command and gasped at the threat to David's honor that Joab considered necessary to get the king out of Jerusalem: "And Joab sent messengers to David, and said, 'I have fought against Rabbah; moreover, I have taken the city of waters. Now, therefore, gather the rest of the people together and encamp against the city and take it, lest I capture the city and it be called after my name'" (2 Sam 12:27–28, RSV).

This finally provokes David into action. At long last he gathers all the people, fights against Rabbah and captures it (2 Sam 12:29). He takes their king's crown and puts it on his head. This is a personal touch that shames the Ammonite in a way that repays the shame David endured in the treatment of his embassy. After this he despoils the city (2 Sam 12:30). He also sets the Ammonite population to work. So, at last, having taken due vengeance on the Ammonites for their original insult, he returns to Jerusalem with the people.

CONCLUSION

By undertaking an investigation of 2 Samuel 10–12 with particular attention to textual data relating to the social dynamics of challenge-and-response and patron/client that were central to its ancient context, I have argued that these chapters form a tightly integrated narrative. They focus upon avenging an insult offered to Israel, but one where the execution of that vengeance is inappropriately delayed and with tragic consequences. By using these social-scientific perspectives heuristically to highlight data in the text—that is, to ask questions which only the data can answer and to see how data so identified fits together—I have been able to produce (it is hoped) significant exegetical gains.

These results allow us to appreciate the very distinctive way in which the narrative of David in 2 Samuel 10–12 compares with other stories that Christopher Booker identifies as manifesting the Voyage and Return plot. David journeys not to another place or time or social milieu but inwardly, to a new immoral state, of adultery, disloyalty and murder—a journey away from this true self, a journey that denies his own good heart that God had previously recognized in him (1 Sam 16:7, 12). Strangely quiescent in the face of the Ammonite insult and culpably inactive in the conduct of the resulting war with Ammon, David has time on his hands and is in a state of mind that allows him to be precipitated out of his usual values when he catches sight from his roof of a beautiful woman bathing. Heroes on their voyage enter a new world that may be exhilarating,[37] and presumably David enjoyed a sense of exhilaration in his liaison with Bathsheba and in the royal power that let him take any woman he liked, but this experience very quickly passed, with Bathsheba falling pregnant while her husband was risking his life on

37. Booker, *Seven Basic Plots*, 105.

behalf of David and Israel in the Ammonite war. So the mood of David's adventure changes and a dark shadow falls over it, a shadow that can only be removed with the murder of Uriah. Normally in these plots the heroes make their escape back to the other world from which they started. The question then arises, "how far have they learned or gained anything from their experience? Have they been fundamentally changed, or was it all 'just a dream'?" [38] Certainly like the Ancient Mariner or the Prodigal Son David has moved from darkness back into light and repents of what he has done: "I have sinned against the Lord" (2 Sam 12:13). But this repentance was only precipitated by the extraordinary intervention of the prophet Nathan and his parable of the poor man and his lamb fired at David with the explosive words: *'atah ha-'iš* ("You are the man!"). But really things could never be the same for David again. Not only has a propensity for evil emerged in the Lord's anointed king no less, but he must live with the consequences for the rest of his life, the sword that will never leave his house. Those consequences begin to appear in the very next chapter of 2 Samuel, in the story of Amnon, Tamar and Absalom, dealt with in the next chapter of this volume. Unlike many heroes of the Voyage and Return plot who move from darkness to light, David has traveled from light to darkness to dimmer light.

Finally, therefore, it is easy to imagine that the original audience of this text would have wondered how, as the years rolled on, David must often have reflected upon his behavior in relation to Ammon and looked forward with foreboding to the problems he now faced. Not the least of those problems was the inevitable question from his bright young son Solomon, posed with natural but misplaced family pride: "What did you do in the Ammonite War, father?"

---

38. Ibid, 106.

10

Dishonor Avenged: Amnon, Tamar, and Absalom (2 Samuel 13)

A TALE OF TERROR AND TRAGEDY

The account of the rape of Tamar by her half brother Amnon and the latter's subsequent slaying by Tamar's full brother Absalom in 2 Samuel 13 is one of the most disturbing narratives in the Old Testament. Not surprisingly, it is the subject of one of the four biblical "texts of terror" analyzed by Phyllis Trible in her rightly influential 1984 work of that name.[1] The aim of this essay is to investigate the narrative in a way that is attuned as closely as possible to its ancient context, so that we can approximate more closely to how the story would have been understood by its original audience. To do this I will draw upon ethnographic research into Mediterranean ethnography in the modern period, for example, Finnish anthropologist Hilma Granqvist's work amongst Palestinian and Jordanian Arabs in the 1920s and 1930s. By situating the narrative more firmly in its ancient context I aim not only to show that it contains even more terror than Trible discerned in it (by focusing more on the destruction of Tamar's life within the culture of ancient Israel), but also to illustrate how such a story relates to a wider literary interest in tragedy and revenge.

1. Trible, *Texts of Terror*, 25–44, 93–100.

The textual history of the books of Samuel is notoriously complicated.[2] In this essay, in line with my practice elsewhere in this volume, I will be focusing on the Masoretic Text. At some stage that version made sense to an ancient audience in Israel, even if it was just to the person responsible for the form that we now have. But I will occasionally refer to textual variants in the Septuagint where they have a particular relevance for my interpretation. I do not assume that Tamar, Amnon and Absalom were historical, although I think it likely that they were. For present purposes they need only to be persons whose experience would have made sense to an ancient Israelite audience of this narrative. My interest, as elsewhere in this volume, is historical in that sense.

Is the story of Amnon's rape of Tamar and his murder by Absalom comparable with any of the seven basic plots identified by Christopher Booker? Victor Matthews and Don Benjamin refer to Amnon at one point as "the sole and tragic protagonist" of this tale.[3] This suggests the relevance of "Tragedy," the sixth plot-type that Booker describes.[4] Yet we will see that, although the comparison of 2 Samuel 13 with "Tragedy" raises illuminating questions, the extent to which Amnon can be described as a tragic protagonist is limited to those stories where the "Tragedy" and "Overcoming the Monster" plots converge to produce the pattern of "the hero as monster."[5]

The essence of tragedy, writes Booker, "is that it shows a hero or heroine who commits some great offence and is then drawn down, step by step, into paying the price."[6] The price that is paid is the hero's or heroine's violent death.[7] This pattern emerges in Shakespeare's plays *Richard III* and *Macbeth*, in Marlowe's *Doctor Faustus*, in Robert Louis Stevenson's *Dr Jekyll and Mr Hyde*, in Nabokov's *Lolita*, in Oscar Wilde's *The Picture of Dorian Gray*, in Tolstoy's *Anna Karenina*, and in Flaubert's *Madame Bovary*, to name only a few.[8] In Amnon we certainly have a "hero" who commits a great offence and eventually pays the price with his violent

---

2. Driver, *Notes on the Hebrew Text* is still useful on the textual questions.

3. Matthews and Benjamin, *Social World of Ancient Israel*, 182.

4. Booker, *Seven Basic Plots*, 153–92.

5. Note the title of chapter 10 of Booker's *Seven Basic Plots*: "Tragedy (III): The Hero as Monster" (181–92).

6. Booker, *Seven Basic Plots*, 183.

7. Ibid, 153–54.

8. Ibid, 153–65.

death, yet we do not see the detailed downward spiral typical of much tragedy. He rapes Tamar, two years are said to pass and Absalom has him killed. This means the narrative is much briefer and less developed as far as the "hero" is concerned than those just mentioned. Nevertheless, the details of Booker's account of "Tragedy" do contain numerous points of comparison with the story of Amnon, Tamar and Absalom.

First comes the Anticipation Stage, when the hero or heroine is in some way incomplete or unfulfilled and is looking forward to some unusual gratification.[9] He or she is tempted by a dream of power (like Macbeth or Dr Faustus) or of sexual excitement (as with Humbert Humbert in *Lolita* or Anna Karenina and Madame Bovary) or a mixture of both (as with Dorian Gray).[10] Then some object of desire or course of action presents itself, and his or her energies have a focus.[11] Amnon's illicit interest in his beautiful half sister Tamar (which we will analyze below) can be readily interpreted in this way. Next comes the Dream Stage, when the hero achieves the gratification he had desired, in Amnon's case by raping Tamar. Third, there is the Frustration Stage, where the hero experiences a sense of dissatisfaction and must commit further "dark acts" that lock him more irrevocably into his course of action. Macbeth is a good example, as he commits murder after murder, but for Amnon, too, we will see that just raping Tamar was not enough. Fourth occurs the Nightmare Stage when the hero feels things slipping seriously out of his control. The fact that Amnon does not experience this stage and the reasons for its absence from this narrative will be considered below. Finally, there is the Destruction or Death Wish Stage, where the hero is destroyed by the forces he has roused against himself or takes his own life, the former applying in Amnon's case.

We will now proceed to explore the narrative of Amnon, Tamar and Absalom, mainly by setting it in its ancient context but also at times relating it to the wider universe of tragedy plots among which its particular social setting means the story is cast in a very distinctive shape.

9. Ibid, 156 (where the other four stages are also described).

10. Ibid, 173–74.

11. Ibid, 156.

KING DAVID'S FAMILY AND HOUSEHOLD IN THE LIGHT OF POLYGYNOUS HOUSEHOLDS IN EARLY TWENTIETH-CENTURY PALESTINE

Before considering the details of the narrative in 2 Samuel 13 we need to address certain features of the context in which the events occur. While at a general level we will need to be continually alert to issues such as honor and shame, group-belonging, patrilinearity, polygyny, patrilocality and so on that were discussed in Chapter 2 of this volume and that crop up in this narrative, the immediate context requiring close attention is the family and household of David, Israel's king, in his capital city, Jerusalem. By the time the original audience of this text encountered 2 Samuel 13, they would have already received considerable information bearing on this subject.

Vital data comes from the description at 2 Sam 3:2–5 of the sons born to David at Hebron: "And sons were born to David at Hebron: his first-born was Amnon, of Ahinoam of Jezreel; and his second, Chileab, of Abigail the widow of Nabal of Carmel; and the third, Absalom the son of Maacah the daughter of Talmai king of Geshur; and the fourth, Adonijah the son of Haggith; and the fifth, Shephatiah the son of Abital; and the sixth, Ithream, of Eglah, David's wife. These were born to David in Hebron" (RSV).

So we have six sons born to six separate mothers, daughters not being considered worthy of mention (though we soon learn there were some). Although later on David was to have other children, for the moment we should note that Amnon was David's first-born, his *bekor*. While primogeniture (whereby the eldest son inherits all the father's property) was not a feature of Israelite society, as we have seen in Chapter 3,[12] the first-born son normally had a status at least somewhat higher than sons who were later born. For any man in a patrilinear society such as this, it must have been a considerable relief when he had produced his first son and had thus secured an heir for this property and the future of his name. Accordingly, it would not have been unsurprising if that son had an elevated status in the home and a special place in his father's heart, as I have argued was the case with Judah and his first-born, Er, in Genesis 38 (see chapter 3).

Yet David only reigned from Hebron for seven years and six months, before taking Jerusalem from the Jebusites and making that city his capi-

---

12. In particular, see Greenspahn, *When Brothers Dwell Together*.

tal (2 Sam 5:6–10). Every king needs a palace, especially one with a family as large as David's, and David had a friend who soon met his need:
"And Hiram king of Tyre sent messengers to David, and cedar trees, also
carpenters and masons who built David a house" (*bayit*; 2 Sam 5:11,
RSV). After only one intervening verse, 2 Sam 5:13 states that David
"took more concubines (*pilagšim*) and wives (*našim*) from Jerusalem,
after he came from Hebron, and more sons and daughters were born
to David." The statement that "more sons and daughters were born to
him" (*'od ledawid banim ubanot*) indicates that David already had some
daughters from the time of his residence in Hebron. The narrator then
provides eleven names, this time only of the sons, not the mothers. One
of those sons is Solomon (2 Sam 5:14–16), the son of Bathsheba (2 Sam
12:24). Daughters pass unnamed even if not, in general terms, unmentioned. It is unclear just how many of these wives, concubines and children a reader is to understand were living in the palace at the time of
events of 2 Samuel 13. Nevertheless, we are certainly looking at a family
with a large and growing number of members.

To understand the circumstances of David's family (including
Amnon, Tamar, and Absalom whom we will soon encounter) in a way
necessary to interpret the narrative, however, we need to bear in mind
the polygynous family arrangements in which they found themselves.
Very few commentators have seen the need for this, which is a salutary
reminder of the need for interpreters to think themselves into a context
that is not the Western one with which most of them are familiar.

Among the Palestinian Arabs with whom Finnish anthropologist
Hilma Granqvist lived in the 1920s and 1930s, a man who married more
than one wife had to provide each wife separate sleeping quarters (with
daytime activities in common space), or even accommodate them in
separate dwellings.[13] This was required by Islamic law, but it also made
good practical sense in preserving a measure of peace and harmony in
the home. Since only one house, one palace, is mentioned in connection
with David, it is likely that he provided each of his wives and concubines
with some space private to themselves and their children, whatever
shared space was allocated for the entire family.

---

13. Granqvist, *Marriage Conditions* 2:191–92. In footnote 1 on p. 192 she reports on
other research among Palestinians and Bedouin showing how Arab men were expected
to provide a separate establishment for each wife if they had the resources (which usually only applied to rich men).

The picture that emerges, therefore, is of a palace where David's women and their respective sets of children live, probably with separate sleeping quarters but shared areas for other purposes. The house Hiram built for David must have been very large! With so many co-wives and concubines and their sons and daughters, the palace would have been a very busy place, with extensive networks of social interactions among David's various women and their children. In addition, the fact that it enjoyed royal resources would have ensured its members a high level of material comfort. Since we learn in 2 Samuel 13 that both Amnon and Absalom had their own houses (vv. 7 and 20), it must have been David's practice to set up his sons, as they reached early adulthood, in their own houses. Daughters no doubt only left the palace when they married.

Yet it is not enough merely to note the domestic arrangements common among polygynous families; we need to ask how children of David's various wives and concubines related to their full siblings by the same mother and to their half siblings by other mothers.

Mention was made in chapter 2 of this volume of the fact that we are dealing with a high context culture, where a huge amount of contextual information was understood by the original audience of this narrative, so that we observe a noticeable sparseness in the story-telling.[14] The nature of the relationships between half and full siblings in a polygynous household, a matter central to its successful functioning, is a good example of this phenomenon; it is something with which an ancient Israelite audience would have already been familiar, so that specific explanation was unnecessary. Modern readers, however, are not in this position and need help from Mediterranean ethnography to appreciate what is going on in the narrative.

Among the Palestinian Arabs observed by Hilma Granqvist there were very strong bonds between brothers and sisters of the same mother and father. Close relationships were built up between brothers and sisters when they were growing up in their father's house. A husband might divorce a woman, but her brother would always be there. That is why one woman, when asked who of a husband, son or brother she would least like to see die, said, "A husband may [always] be had; a son can [also] be born; but a beloved brother, from where shall he come back [when he is once dead]?"[15]

14. See pp. 74–76.
15. Granqvist, *Marriage Conditions* 2:253.

Granqvist makes the following comment on the close connection between brother and sister in the patrilinear culture of the Palestinians that has considerable bearing on what happens to Tamar: "A man is even more responsible for his sister than for his wife and children, she can always take refuge with him even from the husband."[16] We will see later how Tamar seeks refuge with her brother Absalom.

Similarly strong ties between brothers and sisters also exist in another patrilinear (although not polygynous) Mediterranean culture, that of the Greek Sarakatsani: "The idea of 'one blood' which they share in their common filiation to the same parents is the value that underlies the impressive solidarity of siblings in the elementary family and their almost complete identification of interests . . . Whatever, for good or ill, is suffered or achieved by one sibling is held to affect the other siblings to an almost equivalent degree."[17]

In a polygynous context in which there were siblings of different co-wives in the household, the love between full brothers and sisters emerges very strongly. Among the Arab Palestinians whom Granqvist observed, whereas relations between the children of co-wives tended to be strained, only if children had both parents in common did they really feel like brothers and sisters. A child in a polygynous family spoke of his father's child by a co-wife as "my father's son" (not "my brother"). This sense of distance was often accompanied by negative feelings towards half siblings. Thus it was said, "From the son of the co-wife there is no joy" and "Thy father's son is like the people who fought against thee." As a rule, the Palestinians took the view that "They who are from one 'back' (that is, one father) and two (different) wombs (i.e. children of the same father but two different mothers) do not love each other." On the other hand, "thy mother's son (that is, a full brother) is as gold in thy sleeve" and "He who from my father's 'back' came to my mother's womb, he is my brother." The last sentiment was expressed even more vividly: "My brother, that is my mother's son and not (her) co-wife's son, we both turned in the same womb."[18]

These sentiments are likely to occur in another polygynous family located in a patrilinear and patrilocal culture and that is essentially what

16. Ibid., 254.

17. Campbell, *Honour, Family and Patronage*, 172.

18. The material (including quotations) comes from Granqvist, *Marriage Conditions* 2:216–17.

we will find in David's family. In particular, we will observe strong bonds of love between the full siblings Tamar and Absalom, while Amnon, her half brother, will exhibit antipathy to her, although in a particularly shocking way. It should be noted that it appears from the text before us that among the Israelites, unlike modern Palestinians, it was the custom for half siblings to refer to one another as "brother" or "sister."

THE RAPE OF TAMAR

Context and Characters

Let us now address the narrative.

"Now afterwards it came to pass that Absalom, David's son, had a beautiful (*yaphah*) sister, whose name was Tamar; and Amnon, David's son, lusted after her" (*waye'ehabeha*, 2 Sam 13:1). Although we are never told explicitly, the only way that the story makes sense is if Tamar and Absalom mentioned in 2 Sam 13:1 are full siblings, the children of David and Maacah, the daughter of Talmai, king of Geshur, while Amnon is their half brother, the son of David and Ahinoam. As already noted, Amnon was the first son of David born while he was at Hebron and Absalom the third (2 Sam 3:2). Perhaps Tamar was also born during this Hebron period. My previous discussion of full sibling and half sibling relationships in polygynous households will become relevant as we consider the narrative as it develops.

The brief phrase "now afterwards" (*aharey ken*) in v. 1 actually refers back to the momentous events of 2 Samuel 10–12, which contain the beginning and successful conclusion of the war with the Ammonites, in the midst of which occur David's having sexual intercourse with Bathsheba the wife of Uriah the Hittite, his murder of Uriah and the birth of Solomon. I have considered this narrative in chapter 9 of this volume. Although Phyllis Trible notes the allusion to 2 Samuel 10–12, she wrongly considers that here "the narrator leaves these exploits."[19] In fact 2 Samuel 10–12 casts a black cloud over the rest of the narrative in 2 Samuel, beginning with 2 Samuel 13, by virtue of the prophet Nathan's prophecy to David in consequence of his murder of Uriah, which includes the warning: "Now therefore the sword shall never depart from your house, because you have despised me, and have taken the wife of Uriah the Hittite to be your wife" (2 Sam 12:10, RSV). The first person

19. Trible, *Texts of Terror*, 25–26.

to take up that sword will be Absalom. In 2 Samuel 13 we learn just why he did. As J. P. Fokkelman has noted, Absalom looms over the Amnon-Tamar story in vv. 1–22 ("Absalom's presence is the backdrop against which the drama Amnon-Tamar is enacted."). He also views Absalom as the dominant actor in the revenge story in vv. 23–39 and considers that "the story of Amnon and Tamar is a component of Absalom's history."[20] These latter remarks are probably pushing his point too far; Amnon is the tragic protagonist (admittedly, a monstrous one) in 1 Sam. 13:1–33. Absalom serves as the avenging agent in that story and then becomes more central in the ongoing narrative.

Scholars frequently raise the question of the extent to which the actions of Amnon in relation to Tamar parallel those of his father, David, in relation to Bathsheba. Some, like Fokkelman who describes Amnon as "a chip off the old block" regard David and Amnon as fundamentally the same in the their attitudes and character.[21] In fact, as Mark Gray has argued, while there are some similarities between David and Amnon, there are also many differences, especially the undoubted violence with which Amnon rapes Tamar, for which there is no evidence in relation to David's treatment of Bathsheba.[22] In similar vein, Walter Dietrich notes that the text leaves open the question of whether Bathsheba consented to David's advances or not.[23] While this may be true, we should not forget that David did send messengers, who "took her," so that she came to David and he lay with her (2 Sam 11:4), which inevitably raises the question of the extent to which her will was suborned by the king. Nevertheless, Gray puts this issue well when he writes, "I think we are to understand Amnon's action as one of unmitigated brutality, but we are not led by the text to put David's in quite the same category."[24] Accordingly, while David no doubt showed his sons a very poor example, he was not as bad as Amnon as far as the woman he desired was concerned. Although he had sex with Bathsheba and had her husband killed, he did go on to take her as his wife, whereas Amnon, once he had raped Tamar, had her expelled from his house.

20. Fokkelman, *Narrative Art*, 1:101.

21. Ibid., 1:99; Gray, "Amnon," 39–40, summarizes the views of a number of scholars who share this view.

22. Gray, "Amnon," 48. Also see Dietrich, "David, Amnon und Abschalom."

23. Dietrich, "David, Amnon und Abschalom," 119–20.

24. Gray, "Amnon," 48.

Most versions translate *waye'ehabeha* in v. 1 as "he loved her," or "fell in love with her" or some other expression using "love."[25] These are serious mistranslations in the light of Amnon's feelings towards Tamar, described in the next verse, which have nothing whatever to do with love. Similarly doubtful is George Ridout's suggestion that Amnon had "great affection for his half sister."[26] Although Trible takes a step in the right direction by saying Amnon "desired" Tamar,[27] even this translation falls short of the meaning of the verb *'aheb* as far as Amnon was concerned, as we will now see by considering the next verse: "And Amnon was so tormented that he made himself ill because of his sister Tamar; for she was a virgin, and it seemed impossible to Amnon to do anything to her" (2 Sam 13:2, RSV).

In comparison with Christopher Booker's description of the "Tragedy" plot, set out above, this verse describes what he calls the Anticipation Stage, when the "hero" is in some way incomplete or unfulfilled and is looking forward to some unusual gratification. In Amnon's case, the issue concerns sexual excitement focused on a forbidden object (similar to Humbert Humbert's obsession with an underage girl in *Lolita*). Indeed the nature of both the lack of fulfillment and the gratification Amnon seeks make him a most unattractive character. The RSV translation accurately captures the Hebrew, and how dim a view an ancient Israelite audience would have taken of Amnon. His illness derives from the fact that Tamar is a virgin and there is nothing he can do *to her*! Not "with her," for example, but "to her." Let us pause for a moment and reflect on this. Amnon has a half sister, a member of the same extended family to which he belongs, a family whose members enjoy shared honor from belonging to a group in Israel as illustrious as this. Tamar is also beautiful and a virgin. But Amnon does not rejoice in this, even though, as a member of David's family, he is also touched by the honor that comes to it from Tamar's beauty and virginal status. No, he is sick because he can do nothing about it. The problem is that she is physically unavailable to him, as she lives in the no doubt protected environment of the royal palace,[28] a point I will return to below, whereas he is living in his own house. One could imagine someone in Amnon's

25. For example, the KJV, RSV, and the JB.
26. Ridout, "Rape of Tamar," 78.
27. Trible, *Texts of Terror*, 26.
28. So McCarter, *II Samuel*, 321, and most commentators.

position disregarding the fact of their half sibling relationship and wanting to have sex with Tamar simply because she was a beautiful woman.[29]
Such an inclination would not be morally admirable in this setting, but
nor would it necessarily be vicious or pathological. But that is not what
Amnon wants. He is tormented to sickness *because of* Tamar's virginity.
Her beauty and innocent status drive him to distraction. His frustration
at finding it impossible to do anything *to* Tamar can only mean that he
wants to destroy her virginal innocence, not to enjoy sex with her. This
interpretation will be confirmed by subsequent events. In Amnon we
seem to be confronted with an agent of evil that is so vicious and so inexplicable that its motivation and character tend to resist comprehension.

Victor Matthews and Don Benjamin have, nevertheless, recently
proposed a new and provocative explanation of Amnon (one of the few
attempts to make sense of the story of Amnon, Tamar, and Absalom
that uses Mediterranean anthropology), which seeks to account for
his actions in political terms.[30] Their central thesis is that "To force
David to name him heir, Amnon rapes Tamar hoping that his actions
will assure him of the right of becoming monarch."[31] They see Amnon's
actions as directed towards eliminating Tamar's full-brother Absalom
as a contender for the crown. In their view, when a man representing
one household (like Amnon) raped a woman from another (and they
propose Tamar belonged to Absalom's household) that had a position of
honor in the community, and was therefore worthy of this "challenge,"
"it was not only an act of sexual violence but also a hostile takeover
bid. The assailant asserted the right of his household to the resources of
another."[32] Although this is a stimulating reading, and well emphasizes
the importance of family honor and purity codes among the ancient
Israelites, it nevertheless misunderstands the text in many significant
respects, a correct interpretation of which is necessary properly to

29. It is doubtful that incest was a big issue here because in v. 2 her status as his
half sister is not presented as a factor stopping him from doing anything to her (so
Fokkelman, *Narrative Art*, 1:103–4). Also Tamar later says David will let him marry her
(2 Sam 13:13). For a summary of this question, see McCarter, *II Samuel*, 323–24.

30. Matthews and Benjamin, *Social World of Ancient Israel*, 176–86; and Matthews
and Benjamin, "Amnon and Tamar"; the latter is a more fully documented version of
their argument.

31. Matthews and Benjamin, *Social World of Ancient Israel*, 181.

32. Matthews and Benjamin, "Amnon and Tamar," 347; and see Matthews and
Benjamin, *Social World of Ancient Israel*, 180.

grasp the meaning of this narrative in its context. I will critically engage with the interpretation of Matthews and Benjamin during the course of the argument.

Jonadab's Plan

At this juncture a friend of Amnon comes to his aid, in the form of Jonadab, the son Shimeah, David's brother. Shimeah, also known as Shammah or Shimei was Jesse's third son (1 Sam 16:9). So Jonadab is the paternal cousin of Amnon, but also of Tamar and Absalom. Jonadab, we are told, was very cunning (*ḥakam me'od*) (v. 3). He asks Amnon why he looks so haggard every morning and Amnon replies, "I lust after Tamar, my brother Absalom's sister" (2 Sam 13:4). Here "I lust after" translates the same Hebrew word (*'aheb*) as appears in v. 1. Amnon does not give Jonadab the information that the narrator provides the reader/listener in v. 2, that Amnon is sick because there is nothing he can do to Tamar, in which case Jonadab might have thought that Amnon actually did love her. Nevertheless, Jonadab's haste to devise the plan for Amnon's rape of Tamar shows he does not deserve the benefit of the doubt. He knows what Amnon wants.

This plan appears in the next verse in reply to Amnon's admission: "Jonadab said to him, 'Lie down on your bed, and pretend to be ill; and when your father comes to see you, say to him, "Let my sister Tamar come and give me bread to eat, and prepare the food in my sight, that I may see it, and eat it from her hand"'" (2 Sam 13:5 RSV).

Jonadab does not need to say what will happen next; both men know exactly what he has in mind, and he can leave the detailed execution of the plan to Amnon. So here we have Jonadab, just as much the paternal cousin of Tamar as he is of Amnon, dreaming up the scheme that will enable one cousin to rape another.

There must have been a particular horror for an ancient Israelite audience in the fact that Jonadab, a paternal cousin of Tamar, devised her dishonor. David had seven brothers (1 Sam 16:10), all older than him (1 Sam 16:11), of whom the eldest was Eliab (1 Sam 16:6; 17:28), and after him (assuming they are named in order of age) Abinadab and Shammah (1 Sam 16:8–9), the latter being Jonadab's father. In a patrilinear culture a man's brothers have a particularly important role in the life of his family. This ultimately relates to the fact that they will inherit their father's property when he dies. Yet with this privilege come responsibilities. Among Granqvist's Arab Palestinians, when a man died his brother stepped into his place: "He is responsible for his debts but also administers the property and is the natural protector, guardian and person to arrange the marriage of his brother's children. When there is a daughter to inherit it is quite clear, that, if the father's brother (*il-'amm*) has the right, he will be glad to arrange a marriage between his ward and his son and thus bring the property, which he has already learnt to regard as his own, into his family."[33]

Similar arrangements obtained in ancient Israel, where there are many signs of a special role and regard for the father's brother (*dod*) and also for his sons. An excellent example occurs in Lev 25:47–49, where it is provided that if a man falls into financial difficulties and sells himself to a foreigner living amongst the people, he may be redeemed by his brother, his paternal uncle, *his paternal uncle's son* or another member of the family. This looks very similar to the Palestinian attitude and arrangements just mentioned. Among the Bedouin of Egypt a woman's *ibn 'amm* ("father's brother's son," "paternal cousin") stands in a close relation to her, especially as her most suitable marriage partner, and has a duty to avenge affronts to her (and also sexual misconduct by her).[34] In Amos 6:10 the remains of a man who have been burnt in a house are to be brought out by his paternal uncle. In Jer 32:7 a right to possess a man's field is vested in the son of his paternal uncle. In Lev 18:14 there is a prohibition on uncovering the nakedness of the brother (or sister) of one's father, but not the brother of one's mother (only her sister). Numbers 36 relates a ruling by Moses to the effect that where a man only has daughters they must be married off to the sons of their father's brothers; this meant that the property and the line of descent remained within the patrilineage.

From this we may conclude that if David had died leaving young children and his father, Jesse, was also dead, it would have been up to his brothers to make appropriate arrangements for his property and children. If they were dead, the duty would fall on their sons. Perhaps David's eldest brother, Eliab, would have had the dominant role, but raising this scenario indicates the sort of responsibility that a paternal uncle or paternal cousin might have in relation to any young children of

33. Granqvist, *Marriage Conditions* 2:79.
34. Abou-Zeid, "Honour and Shame," 256–57.

David: to see them fed and housed, their property protected and appropriate marriages arranged in due course. Although Amnon and Tamar are both or marriageable age, Jonadab nevertheless grotesquely breaks the obligations he has to her as one of her paternal kinsmen by devising the plan for her rape. His actions would have been regarded as particularly appalling by an ancient Israelite audience because of his violation of the relationship between two paternal cousins. Why did he do so? Presumably to curry favor with the man, a friend of his after all, who, as the David's firstborn, might have seemed most likely to succeed the king after his death. But Jonadab's support should be restricted to this possibility. Contrary to the proposal of Matthews and Benamin, there is no hint that Jonadab's advice to Amnon had the purported aim of helping him gain the kingdom by eliminating Absalom through the rape of Tamar.[35] Jonadab's advice is solely directed to helping Amnon with his physical desire to rape Tamar and to benefit from any cementing of his friendship with Amnon that his might produce. Similarly, their suggestion that Jonadab tells Amnon to ask David to send Tamar to feed him with food prepared in his sight because he fears being poisoned lacks any foundation in the text and requires that Amnon apprehends political machinations against him for which there is equally no evidence.[36] He is simply telling David that his health would be improved with some tender loving care in the form of his sister's presumably excellent cakes fresh from her own baking (as opposed to her making them in the palace and sending them to her by another hand). This device is necessary to get her into his house, but it will also provide him the opportunity to gaze on her, lustfully no doubt, as she does the cooking.

The Plan Is Implemented

Events then followed as Jonadab had suggested: "So Amnon lay down, and pretended to be ill; and when the king came to see him, Amnon said to the king, 'Pray let my sister Tamar come and make a couple of cakes in my sight, that I may eat from her hand'" (2 Sam 13:6, RSV). The next

35. Matthews and Benjamin consider that although Amnon thought Jonadab was his wise and loyal friend, Jonadab had actually supported Absalom's claim all along (*Social World of Ancient Israel*, 82). They even go so far as to suggest that Absalom may have dispatched Jonadab to Amnon to give him bad advice" ("Amnon and Tamar," 353).

36. See Matthews and Benjamin, "Amnon and Tamar," 353.

verse plays a central role in Matthews and Benjamin's argument, and also in revealing its flaws: "Then David sent to Tamar at home (*habbaytah*) saying, "Go to your brother Amnon's house and prepare food for him.""

The word *habbaytah* represents "the house" (*habayt*) in the old accusative form (= the added –*ah*) to express motion towards and literally means "towards the house." But which house? Where is Tamar living? This is an extremely important question for understanding Tamar's eventual fate, as we will see, although one which few commentators explore or Bible translators recognize.[37] Drawn to focus on this issue by their interest in the honor and shame dimensions of this narrative, however, Matthews and Benjamin rightly appreciate its significance. According to them, it is the house of her brother Absalom: "Tamar belongs to the household of Absalom."[38] Certainly at this time Absalom did have a house and Tamar would end up living there (2 Sam 13:20). But that is not where she was living when David sent for her. There can be no doubt that the house to which David sends for Tamar is his own house, the royal palace. Since this conclusion is really fatal to Matthews and Benjamin's political interpretation of Amnon's action—that he rapes Tamar to damage Absalom (in whose house she allegedly lives) and hence eliminate Absalom as a contender for the throne—it requires a little more attention.

The primary consideration here is that mention of "the house" in v. 7, with the definite article but without mention of its owner immediately suggests that this is a house previously mentioned in the narrative and the only candidate is the one provided by Hiram that has come up earlier in the narrative, so that its ownership does not require stating. It is David's house. By contrast, we should note the references to the house of Amnon (2 Sam 13:7, 8) and the house of Absalom (2 Sam 13:20), where the names of the respective owners are expressed. "The house" in v. 7 is "the palace." The word *heykal* is not used, probably because the usual term for "royal palace" in Hebrew is *bayit hammelek*. The natural assumption is that all of David's wives and concubines were housed in this *bayit*, his palace. This would mean, quite realistically, that his palace contained his harem in which all of his wives (of whom seven are known, the six

37. But note the correct translation of the word as "his house" in the Spanish Reina-Valera 1995 version: "Entonces David envió a decir a Tamar a su casa . . ."

38. Matthews and Benjamin, *Social World of Ancient Israel*, 182; and Matthews and Benjamin, "Amnon and Tamar," 354.

mentioned in 2 Sam 3:2–5 and Bathsheba) and his concubines and their children reside, with the various wives and concubines probably having separate sleeping quarters. Furthermore, in 2 Sam 15:16 when David is fleeing Jerusalem, he leaves behind ten concubines (*nashim pilagshim*) to look after "the house" (*habbayit*), again with the article, meaning his palace. His concubines seem to have been expendable in a way his wives were not. The word *bayit* is used in the same sense in 2 Sam 16:21, in the passage (2 Sam 16:20–23) where Absalom has sex with these concubines (*pilagšim*), as predicted by Nathan earlier in the narrative (2 Sam 12:11), although there in relation to wives (*našim*) not concubines. There is further reference to this "house" in 2 Sam 20:3, where David returns to Jerusalem, to the palace and shuts the ten concubines away until the day of their death.

In 1994, Victor Matthews revealed some of the reasoning that led to the view expressed by himself and Don Benjamin that the house was Absalom's when he argued that although a wife had to uphold the honor of her husband, once her son, the prince, "has reached an age when he can maintain his own household separate from the king's," then "the queen technically owes allegiance to the king but belongs to the household of her son, along with any sisters of the prince."[39] Although Matthews cites no evidence for this surprising proposition, some comparable material unhelpful to his position is to be found in the operations of the royal harem in the Ottoman empire. For a period starting from the middle of the fifteenth century a practice developed of sending a royal prince from the capital to be the governor of a province, accompanied by his mother. Her role was to preside over the domestic household of the prince and to help his tutor to train and supervise him. In the capital the sultan's mother was in charge of the household. During the late sixteenth century, however, the princely governorate in the provinces came to an end and "the entire royal family was united in the capital under one roof, rather than, as previously, dispersed throughout the royal domain." From that time onwards there was "only one royal household, over which the senior woman, the sultan's mother, naturally took charge."[40]

This comparable material would lead us to expect that in Israel under David each prince did not go off to found a household with his

---

39. Matthews, "Female Voices," 8.

40. Peirce, *Imperial Harem*, 24. The date of the demise of the princely governorate appears on 91.

mother, because there was no system of princes ruling provinces that would have provided the basis for a royal wife to leave the king's house. In addition, the text of 2 Samuel 13 itself provides strong counterevidence. The evidence points firmly to the fact that David's wives (and concubines) remained as members of his household and in his house. In a patrilinear society (absent extraordinary circumstances such as those in the Ottoman empire in the fifteenth and sixteenth centuries), this is what we would expect. The senior male, *à fortiori* a king, remains in control of his family unless frailty or death prevents him from doing so. Although David had given Amnon and Absalom their own houses, the probable reason was that having young men in a palace in the presence of attractive women who were not their mothers and to whom they had no blood relation, or who were only half sisters, was a recipe for problems, as this narrative itself makes very clear. Perhaps David is also showing some recognition of the growing maturity of his elder sons and their wish to live apart from the women and children of the larger family, especially because they wished to associate freely with men of their age, whose presence in the palace with David's women would have been even more undesirable. This explains why Amnon and Absalom were given their own houses, but letting them have power over their mothers, David's wives, would have been a very different matter for which there is no evidence. In addition, it is clear from the text that Amnon does not have his mother (Ahinoam of Jezreel, 2 Sam 3:2) or any sister living with him, only servants. At 2 Sam 13:9 Amnon asks someone, presumably a servant, to send everyone (literally, "every man") away; these are presumably his (male) friends and companions. We have direct reference to this servant in 2 Sam 13:17–18; it is a man who serves "him," that is, just Amnon, since Amnon has no other family members living with him.

To return to the narrative, David sent to Tamar (in his palace, as just explained), telling her to go to Amnon's house and prepare food for him and so she did, finding him lying down (vv. 7–8).

We need to imagine the scene. Tamar has come to a room in Amnon's house that must contain an oven or at least a fireplace, because she is going to bake the cakes. Amnon's servant and companions are present, until he has them leave (v. 9), and he is on his bed in a separate, internal chamber (*ḥeder*, v. 10) from which he has a view of Tamar kneading the dough and then baking the cakes from it.

The contrast between Tamar and Amnon is stark. On the one hand we have a beautiful young woman engaged in the simple task of preparing food for her sick half brother in accordance with her father's instruction. It is a scene of domestic peace and tranquility. On the other hand we have Amnon in his bed, looking at her. Following Jonadab's advice, Amnon had told David he wanted Tamar to make the cakes in his sight (vv. 5, 7), no doubt to avoid the possibility that the king would ask her to make them but someone else might convey them to Amnon. And Tamar does indeed make the cakes "in his sight" (v. 8). Yet by this means Amnon is also able to gaze, no doubt lustfully, at Tamar as she goes about her duty. Phyllis Trible aptly notes the presence of his eyes and gaze in the scene.[41] Amnon's gaze bears a similarity to the way that Amnon's father, David, once looked upon Bathsheba as she went about another domestic task (2 Sam 11:2), as Walter Dietrich has suggested.[42]

So far, however, nothing has happened that would have given Tamar any cause for concern. This soon changes. She empties the cakes from the pan in front of him, meaning in the cooking area, while he watches from his chamber, but he refuses to eat. Depending on how he did this and what he said, Tamar may have felt the first glimmer of concern. Yet her reaction would certainly have turned to alarm at what came next (v. 9): "And Amnon said, 'Send out every one from me.' So every one went out from him." With no one left to witness what might transpire, Tamar must have apprehended with a sudden sense of shock what Amnon might have in mind. When next he tells her to bring the food into the chamber, "that I may eat from your hand," we can well imagine the nervousness and even fear with which she takes the cakes and brings them to him in his chamber (v. 10). Her fear is immediately realized: "But when she brought them near him to eat, he took hold of her, and said to her, 'Come, lie with me, my sister.'" (v. 11; RSV).

The narrative of Tamar's actual rape in vv. 12–14 is highly condensed and yet remarkably graphic. One aspect of its narrative art is that from the moment that Amnon seizes Tamar, saying, "Come, lie with me, my sister" (v. 11), she is struggling to escape from him. Consider the language in v. 12, with its five negative statements. The reader is compelled to understand Tamar's various statements as spread out and as enunciated in the course of a struggle to escape from Amnon's grip:

---

41. Trible, *Texts of Terror*, 31.

42. Dietrich, "David, Amnon und Abschalom," 120.

"No!" (The force of the Hebrew word *lo'*, meaning "not ever")

"No, my brother!" (The force of the Hebrew word *'al*, meaning 'not now')

"Do not dishonor me, for this is not done in Israel."

"Do not commit this outrage!" (*nebalah*, v. 12).

The Hebrew word *'anah* means to be or afflicted, humbled or put down, a serious problem in an honor-culture, and here "dishonor" translates the piel form of this verb, in the well-attested sense of humbling a woman by violating her (cf. Gen 34:2; Deut 21:14; 22:24, 29; Judg 19:24; 20:5). The word will reappear in vv. 14, 22, and 32.

Another word in this verse steeped in the honor language of ancient Israel is *nebalah*.[43] Here the word conveys the meaning of an outrage that will result in the reputations of both of them plummeting. Marböck aptly notes that its use in v. 12 recalls its appearance in Judges 19:23 where the Levite cautions the men of Gibeah against committing an outrage (*nebalah*) on his concubine: in these two cases the person who commits *nebalah* "callously disregards not only the norms of the community but also human warnings and pleas."[44] The word is also employed in relation to Shechem's rape of Dinah in Gen 34:7. In this sense it is rather like *hubris* in classical Greece, although it is translated as *aphrosynē* in the LXX at this point (and elsewhere), which does not really seem to catch its brutal connotation but does show a movement toward a wisdom interpretation.[45]

Tamar attempts to reason with Amnon, by pointing out the consequences of his raping her, first for herself, "As for me, where could I carry my shame?" and then for him, "and as for you, you would be as one of the base men in Israel." (v. 13). The word for shame here, *heref*, falls into the general semantics of shame and honor in the Hebrew Bible.

Victor Matthews notes that in a tradition-oriented society like that of ancient Israel, where codes of correct conduct were measures of honor or dishonor, family members had a duty to uphold its honor and used speech and actions as a means of social control to achieve this end.[46] According to Matthews, what Tamar says to Amnon is an example of "shaming speech," which is speech that calls on each person to act "hon-

43. See Marböck, "*Nabal*; *nebalah*."

44. Ibid, 168.

45. For the movement towards the wisdom tradition in translating, see ibid., 171.

46. Matthews, "Honor and Shame," 98.

orably, with carefully thought out actions, not in the manner of fools who act in the height of passion, without thinking."[47] It is noteworthy that the reasons she gives are completely taken up with their reputations; she does not mention that what Amnon is intent upon doing represents a breach of divine law. The reasons she offers are the ones that we expect in an honor and shame culture such as this. But nothing she says dissuades Amnon from his course.

Tamar also proposes an alternative to rape; Amnon can have her sexually by marrying her: "Now therefore, I pray you, speak to the king; for he will not withhold me from you" (v. 13). There is probably an implication here that the king would overlook the issue of their being half siblings (which represented a bar to their marriage in some reaches of Israelite tradition, for example, Lev 18:9, 11; Deut 27:22)[48] in granting them permission to marry. The rationale for Tamar's proposal is that through marriage both their reputations will be preserved.

What was the cause of Tamar's concern, which was so tied to the reputations of both of them? To appreciate the terrible reality that Amnon was about to inflict on Tamar and she was to suffer, since it goes far beyond the undoubted physical and psychological horrors of rape with which those of us who live in modern Western cultures are familiar, we must set the action in its cultural context.

The Rape of Tamar in Its Ancient Context

Rape is always a terrible outrage against a woman, involving in Western cultural settings powerlessness, physical assault, pain, injury and defilement, diminished self esteem and various forms of post-traumatic psychological disturbances, an experience for which Dartmouth philosopher Susan Brison, raped, strangled, beaten on the head and left for dead on a visit to France in 1994 has offered powerful testimony.[49] Yet there is good reason to believe that for someone like Tamar, a virgin in this particular cultural context, rape had other very serious consequences in addition to these. Even a commentator like Phyllis Trible,

---

47. Ibid., 99.

48. See McCarter, *II Samuel*, 323–24.

49. For discussion of the effects of rape on women in contemporary Western society from a survivor's viewpoint, see Brison, "Surviving Sexual Violence"; and Brison, *Aftermath*.

very sensitive to the abuse suffered by women in biblical stories such as these, has understated the impact of Amnon's assault on her.

One prominent feature of many cultures around the Mediterranean, past and present, which I mentioned in chapter 2, is a concern that a young woman must be a virgin when she first marries. Researchers who have commented on this feature include Jane Schneider, Carol Delaney, and Maureen Giovannini.[50] Maureen Giovannini has rightly made the following comment (by way of criticizing Michael Herzfeld for his ethnographic particularism): "Despite considerable variation in the content of Mediterranean moral-evaluative systems, some striking parallels exist which cannot be ignored. One of these is the cultural emphasis on female chastity as an indicator of social worth for individuals and their respective kin groups."[51]

Although the cultural equation of female chastity and social worth may not a "cultural universal" of the Mediterranean region, nor in fact restricted to that region, it is very pervasive in that part of the world and is associated with institutionalized practices that influence and reflect "gender-based relations of authority, dominance and coercion." These practices include female seclusion, the veiling of women, the "crime of honour," and ritual displays of virginity (such as bloody sheets and nightgowns).[52] Those who wish to deny the currency or force of such practices will need to reckon with the large number of women in or from Middle Eastern countries who are murdered each year by their fathers or brothers for the reason that they have sex with a man not their husband or are merely suspected to have done so. As I write (on September 26, 2009) one of these cases is going through a court in London.

The Palestinian villagers among whom Finnish anthropologist Hilma Granqvist lived in the 1920s and 1930s shared this circum-Mediterranean concern with the chastity of their women, as seen in the need for a new bride to be able to prove, via the testimony of her husband or the display of the bride's blood-marked sheet or underwear, the fact that

50. See Gilmore, "Introduction," 3–4; Schneider, "Of Vigilance and Virgins," Delaney, *Seeds of Honor*, 35–48; and Giovannini , "Female Chastity Codes," 61. This is not to say that virginity is not valued in other cultures; see Frymer-Kensky, "Virginity in the Bible," 82–84.

51. Giovannini, "Female Chastity Codes," 61.

52. Ibid.

he had ruptured her hymen on their wedding night.[53] This phenomenon was also a feature of life in ancient Israel, since Deut 22:13–21 presents a long discussion, first, concerning a man who falsely denies that his wife was a virgin on their wedding night being shown up by the production of the bloodied garment and, second, of the stoning of a woman who cannot provide such evidence.

The way a woman achieves the best result in life in these societies, meaning both material comfort but also honor (meaning her own view of herself matched by the high regard in which she is held by those who know here), is by marrying well and then having children. Yet if a woman is to enter a favorable and honorable marriage (usually arranged by her father, brothers or other male relatives), it is vital that she does so as a virgin.

There is also a strong link between the honor of a family and the virginity of its unmarried daughters.[54] When a young woman has sex before she is married, the honor of the family is besmirched. Since it is a duty of the men of the family to guard their women against just such an event, they feel the insult most keenly. To have lost control of one of their daughters or sisters badly damages their reputation by casting a deep shadow over their manhood. One way to restore, or at least partially restore, their reputation is by wreaking vengeance on the perpetrators, preferably by killing them. Sometimes they will kill the man concerned, but often the woman herself (their own daughter or sister) also falls victim to their desire for revenge. Honor killings of women who have had sex with men before marriage, or who are even suspected of having done so, are quite common in parts of the Middle East (such as Jordan) even today, and the killers tend to receive light sentences.[55]

---

53. Granqvist, *Marriage Conditions*, 2:126–30.

54. For a discussion of how a woman who engages in sex outside marriage endangers the honor of her family, see Matthews, "Honor and Shame," 102–12.

55. Thus the *Sunday Times Magazine* of July 8, 2001 (pp. 20–25), carried a story of the light sentences Jordanian courts generally give to men who have murdered their sisters or daughters because they have had, or are merely believed to have had, sex with a man outside marriage. One thirty-two-year-old man who had shot and killed his sixteen-year-old sister after she had been raped by her brother-in-law said, "She should die because she made a mistake. If she didn't die, we would kill 1,000 men because of shame." He received a six-months' sentence during which he said he was treated as a hero in jail. Also see Marohl, *Joseph's Dilemma*.

Since a woman who is not a virgin will find it difficult, if not im-possible, to enter into a good marriage with a suitable husband, to rape a woman is to deny her the prospect of a happy and honorable life. Sometimes marriage with a man of low prestige occurs,[56] but even that might not be possible or practical for a highborn woman. A man who rapes a woman in this context will, in most cases, consign his victim to a form of social death.

Very similar cultural patterns also obtained in ancient Israel. That daughters were expected to be virgins when they married, with terrible consequences if they were not, emerges in the laws that appear in Deut 22:13–21 and 22:28–29.[57] Frymer-Kensky rejects the notion that a girl who had been raped would no longer be marriageable, on the basis that there is "no hint" of this in the biblical text; most women would find husbands, she claims, and the only issue was that a man would not have to pay a bride-price to the woman's father if she was not a virgin. Yet Frymer-Kensky's view runs up against the cold facts of Tamar's story who, as we shall see, certainly did consider herself unmarriageable af-ter Amnon had raped her. While this condition may also be related to her high status, it nevertheless provides a counter-example to Frymer-Kensky's proposition. On the other hand, whereas the male relatives of a woman in today's Middle Eastern cultures who has been raped might well kill her, ancient Israelite brothers and fathers seem to have sought to redeem their honor by killing the man responsible (and even the men in his family and town), as revealed in the homicidal anger of Dinah's brothers toward her assailant Shechem in Genesis 34. Unlike the Bedouin of Egypt in the middle of the twentieth century, however, who often killed their sister or daughter who had been seduced or raped as well as the man who had one it,[58] there is no indication that Dinah's brothers killed her and Gen 34:31 provides almost conclusive evidence that they did not.

---

56. Among the Greek Saraksatsani tribe a woman who is not a virgin will some-times be able to marry a man of low prestige or a widower (Campbell, *Honour, Family, and Patronage*, 170).

57. See Frymer-Kensky, "Virginity in the Bible," 79.

58. See the discussion in Abou-Zeid, "Honour and Shame," 256–57.

Violence against Innocence and Reason

Considerations such as these motivated Tamar to try to reason Amnon out of what he was intending to do. Amnon, however, was not to be reasoned out of what he had in mind: "But he would not listen to her; and because he was stronger than her, he dishonored her, and laid her" (v. 14).

Note that the Masoretic Text actually reads "he laid" her, since we have *'otah* (the accusative form in the feminine) and not *'ittah* (= prepositional, "with her"). The Septuagint, however, has "with her." This striking usage in the Hebrew version appears elsewhere in relation to illicit intercourse (Gen 34:2; Lev 15:18, 24; Num 5:13, 19; Ezek 23:8).[59] Here, as in v. 12, "dishonored" translates the piel form of the Hebrew verb *'anah* and means "to humble" a woman in the sense of violating her. What Tamar had urged Amnon not to do, he has done. The expression "he was stronger than her" shows that Tamar actively resisted Amnon but was eventually subdued by his superior strength. Driver translates by saying Amnon "overpowered her."[60] But in this context, lack of consent was irrelevant to a woman's status and position; what mattered was an intact hymen, and that Tamar no longer possessed. In terms of Christopher Booker's "Tragedy" plot Amnon's brief moment of sexual release constitutes the entirety of the Dream Stage, when he has achieves the gratification he had desired, by raping the virginal Tamar. Yet this was the most fleeting of experiences, far briefer than even what Humbert Humbert achieved with Lolita before their relationship soured.

As she lay there in her violated state, Tamar must have wondered what would happen next, and we will see in a moment that even in this situation there was one possible route out of disgrace and social ruin. Yet it is doubtful we should imagine her anticipating the behavior of the creature that was Amnon, which I will translate fairly literally to preserve the flavor of the original: "Then Amnon hated her with a very great hatred, to the extent that the hatred with which he hated her was greater than the lust with which he had lusted after her. And Amnon said to her, 'Get up, be gone'" (v. 15).

This marks Amnon's arrival at a point in the story that Booker refers to as the Frustration Stage of a tragedy, where the "hero" experi-

---

59. Driver, *Notes on the Hebrew Text*, 298.
60. Ibid.

ences a sense of dissatisfaction that impels him to commit further "dark acts" that solidify the evil course of action on which he is embarked. For Amnon, like Macbeth, one evil act was not enough; just raping Tamar was not enough. Initially Amnon had been tortured by the fact that he could not do anything "to" Tamar. Now that he has done what he wanted, his attitude toward her is not just one of disregard; it is positive hatred. According to van Treek, after Amnon had violated Tamar a profound emotional change came over him.[61] Yet this view neglects the fact that Amnon's initial attitude towards Tamar was already a form of hatred that underlay his lust for her; once he has satisfied that lust, there is no great emotional change; rather, the underlying hatred is made manifest and actually exceeds his initial lust.

To see a very different reaction from another man who has violated a woman like Amnon has, consider the case of Shechem in Genesis 34: "Now Dinah the daughter of Leah, whom she had borne to Jacob, went out to visit the women of the land; and when Shechem the son of Hamor the Hivite, the prince of the land, saw her, he seized her and lay with her and dishonored her" (vv. 1–3). Here the language describing Shechem's act is similar to that used of Amnon (*lakah*, "he took her"; *šakab*, "he slept with her," and *'anah*, "he dishonored her").

But Shechem's subsequent feeling toward Dinah is very different from Amnon's for Tamar: "And his soul was drawn to Dinah the daughter of Jacob; he loved the girl and spoke tenderly to her. So Shechem spoke to his father Hamor, saying, 'Get me this girl for my wife'" (vv. 3–4, RSV). What Shechem had done was deeply wrong, but his behavior afterwards in contrast with Amnon's shows just how much more evil was that of Amnon.

Yet even at this dreadful pass, Tamar does not simply collapse but again tries to reason with Amnon, "She said to him, 'No, my brother; for this evil in sending me away is greater than the other which you did to me'" (v. 16). Her words revolve around the issue of her honor. Expressing a viewpoint very different from that current in modern Western cultures yet well known in Mediterranean societies past and present, Tamar makes clear that the act of rape is not as great a problem for her as the social consequences if Amnon himself will not take her as his wife. She must consider no one else will marry her (or at least no one she would care to marry) once what has happened becomes common

61. Van Treek, "Amnón y Tamar," 26.

knowledge. Her point is that Amnon should now keep her as his wife (seeking David's permission after the event). Deut 22:28–29 reflects a very similar situation, by providing that if a man rapes a virgin who is not betrothed, the assailant, when he has been found with the woman, must pay a bride-price to the woman's father and marry her and thereafter never send her away. It is assumed in this law that the only way a man could do justice to such a woman whom he had raped was to marry her himself, because no one else (or no one respectable) would. Tamar's appeal to Amnon was really her last chance to prevent the destruction of her life. Yet her words made no impact on him: "But he would not listen to her. He called the young man who served him and said, 'Put this woman outside, out of my presence, and bolt the door behind her'" (vv. 16–17, RSV). Even in his dismissal of her, Amnon took pain to express his loathing for her, because the Hebrew translated here as "out of my presence" is *me'alay*, which (unlike *me'itiy*), carried the connotation of dismissing a menial (as in v. 9) or one whose presence was obnoxious (Exod 10:28).[62] So the servant put her out, bolting the door behind her.

Before considering Tamar's reaction to this summary ejection, we should consider whether there was any other reason for Amnon acting in this way other than his own vicious nature, in particular the political explanation of Matthews and Benjamin. According to these two interpreters, if a household could not protect its women, then it was declared insolvent or shamed and unable to fulfill its responsibilities to the community as a whole, for which proposition they cite Maureen Giovannini.[63] "Like war, rape was a violent social process for redistributing the limited goods that a society possessed so that it would not be destroyed by the weakness of a single household. The Bible regularly identifies such procedures for social realignment with the formula 'so you shall purge the evil from Israel'" (Deut 22:22).[64] By raping Tamar Amnon has made an attack on the household of Absalom with the aim of smoothing his accession to the throne.

The main problem with this view, as noted above, is that Tamar belonged to David's household, not Absalom's. Yet it further suffers from mixing honor with other types of good in this culture. While a family will be shamed if a woman from it is raped (and here David's

62. See Driver, *Notes on the Hebrew Text*, 299.

63. Giovannini, "Female Chastity Codes," 68.

64. Matthews and Benjamin, *Social World of Ancient Israel*, 180.

family has been shamed), the notion that such a rape impacts on the property of the household (which encompasses the all-important asset of land) lacks support. The high point of this position comes when they assert, "The household of the assailant became the legal guardian for the shamed household, while negotiations to realign its resources and responsibilities took place," for which remarkable proposition they cite Gen 34:4–24; 2 Sam 11:6–26; and 13:15–22 in support.[65] As for the modern ethnography, however, Giovannini does not support such a position, even though she notes (as we would expect) that a man whose female relative has been defiled was believed to be less than a real man and that in a contemporary south Italian community, even where chastity codes were diminishing in significance, a man whose wife was unfaithful would be unlikely to be elected to public office.[66] Nor are the biblical passages they cite evidence for their position. Although Deut 22:22 provides death for both the man who sleeps with another man's wife and for the woman, how does this affect the property of the man's family? The case of Shechem in Genesis 34 actually represents strong biblical counter-evidence. Having raped Dinah but then having fallen in love with her, Shechem was happy to pay her family a huge price for her. The thought of taking over her family's resources was not in his head at any point. Nor does 2 Sam 11:6–26 further their case.

There is no sense, therefore, in which Amnon took over Absalom's household by raping Tamar, or that he had a political motivation for his actions. And certainly there is no mention in the text of his having acted in any way consistent with such an intention in the two years he lived after raping Tamar. Amnon gained no traction whatever in relation to Absalom's household. Rather, he ensured complete alienation between himself and Absalom. The desire he had for purely personal (and, in his case, deeply twisted) gratification in doing something "to Tamar" was the total explanation for his raping her.

Tamar and Absalom

Upon being cast from Amnon's house, Tamar immediately engages in the local rituals of mourning that in this case symbolized not an actual death but nevertheless the destruction of her life. She puts ashes on her

---

65. Ibid., 181.

66. Giovannini, "Female Chastity Codes," 68, 71.

head, she rends the long robe with sleeves she was wearing (the robe worn by the virgin daughters of the king), lays her hand on her head and goes off, crying aloud as she does so (vv. 18–19). She is the very picture of desolation.

The sharp transition to the next scene (v.20) well reveals how this biblical narrative (like so many others) exhibits a high-context disinclination to be too specific and how we must make a deliberate effort to imagine ourselves into the cultural realities of Tamar's world.

It is of utmost importance in understanding Tamar's plight to note that she does not go back to the royal palace from where she had come, only a very short time before, a beautiful and presumably carefree, virginal daughter of the king, having set off from her mother's quarters in the palace to cook for the supposedly sick Amnon. That happy state was destroyed by Amnon's raping her. What could she do? She could not return to the palace because she no longer had a place there. For the palace contained the king, his wives, and their unmarried daughters, together with smaller children. The daughters still there were waiting for their father to secure honorable marriages for them, leading to the production of children, who would make their lives complete. In such a setting Tamar would have been an impossible anomaly. No one would marry her now. She would besmirch her mother and immediate family with shame if she were to return to them. Her only recourse was to move in with her full brother, Absalom, who really did love her, as 2 Sam 13:20 makes clear he did.

In understanding more fully why Tamar moves into her brother's house, we are helped by some comparative material from Palestine. Granqvist notes, "As long as a girl still lives in the circle of her own people in the father's house, she has no reason to pay attention to or reflect upon the brother's love. She lives rather carefree among them and under their protection."[67] But when a young Palestinian woman has married and is living in a new milieu, among strangers, then "she will fully understand the value of having a brother to stand by her,"[68] especially when problems arise. Unlike the Palestinian cases, Tamar did not leave the royal palace to marry, yet she has been excluded from it just as surely as if she had. It is in this situation that she must seek refuge with Absalom, relying on him to take her in and look after her.

67. Granqvist, *Child Problems*, 179.
68. Ibid, 179.

Thus the text proceeds in v. 20 to a meeting between Absalom and Tamar during which he speaks and she is silent: "And her brother Absalom said to her, 'Has Amnon your brother been with you? Now hold your peace, my sister; he is your brother; do not take this to heart.'" At first sight this advice, from a man giving advice to a woman he loves who was in dire straits, seems even more unhelpful than the way Elkanah sought to comfort his barren wife, Hannah, in 1 Sam 1:7–8, a passage considered in chapter 4 of this volume.[69] Nevertheless, we will see below that there was a reason for Absalom seeking to minimize the extent of the outrage that had been wreaked on Tamar. We know that this meeting occurred in Absalom's house from the way the verse ends: "So Tamar dwelt, a desolate woman, in her brother Absalom's house." This is the last we hear of Tamar. There is no solution to her dishonor and nothing more that can be said of her life. It is surely no accident, however, that when, in addition to his three (unnamed) sons, Absalom has a daughter, he names her Tamar (2 Sam 14:27). Phyllis Trible aptly observes, "the anonymity of all the sons highlights the name of the lone female child."[70]

ABSALOM'S REVENGE

Textual Features

Tamar's reliance upon Absalom is only made possible because in ancient Israel women who were raped were not, as they are in some Middle Eastern countries today, regarded as deserving death at the hands of a close male relative. This emerges very clearly in the fact that Dinah's brothers have homicidal anger for Shechem when he has raped her, but not for Dinah herself (Gen 34:7, 13, 26–27, 31). Indeed, not only do Dinah's brothers avenge her rape by killing Shechem, they also slay his father and all the males in their city. Although this is not to say that any character in these narratives denied the catastrophe for the woman involved (which at least Shechem wanted to end by marrying her), it is significant that the woman's relatives did not want to kill her to redeem their own or their families' honor. This response illustrates an attitude also found among the Sarakatsani tribe of contemporary Greece where "The brother is the guardian of his sister from rape and insult and he

---

69. See pp. 128–29.
70. Trible, *Texts of Terror*, 43.

must avenge any violation of her person and character."[71] Absalom was motivated by a very similar desire to kill the man who had dishonored his sister, even if he was his half brother.

Certainly if Absalom did not act against Amnon, no one else would. David was unhelpful: "When King David heard of all these things, he was very angry" (2 Sam 13:21). There are two reasons why David would be angry: first, because Amnon had brought shame on him, as a father who was unable to protect one of his daughters from attack, indeed who had been gulled into placing her in the very situation where the attack occurred; second, we must suppose he had some concern for Tamar and her plight, as one of his own (admittedly very large number) of children. Yet while David is certainly angry at Amnon, he neither says anything to him nor takes any action against him, and he does nothing for Tamar. Earlier in this chapter I suggested that David would have had a special regard for Amnon as his firstborn son, and this explains why David's anger (at Amnon) is the limit of his response. The Septuagintal version confirms this view by stating explicitly, "but he did not grieve the spirit of his son Amnon, because he loved him, for he was his first-born." Robert Alter notes that "For the king, the failure to speak is a sign of domestic and political impotence, leading directly to the calamities that will assail his household and his reign from this point onward."[72] While his comment is accurate, Alter neglects to mention that the primary cause for these "calamities" is not David's failure to deal with Amnon, but the divine punishment previously announced to him by Nathan (2 Sam 12:7–15): that because he had murdered Uriah and taken Bathsheba as his wife the sword would never leave his house and that God would raise up evil against him out of his own house. Amnon's rape of Tamar is what unleashes the sword and the God-sent evil that Nathan had prophesied.

Yet Absalom does not rush to exact revenge on Amnon. As we have just seen, as far as Tamar is concerned, he seeks to wrap what has happened in a cloak of euphemism and reassurance: "Has Amnon your brother been with you? Now hold your peace, my sister; he is your brother; do not take this to heart." On one view, Absalom's words are a feeble attempt at compassion towards his sister. On another view, surely more plausible, they represent his attempt to pacify the situation sufficiently so that he may bring about what he has in store for Amnon.

71. Campbell, *Honour, Family and Patronage*, 178.
72. Alter, *The Art*, 79.

For whatever he says to Tamar, his attitude to Amnon is revealed in his blank refusal to speak to him: "But Absalom spoke to Amnon neither good nor bad; for Absalom hated Amnon, because he had dishonored his sister Tamar" (v. 22).

Robert Alter, having noted (as mentioned above) that David stays silent after Amnon's rape of Tamar, also points to the silence of Absalom, commenting aptly that "for Absalom, the refusal to say anything—to the perpetrator of the sexual crime, the narrator specifies—is ominous in an opposite way because it clearly betokens a grim resolution to act in due time, and will ultimately issue in murder and rebellion."[73]

Vengeance in Mediterranean Perspective

Absalom's response to Amnon's rape of his sister needs to be understood in relation to the prevailing cultural system of ancient Israel where honor was a dominant value, as it has been in many modern Mediterranean countries, at least until quite recently. Pitt-Rivers, in one of the early formulations of the relationship between honor and vengeance in the Mediterranean notes that "a physical affront is a dishonor, regardless of the moral issues involved, and creates a situation in which the honor of the affronted person is in jeopardy and requires 'satisfaction' if it is to return to its normal condition." Such satisfaction can come through an apology, "which is a verbal act of self-humiliation," or, if an apology is not forthcoming, it will require avenging. "To leave an affront unavenged is to leave one's honour in a state of desecration and this is therefore the equivalent of cowardice."[74] Tamar is not able to avenge her dishonor, but in this context Amnon's act is not merely the violation of Absalom's beloved sister but an attack on his own honour too. "When a man reacts to a slight upon the honour of another," writes Pitt-Rivers, "it can only be because his own is involved."[75] Revenge by Absalom is an inevitable consequence of what Amnon had done, given that Tamar is Absalom's full sister.

73. Ibid.
74. Pitt-Rivers, "Honour and Social Status," 26.
75. Ibid., 28.

Absalom's Revenge Delayed

Although Absalom needs to avenge himself on Amnon to redeem the honor of Tamar and of himself, he waits two years before doing so. Before considering why, we should consider Amnon's position. If this narrative were fully comparable with Booker's Tragedy plot, Amnon would now enter a the Nightmare Stage when he would feel things slipping seriously out of his control. Amnon, however, does not have this experience for two reasons. The first, as noted above, is that David, who might have been expected to punish Amnon in some way for what he had done, in fact does nothing because of a soft spot he has for Amnon as his firstborn. Perhaps Amnon had expected all along that his father would indulge him in this way. Second, Absalom himself does nothing, at least initially. While Amnon could hardly have failed to notice that Absalom no longer spoke to him (v. 22), neither had he taken any action against him or his interests, so that Amnon may have begun to wonder if he was going to get away with what he had done to Tamar. The fact that nothing happens to Amnon in the period between his crime and his death makes his a rather attenuated story in comparison with other tragic protagonists, such as Dorian Gray, with their finely chronicled downward progression.

It is unclear why Absalom delays in taking revenge on Amnon. Although among modern people in Western society there is a saying that vengeance is a dish best served cold, this view does not necessarily prevail in the Mediterranean context. Pierre Bourdieu notes that among the Kabyle of North Africa, "Dishonour remains virtual as long as long as the possibility of riposte remains; but it becomes more and more real the longer vengeance is delayed. Thus honour requires that the time lapse between the offence and its reparation should be as short as possible."[76]

Sometimes, however, vengeance is delayed for a very long time; but, once taken, it is all the more meritorious in the eyes of the local community.[77] Both his family and the local people will expect a man to avenge an affront to a family member. The members of his family grow anxious when he defers carrying out the vengeance required. Nevertheless, "When a man is under an obligation to avenge an offence, those about

76. Bourdieu, "The Sentiment of Honour," 214.
77. Ibid.

him carefully avoid reminding him of that fact. But everyone observes his slightest gesture and tries to guess his intentions."[78]

Members of his immediate family, Tamar especially, but also their mother and any full siblings, would have expected, even wanted, Absalom to take vengeance on Amnon, especially as David had done nothing. No doubt other members of royal court, in particular, the extended family of David, including his nephew Jonadab, would have thought some response was likely. The fate of Shechem and his relatives at the hands of Dinah's brothers was an instructive model of the possibilities. Anyone watching Absalom would have been fortified in this belief by the fact that he refused to speak to Amnon and, quite obviously, hated him (v. 22). Jonadab later indicates that he at least recognized the connection between Absalom's slaying of Amnon and Amnon's violation of Tamar (v. 32).

Absalom springs a trap on Amnon structurally similar to the one that Amnon, on Jonadab's advice, had sprung on Tamar. Just as Amnon had tricked David into sending Tamar out of the safety of the royal palace to his house where she would be under his control and he could rape her, so Absalom tricked David into sending Amnon to a context controlled by Absalom, in this case to Baal-Hazor, near Ephraim, to the feasting and drinking that would accompany the sheep shearing being undertaken by Absalom's men, where his servants could kill Amnon (2 Sam 13:23–27). Absalom cunningly first puts pressure on David and his servants to go to the sheep shearing, anticipating that the king will say no but be in a mood to send others to attend in his stead, initially his other sons, but then at Absalom's persistent urging, Amnon as well. David clearly has some misgivings, probably driven by Absalom's not having spoken a word to Amnon in two years, because when Absalom mentions Amnon, the king asks, "Why should he go with you?" (v. 26). Perhaps David reasoned that Absalom's hatred of Amnon (which in this culture and for the cause in question was very likely to lead to violence) was abating. Perhaps the original audience reasoned that in their conversation (the details of which are not provided) Absalom had tricked David into this belief. It is noteworthy that Jonadab is not described as making any attempt to warn either David or Amnon of the danger in Amnon's attendance at Absalom's shearing festivities.

78. Bourdieu, "The Sentiment of Honour," 208.

Second Samuel 13:28 presupposes a banqueting scene, although the very taut narrative style of the biblical narrative does not explicitly mention it. Absalom orders his servants to smite Amnon when he is merry with wine and they do as he commands (v. 29). It is somewhat surprising that Absalom does not kill Amnon himself. Thus we reach the Destruction Stage of the Tragedy, where Amnon is destroyed by the force of Absalom's vengeance that he has roused against himself. Amnon is one tragic protagonist whose death would cause no one to shed a tear.

Upon Amnon's murder, the rest of the king's sons flee the scene on their mules. The narrative then proceeds to the curious incident in which rumor reaches David that Absalom has slain all his sons, so that the king and his servants plunge into mourning (vv. 30–31). It is Jonadab, showing the same cunning that he put at Amnon's disposal, who reassures the king that Absalom has only killed Amnon, something Jonadab has seen coming since Amnon raped Tamar (vv. 32–33). Sure enough, the other princes soon appear (vv. 34–36). Meanwhile, Absalom has fled (v. 34), to Talmai, the son of Ammuhud, king of Geshur (v. 37), but (more important) his mother's father. Why Talmai? Because he is likely to be very sympathetic to a grandson who has had killed the man who raped his granddaughter (that grandson's full sister) and then refused to marry her, especially when Talmai has no blood relationship with rapist. "Then David mourned for Amnon, but after three years his grief was spent and he began to long for Absalom" (vv. 37–39).

CONCLUSION

The story of Amnon, Tamar, and Absalom in 2 Samuel 13 requires close contextualization in the distinctive culture of ancient Israel to be comprehensible. In particular, fully to appreciate the plight of Tamar, who is left desolate less by her violent rape than by her rapist's refusal to marry her, requires a major leap in understanding on the part of modern Western readers, for whom the thought of a woman wanting to marry a man who has raped her will seem very strange indeed.

As for Amnon, the admittedly intriguing notion of Victor Matthews and Don Benjamin that his attack on Tamar was the opening gambit in a campaign to neutralize Absalom as a rival for the throne and eventually to take over the state finds no support in the text. Nothing suggests that Amnon is thinking of anything other than his penetration of Tamar as

he prepares for the act. Nor does he show any interest in the throne in
the two years thereafter that Absalom permits him to live, even though
2 Samuel is not reticent about reporting the ambitions of Absalom in
this regard, nor in reporting the effort, time and expense needed for
the attempt (2 Sam 15:1–6). Cosseted prince, devoted to satisfying his
own urges (and in a way not completely unlike his father), Amnon most
certainly is, Macchiavellian aspirant for the throne of Israel he is not.
The idea that Amnon "is a man who would be king"[79] is unsubstantiated
and unconnected with the text. In this narrative the entirety of Amnon's
ambition and of his character is crystallized in his urge physically to
penetrate Tamar. There is nothing more to him than that.

And yet one can discern in the story of Amnon, Tamar and
Absalom a plot recognizably akin to others that are reasonably classified as "Tragedy" within Christopher Booker's seven basic plots, but
more specifically where this plot intersects with the Overcoming the
Monster type. In Amnon we do not have a tragic hero who is a victim
of his or her own folly, but one who is "the malevolent author of other
people's sufferings."[80] To this extent the narrative falls into place with
many others created in different times and cultures that project a literary
patterning of a particular set of human interactions having an abiding
grip on human imagination. The tragic protagonists most comparable
to Amnon are figures such as Macbeth, Richard III, Dorian Gray, and
Mr. Hyde (in *Dr. Jekyll and Mr. Hyde*).[81] The relative thinness of the story
as far as Amnon is concerned is a product both of the monochromatic
blackness of his character and of the typically sparse nature of much Old
Testament narrative that reflects the high-context culture in which it was
produced, where authors relied far more on shared understandings and
far less on detailed elaboration than we do.

79. Matthews and Benjamin, *Social World of Ancient Israel*, 182.
80. Booker, *Seven Basic Plots*, 182.
81. Ibid, 183.

Epilogue

In chapter 1 I expressed my conviction that Old Testament narratives have an abiding value and deserve the closest attention from a very wide range of readers. I will conclude this volume by briefly reviewing how the eight stories considered here respond to the variety of reasons that I have proposed might stimulate us to read these texts.

For believing Christians and Jews (whether professional or non-professional in their interest in scripture) reading the stories of Tamar, Hannah, Saul, David and his family, and Judith (at least for Catholics and Orthodox) means reminding ourselves that we are committed to an all-absorbing chain of belief and memory that includes these figures. To this extent, members of these religious traditions are less prey to the risk of cultural forgetting that Paul Connerton has recently argued is a feature of modernity.[1] The biblical narratives offer us representations, images, examples of theoretical and practical intelligence, attitudes and behavior from a tradition, which are accepted in the name of the *necessary* continuity between the past and the present.[2] In this way the tradition confers transcendent authority on the past, yet without reducing the complexity of human responses to experience and to divine grace. This complexity is most evident in the cases of Saul and David. These narratives have indelibly colored who we are and how we interpret the world. They are, indeed, part of our life story. Belonging to a tradition such as this means we are engaged in "the act of receiving a sacred, intangible trust, humble and respectful resolve to repeat something already said."[3] As we recollect a past peopled with figures such as these, portrayed in stories such as these, we are recalling a past that gives meaning to the

1. Connnerton, *How Modernity Forgets.*
2. Hervieu-Léger, *Religion as a Chain of Memory*, 87.
3. Ibid, 86.

present and points to or even embraces the future. For the process in which we are engaged is not purely anamnetic. Encountering these narratives, especially with the fresh interpretations that come from reading them like an ancient Israelite would have, also inevitably fires our imaginations to re-adjust or even re-invent the collective memory they feed. Even readers who once counted themselves as believing and Christians or Jews but no longer do so will find this balance of memory grasped, yet reworked and reappropriated, helpful in telling them who they were then and now are.

Religious and nonreligious readers of the Old Testament will have found that the eight narratives discussed in this volume disclose more ample opportunities for being human. Who can forget Tamar's resolution and resourcefulness in arranging for Judah to father a child upon her? Or Hannah's moving prayer to God in the temple at Shiloh to end her barrenness? Or David's reliance on his sling and his God to defeat a giant Philistine? Or his deciding not to kill Saul when he had the chance? We are not the same once we have read them, and that effect is even more pronounced by virtue of our paying close attention to the relationship of the narratives with their distinctive cultural setting. For although we have met characters like Judah and Tamar, Hannah, Saul, David and his children Amnon, Tamar and Absalom with at least something of the force of real people, we cannot forget that the culture into which they were socialized is very different from that of North American and northern European readers. The experience is closer to getting to know a man or woman from a Middle Eastern country today, especially one where there exist patrilinear, patrilocal and polygynous social patterns.

An important consequence of reading these narratives with their ancient audience is that our capacity to become intercultural people, who are able to understand our fellow human beings in different cultures and to translate their meanings from one to the other from a rich mediating position between the two, is enhanced. To become intercultural means to be vested with an understanding of values and behavior that can appreciate examples of these phenomena that stand out as particularly impressive in their context and also of critiquing more limited notions of the human that subsist within the borders of single cultures. As an example of the former, I will cite Tamar's admirable presence of mind as she tries to defend her honor against Amnon (2 Sam 13:12–16), and of the latter, the notion that honesty is only owed to members of one's in-group (an attitude very apparent in Judith's entrapment of Holofernes).

Or if, driven by our human love of mimesis and representation, we are attracted to Old Testament narratives by their power as stories—for the aesthetic pleasure we obtain from entering an imaginative world—we will not have been disappointed by the eight narratives considered here. In these, as in all good stories, "all those purposive relations which determine acting and caring existence have not simply disappeared, but in a curious way acquire a different quality."[4]

To bring this issue of aesthetic pleasure into greater focus, by creatively aligning these biblical narratives with a larger universe of literary productions extending across times and cultures, I have utilized Christopher Booker's *The Seven Basic Plots*. Booker's "Overcoming the Monster" plot provides significant points of comparison with the narratives of David and Goliath, and Judith and Holofernes, while also being comparable with Absalom's slaying of Amnon. The "Rags to Riches" plot lines up with Tamar's securing twin sons from Judah and (in a more compressed form) in Hannah's movement from barrenness to being the mother of a son and the defeat of her rival, co-wife Peninnah. David's transition from fugitive to king in 1 Samuel 19 to 2 Samuel 5:5 is illuminated in comparison with the "Quest" plot, while his passage away from his true self and (partial) return in 2 Samuel 10–12 is usefully compared with the "Voyage and Return" story-line. Finally, the account of Saul's rise and fall in 1 Samuel 8–31 and Amnon's story in 2 Samuel 13 is comparable with "Tragedy," although in Amnon's case only with those examples featuring villainous protagonists (such as Dorian Gray).

We noted in chapter 1 that the selection of regularly recurring features in stories from different cultures almost inevitably results in the isolation of those stories from the original social and cultural context. Nevertheless, using Mediterranean ethnography to develop a richer understanding of the context than is usually possible has allowed these narratives to be firmly contextualized in the setting of ancient Israel even while drawing out the connection of their plots with other works of literature.

Finally, for faithful Christians and Jews it is essential that we go on reading and re-reading the great narratives of the Old Testament, since the future of a religion is closely associated with its collective memory

4. Gadamer, *Truth and Method*, 91.

that exists in a state of constant interaction with its tradition. Central to that memory is the extent to which Yahweh continually intervenes to subvert the established order, by hurling the mighty from their thrones and raising up the lowly. But for all other readers, professional and non-professional alike, these narratives represent a repository of stories that stand up well in relation to other works of world literature and more than repay the effort to take them seriously—by using all the means at our disposal to read them as an ancient Israelite might have.

Bibliography

Abou-Zeid, A. M. "Honour and Shame among the Bedouins of Egypt." In *Honour and Shame: The Values of Mediterranean Society,* edited by J. G. Peristiany, 243–59. NHSS. London: Weidenfeld & Nicolson, 1965.

———. "Migrant Labour and Social Structure in Kharga Oasis." In *Mediterranean Countrymen: Essays in the Social Anthropology of the Mediterranean,* edited by Julian Pitt-Rivers, 41–53. Recherches méditerranéennes: Études 1. Paris: Mouton, 1963.

Abu-Lughod, Lila. "Polygyny." In *Writing Women's Worlds: Bedouin Stories,* by Lila Abu-Lughod, 87–125. Berkeley: University of California Press, 1993.

———. *Veiled Sentiments: Honor and Poetry in a Bedouin Society.* Berkeley: University of California Press, 1986.

Ackroyd, Peter R. *The Second Book of Samuel.* Cambridge Bible Commentary. Cambridge: Cambridge University Press, 1977.

Albera, Dionigi. "Anthropology of the Mediterranean: Between Crisis and Renewal." *History and Anthropology* 17 (2006) 109–33.

Albera, Dionigi, and Anton Blok. "The Mediterranean as a Field of Ethnological Study: A Retrospective." In *Anthropology of the Mediterranean,* edited by Dionigi Albera et al., 15–37. Collection L'atelier méditerranéen. Paris: Maisonneuvre & Larose, 2001.

Albera, Dionigi et al., editors. *: L'anthropologie de la Méditerranée: Anthropology of the Mediterranean.* Collection L'atelier méditerranéen. Paris: Maisonneuvre & Larose, 2001.

Al-Khayyat, Sana. *Honour and Shame: Women in Modern Iraq.* London: Saqi, 1990.

Alonso-Schökel, Luis. "Narrative Structures in the Book of Judith." In *Protocol Series of the Colloquies of the Center for Hermeneutical Studies in Hellenistic and Modern Culture,* edited by W. Wuellner, 1–20. Berkeley, CA: Center for Hermeneutical Studies in Hellenistic and Modern Culture, 1975.

Alter, Robert. *The Art of Biblical Narrative.* New York: Basic Books, 1981.

Amit, Yairah. "'Am I Not More Devoted to You Than Ten Sons?' (1 Samuel 1.8): Male and Female Interpretations." In *A Feminist Companion to Samuel and Kings,* edited by Athalya Brenner, 69–76. FCB 5. Sheffield, UK: Sheffield Academic, 1994.

———. *Reading Biblical Narratives: Literary Criticism and the Hebrew Bible.* Minneapolis: Fortress, 2001.

Anderson, A. A. *2 Samuel.* WBC 11. Dallas: Word, 1989.

Arensberg, Conrad M. "The Old World Peoples: The Place of European Cultures in World Ethnography." *Anthropological Quarterly* 36 (1963) 75–99.

Asano-Tamanoi, Mariko. "Shame, Family, and State in Catalonia and Japan." In *Honor and Shame and the Unity of the Mediterranean*, edited by David D. Gilmore, 104–20. AmAnthAss 22. Washington, DC: American Anthropological Associatio, 1987.

Assmann, Jan. *Das Kulturelle Gedächtnis: Schrift, Erinnerung und Politische Identität in frühen Hochkulturen.* C. H. Beck Kulturwissenschaft. Munich: Beck, 1992.

Auerbach, Eric. *Mimesis: The Representation of Reality in Western Literature.* Translated by Willard R. Trask. Princeton: Princeton University Press, 1953.

Auld, Graeme A., and Craig Y. S. Ho. "The Making of David and Goliath." *JSOT* 56 (1992) 19–39.

Aurelius, Erik. "Wie David ursprünglich zu Saul kam (1 Sam 17)." In *Vergegenwärtigung des Alten Testaments: Beiträge zur biblischen Hermeneutik. Festschrift für Rudolf Smend zum 70. Geburstag*, edited by Christoph Bultmann et al., 44–68. Göttingen: Vandenhoeck & Ruprecht, 2002.

Bailey, F. G. *The Prevalence of Deceit.* Ithaca, NY: Cornell University Press, 1991.

Bal, Mieke. *Death and Dissymmetry: The Politics of Coherence in the Book of Judges.* Chicago Studies in the History of Judaism. Chicago: University of Chicago Press, 1988.

———. "Head Hunting: 'Judith' on the Cutting Edge of Knowledge." In *A Feminist Companion to Esther, Judith and Susannah*, edited by Athalya Brenner, 253–85. FCB 7. Sheffield, UK: Sheffield Academic, 1995.

Bartlett, Frederic C. *Remembering: A Study in Experimental and Social Psychology.* Cambridge Psychological Library. Cambridge: Cambridge University Press, 1932.

Barton, John. "Disclosing Human Possibilities: Revelation and Biblical Stories." In *Revelation and Story: Narrative Theology and the Centrality of Story*, edited by Gerhard Sauter and John Barton, 53–60. Aldershot, UK: Ashgate, 2000.

———. *Ethics and the Old Testament.* London: SCM, 1998.

———. "Reading for Life: The Use of the Bible in Ethics and the Work of Martha C. Nussbaum." In *The Bible in Ethics: The Second Sheffield Colloquium*, edited by John W. Rogerson, Margaret Davies, and M. Daniel Carroll, 66–76. JSOTSup 207. Sheffield, UK: Sheffield Academic, 1995.

Beck, John A. "David and Goliath: A Story of Place: The Narrative-Geographical Shaping of 1 Samuel 17." *Westminster Theological Journal* 68 (2006) 321–30.

Benjamin, Don C. *The Old Testament Story: An Introduction with CD-ROM.* Minneapolis: Fortress, 2004.

Berger, Peter L. and Luckmann, Thomas. *The Social Construction of Reality: A Treatise in the Sociology of Knowledge.* London: Penguin, 1966.

Bertram, Georg. "*hubris*, etc." In *TDNT* 8 (1972) 295–307.

Billig, Michael. "Collective Memory, Ideology and the British Royal Family." In *Collective Remembering*, edited by David Middleton and Derek Edwards, 60–80. Inquiries in Social Construction. London: Sage, 1990.

Billingham, Clyde E. "Goliath and the Exodus Giants: How Tall Were They?" *JETS* 50 (2007) 489–508.

Bird, Phyllis. "The Harlot as Heroine: Narrative Art and Social Presupposition in Three Old Testament Texts." In *Women in the Hebrew Bible: A Reader*, edited by Alice Bach, 99–117. London: Routledge, 1999. (Reprinted from *Semeia* 46 [1989] 119–39).

Blenkinsopp, Joseph. "The Family in First Temple Israel." In *Families in Ancient Israel*, edited by Leo G. Perdue et al., 48–103. Family, Religion, and Culture. Westminster John Knox, 1997.

Blok, Anton. *The Mafia of a Sicilian Village, 1860–1960: A Study of Violent Peasant Entrepreneurs.* 1974. Reprinted, Long Grove, IL: Waveland 1988.

———. "The Peasant and the Brigand: Social Banditry Reconsidered." *Comparative Studies in Society and History* 14 (1972) 494–503 (for Hobsbawm's reply, see 503–5).

Bodner, Keith. "Eliab and the Deuteronomist." *JSOT* 28 (2003) 55–71.

———. *1 Samuel: A Narrative Commentary.* Hebrew Bible Monographs 19. Sheffield, UK: Sheffield Phoenix, 2009.

Bolle, Kees W., editor. *Secrecy in Religions.* Studies in the History of Religion 49. Leiden: Brill, 1987.

Booker, Christopher. *The Seven Basic Plots: Why We Tell Stories.* London: Continuum, 2004.

Borgman, Paul. *David, Saul, and God: Rediscovering an Ancient Story.* Oxford: Oxford University Press, 2008.

Bornkamm, Günther. "The Stilling of the Storm at Sea in Matt. 8.23–27." In *Tradition and Interpretation in Matthew,* by Günther Bornkamm, Gerhard Barth, and Heinz Joachim Held, 52–57. London: SCM, 1982.

Bos, Johanna W. H. "Out of the Shadows: Genesis 38; Judges 4:17–22; Ruth 3." *Semeia* 42 (1988) 37–67.

Bourdieu, Pierre. "The Sentiment of Honour in Kabyle Society." In *Honour and Shame: The Values of Mediterranean Society,* edited by J. G. Peristiany, 191–241. NHSS. London: Weidenfeld & Nicolson, 1965.

Bourguignon, Erika. "Introduction: A Framework for the Comparative Study of Altered States of Consciousness." In *Religion, Altered States of Consciousness, and Social Change,* edited by Erika Bourguignon, 3–38. Columbus: Ohio University Press, 1973.

Bourke, Joseph, OP. "Samuel and the Ark: A Study in Contrasts." *Dominican Studies* 7 (1954) 73–103.

Bowman, Alan K. *The Town Councils of Roman Egypt.* American Studies in Papyrology 11. Toronto: Hakkert, 1971.

Boyd, Jane, and Philip F. Esler. *Visuality and Biblical Text: Interpreting Velázquez' Christ with Martha and Mary as a Test Case.* Arte e Archeologia: Studi e Documenti 26. Florence: Olschki, 2004.

Braemer, Frank. *L'architecture domestique du Levant à l'Age du fer: Protohistoire du Levant.* Paris: Éditions Recherches sur les civilisations, 1982.

Brandes, Stanley. "Reflections on Honor and Shame in the Mediterranean." In *Honor and Shame and the Unity of the Mediterranean,* edited by David D. Gilmore, 121–34. AmAnthAss 22. Washington, DC: American Anthropological Association , 1987.

Brichto, Herbert C. "Kin, Cult, Land and Afterlife—A Biblical Complex." *Hebrew Union College Annual* 44 (1973) 1–54.

Bright, John. *A History of Israel.* 4th ed. Louisville: Westminster John Knox, 2000.

Brison, Susan J. *Aftermath: Violence and the Remaking of the Self.* Princeton: Princeton University Press, 2001.

———. "Surviving Sexual Violence: a Philosophical Perspective." *Journal of Social Philosophy* 24 (1993) 5–22.

Bromberger, Christian. "Bridge, Wall, Mirror: Coexistence and Confrontations in the Mediterranean World." *History and Anthropology* 18 (2007) 291–307.

———. "Towards an Anthropology of the Mediterranean." *History and Anthropology* 17 (2006) 91–107.

Brown, Raymond E., et al., editors. *Jerome Biblical Commentary*. Englewood Cliffs, NJ: Prentice-Hall, 1968.

Brueggemann, Walter. *First and Second Samuel*. Interpretation. Louisville: Westminster John Knox, 1990.

Bruns, E. J. "The Genealogy of Judith." *CBQ* 18 (1956) 19–22.

———. "Judith or Jael?" *CBQ* 16 (1954) 12–14.

Buber, Martin. "Leitwort and Discourse Type: An Example." In *Scripture and Translation*, by Martin Buber and Franz Rosenzweig, 143–50. Translated by Lawrence Rosenwald with Everett Fox. ISBL. Bloomington: Indiana University Press, 1994.

Buber, Martin, and Franz Rosenzweig. *Scripture and Translation*. Translated by Lawrence Rosenwald with Everett Fox. ISBL. Bloomington: Indiana University Press, 1994

Budde, Karl. *Religion of Israel to the Exile*. American Lectures on the History of Religions. New York: Putnam, 1899.

Callaway, Mary. *Sing, O Barren One: A Study in Comparative Midrash*. SBLDS 91. Atlanta: Scholars, 1986.

Campbell, Antony F. *1 Samuel*. FOTL 7. Grand Rapids: Eerdmans, 2003.

Campbell, J. K. *Honour, Family and Patronage: A Study of Institutions and Moral Values in a Greek Mountain Community*. Oxford: Oxford University Press, 1964.

Campbell, Joseph. *The Hero with a Thousand Faces*. New York: Princeton University Press, 1968.

Caponigro, Mark Stephen. "Judith, Holding the Tale of Herodotus." In *No One Spoke Ill of Her: Essays on Judith*, edited by James C. VanderKam, 47–59. Early Judaism and Its Literature 2. Atlanta: Scholars, 1992.

Carlson, R. A. *David, The Chosen King: A Traditio-historical Approach to the Second Book of Samuel*. Stockholm: Almqvist & Wiksell, 1964.

Cazelles, H. "*hll*." In *TDOT* 3 (1978) 411–13.

Chandler, Billy J. *The Bandit King: Limpiao of Brazil*. College Station: Texas A & M Press, 1978.

Chaney, Marvin L. "Ancient Palestinian Peasant Movements and the Formation of Premonarchic Israel." In *Palestine in Transition: The Emergence of Ancient Israel*, edited by David Noel Freedman and David Frank Graf, 39–90. Social World of Biblical Antiquity Series 2. Sheffield, UK: Almond, 1983.

———. "Bitter Bounty: The Dynamics of Political Economy Critiqued by the Eight-Century Prophets." In *Reformed Faith and Economics*, edited by Robert L. Stivers, 15–30. Lanham, MD: University Press of America, 1989.

———. "Study of the Israelite Monarchy." *Semeia* 37 (1986) 53–76.

Chertok, Shlomo. "Mothers, Sons and Infertility: A Study of Barrenness in the Bible." *Le'ela* 21 (2000) 21–27.

Clark, Gordon R. *The Word Hesed in the Hebrew Bible*. JSOTSup 157. Sheffield, UK: JSOT Press, 1993.

Clarke, Simon. *The Foundations of Structuralism: A Critique of Lévi-Strauss and the Structuralist Movement*. Totowa, NJ: Barnes & Noble, 1981.

Clifford, Richard J. "Genesis 38: Its Contribution to the Jacob Story." *CBQ* 66 (2004) 519–32.

Clines, David J. A., and J. Cheryl Exum. "The New Literary Criticism." In *The New Literary Criticism and the Hebrew Bible*, edited by David J. A. Clines and J. Cheryl, Exum, 11–25. JSOTSup 143. Sheffield, UK: Sheffield Academic, 1993.

Coats, George W. "Widow's Rights: A Crux in the Structure of Genesis 38." *CBQ* 34 (1972) 461–66.

Cole, Sally. *Women of the Praia: Work and Lives in a Portuguese Coastal Community.* Princeton: Princeton University Press, 1991.

Connerton, Paul. *How Modernity Forgets.* Cambridge: Cambridge University Press, 2009.

Cook, Joan E. *Hannah's Desire, God's Design: Early Interpretations of the Story of Hannah.* JSOTSup 282. Sheffield, UK: Sheffield Academic, 1999.

Coote, Robert B., and Whitelam, Keith W. *The Emergence of Early Israel in Historical Perspective.* Social World of Biblical Antiquity Series 5. Sheffield, UK: Almond, 1987.

Copeland, Lennie, and Lewis Griggs. *Going International: How to Make Friends and Deal Effectively in the Global Marketplace.* New York: Random House, 1986.

Couffignal, Robert. "David et Goliath: un conte merveilleux. Etude littéraire de 1 Samuel 17 et 18,1–30." *Bulletin de littéraire ecclésiastique* 99 (1998) 431–42.

Cowley, A. E. "The Book of Judith." In *The Apocrypha and the Pseudepigrapha of the Old Testament in English: With Introductions and Critical and Explanatory Notes to the Several Books. Volume 1: Apocrypha*, edited by R. H. Charles, 242–67. Oxford: Clarendon, 1913.

Craven, Toni. "Artistry and Faith in the Book of Judith." *Semeia* 8 (1977) 75–101.

———. *Artistry and Faith in the Book of Judith.* SBLDS 70. Chico, CA: Scholars, 1983.

Crook, Zeba A. "Method and Models in New Testament Interpretation: Critical Engagement with Louise Lawrence's Literary Ethnography." *Religious Studies Review* 32 (2006) 87–97.

———. "Reciprocity—Covenantal Exchange as a Test Case." In *Ancient Israel: The Old Testament in Its Social Context*, edited by Philip F. Esler, 78–91. Minneapolis: Fortress, 2006.

———. *Reconceptualising Conversion: Patronage, Loyalty, and Conversion in the Religions of the Ancient Mediterranean.* BZNW 130. Berlin: de Gruyter, 2004.

———. "Structure vs. Agency in Studies of the Biblical Social World: Engaging with Louise Lawrence." *JSNT* 29 (2007) 277–86.

Cross, Frank M. Jr. "A New Qumran Biblical Fragment Related to the Original Hebrew Underlying the Septuagint." *BASOR* 132 (1953) 23.

Cross, Frank Moore, et al., editors. *Qumran Cave 4: XII: 1–2 Samuel.* Discoveries in the Judean Desert 17. Oxford: Clarendon, 2005.

Crossan, John Dominic. *Dark Interval: Towards a Theology of Story.* Niles, IL: Argus, 1975.

Dabove, Juan Pablo. *Nightmares of the Lettered City: Banditry and Literature in Latin America, 1816–1929.* Illuminations: Cultural Formations of the Americas. Pittsburgh: University of Pittsburgh Press, 2007.

Dancy, J. C. *The Shorter Books of the Apocrypha.* Cambridge: Cambridge University Press, 1972.

Davies, Philip R. *In Search of 'Ancient Israel'.* JSOTSup 148. Sheffield, UK: JSOT Press, 1992.

Davis, Ellen F. *Scripture, Culture, and Agriculture: An Agrarian Reading of the Bible.* Cambridge: Cambridge University Press, 2008.

Davis, John. "Family and State in the Mediterranean." In *Honor and Shame and the Unity of the Mediterranean,* edited by David D. Gilmore, 22–34. AmAnthAss 22. Washington, DC: American Anthropological Association, 1987.

———. *People of the Mediterranean: An Essay in Comparative Anthropology.* Library of Man. London: Routledge & Kegan Paul, 1977.

Davison, Gerald C., and John M. Neale. *Abnormal Psychology.* New York: Wiley, 1990.

Deem, Ariela. "'And the Stone Sank into His Forehead': A Short Note on 1 Samuel XVII 49." *Vetus Testamentum* 28 (1978) 349–51.

Delaney, Carol. "Seeds of Honor, Fields of Shame." In *Honor and Shame and the Unity of the Mediterranean,* edited by David D. Gilmore, 35–48. AmAnthAss 22. Washington, DC: American Anthropological Association , 1987.

Delcor, Matthias. "Le livre de Judith et l'époque grecque." *Klio* 49 (1967) 151–79.

DeMaris, Richard E. and Carolyn S Leeb. "(Dis)Honor and Ritual Enactment in the Jephthah Story: Judges 10:16—12:1." *In Ancient Israel: The Old Testament in Its Social Context,* edited by Philip F. Esler, 177–90. Minneapolis: Fortress, 2005.

Dietrich, Walter. "David, Amnon und Abschalom (2 Samuel 13): Literarische, textliche und historische Erwägungen zu den ambivalenten Beziehungen eines Vaters zu seinen Söhnen." *Text* 23 (2007) 115–43.

———. *Samuel. Biblischer Kommentar VIII/1.* Neuchirchen-Vluyn: Neukirchner, 2003.

Dover, K. J. *Greek Popular Morality in the Time of Plato and Aristotle.* Oxford: Blackwell, 1974.

Driver, S. R. *Notes on the Hebrew Text and the Topography of the Books of Samuel, with an Introduction on Hebrew Palaeography and the Ancient Versions and Facsimiles of Inscriptions and Maps.* Oxford: Clarendon, 1913.

Dubarle, A. M. "La Mention de Judith dans la littérature ancienne, juive et chrétienne." *RB* 66 (1959) 514–49.

Dubisch, Jill. *In a Different Place: Pilgrimage, Gender, and Politics at a Greek Island Shrine.* Princeton: Princeton University Press, 1995.

Du Boulay, Juliet. "Lies, Mockery and Family Integrity." In *Mediterranean Family Structures,* edited by J. G. Peristiany, 389–406. Cambridge Studies in Social Anthropology 13. Cambridge: Cambridge University Press, 1976.

———. *Portrait of a Greek Mountain Village.* Oxford Monographs on Social Anthropology. Oxford: Oxford University Press, 1974.

Dubovsky, Peter. *Hezekiah and the Assyrian Spies: A Reconstruction of the Neo-Assyrian Intelligence Services and their Significance for 2 Kings 18–19.* Biblica et Orientalia 49. Rome: Pontifical Biblical Institute Press, 2006.

Duling, D.C., 2011, 'Memory, collective memory, orality and the gospels', *HTS Teologiese Studies/Theological Studies* 67(1), Art. #915, 103–113. DOI: 10.4102/hts.v67i1.915

Dunn, Ross. "A Life in the Day (sic) of Ahmed Abyyiat." *The Sunday Times Magazine,* 21 December 1997, 46.

Dundes, Alan. "Introduction to the Second Edition." In *Morphology of the Folktale,* by Vladimir Propp, xi–xvii. 2nd ed. Revised and edited with a preface by Louis A. Wagner. New introduction by Alan Dundes. The first edition was translated from the 1928 Russian original by Laurence Scott. Austin: University of Texas Press, 1968.

Dutton, Dennis. "Are There Seven Basic Plots?" (A Review of Christopher Booker's *The Seven Basic Plots: Why We Tell Stories*). *Washington Post Book World,* 2005.

Eissfeldt, Otto. *The Old Testament: An Introduction. The History of the Formation of the Old Testament.* Translated by Peter R. Ackroyd. Oxford: Blackwell, 1966.

Elliott, John H. "The Evil Eye and the Sermon on the Mount: Contours of a Pervasive Belief in Social Scientific Perspective." *BibInt* 2 (1994) 51–84.

———. "The Evil Eye in the First Testament: The Ecology and Culture of a Pervasive Belief." In *The Bible and the Politics of Exegesis*, edited by Norman K. Gottwald, 147–59. Cleveland: Pilgrim, 1991.

———. "The Fear of the Leer: The Evil Eye from the Bible to Li'l Abner." *Forum* 4 (1988) 42–71.

———. "Matthew 20:1–15: A Parable of Invidious Comparison and Evil Eye Accusation." *BTB* 22 (1992) 52–65.

———. "Paul, Galatians and the Evil Eye." *Currents in Theology and Mission* 17 (1990) 262–73.

———. *Social-Scientific Criticism of the New Testament: An Introduction.* London: SPCK, 1995.

Eppstein, Victor. "Was Saul Also among the Prophets?" *ZAW* 81 (1969) 287–304.

Erikson, Erik. *Young Man Luther: A Study in Psychoanalysis and History.* New York: Norton, 1958.

Esler, Philip F. "Ancient Mediterranean *Monomachia* in the Light of Cultural Anthropology: The Case of David and Goliath." In *The Idea of Man and Concepts of the Body: Anthropological Studies on the Ancient Cultures of Israel, Egypt, and the Near East.*, edited by Anjelika Berjelung et al. Oriental Religions in Antiquity. Tübingen: Mohr/Siebeck, 2011 (forthcoming).

———. "The Biblical Paintings of Ivor Williams (1908–1982)." In *Biblical Art from Wales*, edited by Martin O'Kane and John Morgan-Guy, 187–203. Sheffield, UK: Sheffield Phoenix, 2010.

———. *Community and Gospel in Luke-Acts: The Social and Political Motivations of Lucan Theology.* Society for New Testament Studies Monograph Series 57. Cambridge: Cambridge University Press, 1987.

———. *Conflict and Identity in Romans: The Social Setting of Paul's Letter.* Minneapolis: Fortress, 2003.

———. *Galatians.* New Testament Readings. London: Routledge, 1998.

———. "Glossolalia and the Admission of Gentiles into the Early Christian Community." In *The First Christians in Their Social Worlds*, edited by Philip F. Esler, 37–51. London: Routledge, 1994.

———. "Introverted Sectarianism at Qumran and in the Johannine Community." In *The First Christians in Their Social Worlds: Social-Scientific Approaches to New Testament Interpretation*, 70–91. London: Routledge, 1994.

———. "Introduction: Models, Context and Kerygma in New Testament Interpretation." In *Modelling Early Christianity: Social-Scientific Studies of the New Testament in Its Context*, edited by Philip F. Esler, 1–20. London: Routledge, 1995.

———. "Making and Breaking an Agreement Mediterranean Style: A New Reading of Galatians 2:1–14." *BibInt* 3 (1995) 285–314.

———. "Ludic History in the Book of Judith: The Reinvention of Israelite Identity?" *BibInt* 10 (2002) 107–43.

———. *New Testament Theology: Communion and Community.* Minneapolis: Fortress, 2005.

————. "Paul and the Agon: Understanding a Pauline Motif in Its Cultural and Visual Context." In *Picturing the New Testament: Studies in Ancient Visual Images*, edited by Annette Weissenrieder et al., 356–84. WUNT 2/193. Tübingen: Mohr/Siebeck, 2005.

————. "'Remember My Fetters': Memorialisation of Paul's Imprisonment." In *Explaining Christian Origins and Early Judaism: Contributions from Cognitive and Social Science*, edited by Petri Luomanen et al., 231–58. BibIntSer 89. Leiden: Brill 2007.

————. "Social-Scientific Models in Biblical Interpretation." In *Ancient Israel: The Old Testament in Its Social Context*, edited by Philip F. Esler, 3–14. Minneapolis: Fortress, 2006.

Esler, Philip F., and Anselm C. Hagedorn. "Social-Scientific Analysis of the Old Testament: A Brief History and Overview." In *Ancient Israel: The Old Testament in Its Social Context*, edited by Philip F. Esler, 15–32. Minneapolis: Fortress, 2006.

Esler, Philip F., and Ronald A. Piper. *Lazarus, Mary and Martha: A Social-Scientific and Theological Reading of John.* London: SCM, 2006.

————. "The Raising of Lazarus in Early Christian Art." In Philip F. Esler and Ronald A. Piper. *Lazarus, Mary and Martha: A Social-Scientific and Theological Reading of John*, 131–45. London: SCM, 2006.

Exum, J. Cheryl. *Tragedy and Biblical Narrative: Arrows of the Almighty.* Cambridge: Cambridge University Press, 1992.

Fernea, Elizabeth W. *Guests of the Sheik: An Ethnography of an Iraqi Village.* Garden City, NY: Anchor, 1969.

Finke, Andrew. *The Samuel Scroll from Qumran: 4QSam^a Restored and Compared to the Septuagint and 4QSam^c.* STDJ 43. Leiden: Brill, 2001.

Finkelstein, Israel. *'Izbet Sartah: An Early Iron Age Site Near Rosh Ha'ayin, Israel.* Bar International Series 299. Oxford: B.A.R., 1986.

————. *The Archaeology of the Israelite Settlement.* Jerusalem: Israel Exploration Society, 1988.

Firmage, Edwin. "Zoology (Fauna)." In *ABD* 6 (1992) 1109–66.

Fokkelman, J. P. *Narrative Art and Poetry in the Books of Samuel: A Full Interpretation Based on Stylistic and Structural Analyses.* Volume 1, *King David (II Sam. 9–20 & I Kings 1–2).* Studia Semitica Neerlandica 20. Assen: Van Gorcum, 1981.

————. *Narrative Art and Poetry in the Books of Samuel: A Full Interpretation Based on Stylistic and Structural Analyses.* Volume 2, *The Crossing Fates (I Sam. 13–31 & II Sam. 1).* Studia Semitica Neerlandica 23. Assen: Van Gorcum, 1986.

Foster, George M. "Peasant Society and the Image of Limited Good." In *Peasant Society: A Reader*, edited by Jack M. Potter, May N. Diaz and George M. Foster, 300–23. Boston: Little, Brown, 1967 (reprinted from *American Anthropologist* 67 [1965] 293–315).

Fox, Everett. "The Book in Its Contexts." In *Scripture and Translation*, by Martin Buber and Franz Rosenzweig, xiii–xxvii. English translation by Lawrence Rosenwald with Everett Fox. ISBL. Bloomington: Indiana University Press, 1994.

————. "Stalking the Younger Brother: Some Models for Understanding a Biblical Motif." *JSOT* 60 (1993) 45–68.

Frazer, Chris. *Bandit Nation: A History of Outlaws and Cultural Struggles in Mexico, 1810–1920.* Lincoln: University of Nebraska Press, 2006.

Frazer, Sir James George. *The Golden Bough: A Study in Magic and Religion.* 1890. Reprinted, London: Macmillan, 1929.

Freund, Richard A. "Lying and Deception in the Biblical and Post-Biblical Judaic Tradition." *Scandinavian Journal of the Old Testament* 1 (1991) 45–61.

Freyne, Seán. "Bandits in Galilee: A Contribution to the Study of Social Conditions in First-Century Palestine." In *The Social World of Formative Christianity and Judaism: Essays in Tribute to Howard Clark Kee,* edited by Jacob Neusner et al., 50–68. Philadelphia: Fortress, 1988.

Friedl, Ernestine. "Some Aspects of Dowry and Inheritance in Boeotia." In *Mediterranean Countrymen: Essays in the Social Anthropology of the Mediterranean,* edited by Julian Pitt-Rivers, 113–35. Paris: Mouton, 1963.

Frye, Northrop. *Anatomy of Criticism: Four Essays.* Princeton: Princeton University Press, 1957.

Frymer-Kensky, Tikva. "Virginity in the Bible." In *Gender and Law in the Hebrew Bible and the Ancient Near East,* edited by Victor H. Matthews et al., 79–86. JSOTSup 262. Sheffield, UK: Sheffield Academic, 1998.

Funk, Robert W., editor. *Semeia* 1: *A Structuralist Approach to the Parables* (1974).

Gadamer, Hans-Georg. *Truth and Method.* 2nd ed. Translated by William Glen-Doepel. London: Sheed & Ward, 1979.

Gilmore, David D. "Anthropology of the Mediterranean Area." *Annual Reviews in Anthropology* 11 (1982) 175–205.

———, editor. *Honor and Shame and the Unity of the Mediterranean.* AmAnthAss 22. Washington, DC: American Anthropological Association , 1987.

———. "Honor, Honesty, Shame: Male Status in Contemporary Andalusia." In *Honor and Shame and the Unity of the Mediterranean,* edited by David D. Gilmore, 90–103. AmAnthAss 22. Washington, DC: American Anthropological Association, 1987.

———. "Introduction: The Shame of Dishonor." In *Honor and Shame and the Unity of the Mediterranean,* edited by David D. Gilmore, 2–21. AmAnthAss 22. Washington, DC: American Anthropological Association, 1987.

———. *The People of the Plain: Class and Community in Lower Andalusia.* New York: Columbia University Press, 1980.

Gilsenan, Michael. "Lying, Honor, and Contradiction." In *Transaction and Meaning: Directions in the Anthropology of Exchange and Symbolic Behaviour,* edited by Bruce Kapferer, 191–219. Philadelphia: Institute for the Study of Human Issues, 1976.

Giovannini, Maureen J. "Female Chastity Codes in the Circum-Mediterranean: Comparative Perspectives." In *Honor and Shame and the Unity of the Mediterranean,* edited by David D. Gilmore, 61–74. AmAnthAss 22. Washington, DC: American Anthropological Association, 1987.

Golka, Friedemann W. "German Old Testament Scholarship." In *A Dictionary of Biblical Interpretation,* edited by R. J. Coggins and J. L. Houlden, 258–64. London: SCM, 1990.

Good, Edwin M. *Irony in the Old Testament.* Philadelphia: Westminster, 1965.

Gooding, David W. "An Approach to the Literary and Textual Problems in the David-Goliath Story: 1 Sam 16–18." In *The Story of David and Goliath: Textual and Literary Criticism,* edited by Dominique Barthélemy et al., 55–86. OBO 73. Göttingen: Vandenhoeck & Ruprecht. 1986.

Goody, Jack. "Polygyny, Economy and the Role of Women." In *The Character of Kinship,* edited by Jack Goody, 175–90. Cambridge: Cambridge University Press, 1973.

Gordon, Robert P. *1 & 2 Samuel: A Commentary*. Exeter: The Paternoster Press, 1986.

————. "Saul's Meningitis according to Targum 1 Samuel XIX 24." *VT* 37 (1987) 39–49.

Gottwald, Norman K. *The Tribes of Yahweh: A Sociology of the Religion of Liberated Israel 1250–1050 B.C.E.* Maryknoll, NY: Orbis, 1979.

Granqvist, Hilma. *Birth and Childhood among the Arabs: Studies in a Muhammadan Village in Palestine*. 1947. Reprinted, New York: AMS, 1975.

————. *Child Problems among the Arabs: Studies in a Muhammadan Village in Palestine*. Helsinki: Söderstrom, 1948.

————. *Marriage Conditions in a Palestinian Village*. Commentationes Humanarum Litterarum 3.8. Helsinki: Societas Scientiarum Fennica, 1931.

————. *Marriage Conditions in a Palestinian Village*. Vol. 2. Commentationes Humanarum Litterarum 6.8. Helsinki: Societas Scientiarum Fennica, 1935.

Gray, Mark. "Amnon: A Chip Off the Old Block? Rhetorical Strategy in 2 Samuel 13.7–15: The Rape of Tamar and the Humiliation of the Poor." *JSOT* 23 (1998) 39–54.

Greenspahn, Frederick E. *When Brothers Dwell Together: The Preeminence of Younger Siblings in the Hebrew Bible*. Oxford: Oxford University Press, 1994.

Greimas, Algirdas Julien. *Sémantique structurale: recherche de méthode*. Paris: Larousse, 1966.

Gudykunst, William B., and Young Yun Kim. *Communicating with Strangers: An Approach to Intercultural Communication*. 4th ed. Boston: McGraw Hill, 2003.

Gunkel, Hermann. *The Folktale in the Old Testament*. Translated by Michael D. Rutter. Edited by David M. Gunn. Historic Texts and Interpreters in Biblical Scholarship 6. Sheffield, UK: Sheffield Academic, 1987 (the German original of this work was first published in 1917).

————. *Genesis*. Handkommentar zum Alten Testament 1. Göttingen: Vandenhoeck & Ruprecht, 1901. 3rd ed., 1910.

————. *Genesis. Translated and Interpreted by Hermann Gunkel*. Translated by Mark E. Biddle, with a foreword by Ernest W. Nicholson. Macon, GA: Mercer University Press, 1997.

Gunn, David M. *The Fate of King Saul: An Interpretation of a Biblical Story*. JSOTSup 14. Sheffield, UK: JSOT Press, 1980.

Gunn, David M., and Danna Nolan Fewell. *Narrative in the Hebrew Bible*. Oxford Bible Series. Oxford: Oxford University Press, 1993.

Halbwachs, Maurice. *The Collective Memory*. Translated by Francis J. Ditter Jr. and Vida Yazdi Ditter, with an introduction by Mary Douglas. New York: Harper & Row, 1980.

Hall, Edward T. *Beyond Culture*. Garden City, NY: Anchor, 1976.

————. *The Dance of Life: The Other Dimensions of Time*. Garden City, NY: Doubleday, 1983.

Hall, Edward T., and Mildred Reed Hall. *Understanding Cultural Differences: French, Germans and Americans*. Yarmouth, ME: Intercultural Press, 1990.

Halpern Baruch. *David's Secret Demons: Messiah, Murderer, Traitor, King*. The Bible in Its World. Grand Rapids: Eerdmans, 2001.

Hamadeh, Najla'. "The Values and Self-Identity of Bedouin and Urban Women: A Comparative Analysis: Field Study (Bekaa Valley, Lebanon)." Economic and Social Commission for Western Asia, Series of Studies on Arab Women and Development, Number 26, United Nations, New York, 1997 (23 pages).

Hamilton, Victor P. *The Book of Genesis: Chapters 18–50*. New International Commentary on the Old Testament. Grand Rapids: Eerdmans, 1995.

Handy, Lowell K. "Dagon." In *ABD* 2 (1992) 1–3.

Hanson, K. C. "Jesus and the Social Bandits." In *The Social Setting of Jesus and the Gospels*, edited by Wolfgang Stegemann, Bruce J. Malina, and Gerd Theissen, 283–300. Minneapolis: Fortress, 2002.

———. "The Gezer Almanac." Online: www.kchanson.com/ANCDOCS/westsem/gezer .html

Hanson, K. C., and Douglas E. Oakman. *Palestine in the Time of Jesus: Social Structures and Social Conflicts.* 2nd ed. Minneapolis: Fortress Press, 2008

Harrington, Daniel J., SJ, and Anthony J. Saldarini. *Targum Jonathan of the Former Prophets: Introduction, Translation and Notes.* Aramaic Bible 10. Edinburgh: T. & T. Clark, 1987.

Harris, W. V., editor. *Rethinking the Mediterranean.* Oxford: Oxford University Press, 2005.

Hauschild, Thomas et al. "Syncretism in the Mediterranean: Universalism, Cultural Relativism and the Issue of the Mediterranean as a Cultural Area." *History and Anthropology* 18 (2007) 309–32.

Hays, J. Daniel. "The Height of Goliath: A Response to Clyde Billingham." *JETS* 50 (2007) 509–16.

———. "Reconsidering the Height of Goliath." *JETS* 48 (2005) 701–14.

Headland, Thomas N., Kenneth L. Pike, and Marvin Harris, editors. *Emics and Etics: The Insider/Outsider Debate.* Frontiers of Anthropology 7. London: Sage, 1990.

Hellmann, Monika. *Judith—Eine Frau im Spannungsfeld von Autonomie und göttlicher Führung.* Europäische Hochsschulshriften 23/444. Frankfurt: Lang, 1992.

Hendin, David. *Guide to Ancient Jewish Coins (with values by Herbert Kreindler).* New York: Attic, 1976.

Henten, Jan Willem van. "Judith as Alternative Leader: A Rereading of Judith 7–13." In *A Feminist Companion to Esther, Judith and Susannah*, edited by Athalya Brenner, 224–52. FCB 7. Sheffield, UK: Sheffield Academic, 1995.

Hertzberg, Hans Wilhelm. *I & II Samuel: A Commentary.* Translated by J. S. Bowden. Old Testament Library. Philadelphia: Westminster, 1964

Herzfeld, Michael. "'As in Your Own House': Hospitality, Ethnography, and the Stereotype of Mediterranean Society." In *Honor and Shame and the Unity of the Mediterranean*, edited by David D. Gilmore, 75–89. AmAnthAss 22. Washington, DC: American Anthropological Association, 1987.

———. "Honour and Shame: Problems in the Comparative Analysis of Moral Systems." *Man* 15 (1980) 339–51.

———. "The Horns of the Mediterraneanist Dilemma." *American Ethnologist* 11 (1984) 439–54.

Hervieu-Léger, Danièle. *Religion as a Chain of Memory.* Translated by Simon Lee. Cambridge, MA: Polity, 2000.

Herzog, William R. II. *Parables as Subversive Speech: Jesus as Pedagogue of the Oppressed.* Louisville: Westminster John Knox, 1994.

Herzog, Ze'ev. *Beersheba II.* Tel Aviv: Institute of Archaeology, 1984.

Hiebert, Paula S. "'Whence Shall Help Come to Me?' The Biblical Widow." In *Gender and Difference in Ancient Israel*, edited by Peggy L. Day, 125–41. Minneapolis: Fortress, 1989.

Hobbs, T. R. "Reflections on Honor, Shame, and Covenant Relations." *JBL* 116 (1997) 501–3.

Hobsbawm, E. J. *Bandits*. London: Weidenfeld & Nicolson, 1969.

———. *Primitive Rebels: Studies in Archaic Forms of Social Movement in the 19th and 20th Centuries*. Manchester: Manchester University Press, 1959.

———. "Social Banditry." In *Rural Protest: Peasant Movements and Social Change*, edited by Henry A. Landsberger, 142–57. London: Macmillan, 1974.

———. *Social Bandits and Primitive Rebels*. Glencoe, Ill.: Free Press, 1960 (= the US version of *Primitive Rebels: Studies in Archaic Forms of Social Movement in the 19th and 20th Centuries*, 1959).

———. "Social Bandits: Reply." *Comparative Studies in Society and History* 14 (1972) 503–5 (= reply to Blok, "The Peasant and the Brigand").

Hoffner, Harry A. "A Hittite Analogue to the David and Goliath Contest of Champions." *CBQ* 30 (1968) 220–25.

Hofstede, Geert. *Culture's Consequences: International Differences in Work-Related Values*. Beverly Hills, CA: Sage, 1980.

———. *Cultures and Organizations: Software of the Mind: Intercultural Cooperation and Its Importance for Survival*. London: HarperCollins, 1994.

Holladay, John S. Jr. "House, Israelite." In *ABD* 3 (1992) 308–18.

———. "Stable, Stables." *ABD* 4 (1992) 178–83.

Horrell, David G., editor. *Social-Scientific Approaches to New Testament Interpretation*. Edinburgh: T. & T. Clark, 1999.

———. "Whither Social-Scientific Approaches to New Testament Interpretation? Reflections on Contested Methodologies and the Future." In *After the First Urban Christians: The Social-Scientific Study of Pauline Christianity Twenty-Five Years Later*, edited by Todd D. Still and David G. Horrell, 6–20. London: Continuum, 2010.

Horsley, Richard A. "Ancient Jewish Social Banditry and the Revolt Against Rome." *CBQ* 43 (1981) 409–32.

———. "Josephus and the Bandits." *JSJ* 10 (1979) 37–63.

Horsley, Richard A., and John S. Hanson. *Bandits, Prophets, and Messiahs: Popular Movements in the Time of Jesus*. San Francisco: Harper & Row, 1985.

Hughes, H. M. *The Ethics of Jewish Apocryphal Literature*. London: Culley, 1909.

Humphreys, W. Lee. "From Tragic Hero to Villain: A Study of the Figure of Saul and the Development of 1 Samuel." *JSOT* 22 (1982) 95–117.

———. "The Rise and Fall of King Saul: A Study of an Ancient Narrative Stratum in 1 Samuel." *JSOT* 18 (1980) 74–90.

———. "The Tragedy of King Saul: A Study of the Structure of 1 Samuel 9–31." *JSOT* 6 (1978) 18–27.

Hunt, A. S., and C. C. Edgar. *Select Papyri*. Vol. 2: *Non-Literary Papyri Public Documents*. Loeb Classical Library 282. Cambridge: Harvard Univ. Press, 1934.

Hutzli, Jürg. "Mögliche Retuschen am Davidbild in der massoretischen Fassung der Samuelbücher." in *David und Saul im Widerstreit: Diachronie und Synchronie im Wetstreit: Beiträge zur Auslegung des ersten Samuelbuches*, edited by Walter Dietrich, 102–15. OBO 206. Göttingen: Vandenhoeck & Ruprecht, 2004.

Isaac, B. "Bandits in Judaea and Arabia." *Harvard Studies in Classical Philology* 88 (1984) 171–203.

Isser, Stanley Jerome. *The Sword of Goliath: David in Heroic Literature.* SBL Studies in Biblical Literature 6. Atlanta: Society of Biblical Literature, 2003.

James, William. *The Varieties of Religious Experience: A Study in Human Nature: Being the Gifford Lectures on Natural Religion Delivered at Edinburgh in 1901–1902.* London: Longmans, Green, 1902.

Jeremias, Joachim. "*Poimên,* etc." In *TDNT* 6 (1968) 485–502.

Jobling, David. "David and the Philistines (with methodological reflections)." In *David und Saul im Widerstreit: Diachronie und Synchronie im Wettstreit: Beiträge zur Auslegung des ersten Samuelbuches,* edited by Walter Dietrich, 74–85. OB 206. Göttingen: Vandenhoeck & Ruprecht, 2004.

———. "Hannah's Desire." In *1 Samuel,* edited by D. W. Cotter, 131–42. Berit Olam; Collegeville, MN: Liturgical, 1998.

———. *1 Samuel.* Berit Olam. Collegeville, MN: Liturgical, 1998.

Johnson, Roger A., editor. *Psychohistory and Religion: The Case of YOUNG MAN LUTHER.* Philadelphia: Fortress, 1977.

Joseph, G. M. "On the Trail of Latin American Bandits: A Reexamination of Peasant Resistance." *Latin American Research Review* 25 (1990) 7–18.

Kautsky, John. *The Politics of Aristocratic Empires.* Chapel Hill: University of North Carolina Press, 1982.

Kee, Howard Clark. "Testaments of the Twelve Patriarchs." In *The Old Testament Pseudepigrapha.* Volume 1, *Apocalyptic Literature and Testaments,* edited by James H. Charlesworth, 775–828. London: Darton, Longman & Todd, 1983.

Kiev, Ari. *Transcultural Psychiatry.* New York: Free Press, 1972.

Kindler, Arie. *Coins of the Land of Israel: Collection of the Bank of Israel: A Catalogue.* Translation edited by Gabriel Sivan. Jerusalem: Keter, 1974.

Kirk, Alan, and Tom Thatcher, editors. *Memory, Tradition, and Text: Uses of the Past in Early Christianity.* Semeia Studies 52. Atlanta: Society of Biblical Literature, 2005.

Kirmayer, Laurence J. "Beyond the 'New Cross-cultural Psychiatry': Cultural Biology, Discursive Psychology and the Ironies of Globalization." *Transcultural Psychiatry* 43 (2006) 126–44.

Kjaer, Hans, *The Excavation of Shiloh, the Place of Eli and Samuel.* Jerusalem: Breyt-Ul-Makdes Press, 1930.

Klein, Lillian R. "Hannah: Marginalized Victim and Social Redeemer." In *A Feminist Companion to Samuel and Kings,* edited by Athalya Brenner, 77–92. FCB 5. Sheffield, UK: Sheffield Academic, 1994.

Klein, Ralph W. *1 Samuel.* 2nd ed. WBC 10. Nashville: Nelson, 2008.

Kleinman, Arthur. *Patients and Healers in the Context of Culture: An Exploration of the Borderland between Anthropology, Medicine, and Psychiatry.* Comparative Studies of Health Systems and Medical Care 3. Berkeley: University of California Press, 1980.

Kleinman, Arthur and Byron Good, editors. "Introduction: Culture and Depression." In *Culture and Depression: Studies in the Anthropology and Cross-Cultural Psychiatry of Affect and Disorder,* edited by Arthur Kleinman and Byron Good, 1–33. Berkeley: University of California Press, 1985.

Kratz, R. G. *The Composition of the Narrative Books of the Old Testament.* Translated by John Bowden. London: T. & T. Clark, 2005.

Kuemmerlin-McLean, Joanne K. "Demons (Old Testament)." In *ABD* 2 (1992) 138–40.

Kunin, Seth Daniel. *The Logic of Incest: A Structuralist Analysis of Hebrew Mythology*. Journal for the Study of the Old Testament Supplement 185. Sheffield: Sheffield Academic Press, 1995.

Kutsch, E. "*hrp*' II." In *TDOT* 5 (1986) 209–15.

Lang, Bernhard. *Monotheism and the Prophetic Minority: An Essay in Biblical History and Sociology*. Social World of Biblical Antiquity Series 1. Sheffield, UK: Almond, 1983.

Lapp, Paul. "Tell el-Fûl." *Biblical Archaeologist* 28 (1965) 2–10.

Larrington, Carolyne. "Downhill since Milton." A Review of Christopher Booker's *The Seven Basic Plots: Why We Tell Stories*. *The Times Literary Supplement*, 6 February 2005.

Lawrence, Louise Joy. *An Ethnography of the Gospel of Matthew: A Critical Assessment of the Use of the Honour and Shame Model in New Testament Studies*. WUNT 2/165. Tübingen: Mohr/Siebeck, 2003.

———. "Structure, Agency and Ideology: A Response to Zeba Crook." *JSNT* 29 (2007) 277–86.

Leeb, Carolyn S. "Polygyny in the Biblical World: Insights from Rural Haiti." In *Ancient Israel: The Old Testament in Its Social Context*, edited by Philip F. Esler, 50–65. Minneapolis: Fortress, 2005.

———. "The Widow: Homeless and Post-Menopausal." *BTB* 32 (2002) 160–62.

Lemche, Niels Peter. "From Patronage Society to Patronage Society." In *The Origins of the Ancient Israelite States*, edited by Volkmar Fritz and Philip R. Davies, 106–20. JSOTSup 228. Sheffield, UK: Sheffield Academic, 1996.

———. "Kings and Clients: On Loyalty Between the Ruler and the Ruled in Ancient 'Israel.'" *Semeia* 66 (1995) 119–32.

———. *The Old Testament between Theology and History: A Critical Survey*. Louisville: Westminster John Knox, 2010.

Lenski, Gerhard, and Jean Lenski. *Human Societies: An Introduction to Macrosociology*. 5th edition. New York: McGraw-Hill, 1987.

Levenson, Jon D. "1 Samuel 25 as Literature and History." *CBQ* (1978) 40, 11–28.

Levine, Amy-Jill. "Sacrifice and Salvation: Otherness and Domestication in the Book of Judith." In *No One Spoke Ill of Her: Essays on Judith*, edited by James C. VanderKam, 17–30. Early Judaism and Its Literature 2. Atlanta, GA: Scholars Press, 1992.

Lévi-Strauss, Claude C. "The Myth of Asdiwal." In *The Structural Study of Myth and Totemism*, edited by Edmund Leach, 1–48. Translated by Nicholas Mann. London: Tavistock, 1967.

———. "The Structural Study of Myth." *Journal of American Folklore* 68 (1955) 428–44.

———. *La structure et la forme, réflexions sur un ouvrage de Vladimir Propp*. Cahiers de l'Institut de science économique appliquée. Série M 7, 1960, 1–36.

Lewin, L. "The Oligarchical Limitations of Social Banditry in Brazil: The Case of the 'Good' Thief, Antonio Silvino." *Past & Present* 82 (1979) 116–46.

Lewis I. M. *Ecstatic Religion: A Study of Shamanism and Spirit Possession*. 2nd ed. London: Routledge, 1989.

———. *Religion in Context: Cults and Charisma*. Cambridge: Cambridge University Press, 1986.

Lewis, Theodore J. "The Ancestral Estate (*nahalat 'elohim*) in 2 Samuel 14:16." *JBL* 110 (1991) 597–612.

Liddell, Henry George, Scott, Robert and Jones, Sir Henry Stuart. *A Greek-English Lexicon, with a Supplement*. Oxford: Clarendon, 1968.

Lindblom, J. *Prophecy in Ancient Israel*. Oxford: Basil Blackwell, 1962.

Lisowsky, Gerhard. *Konkordanz zum Hebräischen Alten Testament*. 2nd ed. Stuttgart: Würtembergische Bibelanstalt, 1958.

Löhr, Max. *Die Stellung des Weibes zu Jahwe-Religion und -Kult*. Leipzig: Hinrichs, 1908.

Loizos, Peter and Evthymios Papataxiarchis, editors. *Contested Identities: Gender and Kinship in Modern Greece*. Princeton: Princeton University Press, 1991.

Lowth, Robert. *Lectures on the Sacred Poetry of the Hebrews*. Translated by G. Gregory. 1787.

Luomanen, Petri et al., editors. *Explaining Christian Origins and Early Judaism: Contributions from Cognitive and Social Science*. BibIntSer 89. Leiden: Brill 2007.

———. "Introduction: Social and Cognitive Perspectives in the Study of Christian Origins and Early Judaism." In *Explaining Christian Origins and Early Judaism: Contributions from Cognitive and Social Science*, edited by Petri Luomanen et al., 1–33. BibIntSer 89. Leiden: Brill 2007.

Lust, Johann. "David dans le Septante." In *Figures de David à travers la Bible: XVII congrès de l'ACFEB*, edited by Lousi Derousseaux and Jacques Vermeylen, 243–63. Lectio divino 177. Paris: Cerf, 1999.

———. "The Story of David and Goliath in Hebrew and Greek." in *The Story of David and Goliath: Textual and Literary Criticism*, edited by Dominique Barthélemy et al., 5–18. OBO 73. Göttingen: Vandenhoeck & Ruprecht. 1986.

Madhavan, Sangeetha. "Best of Friends and Worst of Enemies: Competition and Collaboration in Polygyny." *Ethnology* 41 (2002) 69–83.

Malina, Bruce J. "Collectivism in Mediterranean Culture." In *Understanding the Social World of the New Testament*, edited by Dietmar Neufeld and Richard E. DeMaris, 17–28. London: Routledge, 2010.

———. *The New Testament World: Insights from Cultural Anthropology*. 1st ed. Atlanta: John Knox, 1981.

———. *The New Testament World: Insights from Cultural Anthropology*. 3rd ed. Louisville: Westminster John Knox, 2001.

———. "Patron and Client: The Analogy Behind Synoptic Theology." *Forum* 4.1 (1988) 2–32.

———. "Reading Theory Perspective: Reading Luke-Acts." In *The Social World of Luke-Acts: Models for Interpretation*, edited by Jerome H. Neyrey, 3–23. Peabody, MA: Hendrickson, 1991.

———. *The Social World of Jesus and the Gospels*. London: Routledge, 1996.

———. *Windows on the World of Jesus: Time Travel to Ancient Judea*. Louisville: Westminster John Knox, 1993.

Malina, Bruce J., and Jerome H. Neyrey. *Portraits of Paul: An Archaeology of Ancient Personality*. Louisville: Westminster John Knox, 1996.

Malina, Bruce J., and Richard L. Rohrbaugh. *Social-Science Commentary on the Synoptic Gospels*. 2nd ed. Minneapolis: Fortress, 2003.

Malina, Bruce J., and Chris Seeman. "Envy." In *Biblical Social Values and Their Meaning: A Handbook*, edited by John J. Pilch and Bruce J. Malina, 55–59. Peabody, MA: Hendrickson, 1993.

Marböck. J. "*Nabal; nebalah*." In *TDOT* 9 (1998) 157–71.

Marcus, Michael A. "'Horsemen Are the Fence of the Land': Honor and History among the Ghiyata of Eastern Morocco." In *Honor and Shame and the Unity of the Mediterranean,* edited by David D. Gilmore, 49–60. AmAnthAss 22. Washington, DC: American Anthropological Association, 1987.

Marohl, Matthew J. *Joseph's Dilemma: "Honor Killing" in the Birth Narrative of Matthew.* Eugene, OR: Cascade Books, 2008.

Matthews, Victor H. "Female Voices: Upholding the Honor of the Household." *BTB* 24 (1994) 8–15.

———. "Honor and Shame in Gender-Related Legal Situations in the Hebrew Bible." In *Gender and Law in the Hebrew Bible and the Ancient Near East,* edited by Victor H. Matthews, Bernard M. Levinson and Tikva Frymer-Kensky, 97–112. JSOTSup 262. Sheffield, UK: Sheffield Academic, 1998.

———. *Manners and Customs in the Bible.* Rev. ed. Peabody, MA: Hendrickson, 1991.

Matthews, Victor H., and Don C. Benjamin. "Amnon and Tamar: A Matter of Honor (2 Sam. 13.1–38)." In *Interconnections: A Festschrift in Honor of Michael Astour,* edited by G. D. Young et al., 339–66. Baltimore: CDL, 1997.

———. "Honor and Shame in Gender-Related Legal Situations in the Hebrew Bible." In *Gender and Law in the Hebrew Bible and the Ancient Near East,* edited by Victor H. Matthews et al., 97–112. JSOTSup 262. Sheffield; UK:Sheffield Academic, 1998.

———. *The Social World of Ancient Israel 1250–587 BCE.* Peabody, MA: Hendrickson, 1993.

Matthews, Victor H., and James C. Moyer. *The Old Testament: Text and Context.* 2nd ed. Peabody, MA: Hendrickson, 2005.

Mbuwayesango, Dora H. "Childlessness and Woman-to-Woman Relationships in Genesis and in African Patriarchal Society: Sarah and Hagar from a Zimbabwean Woman's Perspective (Gen 16:1–16; 21:8–21)." *Semeia* 78 (1997) 27–36.

McCarter, P. Kyle, Jr. *I Samuel.* AB 8. Garden City, NY: Doubleday, 1980.

———. *II Samuel.* AB 9. Garden City, NY: Doubleday, 1984.

McEndarfer, Jodi. "The Chinese Bandit Menace in 1930." (http://www.iusb.edu/~journal/static/volumes/1998/Paper9.html)

Mendelssohn, J. "Samuel's Denunciation of Kingship in the Light of the Akkadian Documents from Ugarit." *Bulletin of the American Schools of Oriental Research* 143 (1956) 17–22.

Mendenhall, George E. "The Hebrew Conquest of Canaan." *Biblical Archaeologist* 25 (1962) 66–87.

Meneley, Anne. *Tournaments of Value: Sociability and Hierarchy in a Yemeni Town.* Toronto: University of Toronto Press, 1996.

Menn, Esther Marie. *Judah and Tamar (Genesis 38) in Ancient Jewish Exegesis: Studies in Literary Form and Hermeneutics.* Supplements to the Journal for the Study of Judaism 51. Leiden: Brill, 1997.

Merideth, Betsy. "Desire and Danger: The Drama of Betrayal in Judges and Judith." *Anti-Covenant: Counter-Reading Women's Lives in the Hebrew Bible,* edited by M. Bal, 63–78. Bible and Literature Series 22. Sheffield, UK: Almond, 1989.

Meshorer, Ya'akov. *Ancient Jewish Coinage.* Vol. 1, *Persian Period through Hasmoneans.* New York: Amphora, 1982.

Meyers, Carol. *Discovering Eve: Ancient Israelite Women in Context.* Oxford: Oxford University Press, 1988.

————. "An Ethnoarchaeological Analysis of Hannah's Sacrifice." In *Pomegranates and Golden Bells: Studies in Biblical, Jewish, and Near Eastern Ritual, Law, and Literature in Honor of Jacob Milgrom*, edited by David P. Wright, David Noel Freedman and Avi Hurvitz, 77–91. Winona Lake, IN: Eisenbrauns, 1995.

————. "The Family in Early Israel." In *Families in Ancient Israel*, edited by Leo G. Perdue et al, 1–47. Philadelphia: Westminster John Knox, 1997.

————. "Hannah and Her Sacrifice: Reclaiming Female Agency." In *A Feminist Companion to Samuel and Kings*, edited by Athalya Brenner, 93–104. FCB 5. Sheffield, UK: Sheffield Academic, 1994.

Middleton, David, and Derek Edwards. "Introduction." In *Collective Remembering*, edited by David Middleton and Derek Edwards, 1–22. Inquiries in Social Construction. London: Sage, 1990.

Miller, Geoffrey P. "Verbal Feud in the Hebrew Bible: Judges 3:12–30 and 19–21." *Journal of Near Eastern Studies* 55 (1996) 105–17.

Moore, Carey A. *Judith*. AB 40B. Garden City, NY: Doubleday, 1985.

————. "Judith." In *ABD* 3 (1992) 1117–25.

————. "Why Wasn't the Book of Judith Included in the Hebrew Bible." In *No One Spoke Ill of Her: Essays on Judith*, edited by James C. VanderKam, 61–71. Early Judaism and Its Literature 2. Atlanta: Scholars, 1992.

Moxnes, Halvor. "Patron-Client Relations and the New Community in Luke-Acts." In *The Social World of Luke-Acts: Models for Interpretation*, edited by Jerome H. Neyrey, 241–68. Peabody, MA: Hendrickson, 1991.

Muilenburg, James. "Form Criticism and Beyond." *JBL* 88 (1969) 1–18.

Murdock, George Peter. *Theories of Illness: A World Survey*. Pittsburgh: University of Pittsburgh Press, 1980.

Neufeld, Dietmar. "Barrenness: Trance as a Protest Strategy." In *Ancient Israel: The Old Testament in Its Social Context*, edited by Philip F. Esler, 128–41. Minneapolis: Fortress, 2006.

Nicholas, Dean Andrew. *The Trickster Revisited: Deception as a Motif in the Pentateuch*. Studies in Biblical Literature 17. New York: Lang, 2009.

Niditch, Susan. "The Wronged Woman Righted: An Analysis of Genesis 38." *HTR* 72 (1979) 143–49.

Nitsche, Stefan Ark. *David gegen Goliath: Die Geschichte der Geschichten einer Geschichte. Zur fächerübergreifenden Rezeption einer biblischen Story*. Altes Testament und Moderne 4. Munich: Lit, 1998.

Nolan, Patrick and Gerhard Lenski. *Human Societies: An Introduction to Macrosociology*. 11th ed. Boulder CO: Paradigm, 2009

Noth, Martin. *The Deuteronomistic History*. JSOTSup 15. Sheffield, UK: JSOT Press, 1981.

————. *A History of Pentateuchal Traditions*. Translated with an introduction, by Bernhard W. Anderson. Chico, CA: Scholars, 1981.

Nussbaum, Martha C. *The Fragility of Goodness: Luck and Ethics in Greek Tragedy and Philosophy*. Cambridge: Cambridge University Press, 1986.

————. *Love's Knowledge: Essays on Philosophy and Literature*. Oxford: Oxford University Press, 1990.

Oakley, S. P. "Single Combat in the Roman Republic." *Classical Quarterly* 35 (1985) 392–410.

Olshansky, Dimitry. "The Birth of Structuralism from the Analysis of Fairy-Tales." *Toronto Slavic Quarterly, University of Toronto: Academic Electronic Journal in Slavic Studies* 25 (2008).

O'Malley, Pat. "Social Bandits, Modern Capitalism and the Traditional Peasantry: A Critique of Hobsbawm." *Journal of Peasant Studies* 6 (1979) 489–501.

Osiek, Carolyn. "Women, Honor, and Context in Mediterranean Antiquity." *Hervormde Teologiese Studies* 64 (2008) 323–37.

Otto, Rudolf. *The Idea of the Holy: An Inquiry into the Non-Rational Factor in the Idea of the Divine and Its Relation to the Rational.* Translated by John W. Harvey. Oxford: Milford, 1923.

Overholt, Thomas W. *Cultural Anthropology and the Old Testament.* Guides to Biblical Scholarship. Minneapolis: Fortress, 1996.

Pagolu, Augustine. *The Religion of the Patriarchs.* JSOTSup 277. Sheffield, UK: Sheffield Academic, 1998.

Parker, Simon B. "Possession Trance and Prophecy in Pre-Exilic Israel." *VT* 28 (1978) 271–385,

Patai, Raphael. *Sex and Family in the Bible and the Middle East.* Garden City, NY: Doubleday, 1959.

Pedersen, Johannes. *Israel: Its Life and Culture.* 4 vols. Translated by A. Møller and A. I. Fausbøll. London: Oxford University Press, 1926–40.

Peirce, Leslie. *The Imperial Harem: Women and Sovereignty in the Ottoman Empire.* Oxford: Oxford University Press, 1993.

Peristiany, J. G., editor. *Contributions to Mediterranean Sociology: Mediterranean Rural Communities and Social Change: Acts of the Mediterranean Sociological Conference, Athens, July, 1963.* Paris: Mouton, 1968.

———. "Honour and Shame in a Cypriot Highland Village." In *Honour and Shame: The Values of Mediterranean Society,* edited by J. G. Peristiany, 171–90. NHSS. London: Weidenfeld & Nicolson, 1965.

———. *Honour and Shame: The Values of Mediterranean Society.* NHSS. London: Weidenfeld & Nicolson, 1965.

———. "Introduction." In *Honour and Shame: The Values of Mediterranean Society,* edited by J. G. Peristiany, 9–18. NHSS. London: Weidenfeld & Nicolson, 1965.

Pilch, John J. "Healing in Mark: A Social Science Analysis." *BTB* 15 (1985) 142–50.

———. *Healing in the New Testament: Insights from Medical and Mediterranean Anthropology.* Minneapolis: Fortress, 2000.

———. "The Health Care System in Matthew: A Social Science Analysis." *BTB* 16 (1986) 102–6.

———. "Interpreting Biblical Healing: Selecting the Appropriate Model." *BTB* 18 (1986) 60–66.

———. "Jesus's Healing Activity: Political Acts." In *Understanding the Social World of the New Testament,* edited by Dietmar Neufeld and Richard E. DeMaris, 147–55. London: Routledge, 2010.

———. "Lying and Deceit in the Letters to the Seven Churches: Perspectives in Cultural Anthropology." *BTB* 22 (1992) 126–57.

———. "Secrecy in the Mediterranean World: An Anthropological Perspective." *BTB* 24 (1994) 151–57.

————. "Sickness and Healing in Luke-Acts." In *The Social World of Luke-Acts: Models for Interpretation*, edited by Jerome H. Neyrey, 181–209. Peabody, MA: Hendrickson, 1991.

————, editor. *Social Scientific Models for Interpreting the Bible: Essays by the Context Group in Honor of Bruce J. Malina*. BibIntSer 53. Leiden, Brill: 2001.

————. "The Transfiguration of Jesus: An Experience of Alternate Reality." In *Modelling Early Christianity: Social-Scientific Studies of the New Testament in Its Context*, edited by Philip F. Esler, 47–64. London: Routledge, 1995.

————. "Visions in Revelation and Alternate Consciousness: A Perspective from Cultural Anthropology." *Listening: Journal of Religion and Culture* 28 (1993) 231–44.

Pina-Cabral, João de. "The Mediterranean as a Category of Regional Comparison: A Critical View." *Current Anthropology* 30 (1989) 399–406.

Pitt-Rivers, Julian. "La conférence de Burg Wartenstein." In *L'anthropologie de la Méditerranée*, edited by Dionigi Albera et al., 59–63. Collection L'atelier méditerranéen. Paris: Maisonneuve & Larose, 2001.

————. *The Fate of Shechem, or the Politics of Sex: Essays in the Anthropology of the Mediterranean*. Cambridge Studies in Social Anthropology 19. Cambridge: Cambridge University Press, 1977.

————. "Honor." In *International Encyclopedia of the Social Sciences*, edited by David Sills, 6:503–11. New York: Free Press, 1968.

————. "Honour and Social Status." In *Honour and Shame: The Values of Mediterranean Society*, edited by J. G. Peristiany, 19–77. London: Weidenfeld & Nicolson, 1965.

————, editor. *Mediterranean Countrymen: Essays in the Social Anthropology of the Mediterranean*. Paris: Mouton, 1963.

————. *The People of the Sierra*. London: Weidenfeld & Nicolson, 1955.

Pitt-Rivers, Julian, and J. G. Peristiany. "Introduction." In *Honor and Grace in Anthropology*, edited by Julian Pitt-Rivers and J. G. Peristiany, 1–17. Cambridge Studies in Social and Cultural Anthropology. Cambridge: Cambridge University Press, 1992.

Prickett, Stephen. *Origins of Narrative: The Romantic Appropriation of the Bible*. Cambridge: Cambridge University Press, 1996.

Propp, Vladimir I. A. *Morphology of the Folk Tale*. 2nd ed. Revised and edited with a preface by Louis A. Wagner. New introduction by Alan Dundes. Translated by Laurence Scott. Austin: University of Texas Press, 1968.

Pury, Albert de, Thomas Römer, and Jean-Daniel Macchi, editors. *Israel Constructs Its History: Deuteronomistic History in Recent Research*. JSOTSup 306. Sheffield, UK: JSOT Press, 2000.

Rad, Gerhard von. *Genesis: A Commentary*. Rev. ed. Translated by John H. Marks and John Bowden. London: SCM, 1972.

————. *The Problem of the Hexateuch, and Other Essays*. Translated by E. W. Trueman Dicken, with introduction by Norman W. Porteous. London: Oliver & Boyd, 1966.

Reis, Pamel Tamarkin, "Collusion at Nob: A New Reading of 1 Samuel 21–22." *JSOT* 62 (1994) 59–73.

Ridout, George. "The Rape of Tamar: A Rhetorical Analysis of 2 Sam 13:1–22." In *Rhetorical Criticism: Essays in Honor of James Muilenburg*, edited by Jared J. Jackson and Martin Kessler, 75–84. Pittsburgh Theological Monograph Series 1. Pittsburgh: Pickwick, 1974.

Rogers, Sally Carol. "Female Forms of Power and the Myth of Male Dominance: A Model of Female/Male Interaction in Peasant Society." *American Ethnologist* 2 (1975) 727–56.

———. "Gender in Southwestern France: The Myth of Male Dominance Revisited." *Anthropology* 9 (1985) 65–86.

Rohrbaugh, Richard L. "A Dysfunctional Family and Its Neighbors: Luke 15:11–32." In *Perspectives on the Parables: Images of Jesus in His Contemporary Setting*, edited by V. G. Shillington, 141–64. Edinburgh: T. & T. Clark, 1997.

———. "Gossip in the New Testament." In *Social Scientific Models for Interpreting the Bible: Essays by the Context Group in Honor of Bruce J. Malina*, edited by John J. Pilch, 239–59. BibIntSer 53. Leiden: Brill, 2001.

———. "Legitimating Sonship—A Test of Honour: A Social-Scientific Study of Luke 4:1–30." In *Modelling Early Christianity: Social-Scientific Studies of the New Testament in Its Context*, edited by Philip F. Esler, 183–97. London: Routledge, 1995.

Roitman, Adolfo D. "Achior in the Book of Judith: His Role and Significance." In *No One Spoke Ill of Her: Essays on Judith*, edited by James C. VanderKam, 31–45. Early Judaism and Its Literature 2. Atlanta: Scholars, 1992.

Römer, Thomas, and Albert de Pury. "Deuteronomistic Historiography (DH): History of Research and Debated Issues." In *Israel Constructs Its History: Deuteronomistic History in Recent Research*, edited by Albert de Pury, Thomas Römer and Jean-Daniel Macchi, 24–142. JSOTSup 206. Sheffield, UK: Sheffield Academic, 2000).

Rosen, George. *Madness in Society: Chapters in the Historical Sociology of Mental Illness*. Chicago: University of Chicago Press, 1968.

Rosenbaum, M., and A. M. Silbermann, in collaboration with A. Blashki and L. Joseph. *Pentateuch with Targum Onkelos, Haphtaroth and Rashi's Commentary*. Translated and Annotated. Jerusalem: Silberman Family, 1973.

Rosenfeld, Henry. "The Contradictions between Property, Kinship and Power as Reflected in the Marriage System of an Arab Village." In *Contributions to Mediterranean Sociology: Mediterranean Rural Communities and Social Change: Acts of the Mediterranean Sociological Conference, Athens, July, 1963*, edited by J. G. Peristiany, 247–60. Publications of the Social Sciences Centre, Athens 4. Paris: Mouton, 1968.

Rosenzweig, Franz. "The Secret of Biblical Narrative Form." In *Scripture and Translation*, by Martin Buber and Franz Rosenzweig, 129–42. Translated by Lawrence Rosenwald with Everett Fox. ISBL. Bloomington: Indiana University Press, 1994.

Rummel, Stan. "Narrative Structures in the Ugaritic Texts." In *Ras Shamra Parallels*, vol. 3, edited by Stan Rummel, 221–332. Rome: Pontifical Institute Press, 1982.

Saller, Richard P. *Personal Patronage under the Early Empire*. Cambridge: Cambridge University Press, 1982.

Samovar, Larry A. et al. *Communication between Cultures*. 6th ed. Belmont, CA: Thomson Wadsworth, 2007.

Sant Cassia, Paul. "Review Article: Navigating an Anthropology of the Mediterranean: Recent Developments in France." *History and Anthropology* 14 (2003) 87–94.

Sarna, Nahum M. *Genesis: Berêshit*. JPS Torah Commentary. Philadelphia: Jewish Publication Society, 1989.

Schearing, Linda S. and Steven L. McKenzie, editors. *Three Elusive Deuteronomists: The Phenomenon of Pan-Deuteronomism.* JSOTSup 268. Sheffield, UK: Sheffield Academic, 1999.

Schlegel, Alice. "Status, Property, and the Value on Virginity." *American Ethnologist* 18 (1990) 719–34.

Schneider, Jane. "Of Vigilance and Virgins." *Ethnology* 10 (1971) 1–24.

Schneider, Jane, and Peter Schneider. *Culture and Political Economy in Western Sicily.* New York: Academic, 1976.

Seybold, K. "*hphk.*" In *TDOT* 3 (1978) 423–27.

Sharon, Diane M. "Some Results of a Structural Semiotic Analysis of the Story of Judah and Tamar." *JSOT* 29 (2005) 289–318.

Shaw, Brent. "Bandits in the Roman Empire." *Past and Present* 102 (1984) 3–52.

———. "Bandits in the Roman Empire." In *Studies in Ancient Greek and Roman Society,* edited by Robin Osborne, 326–74. Cambridge: Cambridge University Press, 2004. (= Shaw's 1984 essay of this title, plus a 2003 postscript (371–74).)

Sheldon, Mary Rose. *Espionage in the Ancient World: An Annotated Bibliography of Books and Articles in Western Languages.* Jefferson, NC: McFarland, 2002.

———. *Spies of the Bible: Espionage in Israel from the Exodus to Bar Kokhba.* St. Paul, MN: MBI, 2007.

Shiloh, Yigael. "The Four-Room House: Its Situation and Function in the Israelite City." *Israel Exploration Journal* 20 (1970) 180–90.

———. "The Population of Iron Age Palestine in the Light of a Sample Analysis of Urban Plans, Areas, and Population Density." *BASOR* 239 (1980) 25–35.

Shimoff, Sandra R. "Shepherds, Sectarianism, and Judaism." In *The Literature of Early Rabbinic Judaism: Issues in Talmudic Redaction and Interpretation,* edited by Alan J. Avery-Peck, 123–31. New Perspectives on Ancient Judaism 4. Latham, MD: University Press of America, 1989.

Silverman, Sydel. "Defining the Anthropological Mediterranean: Before Aix 1966." In *L'anthropologie de la Méditerranée,* edited by Dionigi Albera, Anton Blok, and Christian Bromberger, 43–57. Paris: Maisonneuvre & Larose, 2001.

Simkins, Ronald A. "Patronage and the Political Economy of Monarchic Israel." In *The Social World of the Hebrew Bible: Twenty-Five Years of the Social Sciences in the Academy,* edited by Ronald A. Simkins, and Stephen L. Cook, *Semeia* 87 (1999) 123–44.

Skehan, Patrick W. "The Hand of Judith." *CBQ* 25 (1963) 94–110.

Slatta, Richard W., editor. *Bandidos: The Varieties of Latin American Banditry.* New York: Greenwood, 1987.

———. "Eric J. Hobsbawm's Social Bandit: A Critique and Revision." *A Contracorriente: A Journal on Social History and Literature in Latin America* (2004) 22–30.

Smelik, Klaas A. D. "Genesis 38 Revisited." In *Om voor te lezen—Miqra. Bundel voor F. J. Hoogewoud,* edited by H. Blok, K. A. Deurloo, et al, 114–20. Amsterdamse cashiers voor exegese van de Bijbel en zijn tradities Supplement Series 4. Maastricht: Shaker, 2005.

Smith, Henry Preserved. *The Books of Samuel.* International Critical Commentary. Edinburgh: T. & T. Clark, 1899.

Speiser, E. A. *Genesis.* AB 1. Garden City, NY: Doubleday, 1963.

Sperber, Alexander. *The Bible in Aramaic.* Vol. 2, *The Former Prophets according to Targum Jonathan.* Leiden: Brill, 1959.

Stansell, Gary. "Honor and Shame in the David Narratives." *Semeia* 68 (1996) 55–79.

Sternberg, Meir. *The Poetics of Biblical Narrative: Ideological Literature and the Drama of Reading.* ISBL. Bloomington: Indiana University Press, 1985.

Stewart, Eric C. "Social Stratification and Patronage in Ancient Mediterranean Societies." In *Understanding the Social World of the New Testament*, edited by Dietmar Neufeld and Richard E. DeMaris, 156–66. London: Routledge, 2010.

Stirling, Paul. "The Domestic Cycle and the Distribution of Power in Turkish Villages." In *Mediterranean Countrymen: Essays in the Social Anthropology of the Mediterranean*, edited by Julian Pitt-Rivers, 201–13. Paris: Mouton, 1963.

———. *A Turkish Village.* NHSS. London: Weidenfeld & Nicolson, 1965.

Stone, Ken. *Sex, Honor, and Power in the Deuteronomistic History.* JSOTSup 234. Sheffield, UK: Sheffield Academic 1996.

Stone, Nira. "Judith and Holofernes: Some Observations on the Development of the Scene in Art." In *No One Spoke Ill of Her: Essays on Judith*, edited by James C. VanderKam, 73–93. Early Judaism and Its Literature 2. Atlanta: Scholars, 1992.

Sturrock, John. *Structuralism.* 2nd ed. London: Fontana, 1993.

Sussman, Max. "Sickness and Disease." In *ABD* 6 (1992) 6–15.

Sutton, David E. *Remembrance of Repasts: An Anthropology of Food and Memory.* Oxford: Berg, 2001.

Tefft, Stanton K. editor. *Secrecy: A Cross-Cultural Perspective.* New York: Human Sciences Press, 1980.

Thompson, Stith. *Motif-Index of Folk-Literature: A Classification of Narrative Elements in Folktales, Ballads, Myths, Fables, Mediaeval Romances, Exempla, Fabliaux, Jest-Books and Local Legends.* 6 vols. Rev. ed. Copenhagen: Roskilde & Bagger, 1955–58 (1932–37).

Tov, Emanuel. "The Composition of 1 Samuel 16–18 in the Light of the Septuagintal Version." In *Empirical Models of Biblical Criticism*, edited by Jeffrey H. Tigay, 95–130. 1985. Reprinted, Dove Studies in Bible, Language, and History. Eugene, OR: Wipf & Stock, 2005.

———. "The Nature of the Differences between MT and the LXX in 1 Sam 17–18." In *The Story of David and Goliath: Textual and Literary Criticism*, edited by Dominique Barthélemy et al., 19–46. OBO 73. Göttingen: Vandenhoeck & Ruprecht, 1986.

Triandis, Harry C. "Collectivism vs. Individualism: A Reconceptualization of a Basic Concept in Cross-Cultural Psychology." In *Cross-Cultural Studies of Personality, Attitudes and Cognition*, edited by Gajendra Verma and Christopher Bagley, 60–95. London: Macmillan, 1988.

———. "Cross-Cultural Studies of Individualism and Collectivism." In *Nebraska Symposium on Motivation, 1989: Volume 37. Cross Cultural Perspectives*, edited by Richard A. Dienstbier and John J. Berman, 41–133. Lincoln: University of Nebraska Press, 1990.

———. "Theoretical and Methodological Approaches to the Study of Collectivism and Individualism." In *Individualism and Collectivism: Theory, Method, and Application*, edited by Uichol Kim et al., 41–51. Cross-Cultural Research and Methodology Series 18. Thousand Oaks, CA: Sage, 1994.

Trible, Phyllis. *Texts of Terror: Literary-Feminist Readings of Biblical Narratives.* 1984. Reprinted with a Preface by Jane Craske, London: SCM, 2002.

Ullmann, Manfred. *Islamic Medicine.* Islamic Surveys 11. Edinburgh: Edinburgh University Press, 1978.

Ulrich, Eugene. *The Qumran Text of Samuel and Josephus*. HSM 19. Harvard: Harvard University Press, 1978.

UN News Centre. "Banditry Jeopardizing Humanitarian Work in Eastern Chad, Warns UN." November 13, 2009. Online: http://www.un.org/apps/news/story .asp?NewsID=32949&Cr=chad&Cr1/.

Vancil, Jack W. "Sheep, Shepherd." In *ABD* 5 (1992) 1187–90.

Van Seters, John. "The Problem of Childlessness in Near Eastern Law and the Patriarchs of Israel." *JBL* 87 (1968) 401–8.

Van Treek Nilsson, Mike D. "Amnón y Tamar (2 S 13, 1–22). Ensayo de antropología narrativa sobre la violencia." *Estudios Bíblicos* 65 (2007) 3–32.

Vaux, Roland de. "Single Combat in the Old Testament." In *The Bible and the Ancient Near East*, 122–35. Translated by Damian McHugh. Garden City, NY: Doubleday, 1972.

Wagner, S. "*klm*." In *TDOT* 7 (1995) 185–96.

Walters, S. D. "Hannah and Anna: The Greek and Hebrew Texts of 1 Samuel 1." *JBL* 107 (1988) 385–412.

Walsh, J. P. M. *The Mighty from Their Thrones: Power in the Biblical Tradition*. Overtures to Biblical Theology. Philadelphia: Fortress, 1987.

Watson, Francis. *Text, Church and World: Biblical Interpretation in Theological Perspective*. Edinburgh: T. & T. Clark, 1994.

Weidman, Hazel Hitson. "Falling-Out: A Diagnostic and Treatment Problem Viewed from a Transcultural Perspective." *Society, Science and Medicine* 13 (1979) 95–112.

Weiss, Meir. *The Bible from Within: The Method of Total Interpretation*. Translated by B. Schwartz. Jerusalem: Magnes, 1984 (1962).

Wenham, Gordon J. *Genesis 16–50*. WBC 2. Dallas: Word, 1994.

White, Sidnie Ann. "In the Steps of Jael and Deborah: Judith as Heroine." In *No One Spoke Ill of Her: Essays on Judith*, edited by James C. VanderKam, 5–16. Early Judaism and Its Literature 2. Atlanta: Scholars, 1992.

Whybray, R. N. "Genesis." In *The Oxford Bible Commentary*, edited by John Barton and John Muddiman, 38–66. Oxford: Oxford University Press, 2001.

Wikan, Unni. "Shame and Honour: A Contestable Pair." *Man* 19 (1984) 635–52.

Wildavsky, Aaron. "Survival Must Not be Gained through Sin: The Moral of the Joseph Stories Prefigured Through Judah and Tamar." *JSOT* 19 (1994) 37–48.

Wilson, Robert R. *Prophecy and Society in Ancient Israel*. Philadelphia: Fortress, 1980.

Wintermute, O. S. "Jubilees (Second Century B. C.)." In *The Old Testament Pseudepigrapha. Volume 2. Expansions of the "Old Testament" and Legends, Wisdom and Philosophical Literature, Prayers, and Odes, Fragments of Lost Judeo-Hellenistic Works*, edited by James H. Charlesworth, 35–142. Garden City, NY: Doubleday, 1985.

Yadin, Azzan. "Goliath's Armor and Israelite Collective Memory." *VT* 54 (2004) 373–94.

Author Index

Scripture Index